MW00334341

China–Africa and an Economic Transformation

Praise for the book

'This book's accessible up-to-date assessment on the evolving trade and investment relations between China and Africa is a welcome contribution to a field that is under-studied. The asymmetry in Africa-China relations is recognised and honestly addressed, including insights into governance arrangements. Lin and Oqubay's book is academically rigorous, and also offers immensely practical guidance to Chinese and African stakeholders on how to build this partnership going forward.'

Dr Miriam Altman, PhD, Commissioner in the South African
National Planning Commission

'This is an extremely important volume. In the chatter on China and Africa, the Chinese and Africans are the very ones often left out. The editors themselves represent a departure from "being spoken to" by a Western world with its own distinct interests. They have assembled a set of chapters of deep insights into collaboration in specific countries and which speak to a complex situation that indicates a changed world because of China and Africa.'

Stephen Chan OBE, Professor of World Politics,
SOAS University of London

'This book comes at a critical moment in China-Africa relations, as both sides explore ways to reach their partnership potential. The 2018 FOCAC Beijing Summit launched an ambitious cooperation agenda in support of Africa's development, as encapsulated in Agenda 2063. We also agreed to advance shared priorities on the global stage. The African Union is committed to working with China on our joint objectives towards "building an even stronger community with a shared future". As we move forward, this book, which brings together various intellectual contributions, is a useful resource that captures the concrete achievements of this partnership and highlights the opportunities for even greater impact to the benefit of the two partners.'

Moussa Faki Mahamat, Chairperson of the
African Union Commission

'Arkebe Oqubay and Justin Yifu Lin have assembled a range of eminent scholars from across the globe to update the debate on one of Africa's partners that is here to stay: China. African countries' relations with China are evolving, solidifying, intensifying and diversifying – and they require constant learning and adaptation to understand. With this nuanced book, the authors illustrate that Chinese engagement is no panacea to African countries' development, yet the Chinese positive narrative of Africa is a fresh wind from the east that can be harnessed for home-grown strategic action. A key read for scholars and policy-makers alike!'

Sven Grimm, Head of Programme at German Development Institute and Associate Professor, Stellenbosch University

'A must read – a brilliant up-to-date review of Africa-China economic relationships and how they have evolved over the last 25 years, during the surge of China's own development. The book analyses how Africa-China relationships contrast with past and present Africa's economic relationship with the West, bringing out the positives and new opportunities of trade with China as well as the negatives and possible future problems, such as rising debt and trade deficit gaps. The chapters are analysed by a distinguished panel of well-placed authors, throwing interesting light on what Africa and others can learn from China's own accelerated development. The result is an important document which deserves the attention of national and international policymakers in Africa, the West and China as well as students and analysists following China-African relations.'

Sir Richard Jolly, Honorary Professor and Research Associate, Institute of Development Studies, UK

'If you are a public or private entrepreneur, or anyone with a vision to build more prosperous nations and businesses across the African continent in the next 50 years, then this fascinating book is a must-read. Clearly, China's ability to transform its economy, lift nearly 1-billion people out of poverty, and shape global technological advances—all in a period of less than 50 years—is inspiring and instructive for Africa. It shows that such a transformation is possible. The editors and authors do a stellar job of showing how more strategic approaches by African countries, that navigate the dynamic and complex conditions, are urgently required to unlock unprecedented economic value across the continent and ensure mutual economic benefit going forward. Whether in government or the private sector, anyone with a real commitment to the sustainable and prosperous future of both, will be wise to carefully study this volume and glean actionable insights from its historically grounded and intellectually robust analysis.'

Strive Masiyiwa, Founder Econet

'A compelling and cogent work, *China-Africa and an Economic Transformation* offers an opportunity to engage leading policymakers and senior scholars. Cutting against clichéd representations of relations between China and Africa, the contributing authors provide fresh and original ideas about pathways to development. Oqubay and Lin's volume is timely and challenging. This book is a gem, and that's an understatement.'

James H. Mittelman, Distinguished Research Professor and University Professor Emeritus, American University

'Africa's development and structural transformation must be premised on Africans finding the best development pathways suited to the continent's cultural, social and economic context. This interesting volume by Justin Lin and Arkebe Oqubay is among the first to explore the practical application of China's economic development model to Africa and to examine its successes and failures. It is timely, and a must read in a changing global context of multipolarity that questions what works and what does not in economic development.'

Ngozi Okonjo-Iweala, PhD, former Finance Minister, Nigeria

'African countries are poised to experience sustained growth and development. China is positioned by its own economic development and its external development policies to play a major and expanding role in that process. *China-Africa and an Economic Transformation*, a book edited by Justin Yifu Lin and Arkebe Oqubay, presents a clear and important assessment of the multi-faceted interactions between China and its African trade and investment partners. Among the books many great strengths is its explicit recognition of the dynamic and changing aspects of the relationships, responding to shifts in all of these economies, and in the global context. It will become essential reading for policy makers, businesses and civil society leaders in Africa and China, but also for a global constituency concerned about the SDGs and the inclusiveness of the growth patterns in the global economy.'

Michael Spence, Professor of Economics, Stern School of Business, New York University, Nobel Prize in Economics 2001

'As the role of China in Africa grows, it is critical that policymakers, businesses, and civil society leaders have an in-depth understanding of the relationship in order to make well-informed decisions to maximize opportunities and benefits. The new book edited by Arkebe Oqubay and Justin Yifu Lin, *China-Africa and an Economic Transformation*, will serve as a guide to decision-makers by bringing together a nuanced analysis of the historical lessons from China's own development story, the role of Sino-African relations in Africa's infrastructural development to date, and the potential trajectories for this partnership over the coming decades. Capturing the diverse and dynamic nature of the economic ties between China and Africa and relating it to Africa's transformation is a novel approach of this volume. A must-read for policymakers, practitioners, and researchers working toward a healthy and vibrant economic future for the African continent.'

Mark Suzman, Chief Strategy Officer, and President, Global Policy & Advocacy, Bill & Melinda Gates Foundation

China–Africa and an Economic Transformation

Edited by
Arkebe Oqubay and Justin Yifu Lin

OXFORD

UNIVERSITY PRESS

OXFORD
UNIVERSITY PRESS

Great Clarendon Street, Oxford, OX2 6DP,
United Kingdom

Oxford University Press is a department of the University of Oxford.
It furthers the University's objective of excellence in research, scholarship,
and education by publishing worldwide. Oxford is a registered trade mark of
Oxford University Press in the UK and in certain other countries

© Oxford University Press 2019

The moral rights of the authors have been asserted

First Edition published in 2019
Impression: 1

Published in the United States of America by Oxford University Press
198 Madison Avenue, New York, NY 10016, United States of America

British Library Cataloguing in Publication Data
Data available

Library of Congress Control Number: 2018963936

ISBN 978–0–19–883050–4

Printed and bound in Great Britain by
Clays Ltd, Elcograf S.p.A.

This book is dedicated to Deborah Brautigam, a pioneer in China–Africa research, who inspires many established and up-and-coming scholars.

Preface

With China–Africa economic ties having entered a new phase, it is important to review the past twenty-five years and assess key economic policies and strategies that will shape future China and Africa ties. China's economic rebalancing as it prepares to enter the 'fourth industrial revolution', the recently launched Belt and Road initiative (BRI), and new policy directions announced during FOCAC VII in September 2018 present both opportunities and challenges for African countries. Similarly, the Africa of 2018 is significantly different economically from Africa in 2000 when the first FOCAC was launched. Because of a combination of internal economic reforms and an evolving global economic environment, more than eighteen African countries registered positive economic growth for a decade. This growth was sustained for a shorter episode and the growth has been uneven across the continent. Most African countries have not sufficiently diversified their economy and that growth has not sufficiently translated to structural changes. Furthermore, Africa–China economic ties and outcomes have been uneven across African countries.

Since the first FOCAC summit in 2000, China–Africa economic ties have grown by leaps and bounds. Besides the impressive growth in two-way trade between China and Africa, Chinese investment in the productive sectors of many African economies has played a catalytic role in raising productivity in many sectors—although uneven across African countries. China's role in the development and financing of critical African infrastructure—transport, electricity, and logistics—has been critical in addressing key binding constraints that had long held back the continent's economic potential.

Equally important has been the demonstration effect of China's own development experience to African countries. In this regard, the role played by the Chinese state in guiding the market, and the willingness of the state to intervene and experiment with heterodox policies to generate economic growth, compete in global markets, and reduce poverty in the process has been significant. Heavy investment in vital infrastructure, targeted supports to exporting sectors, active FDI promotion, education, and research and development were complemented by flexible policies designed to enhance competitiveness of local enterprises through technological retooling, the retraining of workers, and progressive deregulation of the market. The lessons from China—policy ownership and strategic planning—increasingly inform national development strategies in many African countries.

As China transits to a 'knowledge-based economy' in the new phase of globalization, it faces many rebalancing challenges that could potentially open up, or alternatively diminish new opportunities for African countries. As one of the top sources of outward FDI and as the world's largest trading and manufacturing nation, China's rise can benefit African countries if they are prepared to take a strategic approach in their dealings with China. For example, pending relocation of China's labour-intensive manufacturing could potentially help generate millions of jobs for African youth, and rising consumption by the growing Chinese middle class of luxury agricultural products could increase African exports of these products to China, thus unleashing the productive potential of African farmers.

The relationship between China and Africa is in its early stages and it is too early to arrive at any conclusion as to whether this relationship is necessarily good or bad. Yet, there is an 'exaggerated' perception of China's power in Africa in the mainstream media. In fact, there is no Chinese exceptionalism when it comes to Africa. China is not the sole player in Africa and it is subject to the same political gravity as other external actors dealing with Africa. There is, hence, a danger in making too broad generalizations about China's role in Africa. There is an urgent need for more detailed research both on individual African countries and at the level of value chains to trace the real economic impact of China on Africa's development. Equally important is the need to be cautious about the over-exuberance of some African leaders about the replicability of the Chinese model. While the example of China is appealing, there is a need for realism on the part of Africans if the trends in the evolving global order are to be correctly read and policies formulated accordingly.

Acknowledgements

We are very grateful to all seventeen contributors to this volume with whom we have had the pleasure of working, and would like to thank them sincerely for their personal commitment and the efforts they have made to ensure the success of this book.

Special thanks are due to our commissioning editor, Adam Swallow, and his team at Oxford University Press, as well as the entire production team for their outstanding support and encouragement. We also wish to thank the anonymous reviewers and the delegates of OUP who approved the final version of our proposal.

We would also like to thank Professor Fantu Cheru (Leiden University, Netherlands), our senior technical adviser on this project, who has provided invaluable guidance, and our prestigious panel of external reviewers, Professor Mohamed Salih (Erasmus University, Netherlands), Professor James Mittleman (American University), Professor Scarlett Cornelissen (Stellenbosch University), and Dr Dirk Willem te Velde (Overseas Development Institute) for their critical reviews and valuable comments provided to improve draft chapters. Our thanks also go to all other participants in the Review Workshop held in Addis Ababa in August 2018 for their insightful presentations, discussion, feedback, and collaboration.

We would also like to acknowledge with gratitude the grant received from the Bill and Melinda Gates Foundation. Our personal thanks go to Haddis Tadesse (Bill and Melinda Gates Foundation) and Tewolde Gebremariam (Ethiopian Airlines) for their continued support and to the Made In Africa Initiative and Ethiopian Airlines which provided operational support to this project.

Our gratitude also goes to Keith Povey Editorial Services Ltd, for copy-editing the volume, and 251 Communications for designing the book cover. And finally, our appreciation and thanks go to our project coordinator, Deborah M. Kefale, and the research team of Meron Tilahun, Yohannes Ghebru, Tsion Kifle, and Edom Haile for their support in the preparation of the manuscript and assistance throughout the project.

Contents

List of Figures and Tables   xv
List of Contributors   xvii

1. Introduction to China–Africa and an Economic Transformation   1
   Arkebe Oqubay and Justin Yifu Lin

Part I. China's Rise and the Changing Global Development Discourse

2. China's Economic Emergence and Implications for Africa   19
   Linda Yueh

3. The Meanings and Global Externalities of China's Economic
   Emergence   35
   Célestin Monga

Part II. Evolving China–Africa Relations: Context, Perspectives, and Framework

4. China–Africa Ties in Historical Context   61
   David H. Shinn

5. Evolving Debates and Outlooks on China–Africa Economic Ties   84
   Chris Alden

6. The Institutional Framework of Sino-African Relations   98
   Ian Taylor

Part III. The Dynamics of China–Africa Economic Ties

7. Chinese Loans and African Structural Transformation   129
   Deborah Brautigam

8. China's Development Finance and African Infrastructure
   Development   147
   Jing Gu and Richard Carey

9. The Changing Dynamics of Chinese Oil and Gas
   Engagements in Africa   173
   Cyril Obi

10. The Political Economy of China's Investment in Nigeria:
    Prometheus or Leviathan?   192
    Omolade Adunbi and Howard Stein

11. Agreements and Dispute Settlement in China–Africa
    Economic Ties   216
    Won L. Kidane

12. Labour Regimes and Workplace Encounters between
    China and Africa   239
    Carlos Oya

Part IV. China and Africa's Economic Transformation

13. China's Light Manufacturing and Africa's Industrialization   265
    Justin Yifu Lin and Jiajun Xu

14. Catalysing China–Africa Ties for Africa's Structural
    Transformation: Lessons from Ethiopia   282
    Fantu Cheru and Arkebe Oqubay

15. The Future of China–Africa Economic Ties: New Trajectory
    and Possibilities   310
    Arkebe Oqubay and Justin Yifu Lin

Name Index   325
Subject Index   327

List of Figures and Tables

Figures

3.1 Contribution to global growth, 1980–2017, top five countries
(US$, current prices)   41

3.2 Contribution to global growth, 1960–2017, top five countries
(US$, current prices)   42

3.3 China: Structure of demand, 1970–2017 (percentage of nominal GDP) 44

3.4 Demand contributions to GDP growth (percentage points)   48

3.5 China: Total debt to GDP, 1995–2017   49

3.6 Income and governance, 2016   54

7.1 Chinese loans to Africa, 2000 to 2017 (US$bn)   134

12.1 Levels of labour regime analytical framework   249

13.1 Manufacturing, value added (per cent of GDP) in sub-Saharan Africa 266

14.1 Ethiopia's export comparison, 2000–17   288

14.2 Ethiopia's import comparison, 2000–17   289

14.3 Total number of new FDI manufacturing firms in Ethiopia, 2000–17 290

14.4 FDI inflow to Ethiopia, 2000–17   291

14.5 New Chinese manufacturing firms in three phases   291

14.6 Employment generated (cumulative) by foreign firms   292

Tables

3.1 China's merchandise exports   40

3.2 China's imports, 1960–2017   43

A4.1 Evolution and characteristics of China–Africa relations   80

7.1 Chinese lending to African governments   133

9.1 Value of China's crude oil imports from African countries
(in percentage terms)   174

10.1 Nigeria–China exports 1995–2017 in US$m, except ratios   198

10.2 Nigeria–China imports 1995–2017 and trade balance in US$m, except ratios 198

10.3 Nigeria–China detailed structure of imports of manufactured goods 1995–2017 in US$m, except ratios 200

10.4 Companies listed as operating in Lekki FTZ in UNDP, 2015 and new companies 2018 208

A12.1 Estimated employment localization rates in Chinese firms in Africa from most significant studies/cases 258

13.1 Details of enterprises by sector and region 271

14.1 Ethiopia's trade deficits with key trading partner countries, 2017 (in US$ millions) 289

A14.1 Destination of Ethiopia's exports, 2000–17 303

A14.2 Ethiopia's import comparison 303

A14.3 Total number of new manufacturing (foreign) firms 303

A14.4 Chinese loan commitments to Ethiopia, 2012/2013 (by creditor and type) 304

A14.5 Chinese engagement in the Ethiopian power sector 304

A14.6 Partial listing of Chinese companies engaged in Ethiopia's road sector (2009) 306

15.1 Strategic approach by African countries to FOCAC VII initiatives (2018–21) 316

List of Contributors

Omolade Adunbi is a political anthropologist and an associate professor in the Department of Afro-American and African Studies and Program in the Environment (Pite), and faculty associate, Donia Human Rights Center (DHRC) at the University of Michigan, Ann Arbor. His areas of research explore issues related to resource distribution, governance, human and environmental rights, power, culture, transnational institutions, multinational corporations, and the postcolonial state. His latest book is *Oil Wealth and Insurgency in Nigeria* (Indiana University Press, 2015). He is currently working on two interrelated projects: China's growing interest in Africa's natural resources; and infrastructural projects, oil refineries, and special economic zones.

Chris Alden is a professor in the International Relations Department, London School of Economics and Political Science. He has held fellowships at several universities, including Cambridge University, Tokyo University, Ecole Normale Supérieure, and University of Pretoria. He has authored/co-authored numerous books, including *New Directions in Africa–China Studies,* co-edited with Dan Large (Routledge/SSRC, forthcoming); *Apartheid's Last Stand: The Rise and Fall of the South African Security State* (Palgrave, 2017); *Brazil and Mozambique: Forging New Partnerships or Developing Dependency?,* co-edited with Sergio Chichava and Ana Cristina Alves (Jacana/IESE/SAIIA, 2017); and *China and Africa: Building Peace and Security Cooperation on the Continent,* co-edited with Abiodun Alao, Laura Barber, and Zhang Chun (Palgrave, 2017).

Deborah Brautigam is the Bernard L. Schwartz Professor of Political Economy, director of the International Development Program, and director of the China–Africa Research Initiative at Johns Hopkins University School of Advanced International Studies (SAIS). Her most recent books include *The Dragon's Gift: The Real Story of China in Africa* (OUP, 2010) and *Will Africa Feed China?* (OUP, 2015). Before joining SAIS in 2012, she taught at Columbia University and the American University. Dr Brautigam's teaching and research focus is on international development strategies, governance, and foreign aid. She has a PhD from the Fletcher School of Law and Diplomacy, Tufts University.

Richard Carey is a former OECD director of development cooperation, supporting the OECD Development Assistance Committee (DAC). During his career at the OECD (1980–2010) he led on development issues, including aid effectiveness, aid for trade, participatory development and good governance, policy coherence, development finance, and conflict and fragility. He was the founding co-chair of the China-DAC Study Group in 2009. He has also been active in multilateral work, including MDGs, debt statistics, and multilateral coordination, and in developing a close relationship with the UN Economic Commission for Africa.

Fantu Cheru is emeritus professor of International Relations, American University (Washington, DC) and a senior researcher at the African Studies Centre, Leiden University (The Netherlands). From 2007–12 he was a research director at the Nordic Africa Institute in Uppsala, Sweden and a member of UN Secretary-General Kofi Annan's Panel on Mobilizing International Support for the New Partnership for African Development. Professor Cheru serves on the editorial board of several scholarly journals, and among his publication are: *Oxford Handbook of the Ethiopian Economy* (with Cramer and Oqubay (OUP, 2019)); *Agricultural Development and Food Security in Africa: The Impact of Chinese, Indian and Brazilian Investments* (Zed Books, 2013); *Africa and International Relations in the 21st Century* (with Cornelissen and Shaw (Palgrave Macmillan, 2011)); *The Rise of China and India in Africa* (Zed Books, 2010).

Jing Gu, PhD, is the director of the Centre for Rising Powers and Global Development at the Institute of Development Studies. She has an interdisciplinary background in law, economics, and international development. She has led many interdisciplinary research projects involving multi-country teams, including the ground-breaking pioneering research on China in Africa which involved field research in fifteen African countries and ten Chinese provinces from 2007 to 2017. She has published widely on the BRICS in international development, China and emerging powers, China's international development role, and China-Africa relations. She is a senior advisor to the China International Development Research Network, and a member of the international editorial board of *Third World Quarterly*.

Won L. Kidane is a tenured associate professor of law at the Seattle University School of Law. He teaches, writes, and practices in the areas of international arbitration and litigation. Professor Kidane has published four books (two co-authored) and dozens of law review articles. Among his notable books are: *The Culture of International Arbitration* (OUP, 2017), *Litigating War* (with Murphy and Snider, OUP, 2013), and *Global Issues in Immigration Law* (with Aldana, Lyon, and McKanders, West Academic, 2013). He holds an SJD (Georgetown), JD (University of Illinois), and LLM (University of Georgia).

Justin Yifu Lin is dean of the Institute of New Structural Economics and Institute of South–South Cooperation and Development, and professor and honorary dean of National School of Development at Peking University. He was the senior vice president and chief economist at the World Bank, 2008–12. Prior to this, he served for fifteen years as founding director and professor of the China Centre for Economic Research (CCER) at Peking University. He is a councillor of the State Council and a member of the Standing Committee, Chinese People's Political Consultation Conference. He is the author of more than twenty books including *Beating the Odds: Jump-Starting Developing Countries* (Princeton University Press, 2017); *Going beyond Aid: Development Cooperation for Structural Transformation* (CUP, 2017); *The Quest for Prosperity: How Developing Economies Can Take Off* (Princeton University Press, 2012); *New Structural Economics: A Framework for Rethinking Development and Policy* (World Bank, 2012); *Against the Consensus: Reflections on the Great Recession* (CUP, 2013); and *Demystifying the Chinese Economy* (CUP, 2012). He is a corresponding fellow of the British Academy and a fellow of the Academy of Sciences for the Developing World.

Célestin Monga, PhD, is vice president of the African Development Bank. Prior to that he was managing director at the United Nations Industrial Development Organization (UNIDO) and senior adviser and programme director at the World Bank. He has held various senior positions in academia and financial institutions. A graduate of MIT, Harvard, and the Universities of Paris 1 Pantheon-Sorbonne, Bordeaux, and Pau, Dr Monga has authored and co-edited several books on Africa including *The Oxford Handbook of Africa and Economics*, Vols 1 and 2 (OUP, 2015) with Justin Lin. He was also the economics editor for the five-volume *New Encyclopedia of Africa* (Charles Scribner's, 2007).

Cyril Obi, PhD, is a programme director at the Social Science Research Council (SSRC) and leads two Africa-related programmes: the African Peacebuilding Network (APN) and the Next Generation Social Sciences in Africa (NGSSA). Dr Obi is also a research associate at the Department of Political Sciences, University of Pretoria, South Africa. His publications include *The Rise of China and India in Africa: Challenges, Opportunities and Critical Interventions* (Zed Books, 2010), co-edited with Fantu Cheru.

Arkebe Oqubay, PhD, is a senior minister and special adviser to the Ethiopian Prime Minister and has been at the centre of policymaking for over twenty-five years. He is the former mayor of Addis Ababa and was awarded the Best African Mayor of 2006 by ABN, a finalist World Mayor Award 2006, for transforming the city. He currently serves as board chair of several leading public organizations and international advisory boards, and is a recipient of the Order of the Rising Sun, Gold and Silver Star, presented by the Emperor of Japan. He is a research associate at the Centre of African Studies in the University of London, and holds a PhD in development studies from SOAS, University of London. His recent works include his path-breaking *Made in Africa: Industrial Policy in Ethiopia* (OUP, 2015); *The Oxford Handbook of the Ethiopian Economy* (OUP, 2019), with Cheru and Cramer; *How Nations Learn: Technological Learning, Industrial Policy, and Catch Up* (OUP, 2019), with Ohno; *African Economic Development: Evidence, Theory, and Policy* (OUP, forthcoming), with Cramer and Sender; and *The Oxford Handbook of Industrial Hubs and Economic Development* (OUP, forthcoming), with Lin. Dr Arkebe was recognized by the *New African* as one of the 100 Most Influential Africans of 2016 and a "leading thinker on Africa's strategic development" for his work, both practical and theoretical, on industrial policies. His research focus includes structural transformation, catch-up, industrial policy, and policymaking, with a special emphasis on Africa.

Carlos Oya, PhD, is reader (associate professor) in the political economy of development at SOAS, University of London. His main research interests are labour relations and employment, agrarian political economy, development policy, poverty, and research methodology. He is currently leading a project on structural transformations and employment dynamics in the infrastructure construction and manufacturing sectors in Ethiopia and Angola, with a special focus on Chinese firms.

David H. Shinn, PhD, has been teaching in the Elliott School of International Affairs at George Washington University since 2001. He previously served for thirty-seven years in the US foreign service with assignments at embassies in Lebanon, Kenya, Tanzania, Mauritania, Cameroon, and Sudan, and as ambassador to Burkina Faso and Ethiopia. He is the co-author of *China and Africa: A Century of Engagement* (University of Pennsylvania Press, 2012) and *Historical Dictionary of Ethiopia* (Scarecrow Press, 2013) and author of *Hizmet in Africa: The Activities and Significance of the Gülen Movement* (2014). He has a PhD from George Washington University.

Howard Stein is a professor in the Department of Afro-American and African Studies (DAAS) and Epidemiology at the University of Michigan. He is a development economist educated in Canada, the United States, and the United Kingdom. He has held university appointments in Japan, Tanzania, the Netherlands, the United Kingdom, the United States, Canada, Ireland, and Portugal. He is the editor or author of more than a dozen books and edited collections. His research has focused on foreign aid, finance and development, structural adjustment and neoliberalism, health, gender and development, institutional transformation, industrial policy, export-processing zones, agricultural policy, poverty and rural property rights transformation, and Chinese and African economic relations.

Ian Taylor is a professor in international relations and African political economy at the University of St Andrews and also chair professor in the School of International Studies, Renmin University of China. He is interested in sub-Saharan Africa's political economy and its international relations, the history of Afro-Asian diplomacy, the notion of 'rising powers', and the implications for global governance and development (and for Africa specifically). Focusing largely on sub-Saharan Africa, he has authored eight academic books, edited another eleven, and published over seventy peer-reviewed scholarly articles. He holds a DPhil from the University of Stellenbosch.

Jiajun Xu is an assistant professor and the executive deputy dean of the Institute of New Structural Economics at Peking University. Xu worked at the United Nations and World Bank and currently acts as the general secretary of the Global Research Consortium on Economic Structural Transformation. Her research focuses on development financing and global economic governance. She has published in academic journals in the field of international development. Her academic monograph *Beyond US Hegemony in International Development* was published by Cambridge University Press in 2017. Xu holds a DPhil (PhD) from the University of Oxford.

Linda Yueh, DPhil, is fellow in economics at St Edmund Hall, University of Oxford where she is director of the China Growth Centre. She is also adjunct professor of economics at the London Business School and visiting senior fellow at the London School of Economics and Political Science. She was visiting professor of economics at Peking University. Her books include: *China's Growth: The Making of an Economic Superpower* (OUP, 2013); *Enterprising China: Business, Economic and Legal Development Since 1979* (OUP, 2011); and *What Would the Great Economists Do? How Twelve Brilliant Minds Would Solve Today's Biggest Problems* (Picador, 2019).

1

Introduction to China–Africa and an Economic Transformation

Arkebe Oqubay and Justin Yifu Lin

1.1 The Context of China–Africa Ties

The last quarter of the twentieth century brought tremendous advances in the way human beings organize production, work, trade, and many aspects of social activities. Accelerated advancements in science and technology, the balance between the relative roles of states and markets, transformations in global trade and investment regimes, and the global compacts on environment and social policies have been far reaching. A developing country that has successfully taken advantage of the opportunities from globalization's tidal wave to achieve structural transformation has been China. In a relatively short four decades, China has emerged as the second-largest economy in the world with a huge industrial complex and manufacturing base; it has lifted more than 700 million of its population out of poverty in just a generation and established itself as one of the most influential countries in global affairs.[1] China has become an engine of global economic growth. Since the global financial crisis of 2008, China's annual contribution of at least 30 per cent to global growth has been far more than that of any other economy (see Chapter 2). China is also the largest global trader and net exporter of outward foreign direct investment (FDI) (see Chapter 2). China's economic rise can, therefore, be viewed as a 'global public good', with enormous positive impact on the economic fortunes of many countries across the world, including Africa.

---

[1] National Intelligence Council (2012) *Global Trends 2030: Alternative Worlds*; Linda Yueh (2013), *China's Growth: The Making of an Economic Superpower*; Justin Lin (2012) *Demystifying the Chinese Economy*.

China was trapped in poverty for centuries before its recent rise and the series of reforms launched by Deng Xiaoping at the end of 1978. China's rise from a country with less than one-third of sub-Saharan African countries' per-capita GDP in the late 1970s has been an inspiration, showing that poverty is not a destiny and transformation is possible. The historical example of China certainly has some unique features, but it is not exceptional. China's industrialization has in many ways reproduced historical patterns, especially from other East Asian latecomers, at fast speed and greater scale, and has followed a pattern of 'directed development' or 'pragmatic experimentation' (Ang, 2016). Thus, besides China, other historical experiences offer important lessons for African economies; most share the Chinese trajectory of experimentation and show that its fundamentals—fast infrastructure building coupled with careful FDI management, among other ingredients—are common to other Asian experiences.[2] In the African context, Ethiopia is one country that has followed the Chinese and other East Asian model of industrialization (see Chapter 14).

Over the past decade and a half, China has emerged as Africa's largest trading partner, as among its top five major investors, and as a major source of development finance and contractor of major infrastructure projects for the continent (see Chapters 2, 3, 8, and 9). Chinese demand for African oil and other raw materials has had a huge impact on the performance of African economies over the past decade. In addition, expanded Chinese investments in the infrastructure sector—roads, power generation, ports, and new airports—have opened up opportunities for African producers to increase production and move goods to local, regional, and global markets relatively quickly, resulting in increased incomes to Africans (Brautigam, 2009; Cheru and Obi, 2010; see also Chapters 8, 9, 14, and 15).

It is, however, important to establish at the outset that China is not a newcomer to Africa; indeed, it never left the continent in the first place. While Chinese foreign policy in the 1950s and 1960s was primarily focused on supporting African countries in their struggle against colonialism and imperialism, in the post-Cold War period pragmatic pursuit of mutually beneficial economic cooperation has become the centrepiece of Chinese policy towards Africa (Shinn and Eisenman, 2012) (see Chapter 4). Since the introduction of opening and reform by Deng Xiaoping in 1978, China has pursued its dream of becoming a leading industrial power by embracing globalization and global integration as a development strategy.[3] China's emergence as the

---

[2] We are grateful to James Mittelman and Carlos Oya for important comments and inputs to this section.

[3] Deng Xiaoping was a deputy prime minister in 1978, resigned from that position in 1980, and retained the position of chairman of the Central Military Committee until 1990. After that, Deng did not have any formal title. However, he was China's supreme leader until his death in 1997.

leading player in FDI outflow from emerging economies is linked to the pursuit of its 'Going Global' strategy and its vision for a different kind of international system. China's foray into Africa must, therefore, be understood within this wider context.

It is no accident that China became Africa's most valuable partner in the post-1990 period at a time when prescriptions from neoliberal quarters and structural adjustment reform were coming to be seen as empty promises. Hence, China's rise in Africa began at a time when Africans themselves were engaged in a major soul-searching exercise to find out why the continent's development path had gone wrong after more than fifty years since the end of colonial rule (for most African countries) despite the continuous ties with Europe and North America since the end of colonial rule. The growing fatigue with neoliberal policy experiments that is driving a search for an alternative development model has led many African leaders to take a closer look at China's recent development experience in the hope of drawing important lessons from it (see Chapter 14 on Ethiopia). China's historical experience as a former semi-colony and its spectacular growth experience since the late 1970s under the guidance of a strong developmental state have raised African interest in the pursuit of an alternative development strategy that departs from the conventional neoliberal Washington Consensus policy prescriptions. Of interest to African policymakers have been the homegrown domestic policy lessons and the role played by the Chinese state in experimenting with 'heterodox' policies to accelerate economic growth, emerge as a manufacturing powerhouse and major exporter, and reduce poverty while gradually moving towards the expansion of the markets (see Chapters 2 and 13).

There are also non-material reasons for Africa's attraction to China. In contrast to the paternalistic (and often pessimistic) view of Western partners towards Africa, segments within the Chinese state bureaucracy and varied private-sector groups hold the view that Africa is a dynamic continent on the threshold of a developmental take-off. Its pronounced position of partnership embraces the language of solidarity, mutually beneficial economic cooperation, 'common prosperity', and shared 'developing country' status. Such positive narratives are music to the ears of African policymakers who are wary of perceived Western paternalism and tired of losing policy space because of Western aid-induced policy recommendations. China makes no paternalistic pretence of being in Africa to help poor Africans develop, or to teach them how to govern themselves. China is in Africa to conduct business based on mutual benefit, cooperation, and non-interference in the internal affairs of African countries (People's Republic of China, 2006).

The growing economic partnership between China and Africa has generated much excitement as well as anxiety in many quarters. On the one side stand the 'China bashers' in the West, who accuse China of 'neo-colonialism' by engaging in exploitative economic relations with weak African states, contributing to their indebtedness while gorging on Africa's oil and strategic minerals without having to abide by accepted international norms on human rights, labour, and environmental standards. At the other extreme stand African governments who see China as 'Africa's salvation', pointing to huge Chinese investments in the long-neglected African infrastructure sector, increased access to low-interest loans, and higher returns from commodities as a result of the growing Chinese demand for Africa's natural resources. The relationship between China and Africa is much more complex than that depicted by anti-China and pro-China camps. The contributors in this volume are all in agreement that China's rise has been more of a blessing than a curse for African countries. The 'China effect' on Africa's economic growth, economic diversification, job creation, improved connectivity, increased welfare, and integration into the globalized economy is hard to ignore. The direct contribution that Chinese finance and contractors are making to the economic infrastructure is a necessary condition for the industrialization prospects of African countries.

1.2 Analytical Framework and Aims of the Book

Although the literature on China–Africa relations has proliferated over the past decade, there is a paucity of empirically based literature on Africa's economic development and even less on the potential catalytic role of China–Africa economic ties in Africa's industrialization and structural transformation. In reflecting the rapidly changing dynamics, therefore, this volume makes an important contribution to filling the gap in the existing literature. A key theme of the book is the potential catalytic role of Chinese investment for Africa's industrialization and structural transformation.

China's engagement with African countries is uneven across the continent. Some countries (such as South Africa, Angola, Tanzania, Kenya, Ethiopia, Zambia, Democratic Republic of Congo, Nigeria, and Algeria) have multifaceted economic cooperation with China, while this is not the case for many other African countries. For instance, fewer than ten countries are major destinations of Chinese outward FDI, and the nature of FDI is different across these countries. While about two-thirds of Chinese firms in Ethiopia are in the manufacturing sector, only 30 per cent of all Chinese firms in Africa are, and their impact as driver and catalyst of economic transformation is uneven (McKinsey, 2017; World Bank, 2012).[4] The book interrogates key factors

---

[4] McKinsey (2017) *Dance of the Lions and Dragons: How Are Africa and China Engaging and How Will the Partnership Evolve?;* World Bank (2012) 'Chinese FDI in Ethiopia: A World Bank Survey'.

accounting for this variation and for development outcomes in different African countries. It also examines how lessons from China's development experience can inform policy decisions on industrialization in Africa. African agency is indeed a major factor contributing to the variation of outcomes observed across countries. Included in the volume is a case study of Ethiopia's successful industrialization strategy which demonstrates that it is possible to attract FDI and infrastructure finance from China to kick-start national industrialization, if African policymakers implement strategic actions in their engagement with China to steer the process of economic transformation.

An overarching theme of this volume is economic development in core areas relevant to Africa's economic transformation and where major shifts are observed, such as international trade, investment and industrialization, and infrastructure development and financing. Contributors to the volume interrogate the conditions under which Chinese trade, investment, and infrastructure loans can have a catalytic role in Africa's transformation, as well as the instructive lessons that African countries can draw from the Chinese development experience of the past forty years. Contributors to the volume agree that the Chinese experience shows the importance of writing one's own script in the global political economy, designing a homegrown strategy, instilling self-confidence, selectively dialling into the world system and sequencing openings, investing in human resources, and responding to challenges in a creative manner and with clear vision.

Moreover, as China undergoes major economic rebalancing to enter the fourth industrial revolution and upgrade to an innovation-driven economy, this is bound to affect China–Africa relations in multiple ways offering both opportunities and challenges (see Chapter 2). For example, China's new internationalization strategy—the Belt and Road Initiative (BRI)—covers not only Africa, but other continents, reflecting China's 'Going Global' strategy, greater emphasis on 'industrial cooperation', and the potential to attract manufacturing FDI in light manufacturing. Reaping the opportunities offered by China's economic rebalancing and the 'going out' of Chinese enterprises will primarily depend on the capacity of African actors to make the most of these opportunities. Considering China's global ambitions, African policymakers need to understand the contributions as well as the limitations of the economic ties with China in a rapidly changing context. This will distinguish the scope of this volume from other books that largely address governance, international diplomacy, and social issues (Alden and Large, 2019).[5]

[5] For an up-to-date compendium of research on Africa–China issues see Alden and Large (2019) *New Directions in Africa-China Studies*. This book contains two chapters (18 and 19) that are directly connected to the main focus of this volume.

China–Africa economic relations cannot be understood in isolation from the dynamics and operations of the global economy, and the position each occupies in the global division of labour. While China has been able to transform itself from the relatively poor and underdeveloped country of forty years ago to become one of the leading industrialized economies in the world today, the African continent has lagged far behind notwithstanding the impressive economic growth registered in many African countries in recent years and the rise of a sizeable middle class as a result of globalization. To account for the variation in development outcomes between China and Africa, and to understand the lessons African countries can draw from China regarding the 'pathways' to industrialization and structural transformation, requires a heterodox political-economy approach, with a clear focus on the changing global division of labour and power. This framework requires an understanding of the shifting political-economy conditions currently shaping China's development trajectory, which affect the way China's ties with Africa impact on the prospects for African structural transformations. Likewise, structural and shifting conditions in African settings also influence how opportunities for social and economic transformations are reaped (or not). Such an approach to the book seeks to bind chapters together without constraining individual contributors into an inflexible framework.

The shift in manufacturing to the global South and the 'global business revolution' (Nolan et al., 2007) in the second half of the twentieth century has had an enormous impact on national economies and the international division of labour. Driven by differences in comparative advantages and by the technological and communications revolution, a global manufacturing system has emerged, linking different regions and countries of the capitalist economy.[6] A system of flexible accumulation has given rise to global production networks that coordinate supply chains across multiple frontiers, incorporating both capital and labour from an ever-growing number of developing countries. The unfurling global division of labour creates variations in the regional division of labour, together with distinctive development possibilities (Fröbel, Heinrichs, and Kreye, 1980).[7] The East Asian economies—South Korea, Taiwan, and Japan—were the first to benefit from the new global economy, with China following in their footsteps after 1978. African countries, by and large, have failed to benefit from the unfolding global division of labour. The aim of this book is, therefore, to interrogate what Africa can learn from East Asia and China to embark on a path of industrialization and

---

[6] We are grateful to Professor James Mittelman for his insightful comments and suggestions for this section.

[7] F. Fröbel, J. Heinrichs, and O. Kreye (1980) *The New International Division of Labour: Structural Unemployment in Industrialised Countries and Industrialisation in Developing Countries.*

structural transformation, and whether emerging ties with China can contribute to this path.

1.3 The Structure of the Book

The fifteen chapters of the book are structured in four thematic sections which primarily focus on the progress, foundations, challenges, and future trajectory of China–Africa cooperation. Under the overarching theme of economic development, core areas are examined that have long-term implications for Africa's economic transformation, such as trade, investment, industrialization, infrastructure development, and financing.

1.3.1 *Part I: China's Rise and the Changing Global Development Discourse*

The contributors in this section set out to understand the meanings and global externalities of China's economic emergence in an era of globalization—in a period which has witnessed economic integration and interdependence among nation-states to a hitherto unprecedented degree. Linda Yueh (Chapter 2) and Célestin Monga (Chapter 3) explore the drivers of China's emergence as an economic superpower and its global impact. They argue that while globalization has assisted China's rise, the government's pragmatic economic experimentation with an East Asian-style development strategy and its success in the global quest for prosperity constitute an important chapter in the world's intellectual and political history.

As African countries see China more and more as an example to emulate, the contributors agree that African countries must focus more on learning from China's past domestic reforms process rather than trying to replicate it uncritically and without considering the local African context. Understanding the industrial policy framework is critical to understanding China–Africa economic ties as China moves upwards towards an indigenously driven innovation-led economy.[8]

1.3.2 *Part II: Evolving China–Africa Relations: Context, Perspectives, and Framework*

The contributors in this section examine China–Africa ties in their historical context, the institutional framework for promoting cooperation, and key policy instruments (trade, investment, loans, and technical assistance) that

---

[8] Xi Jinping (2012) *The Governance of China.* See also Ezra Vogel (2011) *Deng Xiaoping and the Transformation of China;* Justin Lin (2012) *Demystifying the Chinese Economy.*

the Chinese state deploys to cement its economic ties with Africa. It must, however, be noted that the Chinese way of catalyzing trade and investment in Africa is not exceptional although the scale may be different, given China's deep pockets. The strategy is clear: to create a paradigm of globalization that is favourable to China while benefiting partner countries.

In Chapter 4, David Shinn methodically presents the evolution of China–Africa interaction from the 1950s to the present, corresponding roughly to China's changes of leadership. From Mao Zedong's seizure of power in 1949 until the early 1990s, China focused more intensely on its political relationship with Africa than on its economic ties. During this period China was more concerned about support for African liberation movements, competition with Taiwan, the 'One China' principle, and dealing with internal challenges such as the Great Leap Forward and the Cultural Revolution. Major economic engagement such as construction of the Tanzania–Zambia railway in the 1970s, was the exception. The Jiang Zemin period in the mid-1980s set the stage for significant advancement. With Hu Jintao's arrival early in the twenty-first century, the China–Africa relationship came to be based predominantly on economic interests, especially China's desire to access African raw materials. It began with trade and expanded into Chinese outward investment in Africa, financing and construction by Chinese companies of infrastructure projects, increased foreign aid, and the movement of Chinese entrepreneurs and small traders to Africa. By 2009, China had overtaken the United States as Africa's largest trading partner. So far, the Xi Jinping era has resulted in a greater focus on deepening China–Africa economic ties, and greater support for African peace and security efforts.

In Chapter 5, Chris Alden traces the evolution of China–Africa economic ties over time, from the tentative commercial engagements of the early 1980s to the comprehensive infrastructure loans and increased foreign direct investment being pursued across all sectors today. As African economies came to demonstrate sustained patterns of higher rates of growth and two-way trade with China grew proportionally, the debate shifted towards one that focused on economic complementarities between them and Africa's integration into global value chains. This marks yet another stage in the progressive development of economic relations between China and Africa. The relentless dynamism of Chinese economic prowess, coupled with Africa's own rapid development, is promising a new cycle of growth and change in both economies. The Belt and Road Initiative, for example, aims to increase economic integration both within Asia and between Asia, Europe, and Africa through a variety of activities, with infrastructure connectivity at its core. This new initiative is bound to have an impact on the future of China–Africa economic relations. It will be up to individual African countries to do their homework in order to take advantage of this new opportunity.

In Chapter 6, Ian Taylor details the institutional framework within which Sino-African relations are constructed and identifies the maze of competing Chinese government institutions involved in shaping China's policy towards Africa. The multiplicity of institutional actors has created major coordination challenges that are often associated with the operations of Africa's Western development partners. Taylor's chapter contradicts the ideas of Chinese exceptionalism. The establishment of the Forum on China–Africa Cooperation (FOCAC) was expected to address problems of coordination and serve as a permanent dialogue platform. Eighteen years on, however, FOCAC has not yet achieved its stated objectives; the time has now come to restructure FOCAC so that it can become both a dialogue forum and coordinator of China–Africa economic ties (see Chapters 4 and 8).

1.3.3 *Part III: The Dynamics of China–Africa Economic Ties*

The Chinese approach to doing business in Africa is no different from those pursued by advanced capitalist countries of the West. However, the focus is quite different from the objectives and goals of Western partners. China focuses to a much greater extent on economic infrastructure and there is deliberate promotion of industrial investments, something that has been completely absent in the dominant Western approach at least until recently. And this has implications for prospects for structural transformation. The Chinese government employs a variety of means to promote FDI to Africa, and to create a more secure climate for Chinese investors in the continent. These include infrastructure loans, preferential trade, and the establishment of special economic zones (SEZs).

Chinese loans to Africa for infrastructure development have played a critical role by removing binding constraints on growth. In Chapter 7, Deborah Brautigam examines the changing actors involved in lending to Africa and the different types of loan instruments over the period 2000–16. The Bank of China, the Export-Import Bank of China, and the Agricultural Development Bank are key institutions that provide such loans, including syndicated loans and resource- or commodity-secured finance. The chapter details the trends in loan finance, regional distribution of loans, and sectors financed by Chinese loans, and examines the degree to which African borrowers have used these loans directly or indirectly to support structural transformation projects. The chapter concludes by examining the implications of rising debt levels in several African cases and the modalities of crafting debt work-out mechanisms between African debtors and Chinese creditors to avert default.

Complementing Deborah Brautigam's chapter on Chinese loans, Richard Carey and Jing Gu (Chapter 8) examine China's financing of Africa's infrastructure development. Carey and Gu argue that China brings a 'public entrepreneurship' model to bear in its state–market relations, combining vision, action, and learning in a governance structure with a vertical and horizontal component in the form of decentralization via provinces and cities, including both state-owned enterprises (SOEs) and private companies. China's capacity to supply large amounts of infrastructure financing and project implementation services in Africa and across the world is explained by three factors: (a) the public entrepreneurship approach of China's 'policy banks'; (b) the strengthening of the BRI programme; and (c) the importance of FOCAC as the overarching policy framework for China's multifaceted relations with the African continent. While the volume of funding is important, it is the 'public entrepreneurship' approach linking visions, action, and learning processes, and the co-evolution of state and market through directed improvisation that make the real difference.

In Chapter 9, Cyril Obi focuses on China's search for oil in Africa, and the strategies used by three Chinese oil corporations—China Petroleum and Chemical Corporation (Sinopec), China National Offshore Oil Corporation (CNOOC), and China National Petroleum Corporation (CNPC)—to establish their presence in Nigeria, Angola, and Sudan. The chapter details the structural challenge these Chinese corporations have faced in operating in these countries and how, through trial and error, they came to reach an accommodation with influential local political elites who were prepared to block any oil exploration and drilling contracts unless they were given their fair share of the revenue from oil or other forms of compensation by the corporations involved. While the hard bargaining by local elites was often conducted under the pretext of protecting the national interest, revenues from oil rarely benefit ordinary citizens. The chapter clearly shows that, despite the often-assumed powerful influence of giant oil companies, they exert little control over the decisions of powerful local elites regarding strategic resources such as oil and gas. In short, Chinese oil corporations are also learning in Africa and they do not yet have a clear advantage in the extractive sectors.

The role of SEZs in promoting industrialization is discussed in Chapter 10 by Omolade Adunbi and Howard Stein. To reduce Nigeria's dependency on oil, the government entered into several economic agreements with Chinese firms to increase investment in enterprises that will help generate a growth-oriented diversified economy. The chapter specifically looks at the construction of Free Trade Zones in Lagos and Ogun states and assesses the nature and impact of Chinese investment projects in different regions of Nigeria. The authors conclude that Nigerian zones have performed poorly in terms of attracting Chinese manufacturing capital with the potential to generate jobs, foreign exchange through exports, technological spillovers, management and labour training, and forward, backward, and demand linkages. This is largely attributed to poor infrastructure, especially electricity, bureaucratic gridlock, and corruption.

In Chapter 11, Won Kidane critically appraises China's use of international trade agreements and dispute settlement mechanisms in its economic relations with its African counterparts. The term 'agreements' is used in its broadest sense to include not only state-to-state international treaties, but also transnational commercial and infrastructure contracts concluded between Chinese state-owned enterprises and African governments or other African-owned interests. The chapter further discusses China's agreements and dispute settlement in three broadly classified areas: trade, investment, and commerce. In trade relations, China and most of its African trade partners operate within the multilateral trading system of the GATT/WTO legal regime, sharing not only the fundamental substantive rules and principles but also the mechanisms of dispute settlement under the Dispute Settlement Understanding. More importantly, however, it is fair to assume that China's bilateral trade agreements with more than forty African states provide more favourable trade terms and concessions than required under the WTO on reciprocal terms. It also appears that China routinely offers unilateral trade concessions to many African states beyond the bilateral treaties. The current flexible institutional arrangement can potentially facilitate manufactured exports from Africa to China in the future.

In Chapter 12, Carlos Oya takes up the issue of labour regimes and workplace encounters between China and Africa in the context of Chinese FDI and building contractors. The chapter counters the most popular claims about conditions in Chinese firms in Africa—limited job creation because of reliance on Chinese labour, poor working conditions, and limited skills transfer—and offers a more empirically nuanced view of the realities of job creation and employment dynamics in Chinese companies across Africa than is usually recognized in mainstream media reporting. The chapter points out that labour practices and outcomes are fluid and that the frequent assumption of Chinese 'exceptionalism' in labour relations is misplaced. It is, therefore, crucial to understand and document the diversity of 'Chinese capitals' (state and private capital, large and small, in construction or manufacturing), the importance of the African labour market context, and the particularities and structural features of the different sectors in which Chinese firms are investing and operating. The evidence of this chapter suggests a potential transformative role of Chinese firms in creating new jobs in construction and manufacturing, as it contributes to the process of building an industrial workforce in Africa.

1.3.4 *Part IV: China and Africa's Economic Transformation*

The contributors in this section discuss the conditions under which Chinese engagement in Africa can play a catalytic role in Africa's industrialization and structural transformation. In Chapter 13, Justin Lin and Jiajun Xu examine the conditions under which Chinese light manufacturing transfer can help drive Africa's industrialization from the historical perspective of the 'flying geese' pattern, the rising cost of labour in China and the likelihood of Chinese manufacturing firms relocating their production to Africa, and what African countries must do to seize this opportunity. Based on first-hand survey data, the authors explore how Chinese light manufacturing firms have coped with rising labour costs, what type of firms are more likely to relocate their manufacturing capacity to low-wage destinations, and where firms tend to relocate their production line. The authors estimate that about 85 million factory jobs will potentially move to other destinations as China loses its competitiveness in labour-intensive industries (see Chapter 14). In order to take advantage of new opportunities as a result of China's economic rebalancing, Lin and Xu offer several recommendations on how to mitigate binding constraints to help African countries seize the window of opportunity of industrial transfer from China to achieve economic structural transformation.

In Chapter 14, Fantu Cheru and Arkebe Oqubay argue that China–Africa economic ties must be examined from a structural transformation perspective in order to adequately evaluate the catalytic effect of Chinese engagement on economic growth, diversification of African economies, the development of domestic capabilities, and Africa's successful insertion into the globalized economy. This will primarily depend on the capacity of African actors to steer the process of economic transformation strategically. So far, the catalytic effect of China–Africa engagement on economic transformation of African countries has been uneven, due mainly to a lack of strategic approach on the part of individual African countries to harnessing the new opportunity, but partly also to the limited size of the Chinese manufacturing presence in Africa relative to China's manufacturing power. Ethiopia is one of a few African countries that has taken a more strategic approach to engaging China while maintaining strong ties with its traditional Western development partners. This pragmatic approach has enabled Ethiopian policymakers to mobilize large amounts of investment from China, other emerging economies, and traditional partners to embark upon a process of industrialization and structural transformation. Unfortunately, the Ethiopian example is not yet replicated by most other African countries.

There is considerable room for enhanced China–Africa economic ties in the years ahead. China's economic rebalancing and the 'Going Global' of Chinese enterprises will primarily depend on the capacity of African actors to make the most of these opportunities. Therefore, African agency and the direction that African policymakers take to steer their process of economic transformation are the key mediators in Africa–China relations. In this regard, Ethiopia's successful experience in attracting Chinese manufacturing firms can be taken as an example for other African countries, showing that it is indeed possible to act to direct Chinese engagement towards industrialization. If African countries fail to take a proactive and strategic approach towards China, many of the 85 million jobs could well go to other global destinations, such as India and, to some extent, China's hinterlands.

The concluding chapter (Chapter 15) pulls together the underlying themes, analytical perspectives, and pathways to Africa's economic transformation, and the catalytic role of Chinese investment and trade for Africa's industrialization and long-term growth. It also reviews FOCAC VII (September 2018) as signalling new directions in China–Africa economic ties for the coming decades. China's economic rebalancing as it enters the fourth industrial revolution can potentially offer new possibilities for African countries to become a preferred destination for Chinese firms planning to relocate to low-cost destinations. African countries must, therefore, take a strategic approach in their relationship with China.

1.4 The Pursuit of a Complementary China–Africa Economic Partnership

China–Africa economic cooperation is both dynamic and work in progress. It is not a marriage made in heaven and there is immense potential for improvement. There will always be areas of tension as is to be expected in any relationship between countries, particularly between countries with unequal power and strength. Some of the contentious issues are: limited spillover effects to the local economy either in the form of employment creation, knowledge transfer, or sub-contracting opportunities to African-owned firms; limited attention to social and environmental issues by Chinese investors; and relatively conflictive labour relations.

To its credit, the Chinese government has not been complacent in seeking remedies for some of these sensitive issues. It has put in place policies and strategies to improve the sustainability of its overseas trade and investment projects. Nevertheless, there is always a gap between what the government legislates in Beijing and the actual compliance of individual Chinese companies operating in Africa. The problem is exacerbated by the limited capacity of host-country African governments to monitor project performance and ensure that Chinese companies are complying with local laws and regulations.

Contributors to the volume have also raised a red flag on two important areas that both Chinese and African governments must address through dialogue and careful review of the evidence. These are: (a) the unsustainable level of debt that countries owe to China and (b) the persistent trade imbalance with China. The debt issue is intrinsically linked to the trade deficit issue. The imbalance is unsurprising in the absence of sufficient structural change and given the liberal trade frameworks of most African countries. Measures to address the problem of indebtedness will not bear fruit unless they are linked to improving the trade imbalance, supporting the export sector, and expanding quality FDI investment in the productive sectors of the economy.

Despite these differences, the opportunities presented by evolving China–Africa relations far outweigh the threats. China presents an enormous economic opportunity for Africa, given its potentially large purchasing power, its links to export markets, its technological prowess, and its commitment to increase investment and trade. As the second-largest economy in the world, China is the top source for outward FDI in manufacturing, and the number one source of infrastructure finance, two pillars of the future structural transformation in Africa. For Africa, China's economic rebalancing is opening up clear opportunities for economic transformation in sectors like light manufacturing. These sectors are critical for most countries because they help confront the two challenges that currently threaten the economic and political stability of the region: export performance and job creation. With increasing labour costs in China, African countries can become the best destination for manufacturing firms planning to relocate in low labour-cost economies. In addition, Africa's proximity to markets in Europe as well as automation and technological advances are contributing to the quick turnaround of production processes. For example, speed to market is one top reason why Chinese manufacturing firms are investing in Ethiopia. In addition, Chinese finance and contractors are making a direct contribution to the economic infrastructure that is a necessary condition for the industrialization prospects of African economies. It is evident that African governments need to develop coherent national policies and an integrated regional/continental strategy for engaging China from a systematic, strong, and much better-informed long-term perspective. Part of this should include an African agenda for closing the technology gap and transforming the asymmetrical pattern of trade between the continent and China. There is also a need for Africans to study and understand the broad ramifications of Chinese history, culture, and engagement with the continent and the world. Likewise, there is a need for Chinese actors, and especially entrepreneurs, to understand the diversity of histories, local cultures, and social norms in Africa. Such knowledge will form the cornerstone for a long-term African strategic leadership and vision for its engagement with China.

References

Alden, Chris, and Daniel Large (2019) *New Directions in Africa–China Studies*. London: Routledge.

Ang, Y. Y. (2016) *How China Escaped the Poverty Trap*. Ithaca, NY: Cornell University Press.

Brautigam, D. (2009) *The Dragons Gift: The Real Story of China in Africa*. Oxford: Oxford University Press.

Cheru, Fantu and Cyril Obi (2010) *The Rise of China and India in Africa: Challenges, Opportunities and Critical Interventions*. London: ZED Books.

Fröbel, F., J. Heinrichs, and O. Kreye (1980) *The New International Division of Labour: Structural Unemployment in Industrialised Countries and Industrialization in Developing Countries*. Cambridge: Cambridge University Press.

Lin, Justin (2012) *Demystifying the Chinese Economy*. Cambridge: Cambridge University Press.

McKinsey (2017) *Dance of the Lions and Dragons: How Are Africa and China Engaging, and How Will the Partnership Evolve?* June. Irene Yuan Sun, Kartik Jayaram, and Omid Kassiri (eds). New York: McKinsey.

Nolan, P., J. Zhang, and C. Liu (2007) 'The Global Business Revolution, the Cascade Effect, and the Challenge for Firms from Developing Countries', *Cambridge Journal of Economics*, 32(1): 29–47.

National Intelligence Council (2012) *Global Trends 2030: Alternative Worlds*. Washington, DC: National Intelligence Council Report.

People's Republic of China (2006) 'Declaration of the Beijing Summit and Beijing Action Plan, 2007–2009', Forum on China–Africa Cooperation (FOCAC), Ministry of Foreign Affairs, the People's Republic of China, Beijing.

Shinn, David, and Joshua Eisenman (2012) *China and Africa: A Century of Engagement*. Philadelphia, PA: University of Pennsylvania Press.

Vogel, Ezra (2011) *Deng Xiaoping and the Transformation of China*. Cambridge, MA: Harvard University Press.

World Bank (2012) 'Chinese FDI in Ethiopia: A World Bank Survey'. Washington, DC and Addis Ababa: World Bank.

Xi Jinping (2012) *The Governance of China*. Beijing: Foreign Languages Press.

Yueh, Linda (2013) *China's Growth: The Making of an Economic Superpower*. Oxford: Oxford University Press.

Part I
China's Rise and the Changing Global Development Discourse

2

China's Economic Emergence and Implications for Africa

Linda Yueh

2.1 China's Economic Rise and Global Impact

China's emergence as the world's second-largest economy in less than four decades has transformed not only the earth's most populous nation but also the global economy. China has affected the rest of the world by creating another source of consumers as well as a place for production. As is consistent with becoming a major economy with companies that have matured enough to invest overseas, since 2014 China has emerged as a net capital exporter, investing more abroad than it receives in inward foreign direct investment (FDI). The clearest manifestation of this outward investment can be seen in the 'Going Global' policy for Chinese firms launched in the early 2000s and in the Belt and Road Initiative (BRI) that started in 2013. The latter has significant implications for Africa as well as along the old Silk Road of Central Asia to the Middle East, and also South-east and South Asia.

Whether China will continue to exert such an impact depends on its economic growth. This chapter explores the drivers of China's emergence as an economic power and the factors determining the sustainability of its growth, focusing on the importance of global integration, and exploring aspects of the country's wider world impact. We begin with an assessment of China's economic rise and continued growth prospects, followed by an analysis of how the global economy has been affected, and concluding with a case study of China's Belt and Road Initiative, specifically with respect to sub-Saharan Africa's development, notably in respect of Chinese infrastructure investment in Kenya.

2.2 China's Economic Emergence

China has accomplished a remarkable feat in transforming itself from one of the poorest countries into the second-largest economy in the world in just thirty years (Borensztein and Ostry, 1996; Chow, 1993; Jefferson, Hu, and Su, 2006; Lin and Zhang, 2015; Song, Storesletten, and Zilibotti, 2011). Market-oriented reforms were launched in 1979, gradually dismantling the centrally planned economy. By doubling its GDP and average income every seven to eight years, it is on the cusp of eradicating extreme poverty (those living on less than US$1.90 per day adjusted for purchasing power parity), and has also lifted hundreds of millions of people into the middle class. With its 1.3 billion accounting for one-fifth of the global population, China's economic growth has begun to shape the world.

China's economy has unusual features. It is a transition economy that has dismantled most, but not all, of its state-owned enterprises and banks. But it is also a developing country where half the population remains rural even though urbanization has proceeded quickly since the 1980s. It does not fit neatly into studies of institutions and growth, as China remains a Communist state. It is not surprising that market-supporting institutions, such as private property protection, are weak, giving rise to the 'China paradox' whereby the country has grown well despite not having a strong set of institutions (Allen, Qian, and Qian, 2005; Yao and Yueh, 2009). China's economic growth is therefore both impressive and puzzling. Also, like any other fast-growing country, it is not assured of sustaining such growth (Zheng, Bigsten, and Hu, 2009). After all, most countries slow down as they become middle-income economies and the few that have become prosperous have done so by increasing their productivity and innovation. Those that have joined the ranks of rich countries such as South Korea are also globally integrated, a trait shared by China.

Key to China's past growth are investment and improvements in education. Looking ahead, these factors, together with technology and innovation, particularly when achieved through global integration that stimulates total factor productivity (TFP), will play important roles.

Focusing on these important components, investment and technology, there have been a large number of studies on the impact of technology and innovation on Chinese growth, particularly in terms of knowledge spillover from foreign direct investment. The Chinese government recognized the importance of innovation early on and enacted a patent law in 1985 followed by associated copyright and trademark legislation. With the imposition of tougher intellectual property rights (IPR) requirements after WTO (World Trade Organization) accession in 2001, Chinese firms have devoted more resources to innovative activities, including patent applications (Hu and

Jefferson, 2009). For example, Zheng, Liu, and Bigsten (2003) find that TFP growth in China has been achieved more through technical progress than through efficiency improvements.

But in the early part of the reform period, China's policies focused on attracting FDI and promoting international trade in order to benefit from the positive spillovers of technology and know-how that characterize the 'catch-up' phase of economic development, during which a country far from the technology frontier learns and imitates rather than re-invents or innovates. The location of FDI is encouraged by geographical and policy factors, such as proximity to major ports and decisions to create free trade areas, by institutions such as laws and regulations, contract enforcement, and local expenditure on infrastructure, and by labour market conditions (Yueh, 2011).

There are several mechanisms through which FDI and trade boost economic growth (Gylfason, 1999). One of the widely recognized avenues is technology transfer. A significant benefit of FDI is that new technology is brought into the country by foreign firms. Technology transfer occurs through new technologies sold directly through licensing agreements or the implicit transfer of new technology to domestic firms working alongside foreign investors. Also, international trade generates technology spillovers through learning-by-exporting or imitating technologies embodied in the imported intermediate goods. Productivity can be boosted as well by domestic firms facing competition at a global level. That FDI and international trade served as major driving forces contributing positively to China's faster growth during the late 1980s to mid-1990s is widely recognized (Chen, Chang, and Zhang, 1995; Harrold, 1995; Liu, Burridge, and Sinclair, 2002; Pomfret, 1997; Shan, 2002). Wei (1993) concludes that FDI contributes to economic growth through technological and managerial spillovers between firms as opposed to simply providing new capital. This is supported by studies such as those by Dees (1998) and Sun and Parikh (2001) who conclude that inward FDI affects China's economic growth in ways beyond simple capital formation. For China, FDI has also facilitated the transformation of the state-owned and the collectively owned sectors by introducing foreign partners and competition that helps to raise the efficiency of some of those state-owned and collectively owned enterprises (Liu, 2009).

Thus, FDI has played an important role in both China's TFP and its remarkable growth (Islam, Dai, and Sakamoto, 2006). The classic catch-up mechanism in neoclassical growth models is for capital to flow from developed to developing countries, bringing with it technology and know-how. China has certainly been the recipient of a large amount of FDI since its 'open door' policy took off in the early 1990s. Whalley and Xin (2010) find that foreign-invested enterprises (FIEs), which are often joint ventures between Chinese and foreign companies, account for around half of China's international trade.

It follows that FDI has been found to have positive effects on China's economic growth. Using econometric methods to regress GDP (or GDP growth) on FDI and other variables, many studies find a positive and significant coefficient on FDI, which points to foreign investment having played a notable part in China's economic growth (Berthelemy and Demurger, 2000; Borensztein, De Gregorio, and Lee, 1998; Chen, Chang, and Zhang, 1995; Dees, 1998; Graham and Wada, 2001; Lemoine, 2000; Liu, Burridge, and Sinclair, 2002; Sun and Parikh, 2001; Tseng and Zebregs, 2002; Wei, 1993; Wei et al., 1999).

Fleisher, Li, and Zhao (2010) find that FDI had a much larger effect on TFP growth before 1994 than after. After the mid-1990s, they find a much smaller, even insignificant, economic impact of FDI. They contend that the drop in the effect of FDI after 1994 can be attributed in part to the growth of the non-state sector. Since then, private and 'red cap' enterprises (nominally rural collectives, but effectively privately owned) and the evolution of township and village enterprises (TVEs) from collectives to private firms have become relatively more important sources of growth, while the relative importance of FDI-led growth has declined. Consistent with this finding, Wen (2007) reports that at least since the mid-1990s, FDI has tended to crowd out domestic investment, more so in the non-coastal regions. Similar findings are reported for later years by Ran, Voon, and Li (2007) and Jiang (2011).

But there is likely to be a degree of endogeneity in these relationships between FDI and TFP growth if the latter encourages more FDI (Li and Liu, 2005). A number of studies conclude that technology transfers and the spillover effects are limited, and much of the correlation between FDI and stronger growth is due to reverse causality (Lemoine, 2000; Woo, 1995; Young and Lan, 1997). Woo (1995) argues that the role of FDI in spillover effects is overstated because foreign investment is located in more market-liberalized regions, including in export zones. Rodrik (1999) also expresses doubts over spillover effects, arguing that greater productivity in domestic firms that export does not necessarily suggest efficiency spillovers from foreign firms, since more productive firms, domestic or foreign, tend to locate in export-oriented areas.

Turning to studies of the role of research and development (R&D), which is key to raising economic growth rates, this research focuses not only on innovation but also on absorptive capacity for utilizing new technology. Lai, Peng, and Bao (2006) find that domestic R&D has a positive and statistically significant impact on growth. Their estimates indicate that technology spillovers depend on the host province's absorptive ability as measured by human capital investment and the degree of openness to international trade. Kuo and Yang (2008) assess the extent to which knowledge and technology spillover contribute to regional economic growth in China. They consider a region's absorptive ability by measuring its capacity to absorb knowledge embodied in

FDI and imports, which then contribute to regional economic growth (for example, the ability of educated workers to use acquired advanced foreign technologies). They find suggestions of the existence of R&D spillover as well as international knowledge spillover. Thus, they conclude that knowledge capital, both in terms of R&D investment and technology imports, contributes positively to regional economic growth.

Along the same lines, Dobson and Safarian (2008) use the evolutionary approach to growth, in which institutions that support technical advance and enterprises develop capacity for learning and innovation. They examine China's transition from an economy in which growth is based on labour-intensive production and imported ideas and technology into one where growth is driven by domestic innovation. They find that increasing competitive pressure on firms encourages learning. Their survey of privately owned small and medium-sized enterprises in high-tech industries in Zhejiang province found evidence of much process, and some product, innovations. These enterprises respond to growing product competition and demanding customers by promoting internal learning and investment in R&D, and also by building international and research linkages.

The role of international knowledge spillover in generating endogenous economic growth, which is when technological innovation is determined by human capital and R&D investment within an economy, has long been emphasized (see, e.g. Grossman and Helpman, 1991). The empirical studies cited above and for other countries find that international technology spillovers are a major source of productivity growth (see Coe and Helpman, 1995; Eaton and Kortum, 1996; Keller, 2000). This crucial and still relatively under-explored issue could provide the basis for more sustainable growth for China in the coming decades.

In Van Reenen and Yueh (2012), we used a specially designed data set with measures of technology spillover at the Chinese firm level to examine this topic. We found positive contributions of Chinese–foreign joint ventures and FDI more generally. In other words, in our estimation, had China not attracted FDI, it would have grown more slowly. This is because Chinese–foreign joint ventures (JVs) are a quarter more productive than other firms, and JVs with technology transfer agreements that benefit from foreign know-how are 73 per cent more productive.

Putting all this together, we calculate that had China not attracted FDI and JVs in particular with their potential to allow for 'catching up' via technology transfers and other indirect avenues of learning, then China's annual GDP growth could have been from a half to more than one percentage point lower (i.e. as low as 8.5 per cent) over the past thirty years. As JVs were more important as a share of investment during the 1990s, accounting for around one-quarter of total investment, this is a conservative estimate. The contribution of joint ventures is therefore sizeable, as one percentage point in compound growth terms translates into large differences in income levels.

Summarizing the studies of Chinese growth, capital accumulation has contributed around half of China's economic growth, which is in line with other estimates that find that capital accumulation rather than TFP growth has driven growth during the reform period to date (see, e.g. Yueh, 2013 for a summary). Labour force growth accounts for much less, around one-tenth to one-fifth of GDP growth. Human capital accounts for another 11 to 15 per cent of China's growth. Factor accumulation (capital and labour) thus accounts for about 60–70 per cent of GDP growth. Once human capital is accounted for in the 'residual', the contribution of TFP to economic growth looks smaller. Within TFP, there is a further need to separate the one-off productivity gains due to factor reallocation during the reform process. By the 2000s, reallocation of workers accounted for around 10 per cent of TFP gains, though there were higher contributions in the previous decades. Van Reenen and Yueh (2012) show that positive spillovers and learning from existing know-how may account for between one-third and two-thirds of TFP. Given the poverty of China when it started market-oriented reforms in 1978 and the apparent 'catch-up' potential, this is not surprising. The challenge will be to increase domestic innovation, of which there are numerous signs, including the competitiveness of Chinese firms which are increasingly testing themselves in the global market, following on from China's decision to promote its firms 'Going Global' in the 2000s.

To achieve its ambition of becoming prosperous, China will need to improve technological and human capital as well as to re-balance its economy. Re-balancing the economy will involve boosting domestic demand (consumption, investment, government spending) to grow more quickly than exports, a shift towards services (including non-tradable sectors) and away from agriculture, increased urbanization to raise incomes, and greater opening up of the financial sector, including the internationalization of the RMB (Corden, 2009; Sato et al., 2012). To achieve these aims will also require the legal system to be examined, together with all the current state-owned enterprises and banks, which impair the efficiency of China's markets and thus its ability to overcome the middle-income-country trap, whereby countries start to slow after reaching upper-middle-income levels (Prasad and Rajan, 2006). For China to realize its potential as an economic superpower requires not only reform of the drivers of productivity but also the continuing transformation of the structure of its economy. China's integration with the world has helped its economic growth thus far, and could help its future prospects. Greater competition against the best firms in the world should stimulate innovation and improve the competitiveness of Chinese multinational corporations.

2.3 China's Global Impact

Given the importance of global integration for China's growth path, the emergence of such a sizeable country has had a significant impact on the rest of the world (Rodrik, 2010). Even though China remains a middle-income country, it is a major force in the world economy, alongside rich America, Europe, and Japan.

China's size and integration with the global economy have contributed to global prices as it is a large, open economy, similar to the United States. These countries are able to influence world prices, whereas smaller economies are 'price takers'. With China's emergence as the world's biggest trader, its exports have also affected other countries. More recently, the impact of China's overseas investments has begun to be felt across the world. Importantly, China has generated incremental growth in the global economy that has made its success significant for the welfare of other countries.

The 'China effect' has been acutely felt in terms of commodity prices. The reform of the state sector in the 1990s and the rise of the non-state sector have heralded a second wave of industrialization in China, which requires energy and raw materials. Since the mid-1990s, China has become a net oil importer even though it is also one of the top ten world producers of oil (Victor and Yueh, 2010). While these commodities constitute a relatively small share of total Chinese imports, their quantities have been large enough to have an impact on world markets. One effect of this is to redistribute income between other countries in the world. Thus, primary commodity exporters have experienced improvements in their export earnings and terms of trade (prices of exports to imports), which have been paid for by importers of these commodities, some of them developed countries.

At the same time, Chinese exports of a range of manufactures have resulted in some substantial price falls, which have benefited developed economies. Lower import prices contributed to a weaker inflationary environment in the United States, the European Union, and others. In this manner, China's rapid global integration and remarkable growth generated a favourable terms-of-trade shock that led to lower than expected levels of inflation in the global economy in the 1990s and early 2000s.

But in terms of exports, China poses a competitive threat. In Latin American countries such as Chile, Costa Rica, and El Salvador, 60–70 per cent of exports are directly threatened by China (Lall, Weiss, and Oikawa, 2005). Bangladesh and Sri Lanka, which compete in lower-end manufacturing, were also affected. And while China's rise has induced more imports from its Asian neighbours, this has not been enough to offset displacement of their exports in third-country markets (Bown and Crowley, 2010; Greenaway, Mahabir, and Milner,

2008). But exports of labour-intensive products like clothing, apparel, textiles, and footwear are a rapidly declining share of China's trade, as more advanced manufactured products, particularly electrical equipment, become a bigger part of its exports (Jarreau and Poncet, 2012; Kaplinsky, Terheggen, and Tijaja, 2011).

A key aspect of this technological upgrading is the growth of high levels of two-way trade in similar items, notably consumer electronics. This 'intra-industry trade' reflects cross-border production networks. Since around half of China's exports have been produced by foreign-owned enterprises since the mid-1990s, the rise of intra-industry trade follows. Multinational corporations seek low-cost manufacturing bases, and diversify their production and supply chains by investing in different countries.

Notably, China's comparative advantage is no longer being driven by low-cost, abundant labour. Some interior provinces may still compete on that basis, but for areas on the coast this advantage has been substantially eroded and the country's competitive advantage is increasingly based on skills. This upgrading will alter the set of industries that experience competitive pressure from China (Yao and Zhou, 2011).

The global financial crisis and the ensuing Great Recession hit China in the autumn of 2008 when exports collapsed. China had suffered some losses from the failure of Lehman Brothers in America, but it did not become embroiled in a financial crisis and thus only suffered the real economy effects on account of the decline in global trade. It did, though, re-shape its outlook towards re-balancing its growth drivers, which is also consistent with becoming a large, open economy that depends more on its own consumers than foreign ones for economic growth (Yueh, 2011).

At the height of the crisis exports collapsed. The severity of the Great Recession led to global trade contracting for the first time in thirty years. Exports account for around one-third of China's GDP and the closure of exporting factories resulted in an estimated 20 million unemployed rural–urban migrants. It propelled China to think about achieving a more stable growth model, including improving the structure of the economy towards a model suitable for a large, open economy. By re-structuring itself as an economy that recognizes the benefits of global integration while maintaining a strong domestic demand base, it can better shield itself from the worst external shocks (see Bagnai, 2009).

China's gradual liberalization of its capital account, in particular the 'going out' policy, has also begun to change the global investment and multinational corporation landscape. State-owned enterprises, and increasingly, private firms were encouraged by the Chinese government to 'go out' and compete on global markets. Launched in 2000, 'Going Out' is intended to create Chinese multinational corporations that are internationally competitive.

Thus, the first commercial outward investment by a Chinese firm occurred in 2004 with TCL's purchase of France's Thomson.

Through this 'Going Global' strategy, China aims to become more than a producer of low-end manufacturing goods, branded under the moniker of Western firms. The ability to produce branded goods is an indicator of industrial upgrading, the very thing that China needs to ensure a sustained growth rate. If its firms are innovative and productive as against leading global companies, that is a sign of innovation. For instance, although Haier is the largest white goods maker in China and is sold in Walmart, it does not command brand recognition and loyalty in world markets. The strategy of Lenovo, therefore, was to not only purchase IBM's PC business but also licence the use of the brand name for five years so that Lenovo could eventually assume the trusted name of IBM in world markets. Chinese brands are now better known, for example, e-commerce website Alibaba and tech firm Tencent, Asia's biggest listed company. By the late 2010s, the only Chinese brand to have broken into the top 100 global brands is Huawei, the world's largest telecoms equipment company.

Previously, most outward FDI consisted of state-led investments in energy and commodities, but the maturing of Chinese industry indicates that the trend is changing as China seeks to move up the value chain and develop multinational companies. This was a trait shared by Japan and South Korea. Unlike most middle-income countries, they managed to join the ranks of the rich economies by having innovative and technologically advanced firms that enabled them to overcome what is sometimes termed the 'middle-income-country trap' (Yueh, 2013). Nations start to slow down in growth when they reach a per-capita income level of around US$14,000. Growing by adding labour or capital (factor accumulation) slows or reaches its limit, and most countries are unable to sustain the double-digit growth rates experienced at an earlier period of development. China is keen to avoid this trap and its policy-makers are attempting to join the ranks of prosperous countries. China is more likely to maintain a strong growth rate by increasing productivity through industrial upgrading that is stimulated by international competition. The demand for energy and upgrading industrial capability had been the motivating forces for China to invest overseas. But, with the focus on overcoming the middle-income-country trap and the need for its firms to face more competition from the biggest companies in the world, China has encouraged the development of Chinese multinational corporations with its 'Going Global' policy (Yueh, 2011).

As a result, there has been explosive growth of outward FDI since the mid-2000s, which points not only to state investment in commodity sectors but also to commercial M&As for private companies. Becoming a net capital exporter is also viewed as a mark of a country reaching a level of industrial development; its firms can compete on world markets. 'Going Out' or 'Going Global' has recently been extended to also encompass the 'Made in China 2025' plan that seeks to introduce artificial intelligence and advanced technology into Chinese companies at home and abroad. With outward FDI overtaking inward FDI by the middle of the 2010s, China appears to have changed its growth model from one that relied on foreign investment to an economy that has its own competitive, multinational companies producing and investing at home and abroad. This trend is increasingly affecting recipient countries of Chinese FDI, particularly with the launch of its Belt and Road Initiative in 2013.

2.4 China's Impact on Africa: The Belt and Road Initiative and Kenya

Alongside the promotion of outward foreign investment by Chinese firms, the Chinese government has also implemented a large international infrastructure investment plan (Fan, 2018; Huang, 2016). The Belt and Road Initiative, launched in 2013, encompasses sixty-five countries at present and the Chinese government intends to invest up to US$1 trillion for another five years from 2018. The BRI builds infrastructure on the maritime road traversing South-east Asia to East Africa while the overland belts encompass the old Silk Road and extend into Central Asia and the Middle East as well as Central and Eastern Europe. That is a substantial amount of foreign direct investment coming from China. And it's coming at a time when there is a dearth of investment not just in the developing world, for which this is a perennial issue, but also in advanced economies.

The OECD, for instance, estimates that in many advanced economies, investment levels are about 15 per cent below what they were before the global financial crisis (OECD, 2017). The United Nations has highlighted a large funding gap in the global economy in order to achieve the Sustainable Development Goals (SDGs) by 2030. The seventeen SDGs are geared towards eradicating poverty and preventable diseases, and ensuring a good quality of life for everyone on the planet. The Belt and Road Initiative fills in some of this gap, particularly in Africa which has been estimated to have only a fraction of the investment it needs to grow, and has the potential to support crucial infrastructure at a critical time (see, e.g. Callaghan and Hubbard, 2016; Luft, 2016).

The BRI is prominently seen in Kenya. It is the most developed country in East Africa, but Kenyan average incomes are only US$1,500 per capita. It sorely lacks investment and the funds for industrialization. China has invested a great deal in Kenya, as it also has in Ethiopia and other countries in sub-Saharan Africa.

On a visit in 2017, I observed Chinese construction firms building the railway connecting the capital Nairobi to Mombasa on the coast, Kenya's largest rail project in more than half a century. To win these contracts, Chinese contractors had cut their costs to rock bottom to secure funding from the Belt and Road Initiative to build railways and roads, making it hard for other companies to compete. It would be a challenge to find Western companies that would do the same work for the same low cost as Chinese companies are willing to do it for.

China had been a significant funder of infrastructure projects in Kenya even before the Belt and Road Initiative. For instance, it was one of the joint funders of the Thika Road, Kenya's first modern multi-lane highway which cut the journey time between Nairobi and Thika, which is in the industrial part of Kenya, from two hours to just 40 minutes.

When China invests in these projects in other countries, bilateral investment agreements are negotiated with different governments, often with different terms. For instance, during fieldwork around Nairobi, I discovered that the agreement in Kenya is that Chinese contractors must hire 70 per cent local workers. But who constitutes that 70 per cent is open to interpretation. The Chinese contractors view the 70 per cent as hiring 70 per cent Kenyans. But the Kenyan workers disagree. They believe 70 per cent locals means local workers and not just Kenyans. For instance, during the current railway extension being built near the Masai Mara national park, the Masai tribe were unhappy because the 70 per cent was interpreted as including other tribes, and not only them. Chinese firms were bringing with them local hires from other Kenyan tribes, which led to friction at railway construction sites. These disagreements were resolved, however, because the Kenyans saw the Chinese investment as a source of much needed employment in rural areas. It was striking how much the Kenyans wanted to work on the Chinese railway projects. It is gruelling work that pays around US$5 per day, and yet Masai people were camped outside the Chinese contractor's camp seeking work. Some had been camped there for months.

Another aspect of these investments is that the Chinese contractors do not enter into joint ventures with local firms or hire Kenyan managers. Thus, the potential for positive spillovers in these African nations is less. Learning from more advanced foreign firms was one of the ways China benefited so much from foreign direct investment (Yueh, 2013). While in its own growth trajectory and catch-up China had required foreign investors to hire local Chinese managers as well as local workers, this wasn't happening much in Kenya. Even in the most developed country in East Africa, there was a dearth of skilled managerial staff. Training was not being offered by the Kenyan government, probably due to a lack of teachers with relevant experience since these skills tend to be gained through working on major infrastructure projects. Thus, it was Chinese firms that were training Kenyans to improve their managerial and technical skills. The other side of the issue was apparent when I asked African policymakers why they do not insist on Chinese firms hiring local managers. Their answer was that they were worried that China would abandon their country and invest in another one instead. Therefore, for African nations such as Kenya to benefit from positive spillovers from foreign direct investment would require their workers to be integrated with Chinese management and technical staff. More needs to be done in that respect by both African nations and China.

Still, China is providing much needed investment in Africa that has the potential to help these nations industrialize (Harrison, Lin, and Xu, 2014; see also Chapter 13). If an industrial area is better connected to the consumers in the capital as well as those overseas through linking commercial centres with ports, then industrialization is more likely to take off. In other words, selling to global markets offers Kenyan firms larger-scale opportunities than the domestic market (see also Chapter 14). Rail, roads, and other improvements to logistics would facilitate Kenya connecting to global markets particularly for light manufacturing, which was what China did when it opened up so it was able to grow without relying solely on the consumption power of its domestic economy. Globalization relaxes the constraints of scale often faced by smaller economies, and such investments are key to achieving global integration. Infrastructure such as the Kenyan roads and railways that China is investing in benefit not only Chinese development, by improving the transport of commodities back to China, but also the host nation. Investment leading to industrialization is important for sustaining African economic development.

2.5 How China's Emergence can Help Transform Growth in Sub-Saharan Africa

China's emergence as an economic power has taken less than four decades. Its growth drivers have changed during this period and increasingly incorporate technology along with outward investment, which means that China's economy has affected the global economy in numerous respects. The era of cheap manufacturing in China has been replaced by a more technologically competitive set of companies emerging to compete in global markets. With companies 'going out' and the large-scale Belt and Road Initiative, outward investment has begun to exceed inward investment in the world's second-biggest economy. The impact on developed economies from Chinese multinational companies is varied, but for developing countries in Africa, investment from China is potentially transformative.

The Belt and Road Initiative has seen billions invested in much needed infrastructure in countries such as Kenya. Linking key cities and ports with road and railways provides the foundation for industrialization. The interest in industrial jobs and the benefits from infrastructure for the economy means that Africa can benefit from China's Belt and Road Initiative. It may even be the key to economic development for Kenya and other countries in sub-Saharan Africa.

References

Allen, F., J. Qian, and M. Qian (2005) 'Law, Finance and Economic Growth in China', *Journal of Financial Economics*, 77(1): 57–116.

Bagnai, A. (2009) 'The Role of China in Global External Imbalances: Some Further Evidence', *China Economic Review*, 20(3): 508–26.

Berthelemy, J. C., and S. Demurger (2000) 'Foreign Direct Investment and Economic Growth: Theory and Applications to China', *Review of Development Economics*, 4(2): 140–55.

Borensztein, E., J. De Gregorio, J., and J. W. Lee (1998) 'How Does Foreign Direct Investment Affect Economic Growth?', *Journal of International Economics*, 45(1): 115–35.

Borensztein, E. and J. D. Ostry (1996) 'Accounting for China's Growth Performance', *American Economic Review*, 86(2): 225–8.

Bown, C. P. and M. A. Crowley (2010) 'China's Export Growth and the China Safeguard: Threats to the World Trading System?' *Canadian Journal of Economics*, 43: 1353–88.

Callaghan, M. and P. Hubbard (2016) 'The Asian Infrastructure Investment Bank: Multilateralism on the Silk Road', *China Economic Journal*, 2: 116–39.

Chen, C., L. Chang, and Y. M. Zhang (1995) 'The Role of Foreign Direct Investment in China Post-1978 Economic Development', *World Development*, 23(4): 691–703.

Chow, G. C. (1993) 'Capital Formation and Economic Growth in China', *Quarterly Journal of Economics*, 108(3): 809–42.

Coe, D. and E. Helpman (1995) 'International R&D Spillover', *European Economic Review*, 39(5): 859–87.

Corden, M. (2009) 'China's Exchange Rate Policy, its Current Account Surplus and the Global Imbalances', *The Economic Journal*, 119(541): F430–41.

Dees, S. (1998) 'Foreign Direct Investment in China: Determinants and Effects', *Economics Planning*, 31(2–3): 175–94.

Dobson, W. and A. E. Safarian (2008) 'The Transition from Imitation to Innovation: An Enquiry into China's Evolving Institutions and Firm Capabilities', *Journal of Asian Economics*, 19(3): 301–11.

Eaton, J. and S. Kortum (1996) 'Trade in Idea: Patenting and Productivity in the OECD', *Journal of International Economics*, 40(3–4): 251–78.

Fan, Z. (2018) 'China's Belt and Road Initiative: A Preliminary Quantitative Assessment', *Journal of Asian Economics*, 55: 84–92.

Fleisher, B., H. Li, and M. Q. Zhao (2010) 'Human Capital, Economic Growth, and Regional Inequality in China', *Journal of Development Economics*, 92(2): 215–31.

Graham, E. M. and E. Wada (2001) 'Foreign Direct Investment in China: Effects on Growth and Economic Performance', Working Paper 01–03, Institute for International Economics.

Greenaway, D., A. Mahabir, and C. Milner (2008) 'Has China Displaced Other Asian Countries' Exports?' *China Economic Review*, 19(2): 152–69.

Grossman, G. M., and E. Helpman (1991) *Innovation and Growth in the Global Economy*. Cambridge, MA: MIT Press.

Gylfason, T. (1999) 'Exports, Inflation and Growth', *World Development*, 27(6): 1031–57.

Harrison, A. E., J. Y. Lin, and L. C. Xu (2014) 'Explaining Africa's (Dis)advantage', *World Development*, 63(C): 59–77.

Harrold, P. (1995) 'China: Foreign Trade Reform: Now for the Hard Part', *Oxford Review of Economic Policy*, 11(4): 133–46.

Hu, A. G. Z. and G. Jefferson (2009) 'A Great Wall of Patents: What Is behind China's Recent Patent Explosion?' *Journal of Development Economics*, 90(1): 57–68.

Huang, Y. (2016) 'Understanding China's Belt and Road Initiative: Motivation, Framework, and Assessment', *China Economic Review*, 40: 314–21.

Islam, N., E. Dai, and H. Sakamoto (2006) 'Role of TFP in China's Growth', *Asian Economic Journal*, 20(2): 127–59.

Jiang, Y. (2011) 'Understanding Openness and Productivity Growth in China: An Empirical Study of Chinese Provinces', *China Economic Review*, 22(3): 290–8.

Jarreau, J. and S. Poncet (2012) 'Export Sophistication and Economic Growth: Evidence from China', *Journal of Development Economics*, 97(2): 281–92.

Jefferson, G., A. G. Z. Hu, and J. Su (2006) 'The Sources and Sustainability of China's Economic Growth', *Brookings Papers on Economic Activity*, 2: 1–60.

Kaplinsky, R., A. Terheggen, and J. Tijaja (2011) 'China as a Final Market: The Gabon Timber and Thai Cassava Value Chains', *World Development*, 39(7): 1177–90.

Keller, W. (2000) 'Do Trade Patterns and Technology Flows Affect Productivity Growth', *World Bank Economic Review*, 14(1): 17–47.

Kuo, C. C. and C. H. Yang (2008) 'Knowledge Capital and Spillover on Regional Economic Growth: Evidence from China', *China Economic Review*, 19(4): 594–604.

Lai, M., S. Peng, and Q. Bao (2006) 'Technology Spillovers, Absorptive Capacity and Economic Growth', *China Economic Review*, 17(3): 300–20.

Lall, S., J. Weiss, and H. Oikawa (2005) 'China's Competitive Threat to Latin America: An Analysis for 1990–2002', *Oxford Development Studies*, 33: 163–94.

Lemoine, F. (2000) 'FDI and the Opening up of China's Economy', CEPII Working Paper 2000–11.

Li, X. and X. Liu (2005) 'Foreign Direct Investment and Economic Growth: An Increasingly Endogenous Relationship', *World Development*, 33(3): 393–407.

Lin, J. Y. and F. Zhang (2015) 'Sustaining Growth of the People's Republic of China', *Asian Development Review*, 32(1): 31–48.

Liu, X., P. Burridge, and P. J. N. Sinclair (2002) 'Relationships between Economic Growth, Foreign Direct Investment and Trade: Evidence from China', *Applied Economics*, 34(11): 1433–40.

Liu, Z. (2009) 'Foreign Direct Investment and Technology Spillovers: Theory and Evidence', *Journal of Development Economics*, 85(1–2): 176–93.

Luft, G. (2016) 'China's Infrastructure Play: Why Washington Should Accept the New Silk Road', *Foreign Affairs*, 95(5): 68–75.

OECD (2017) 'OECD Economic Outlook', Vol. 2017 (2): 19, OECD, Paris.

Pomfret, R. (1997) 'Growth and Transition: Why Has China's Performance Been So Different?', *Journal of Comparative Economics*, 25(3): 422–40.

Prasad, E. S. and R. G. Rajan (2006) 'Modernizing China's Growth Program', *American Economic Review*, 92(2): 331–6.

Rodrik, D. (1999) 'The New Global Economy and Developing Countries: Making Openness Work', Policy Essay No. 24, Overseas Development Council (Baltimore, MD).

Rodrik, D. (2010) 'Making Room for China in the World Economy', *American Economic Review*, 100(2): 89–93.

Sato, K., J. Shimizu, N. Shrestha, and Z. Zhang (2012) 'New Estimates of the Equilibrium Exchange Rate: The Case for the Chinese Renminbi', *World Economy*, 35: 419–43.

Shan, J. (2002) 'A VAR Approach to the Economies of FDI in China', *Applied Economics*, 34(7): 885–93.

Song, Z., K. Storesletten, and F. Zilibotti (2011) 'Growing Like China', *American Economic Review*, 101(1): 202–39.

Sun, H. S. and A. Parikh (2001) 'Exports, Inward Foreign Direct Investment and Regional Economic Growth in China', *Regional Studies*, 35(3): 187–96.

Tseng, W. and H. Zebregs (2002) 'Foreign Direct Investment in China: Some Lessons for Other Countries', Policy Discussion Paper 02/3, IMF.

Van Reenen, J. and L. Yueh (2012) 'Why Has China Grown So Fast? The Role of International Technology Transfers', University of Oxford Department of Economics Working Paper 592; London School of Economics and Political Science Centre for Economic Performance CEP Discussion Paper DP1121, pp. 1–24.

Victor, D. and L. Yueh (2010) 'The New Energy Order: Managing Insecurities in the 21st Century', *Foreign Affairs*, 89(1): 61–73.

Wei, S. J. (1993) 'The Open Door Policy and China's Rapid Growth: Evidence from City-Level Data', Working Paper No. 4602, NBER.

Wei, Y. Q., X. M. Liu, D. Parker, and K. Vaidya (1999) 'The Regional Distribution of Foreign Direct Investment in China', *Regional Studies*, 33(9): 857–67.

Wen, M. (2007) 'A Panel Study on China—Foreign Direct Investment, Regional Market Conditions, and Regional Development: A Panel Study on China', *Economics of Transition*, 15(1): 125–51.

Whalley, J., and X. Xin (2010) 'China's FDI and Non-FDI Economies and the Sustainability of Future High Chinese Growth', *China Economic Review*, 21(1): 123–35.

Woo, W. T. (1995) 'Comments on Wei's (1995) Foreign Direct Investment in China: Sources and Consequences', in A. Krueger (ed.), *Financial Deregulation and Integration in East Asia*. Chicago, IL: University of Chicago Press, pp. 166–89.

Yao, X. and M. Zhou (2011) 'China's Economic and Trade Development: Imbalance to Equilibrium', *World Economy*, 34: 2081–96.

Yao, Y. and L. Yueh (2009) 'Law, Finance and Economic Growth in China: An Introduction', *World Development* (Special Issue on Law, Finance and Economic Growth in China), 37(4): 753–62.

Young, S. and P. Lan (1997) 'Technology Transfer to China through Foreign Direct Investment', *Regional Studies*, 31(7): 669–79.

Yueh, L. (2011) 'Re-balancing China: Linking Internal and External Reforms', *Asian Economic Papers*, 10(2): 85–109.

Yueh, L. (2013) *China's Growth: The Making of an Economic Superpower*. Oxford: Oxford University Press.

Zheng, J., A. Bigsten, and A. Hu (2009) 'Can China's Growth Be Sustained? A Productivity Perspective', *World Development*, 37(4): 874–88.

Zheng, J., Xiaoxuan Liu, and Arne Bigsten (2003) 'Efficiency, Technological Progress, and Best Practices in Chinese State Enterprises (1980–1994), *Journal of Comparative Economics*, 31(1): 134–52.

3
The Meanings and Global Externalities of China's Economic Emergence

Célestin Monga

3.1 Introduction

On 30 June 1984, Deng Xiaoping, who had been anointed as the de facto leader of the Communist Party of China, boldly articulated the reasons why his country would rely on a new ideological framework and adopt a development path quite different from previous practice. He explained the rationale for 'building a socialism with specifically Chinese character.' He said:

> At the founding of the People's Republic [in 1949], we inherited from old China a ruined economy with virtually no industry. There was a shortage of grain, inflation was acute, and the economy was in chaos. But we solved the problems of feeding and employing the population, stabilized commodity price and unified financial and economic work, and the economy rapidly recovered. On this foundation we started large-scale reconstruction. What did we rely on? We relied on Marxism and socialism. But by Marxism we mean Marxism that is integrated with Chinese conditions, and by socialism we mean a socialism that is tailored to Chinese conditions and has a specifically Chinese character.[1]

Deng's confident and positive assessment of China's economic performance, so early into the implementation of his reform programme, was dismissed by many analysts who had in mind the heavy human, political, economic, and social costs of the Cultural Revolution, which many researchers estimated had durably impoverished and weakened China during the twentieth century. With hindsight, it is now clear that Deng's optimistic comments were based

---

[1] Remarks at the talk with the Japanese delegation to the second session of the Council of Sino-Japanese Non-Governmental Persons, in Deng (1994), pp. 72–3.

on a long view of history (the *'longue durée,'* as Fernand Braudel stated it), and reflected the strong belief that an audacious *aggiornamento* of socialist ideals with capitalist instruments in the new reality of an increasingly interconnected world was the appropriate balancing act to give China a chance to rejuvenate its economy while remaining true to its philosophical soul—and to its rejection of social divisions and deep inequality.

On 16 November 2009, United States president Barack Obama visited China for the first time in his life. He praised a 'majestic country' and claimed to see in Shanghai the growth that had caught the attention of the world. He said:

> China has lifted hundreds of millions of people out of poverty—an accomplishment unparalleled in human history—while playing a larger role in global events...
> There is a Chinese proverb: 'consider the past and you shall know the future'.
> Surely, we have known setbacks and challenges over the past 30 years. Our relationship has not been without disagreements and difficulty. But the notion that we must be adversaries is not predestined—not when we consider the past. Indeed, because of our cooperation, both the U.S. and China are more prosperous and more secure.[2] (Obama, 2009)

Obama's seemingly innocuous statement generated controversy in America where many felt offended by such words from the 'leader of the free world' challenging the permanent supremacy of the United States as the only 'indispensable nation'. It asserted that China's emergence as a major economic superpower was nothing to be surprised about: in each period of human history, there have been successful cities and nations in the development of capitalism, 'world-economies' (*'économie-monde'*) as Braudel (1958) put it, and China today just happens to be one of these ordinary phenomena.

Yet China's economic emergence in the late twentieth century has been anything but banal. In fact, the pace, depth, scope, and ramifications of China's economic transformation since 1979 are indeed unique in economic history. With 9.6 per cent annual growth for nearly four decades, China lifted over 700 million people out of poverty in just one generation and become the second-largest economy in the world. Widely seen as a place of failed economic experiments for centuries and until only three decades ago, China is now projected to soon become the largest economy in the world and to dominate the global scene for the foreseeable future. In a world of frequent global economic and financial crises, constant social tensions and conflicts fuelled by poverty, inequities, large-scale unemployment, despair, and big

---

[2] In 1979, trade of goods and services between the United States and China stood at about US$5 billion. In 2017, it had risen to US$712 billion (source: US Bureau of Economic Analysis https://www.bea.gov/data/intl-trade-investment/international-trade-goods-and-services). In many ways, the two leading economies in the world have become so mutually dependent that neither one would truly benefit from a sustained trade war. See Monga (2012) for a theoretical framework of economic interdependence between the economies of the United States and China.

waves of illegal migrations, China's economic transformation and stable performance have resonance and meanings well beyond its borders and neighbourhood: 'As China's domestic market continues to grow, so, too, does its economic power and ability to set global rules' (Spence, 2017).

This chapter posits that the Chinese economy has become a multifaceted global public good. Section 3.2 highlights several global externalities of China's economy, and examines the opportunities and challenges they present. We then discuss some of China's major macroeconomic risks and possible negative externalities to the world economy before offering concluding remarks.

3.2 The Chinese Economy as a Global Public Good

Public goods have long been part of the analytical frameworks used by researchers for the economic analysis of government policy at the national level. With the acceleration of globalization, it has become increasingly clear that issues once viewed as national policy are actually issues of transnational importance and concern. For instance, it is widely recognized that carbon emissions and global warming not only affect the nation involved in their production, but also impact significantly on other nations. Likewise, with increased global mobility, communicable diseases are problems against which no single country can implement an effective national strategy to protect the health of its population.

Making the case that the Chinese economy has become something of a global public good requires some conceptual justification before evidence is provided to support this statement. Global public goods are often narrowly defined as 'goods with benefits and/or costs that potentially extend to all countries, people, and generations. Global public goods are in a dual sense public: they are public as opposed to private; and they are global as opposed to national. Like publicness in general, *globalness* is in most instances a matter of policy choice' (Kaul and Mendoza, 2003). In that sense, 'few global public goods are global and public by nature. The ozone layer is one of these few naturally global and public goods. Most other global public goods are national public goods that have become interlinked in the wake of increasing openness of borders and as a result of increasing international regime formation and policy harmonization behind national borders' (Kaul and Mendoza, 2003).

A broader definition of global public goods, used in this chapter, is the one provided by the International Task Force on Global Public Goods: 'issues that are broadly conceived as important to the international community, that for the most part cannot or will not be adequately addressed by individual countries acting alone and that are defined through a broad international consensus or a legitimate process of decision-making' (2006: 13).[3]

Global public goods have shared benefits and costs across boundaries, with two characteristics: first, they produce benefits that are impossible to prevent everyone from enjoying, or costs which no one can avoid (non-rivalry). Second, consumption by any one individual or nation does not detract from that of another (non-excludability). Typical examples of such 'pure' public goods are air quality or control of epidemic diseases. If only one of these characteristics is satisfied, public goods are said to be impure, which is the way the Chinese economy is analyzed in this chapter. Thanks to its size and performance, China has been contributing about one-third of global growth, constantly expanding global demand, and therefore driving the world quest for prosperity, social inclusion, and social peace. It has become indeed an impure global public good.

China's economic transition started in the late 1970s at a time when the world economy was undergoing profound transformations. The most important change was the unilateral decision by the United States to end the international monetary system set up after World War II (Bretton Woods system) and to end dollar convertibility to gold.[4] That decision abruptly changed the rules of global finance and world trade, and laid the grounds for the reshaping of the global economy. The end of the old international system was accelerated with the subsequent oil price shocks (1973 and 1979), which foreshadowed not just bad news (an international debt crisis in the 1980s) but

---

[3] The International Task Force also provides definitions of various categories of public goods: A local public good benefits [or costs] all the members of a local community, possibly to include the citizens of more than one country. A national public good benefits [or costs] all the citizens of a state. A domestic public good benefits [or costs] all the members of a community situated within a single state. National public goods are domestic public goods, but domestic public goods need not be national public goods. A regional public good benefits [or costs] countries belonging to a geographic territory. A global public good benefits [or costs] all countries and, therefore, all persons.

An international public good benefits [or costs] more than one country. Global and regional public goods are both international public goods. However, some international public goods may be neither regional nor global. The public good of collective defence under NATO, for example, applies to North America and Europe. See Hartley and Sandler (1999) and Marè (1988).

[4] At the Bretton Woods Conference, forty-four countries agreed to keep their currencies fixed (but adjustable in exceptional situations) to the dollar, and the dollar fixed to gold. The United States committed to keeping the dollar price of gold fixed and had to adjust the supply of dollars to maintain confidence in future gold convertibility. The system became operational in 1958 and worked reasonably well, as the United States held about three-quarters of the world's official gold reserves and the system seemed secure. Japan and Europe were still rebuilding their post-war economies and demand for US goods and services—and dollars—was high. But in the 1960s, when European and Japanese exports became more competitive and the US share of world output decreased, it quickly appeared that there was lower demand for dollars, which made gold more desirable. Because the gold supply had increased only marginally, there were more foreign-held dollars than the United States had gold. The United States became vulnerable to a run on gold and there was a loss of confidence in the US government's ability to meet its obligations, thereby threatening both the dollar's position as reserve currency and the overall Bretton Woods system. Hence the decision by the Nixon administration to abandon the dollar–gold link.

also the (re)birth of a multipolar world, exemplified by the rise of Japan and other East Asian economies.

China initiated its process of structural change in an era marked by continuous disruptions which also brought new opportunities. Technological advances, and innovations in satellite communications and shipping, made it economical for manufacturing industries to shift from high-wage developed countries to Asia's low-wage economies:

> Advanced economies moved up the value chain with successful high-tech and service sectors, especially financial services. Emerging economies in Asia began to industrialise rapidly and demanded access to developed economy markets during the 1986 Uruguay round—an attractive proposition for western companies. Consumers in developed economies benefited from lower manufacturing prices. The US accrued huge trade deficits as the world invested its savings in US Treasury securities. (Desai, 2018)

China's economic development strategy took advantage of the new global conditions and focused on export-led growth based on the country's comparative advantage. Like all socialist and many developing economies in previous decades, China had pursued the goal of building modern, capital-intensive industries through investment-led growth in the 1950s to the 1970s. While there had been some visible successes, productivity levels had remained very low and that strategy was inconsistent with China's endowment structure of low capital and large supply of labour and land. In fact, given the country's low-income and weak fiscal base at the time, the modernization strategy could only be implemented with soft budget constraints, financial repression, which created major economic distortions, pervasive rent-seeking practices, and inefficiencies. Serious macroeconomic instability could only be contained by excessive state interventions in the economy.

With GDP per capita standing at only US$154 in 1979, the authorities changed gear to successfully reposition China in the post-Bretton Woods global economy. They initially targeted the industries more in tune with the country's comparative advantage and endowment structure at that time. In 1979 primary and processed primary goods accounted for more than 75 per cent of China's exports, which spurred growth, brought much-needed foreign reserves and fiscal revenues, and created employment to absorb the large and still largely low-skilled labour force. However, close attention was paid to the economy's evolving endowment structure and comparative advantage, and a carefully designed industrial upgrading strategy was adopted to stimulate the production of more sophisticated export goods, at a realistic pace. By 2009 the share of manufactured goods had increased to more than 95 per cent. 'Moreover, China's manufactured exports upgraded from simple toys, textiles,

Table 3.1. China's merchandise exports

Top ten product groups exported in 2017 and trends in exports over 1990–2016

Country	1990	2000	2010	2016
billions of US$				
Electrical machinery, apparatus, and appliances	3.96	41.50	361.63	549.06
Machinery, other than electric	2.72	25.89	309.29	330.62
Footwear	9.61	36.00	129.24	157.32
Miscellaneous manufactured articles, nes	3.92	27.49	113.63	151.98
Textile yarn, fabrics, made up articles, etc.	7.20	16.08	76.33	103.95
Road motor vehicles	4.07	8.89	87.46	91.13
Manufactures of metal, nes	1.43	8.00	51.09	75.51
Scientific and control instruments, photographic goods, clocks	1.30	8.26	52.87	68.27
Furniture	0.32	4.59	39.26	56.11
Iron and steel	1.28	4.92	38.64	55.63
Total Exports	**62.09**	**249.20**	**1,577.76**	**2,097.64**
Percentage of total exports (%)				
Electrical machinery, apparatus, and appliances	6.4	16.7	22.9	26.2
Machinery, other than electric	4.4	10.4	19.6	15.8
Footwear	15.5	14.4	8.2	7.5
Miscellaneous manufactured articles, nes	6.3	11.0	7.2	7.2
Textile yarn, fabrics, made up articles, etc.	11.6	6.5	4.8	5.0
Road motor vehicles	6.5	3.6	5.5	4.3
Manufactures of metal, nes	2.3	3.2	3.2	3.6
Scientific and control instruments, photographic goods, clocks	2.1	3.3	3.4	3.3
Furniture	0.5	1.8	2.5	2.7
Iron and steel	2.1	2.0	2.4	2.7
Total Exports	**100.0**	**100.0**	**100.0**	**100.0**

Source: World Bank World Development Indicators, July 2018

and other cheap products in the 1980s and 1990s to high-value and technologically sophisticated machinery and information and communication technology products in the 2000s' (Lin, 2011a speech). Table 3.1 provides some indication of China's changing endowment structure: in 1990, the footwear industry was the most important export, representing 15.5 per cent of the total. Sophisticated, capital-intensive industries such as electrical machinery, apparatus, and appliances, and machinery other than electric accounted for 10.8 per cent of total exports. By 2016, they represented 7.5 per cent and 42 per cent of exports, respectively.

The export-led strategy designed and implemented to reflect the gradually evolving endowment structure paid off handsomely, not just for China but also for the world economy. With 9.6 per cent annual growth for nearly four decades, China has lifted over 700 million people out of poverty in just one generation, moving from US$154 GDP per capita in 1979 to about US$9,000 in 2017 in a country of 1.3 billion people—and becoming the second-largest economy in the world.

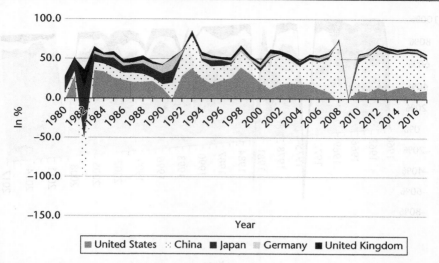

Figure 3.1. Contribution to global growth, 1980–2017, top five countries (US$, current prices)

Source: World Development Indicators, World Bank (2018)

China's contribution to global GDP growth rose from just 2 per cent in 1979 to about 27 per cent in 2017 (World Bank data—see Figures 3.1 and 3.2).[5]

As of 2018, China's economy was larger than the entire Eurozone, two-and-a-half times larger than Japan's, and five times larger than India's. Perhaps even more impressive is the fact that in just one year, say 2017, China's economy expanded by US$1.5 trillion in nominal terms, which is a truly remarkable performance. As observed by O'Neill, 'it essentially created a new economy the size of South Korea, twice the size of Switzerland, and three times the size of Sweden' (O'Neill, 2018).

By lifting itself so rapidly out of low-income status, China has become a major source of global demand and an important market for its trading partners around the world. While China has expanded its exports in recent decades, it has also imported goods and services from all regions of the world. In 1970, its imports amounted to US$2.3 billion (an amount lower than

[5] The World Bank bases its calculations on GDP at constant 2010 US$. Real GDP data for all countries are rebased on a common base year, 2010, and calculated at constant 2010 US$. Aggregate growth for the world or a region is calculated by summing the individual country GDPs at constant 2010 US$ and computing the percentage change. Data is available in the WDI for a longer period, 1960–2017. Other institutions such as the African Development Bank and the IMF use individual country growth rates weighted by GDP based on purchasing-power-parity (PPP) valuation of country GDP, which yields an even bigger contribution of the Chinese economy to world growth. Data is available in the IMF WEO database over the period 1980–2018.

41

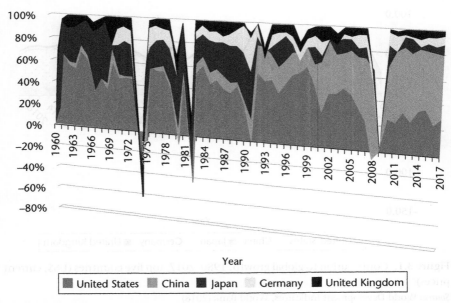

Figure 3.2. Contribution to global growth, 1960–2017, top five countries (US$, current prices)

Source: World Development Indicators, World Bank (2018)

in 1960). In 2017, China's imports amounted to US$1.8 trillion, or 10.2 per cent of the world's imports (Table 3.2).

Second, China has become, in some ways, the financier of choice if not of last resort for several major high-income countries. China holds the world's largest foreign-exchange reserves and regularly assesses its strategy for investing them. For instance, China is the single biggest foreign holder of US government debt. China has also been purchasing large amounts of bonds from other Western countries and therefore financing their fiscal deficits at low costs. Most of China's holdings are in long-term securities with maturities over one year. The US economy and the world economy benefit enormously from such massive and relatively cheap financing from China.

There are legitimate concerns in policy circles that China could try to use its position as the biggest foreign creditor of the United States as leverage in a stand-off on trade issues or other political disagreements. A decision to slow or halt purchases of US Treasuries could indeed disrupt bond markets around the world, with repercussions on interest rates and economic cycles everywhere.

So far, such fears have not materialized, and for good reasons. However, China's Treasury purchases are driven by its trade deficit with the United States, using dollars acquired from sales of goods to the United States to buy

Table 3.2. China's imports, 1960–2017

Top ten importers in 2017 and trends in imports over 1960–2017

Country	1960	1970	1980	1990	2000	2005	2010	2015	2016	2017*
billions of US$										
United States	16.4	42.4	257.0	517.0	1,259.3	1,732.7	1,969.2	2,315.3	2,250.2	N.A
China	2.6	2.3	19.9	53.3	225.1	660.0	1,396.2	1,679.6	1,587.9	1,841.9
Germany	10.2	29.9	188.0	355.7	497.2	777.1	1,054.8	1,051.4	1,055.7	1,167.0
United Kingdom	13.0	21.9	115.5	223.0	348.1	519.3	591.1	626.4	636.4	644.1
Japan	4.5	18.9	141.3	235.4	379.5	515.9	694.1	648.0	607.6	671.9
France	6.3	19.1	134.9	234.4	338.9	504.1	611.1	573.4	572.2	624.7
Hong Kong SAR, China	1.0	2.9	23.0	84.7	214.0	300.2	441.4	559.4	547.3	589.9
Netherlands	5.4	15.7	78.0	126.1	218.3	363.8	516.4	512.4	505.1	574.3
Canada	6.1	14.3	62.5	123.2	244.8	322.4	402.7	429.0	413.0	441.7
Italy	4.7	15.0	100.7	182.0	238.8	384.8	487.0	411.1	406.9	452.6
World	130.6	316.9	2,018.9	3,566.9	6,691.5	10,835.1	15,490.7	16,767.5	16,283.1	18,133.2
Percentage share of World (%)										
United States	12.5	13.4	12.7	14.5	18.8	16.0	12.7	13.8	13.8	N.A
China	2.0	0.7	1.0	1.5	3.4	6.1	9.0	10.0	9.8	10.2
Germany	7.8	9.5	9.3	10.0	7.4	7.2	6.8	6.3	6.5	6.4
United Kingdom	10.0	6.9	5.7	6.3	5.2	4.8	3.8	3.7	3.9	3.6
Japan	3.4	6.0	7.0	6.6	5.7	4.8	4.5	3.9	3.7	3.7
France	4.8	6.0	6.7	6.6	5.1	4.7	3.9	3.4	3.5	3.4
Hong Kong SAR, China	0.8	0.9	1.1	2.4	3.2	2.8	2.8	3.3	3.4	3.3
Netherlands	4.1	5.0	3.9	3.5	3.3	3.4	3.3	3.1	3.1	3.2
Canada	4.6	4.5	3.1	3.5	3.7	3.0	2.6	2.6	2.5	2.4
Italy	3.6	4.7	5.0	5.1	3.6	3.6	3.1	2.5	2.5	2.5
World	100.0	100.0	100.0	100.0	100.0	100.0	100.0	100.0	100.0	100.0

Source: World Bank World Development Indicators, July 2018

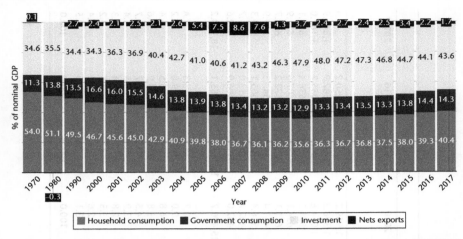

Figure 3.3. China: Structure of demand, 1970–2017 (percentage of nominal GDP)
Source: Statistics Department, AfDB, based on United Nations data

the bonds. The decision to sell or even stop purchases would negatively affect the value of China's large portfolio of US government debt. Therefore, it would not serve China's interest to sell its US bond holdings in mass quantities as a threat, while maintaining such a large position that would be hurt by the move. In fact, beyond the issue of bond holdings, the US and the Chinese economies have become so mutually dependent that unilateral policies by one country aiming at sanctioning the other would be costly even before retaliation (Monga, 2012).

Third, even as China carefully and gradually rebalances its growth model from export-led to domestic consumption (Figure 3.3), it will also help address issues of global imbalances. Still, during that internal adjustment process, China will absorb increasingly large quantities of exports from around the world[6]—including from developing countries that can strategically position themselves to competitively supply goods and services in light manufacturing and low-skilled industries which China dominated at earlier stages of its economic take-off.

In addition to becoming a large and growing market for developing-country exports, China provides new financial, commercial, and managerial resources, and new opportunities to speed up the industrialization of the latecomers.

---

[6] On 30 March 2018, Chinese foreign minister Wang Yi was quoted by Reuters as stating that 'China will import $8 trillion of goods and attract $600 billion of foreign investment in the next five years'.

China is already funding infrastructure investment around the world,[7] and successfully relocating some of its labour-intensive industries to lower-wage countries (Lin, 2012; Oqubay, 2015). The upcoming economic 'graduation' of large emerging countries such as China, Brazil, Indonesia, or India from low-wage, labour-intensive industries will open up enormous growth and job-creation opportunities for low-income countries—provided that they can organize themselves to attract those jobs with more competitive wages and lower transaction costs.

Beyond its new status as a major investor and trade partner (with no political or even policy conditionality to its loans) to high-, middle-, and low-income countries around the world, China's financing, under the right circumstances, comes with valuable ideas, knowledge, and experience, which can foster and sustain learning—especially in African countries. Learning and knowledge transfer often takes place in special economic zones and industrial parks, which generate Marshallian externalities (Monga, 2013a, 2013b; Zeng, 2011; Zhang, 2017).

These attributes of the Chinese economy as an impure global public good also imply possible negative externalities for the world economy, which are discussed in Section 3.3.

3.3 Potential Negative Externalities and Mitigation Factors

The flip side of being a global public good which has brought enormous economic development opportunities to the world is that the Chinese economy also carries potential risks to other nations. It is therefore understandable that researchers and policymakers around the world have been monitoring and even anticipating some of the negative externalities which may be caused by unpleasant economic developments in China. Perhaps unsurprisingly, much of the intellectual and policy discussions about the global 'economic threats' posed by China have been fuelled by fears and pessimism, consistent with the primal and persistent scepticism about the country's trajectory as an enormous and unprecedented experiment in economic and social transformation. This section briefly assesses some of the key issues which deserve serious consideration.

The first scenario which would be of global concern is a sustained slowdown in investment in China, with important implications for global demand and the world economy. During China's initial phase of economic development

---

[7] It should be noted that Hurtley et al. (2018) argue that China's Belt and Road Initiative—which plans to invest as much as US$8 trillion in infrastructure projects across Europe, Africa, and Asia—raises serious concerns about sovereign debt sustainability in eight countries it funds.

and for decades (say from the 1980s through much of the 2000s), export-led growth was the country's winning economic formula. The 2008 financial crisis forced all major economic players to change their growth models: the so-called Great Recession led to a substantial decline in China's net exports, which the authorities analyzed as permanent. China's response to the global financial and economic downturn was a very robust and sustained investment programme amounting to about 12.5 per cent of GDP: 'probably the biggest ever peacetime stimulus', as Wolf (2018) put it. The rapid investment surge, carefully targeted to productive infrastructure and competitive industries and sectors, was a major growth driver for China and for the world economy post 2008.

Maintaining China's investment rate at such high levels (above 50 per cent of GDP on average in the period 2008–18) is unsustainable, and a change in the country's growth model ('rebalancing') will be needed to ensure a soft landing, and stability in global output. Fears of a hard-landing scenario due to a sharp reduction in investment have intensified after some researchers warned that the quality of investment in China has been declining (Chen and Kang, 2018).

However, the declining trend in China's incremental capital-output ratio (ICOR), often interpreted by some analysts as evidence of the ineffectiveness of investment in the country, is misleading. It is based on the unrealistic assumption that the relationship between investment and growth is linear over the short to the medium term.[8] Without the theoretical assumption of linearity, the ICOR is not a constant and therefore, the relationship between investment and growth is also not a linear one.

In addition, variations in the ICOR do not necessarily represent changes in the quality of investment. Easterly offers the example of a Solow-type neoclassical model in which an exogenous increase in investment raises growth temporarily during the transition from one steady state to another. In such a model there is no permanent causal relationship between investment and growth. Under such circumstances, the ICOR reflects much more than quality of investment: 'The measured ICOR during the transition is higher, the higher is the initial level of the investment rate and the lower is the change in the investment rate. Also, the ICOR is higher in steady state the lower is the population growth rate. None of these factors reflect "quality of investment"' (Easterly, 2003: 31–2). In fact, all the other important inputs

---

[8] Such an assumption is derived from the *Leontief production function* or fixed-proportions *production function*, which implies the factors of *production* will be used in fixed (technologically pre-determined) proportions, as there is no substitutability between factors. Solow (1957) and other researchers have shown that it is an unrealistic assumption. For instance, Easterly (2003) notes that: 'In labor-abundant Ethiopia, roads are built with labor crews breaking up rocks with picks. In labor-scarce New York, roads are built with many fewer laborers driving heavy equipment.'

identified by endogenous growth theories (physical capital, new technology, human capital, intermediate new goods, managerial know-how, social capital, etc.) would substantially change the ICOR. As a result, the relationship between investment and growth would be unstable and non-linear, and ICOR would not measure 'investment quality'.

Finally, China's lower growth rate after its economy had steadily risen to become the second-largest in the world and has approached the global technological frontier should not be used mechanically to compute an ICOR and interpret it as evidence of inefficiency in credit and investment. An elephant growing in size at 6.5 per cent a year is still more impressive than a cat growing at 10 per cent.

While the efficiency of investment in China cannot be measured in a rising ICOR, one should still consider the global economic implications of a substantial and permanent slowdown in investment, not just for China but for the world economy. Conventional wisdom among mainstream researchers has been that rebalancing of the Chinese economy should take place so that growth is mainly driven by domestic consumption and not by investment (Chen and Kang, 2018). Yet it is also acknowledged that too rapid an adjustment could generate an outright recession in China and in many other countries.

If there is a clear policy lesson from the history of the forty-year period 1979–2018, it is the quasi-certitude that the Chinese authorities will not let such a scenario occur. The deceleration in Chinese exports to high-income countries and the need to keep the trade surplus at manageable levels have led the authorities to pursue their prudent strategy for rebalancing growth. Thanks to a tightly coordinated set of macroeconomic policies (fiscal and monetary), rebalancing has already been occurring but at a carefully choreographed pace— see Figure 3.4. As explained by Lin (2011b): 'Much is said about stimulating consumption, but the process should be balanced between consumption and continuing strong growth in investment. The latter is critical for industrial upgrading and sustainable increases of per capita income, as well as developing green economy sectors and investing in environmental protection.'

The second economic issue facing China and of great interest to other nations is the size of its debt, the pace of accumulation of financial liabilities, and the risks that it entails. High debt is a global concern,[9] and China is better placed

---

[9] At US$164 trillion in 2016 (225 per cent of the world's GDP), *global total debt* (public and private) stood at historic highs among advanced and emerging market economies. The world was 12 per cent deeper in debt than the previous peak in 2009 at the height of the global financial crisis, with China as a driving force. As of end 2016, governments around the world have accumulated US$63 trillion in *total public debt*, with the United States holding 31.8 per cent of it, followed by Japan (18.5 per cent share) while China, Italy, and France holding shares of 7.9 per cent, 3.9 per cent, and 3.8 per cent. These five countries together hold a total of US$ 41.6 per cent of world debt, equivalent to 66 per cent of total world debt. Source: IMF (2008) Fiscal Monitor.

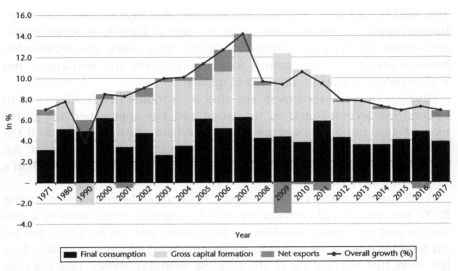

Figure 3.4. Demand contributions to GDP growth (percentage points)
Source: Statistics Department, AfDB, based on United Nations data

than most countries to handle hers. Still, it requires close monitoring. Prior to the 2008 global financial crisis, China's debt was already higher than the average for emerging economies. But it was manageable given the country's rapid growth rates for several decades.

The current much higher trend in indebtedness truly began with the 2008 Great Recession. Strong investment and output performance in China in response to the crisis era was supported by rapid credit growth, which also led to high debt, mainly to non-financial corporations (Figure 3.5) and to off-balance-sheet local government financing vehicles—another issue of global importance.

This has led some researchers to raise concerns about financial stability which could be costly to the world economy, and to even warn that a financial crisis could be looming (Wolf, 2018). Such concerns are based on historical experience, which shows that very rapid credit growth is typically not sustainable and often ends with financial crises (Gourinchas and Obstfeld, 2012) and/or slowdowns in growth (Eggerston and Krugman, 2012; Jones et al., 2018).

Credit cycles can indeed stimulate excessive risk-taking and leverage, which tend to artificially accelerate asset appreciation during the growth period but also to worsen asset depreciations in downturns. According to Chan and Kang:

International experience suggests that China's current credit trajectory is danger-ous with increasing risks of a disruptive adjustment and/or a marked growth slowdown. To find analogues for China, we identified 43 cases of credit booms in which the credit-to-GDP ratio increased by more than 30 percentage points over

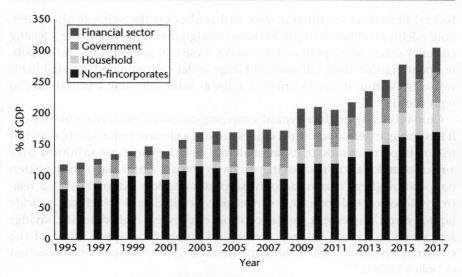

Figure 3.5. China: Total debt to GDP, 1995–2017
Source: IIF

a 5-year period. Among these, only five ended without a major growth slowdown or a financial crisis in the immediate aftermath. However, once considering country-specific factors, these five countries provide little comfort. In addition, all credit booms that began when the ratios were above 100 per cent—as in China's case—ended badly. (Chen and Kang, 2018: 8)[10]

However, China's economic trajectory and performance in the forty-year period 1979–2018 shows that historical precedents do not apply: the empirical regularities of booms and busts observed elsewhere and appearing in cross-country regression analyses on the likelihood of financial crises and sharp growth slowdowns. Debt and currency crises typically occur in emerging economies with a dual problem: excessive government spending to fund unproductive investment or consumption and other generous, untargeted transfer policies, with heavy reliance on foreign lenders to support such profligate habits; and large borrowing in foreign currencies—when the US

---

[10] To try to assess the sustainability and potential risks from China's credit boom, Chen and Kang (2018) use a standard time-series model of private credit determinants. Using data from quarterly observations during nearly a decade, they find that loose monetary policy has been a key driver of rapid credit growth, but also that industrial structure matters a lot: more credit has flown into the provinces relying on fixed asset investment—especially infrastructure investment. For example, average bank loan growth for five provinces with heavy exposure to mining sectors (Heilungjiang, Jilin, Liaoning, Shanxi, and Inner Mongolia) was higher than national growth rate by 3 percentage points in 2015 despite slower deposit growth and lower GDP growth.

Federal Reserve raises interest rates and pushes up the value of the dollar, dollar debts are difficult to pay back and foreign investors start to flee, causing currency crises. Some policymakers make these two problems (excessive public spending that fuels inflation and large dollar-denominated external debt) worse by setting domestic interest rates at artificially low levels (financial repression).

China is clearly not in a 'typical' emerging-country situation. Unlike others, it has strong external accounts: it does not run a chronic trade deficit, does not rely on imports for most of its raw materials, and does not have to borrow large amounts in dollars to finance its purchases abroad. China has a strong external position (large current account surpluses and low external debt), a relatively closed capital account, a very effective central bank which can provide liquidity and implement capital controls effectively, high domestic savings and strong corporate balance sheets, and ample fiscal space. None of the countries which suffered banking and financial crises had such a combination of policy buffers.[11]

While these country-specific factors make China less vulnerable to traditional emerging-economy debt crises, its economy may be suffering from a strong dollar for other reasons: the post-2008 stimulus led to large amounts of domestic loans—including to households and firms interested in higher returns. Besides striving to ensure that interest rate differentials between China and the United States are minimized to limit incentives for capital flight, monetary authorities in Beijing will be maintaining tight currency controls for the foreseeable future. However, in the medium and long term, China's main economic policy to maintain macroeconomic stability, sustain growth beyond upper-middle-income status, and honour its role as the main engine of global growth, will be to pursue the carefully targeted industrial upgrading which has allowed the country to remain true to its evolving comparative advantage and endowment structure.

A third major source of uncertainty for the world economy, which could arise from China's status as a global public good, has to do with the stability of the renminbi. A recurrent fear among policymakers and researchers around the world is whether the authorities in Beijing may decide to 'weaponize' the national currency by actively orchestrating depreciations as a way to maintain export competitiveness in trade wars with other major economies (mainly the United States and the European Union) or with neighbouring countries. Besides weakening China's publicly stated commitment to globalization and the credibility of its leaders on the global economic scene,[12] such an obvious

---

[11] I refer here to the US savings and loan crisis in the 1980s and to Japan's 1997 banking crisis.
[12] At the 2017 World Economic Forum in Davos (Switzerland), President Xi Jinping declared that China would not engage in currency wars.

change in exchange rate strategy would trigger beggar-thy-neighbour tactics and contagion across the Asia region where China is currently asserting its economic and political leadership. The end result of these 'currency wars' would be detrimental to everyone.

Even without active attempts by the Chinese central bank to systematically influence the renminbi exchange rate vis-à-vis major currencies, market forces can provoke similar movements, with considerable potential consequences for the world economy. A sustained appreciation of the renminbi not accompanied by productivity increases in China would reflect a loss of competitiveness for the country contributing most of global growth. This would result in lower than expected global demand, growth below potential in China, and fewer opportunities to absorb imports—including from developing countries relying on China for a substantial share of their external demand and export revenues.

On the other hand, sustained depreciation of the renminbi due to market forces also poses serious threats domestically and globally. It would signal vulnerabilities within the Chinese economy—and weaken the renminbi's status/credibility as an anchor of stability in Asia and beyond. Each of the three main policy options to address such a problem would carry costs and risks for China and the world economy. First, central bank interventions to buy dollars and sell renminbi require using foreign currency reserves, whose high volume is a signature asset for the Chinese economy. Using reserves to boost the value of the renminbi carries psychological costs (as it is seen as reflecting excessive fears of capital flight) and therefore cannot be an easy decision. Moreover, the resources used by the central bank to protect the renminbi would be in diminution of China's 'war chest' and global financial influence—lessening its ability to finance fiscal deficits and help macroeconomic stabilization elsewhere through the buying of bonds and other treasury bills. A financially weaker Chinese central bank would not be good news for the world economy.

The second tool for shoring up the renminbi in case of depreciation would be to raise domestic interest rates and make the currency more attractive relative to the dollar. While this would strengthen the renminbi (especially when the convergence in US and Chinese bond yields has contributed to capital flows), it would also slow down domestic credit, investment, and growth. Yet the world economy needs a continuously growing Chinese economy.

The third policy option to withstand depreciation would be the use of capital controls—including stricter administrative limits on fund outflows. It is generally an effective tool where it can be enforced, especially over short periods of time, before investors figure out ways of circumventing it. It would run countercurrent to China's stated goal of making the renminbi an international currency. Meanwhile, the dollar, its main competitor, is sought after by economic agents around the world: despite a declining share of world GDP from a peak of 32 per cent in 2001 to 23 per cent in 2018, the United States still enjoys the enormous privilege of having its currency used for more than 60 per cent of the foreign reserves held by central banks around the world. Therefore, a major drawback of using stringent capital controls for too long would be a loss of credibility in the ability of policymakers to move markets through signalling, and unnecessary delays in the implementation of the strategy for making the renminbi a global currency. Ultimately, keeping the renminbi generally stable is in China's interest and in the interest of the global economy.

Political-economy risks from within China represent a fourth topic of concern to the global economy. Perhaps the most recurrent warning about China is the risk of social disruptions and a disorderly political transition there, with important potential repercussions for the world economy. China's growth model based on a consistent strategy that follows comparative advantage and reflects a constantly changing endowment structure has already generated inequality, with the Gini coefficient rising from less than 30 per cent in the 1970s to above 40 per cent. With industrial upgrading, the economy is becoming less labour dependent and more capital and technology dependent. This trend fuels income disparities, as poor people draw their incomes mainly from labour, whereas the rich rely more on capital and technology.

Inequality is also worsened by the movement of some workers to new sectors where they first have higher productivity and higher incomes. According to Spence (2007):

> The result is a pronounced tendency for income inequality to rise, and for an extended period. While this is a natural consequence of the process, it presents a challenge. Excessive inequality of income and wealth is not only a normative problem in most societies; it is also socially and politically disruptive and can threaten the support for the policies and public sector investments that in part sustain the growth process. As a result it needs to be mitigated through the redistribution of income or other important services such as health care, education and pensions, and by ensuring that access to infrastructure (clean water, transportation, power) is reasonably equitable.

With the implementation of robust infrastructure programmes across the country, the Chinese government has been largely successful in mitigating the important social risks due to persistently high levels of inequality.

Many experts also doubt that a country with such a large population, growing fast from low to upper-middle income, and on its way to high income, would be able to maintain intact the authoritarian political system under which it has been operating for so long. Economic prosperity brings additional human needs beyond income and material welfare, and also new conceptions of individual freedom and new social demands, which would be impossible for the Chinese Communist Party to accommodate within its current structure and mode of functioning. Speculation and dark predictions from the Cassandras typically refer to the 1989 Tiananmen revolt as an indication that the quest for Western-style, multi-party politics and 'democratization' is an inescapable trajectory for China, especially in an era of enhanced globalization and global citizenship fostered by the development across boundaries of social media and other technological innovation.

The socio-political threat from within—which could be triggered by a large number of low-skilled workers left unemployed by industrial restructuring, the burst of a real-estate bubble leading to a major financial crisis, uncontrolled social unrest, and new political demands that exceed the political supply from existing institutions—has been the subject of debate and even tensions among Chinese political leaders for decades. They have always understood the critical importance of maintaining social peace, even when this meant implementing economic policies that were viewed from afar as second best. The dual economic development strategy adopted after the transition was a major commitment to mitigate the risks of costly social disruptions.

On the one hand, the authorities focused on improving productivity by providing market incentives in the gradual liberalization of agriculture, and by allowing the workers in collective farms and state-owned firms to be residual claimants and to set the prices for selling at the market after delivering the quota obligations to the state at fixed prices (Lin, 1992). Because of the urgent need to create employment—including for low-skilled workers—policymakers in China also embarked upon a controlled capitalist path by opening up some of the previously repressed labour-intensive industries in which it had comparative advantage: entry barriers were lifted, joint ventures encouraged, and foreign direct investment welcomed, if not actively sought.

On the other hand, China maintained strong financial support and protectionist measures to shield from competition many economically non-viable firms operating in priority sectors with large numbers of workers. The economic and political pay-offs were enormous: China went through its transition from communism to a market economy without suffering the heavy social costs of enterprise restructuring and industrial reconfigurations. In addition, the development of labour-intensive industries in newly liberalized sectors absorbed labour and led to sustained growth, which eventually allowed for smooth reforms in the old, low-productivity sectors (Lin, 2009, 2011b).

It seems logical that China's continuing economic progress in income per capita and into the club of advanced economies will eventually translate into new political demands for its citizens. But the nature, scope, and manifestation of these demands are likely to remain country specific, and beyond scholarly speculation. The quest for freedom and for more legitimate modes of

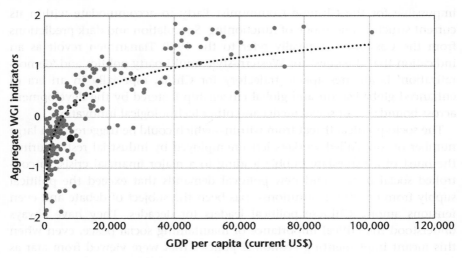

Figure 3.6. Income and governance, 2016
Source: World Development Indicators, World Bank

governance are universal values but China's socio-political itinerary need not to be similar to what was observed in Western countries. The Chinese authorities have always given priority to political stability and social peace, which they consider prerequisites to economic performance.[13] They have also stressed meritocracy and competition within the Communist Party as a more 'objective' way of organizing economic and political governance.[14] In any case, international measures of good governance remain largely based on subjective perception indicators. Figure 3.6 shows that they are correlated with income per capita, with China below the logarithmic trend line (large dark dot).

The fact that China's governance indicators remain quite low despite its rapid and sustained growth rate and it is ranked below countries with poor growth records mainly reflects conceptual issues and methodological biases in the empirical tools used (Lin and Monga, 2017). It may only be a matter of time before China's ranking improves on these perception indicators.

---

[13] When Communist Party leader Zhao Ziyang opposed the use of force to stop demonstrations in Tiananmen Square in 1989, Deng Xiaoping sacked him and appointed Jiang Zemin to succeed him (Vogel, 2013).

[14] In 2016 China's Communist Party (CPC) issued a widely distributed cartoon explaining how leaders are selected at all levels in the country. The preface reads that the CPC 'has always attached importance to the selection and appointment of leading officials, as it bears on not only the Party's capacity to govern, but also the quality of its governing, its successes, and its failures. For this reason, the CPC is constantly striving to improve the system and procedures for the selection and appointment of Party and government leading officials, making it more standardized, scientific, and democratic.' See http://www.idcpc.org.cn/english/picgroup/201605/t20160503_82487.html.

3.4 Conclusion

For several decades, China has been an enormously positive contributor to the world economy and to world stability and peace—an impure global public good. Its industrial upgrading strategies, which reflect changes in its endowment structure, have defied mainstream economic prescriptions. Its stubbornness in designing and implementing steadfastly policy frameworks that identify potentially competitive industries and facilitate their emergence (while accounting for social and political constraints and realities) could provide useful blueprints for all developing countries.

Because of the size of its economy, China has become the anchor of the international financial system, a magnet for global trade and investment, while positioning itself as an intellectual and policy model for other developing countries where leaders are convinced that they can replicate its success. China's continuous dominance will extend into the foreseeable future. Still, the manageability of its domestic issues (pace of the rebalancing of its growth model, domestic debt, inequality, and potential political-economy issues) are of great importance for the many economies whose imports and financing flows depend on it. It is therefore not surprising that fears arise regularly about China's ability to maintain its spectacular performance in an era of increased volatility of national economic policies while also entering a level of development that takes its industries, firms, institutions, and capabilities much closer to the challenges of the global technological frontier. Even its own political leaders have expressed concerns about the enormity of the country's economic challenges.[15] This chapter has argued that the Chinese economy deserves careful and constant analysis and monitoring.

References

Braudel, F. (1958) 'Histoire et Sciences sociales: La longue durée', *Annales*, 13–4: 725–53.
Chen, S. and J. S. Kang (2018) 'Credit Booms—Is China Different?' Working Paper WP/18/2, IMF, Washington, DC.
Deng, X. (1994) *Selected Works of Deng Xiaoping, vol. III (1982–1992)*. Beijing: Foreign Languages Press.
Desai, M. (2018) 'Welcome to the Multipolar World: Trump and China Roles in Transformation', *Omfif Analysis*, 13 August.

---

[15] In 2007, China's prime minister Wen Jiabao declared that his country's growth was 'unstable, unbalanced, uncoordinated, and unsustainable' (quoted by Wolf, 2018). Despite such a sombre assessment, China went on to average about 8 per cent GDP growth in the following decade.

Easterly, W. (2003) 'Can Foreign Aid Buy Growth?' *Journal of Economic Perspectives*, 17(3): 23–48.

Eggerston, G. and P. Krugman (2012) 'Debt, Deleveraging, and the Liquidity Trap: A Fisher-Minsky-Koo Approach', *Quarterly Journal of Economics*, 127(3): 1468–513.

Gourinchas, P.-O. and M. Obstfeld (2012) 'Stories of the Twentieth Century for the Twenty-First', *American Economic Journal: Macroeconomics*, 4(January): 226–65.

Hartley, K. and T. Sandler (1999) 'NATO Burden-Sharing: Past and Future', *Journal of Peace Research*, 36(6): 665–80.

Hurtley, J., S. Morris, and G. Portelance (2018) *Examining the Debt Implications of the Belt and Road Initiative from a Policy Perspective*. Washington, DC: Center for Global Development.

International Monetary Fund (2018) *Fiscal Monitor: Capitalizing on Good Times*. Washington, DC, April.

International Task Force on Global Public Goods (2006) 'Meeting Global Challenges: International Cooperation in the National Interest, Final Report', Stockholm.

Jones, C., V. Midrigan, and T. Philippon (2018) 'Household Leverage and the Recession', Working Paper No. 16965, NBER.

Kaul, I. and R. U. Mendoza (2003) 'Advancing the Concept of Global Public Goods', in Inge Kaul, Pedro Conceição, Katell Le Goulven, and Ronald U. Mendoza (eds) *Providing Global Public Goods: Managing Globalization*. New York: Oxford University Press, pp. 78–111.

Lin, J. Y. (1992) 'Rural Reforms and Agricultural Growth in China', *The American Economic Review*, 82(1): 34–51.

Lin, J. Y. (2009) *Economic Development and Transition: Thought, Strategy and Viability* (Marshall Lectures). New York: Cambridge University Press.

Lin, J. Y. (2011a) 'China and the Global Economy', Luncheon Address, Asia Economic Policy Conference, San Francisco, Federal Reserve Bank.

Lin, J. Y. (2011b) *Demystifying the Chinese Economy*. New York: Cambridge University Press.

Lin, J. Y. (2012) 'From Flying Geese to Leading Dragons: New Opportunities and Strategies for Structural Transformation in Developing Countries', *Global Policy*, 3(4): 397–409.

Lin, J. Y. and C. Monga (2017) *Beating the Odds: Jump-Starting Developing Countries*. Princeton, NJ: Princeton University Press.

Marè, M. (1988) 'Public Goods, Free Riding and NATO Defence Burden Sharing', *The International Spectator: Italian Journal of International Affairs*, 23(1): 7–15.

Monga, C. (2012) 'The Hegelian Dialectics of Global Imbalances', *Journal of Philosophical Economics*, 6(1): 2–51, https://jpe.ro/poze/articole/83.pdf.

Monga, C. (2013a) 'Winning the Jackpot: Jobs Dividends in a Multipolar World', in Joseph E. Stiglitz, Justin Yifu Lin, and Ebrahim Patel (eds) *The Industrial Policy Revolution II: Africa in the 21st Century*. New York: Palgrave MacMillan, pp. 135–171.

Monga, C. (2013b) 'Theories of Agglomeration: Critical Analysis from a Policy Perspective', in J. E. Stiglitz and J. Y. Lin (eds) *The Industrial Policy Revolution I: The Role of Government beyond Ideology*. New York: Palgrave, pp. 209–24.

Obama, B. (2009) Remarks at the Townhall with China's Youth, Shanghai, 16 November.

O'Neill, J. (2018) 'China's Irresistible Rise', *Project Syndicate*, January.

Oqubay, A. (2015) *Made in Africa: Industrial Policy in Ethiopia*. Oxford: Oxford University Press.

Solow, R. (1957) 'Technical Change and the Aggregate Production Function', *Review of Economics and Statistics*, 39(3): 312–20.

Spence, M. (2007) 'Why China Grows So Fast', *The Wall Street Journal*, 23 January.

Spence, M. (2017) 'The Global Economy's New Rule-Maker', *Project Syndicate*, 29 August.

Vogel, E. F. (2013) *Deng Xiaoping and the Transformation of China*, Cambridge, MA: Harvard University Press.

Wolf, M. (2018) 'China's Debt Threat: Time to Rein in the Lending Boom', *Financial Times*, 25 July.

Zeng, D. Z. (2011) 'How Do Special Economic Zones and Industrial Clusters Drive China's Rapid Development?' Policy Research Working Paper WPS 5583, World Bank, Washington, DC.

Zhang, X. (2017) 'Building Effective Clusters and Industrial Parks', How They Did It series, vol. 1, no. 1, Abidjan, African Development Bank.

Part II
Evolving China–Africa Relations

Context, Perspectives, and Framework

Part II

4

China–Africa Ties in Historical Context

David H. Shinn

4.1 Introduction

China began trading with North-east Africa before the Christian era. Several Chinese travellers reportedly visited Africa during the early part of the Christian era. China's first significant contact with Africa occurred during the Ming Dynasty when the fifth and sixth voyages of the famous Zheng He naval fleet reached the north-east of Africa during the first quarter of the fifteenth century. The voyages were, however, an anachronism in Chinese history and were followed by a return to China's inward-looking approach to the rest of the world (Snow, 1988: 30–1). A hiatus in the China–Africa relationship then set in for several centuries until Chinese labourers and traders came to several regions of Africa beginning in the latter part of the eighteenth century (Shinn and Eisenman, 2012: 17–26).

After taking power in 1912, Sun Yat Sen and the Republic of China (ROC) developed official relations with South Africa, where a Chinese community had become well established. South Africa soon became and remains the country with the largest number of persons of Chinese origin on the African continent. Most of the early migrants retained a strong allegiance to China and supported the Chinese nationalist party, the Kuomintang. The Second Sino-Japanese War (1937–45) united the Chinese community in South Africa with China and led to fund-raising campaigns in support of the ROC (Yap and Man, 1996: 255–77). The ROC had brief interaction with independent Liberia and was in contact with the Chinese community in the French colony of Madagascar. Challenges to its ability to rule China severely limited its engagement with Africa (Shinn and Eisenman, 2012: 26–9).

Relations between the People's Republic of China (PRC) and Africa were slow to develop because of Mao Zedong's need to consolidate power and the fact that there were few independent African nations in 1949. Several themes subsequently developed in the China–Africa relationship as it became more intense.

First, there have been different phases in China's relations with Africa that depend largely on global issues, and political and economic developments in China, not in Africa. They began with China's support for African revolutionary movements, the Great Leap Forward, the Cultural Revolution, the Cold War, and the Sino-Soviet split during the leadership of Mao Zedong. This was followed by China's more pragmatic foreign policy, a focus on China's domestic reform, and a pulling back from Africa under Deng Xiaoping. Jiang Zemin, partly concerned by negative fallout from the Tiananmen Square events, again reached out to Africa and set the stage for a major expansion of the China–Africa relationship. Hu Jintao took advantage of his efforts and significantly increased China's trade, aid, and investment with Africa. Xi Jinping has continued the economic engagement begun by Hu Jintao and expanded China's involvement in the security and political sectors, especially party-to-party cooperation.

Second, implicit in the first theme, it is nearly always China that initiates important developments in the China–Africa relationship. This is not surprising and could also be said for the US relationship with Africa. A single large and powerful country can more easily initiate ideas and projects than can fifty-four countries, many of which are small and weak. Although the African Union is slowly improving its ability to speak for the continent, it is not even close to functioning like a national government.

Third, the China–Africa relationship has always been asymmetric. The second theme is the most obvious manifestation of this asymmetry. Interestingly, however, economic but not political asymmetry once favoured Africa. For example, from 1980 to 1984, Africa's global merchandise exports averaged US$79 billion annually. In 1983, China exported only US$50 billion worth of goods. In the years immediately after Mao Zedong came to power in 1949, even the economies of South Africa and Egypt were probably stronger than the economy of China. By the 1990s, however, China had a significant political and economic advantage over African countries individually and collectively. In 2016, China's global merchandise trade was US$3.7 trillion; Africa's was US$790 million. As with the United States, it is a highly asymmetric relationship that has only increased with the passage of time.

4.2 Mao Zedong and Relations with Africa (1949–76)

Although I am not familiar with Africa, as I see it, according to the circumstances of the past ten years, it can be said that there will be still greater

changes in the next ten years ... Asia, Africa, and Latin America, these three
continents all have conditions for revolution at the present time.

(Comment by Mao Zedong to a visitor from Zanzibar in 1964)

It is our African brothers who have carried us into the UN.

(Quotation attributed to Mao Zedong in 1971
after the PRC received from African countries 34 per cent
of UN votes to replace Taiwan)

The seizure of power by the Communist Party of China (CPC) in 1949 did not
result immediately in any significant outreach to Africa. Mao Zedong was
preoccupied with consolidating his rule in the early years of the new regime.
In addition, African countries only began to become independent in significant numbers when Sudan, Tunisia, and Morocco led the way in 1956 followed by Ghana in 1957 and Guinea in 1958. The floodgates opened with
seventeen more independent countries in 1960.

During its first several decades, the PRC struggled economically and could
offer only limited assistance to Africa. Trade with Africa was modest in the
early years and did not begin to rise until the 1990s (Larkin, 1971: 87–96;
Shinn and Eisenman, 2012: 112). China's foreign direct investment was also
negligible. Consequently, China emphasized the establishment of diplomatic
relations with independent African states, strong political ties with ideologically like-minded African governments, and support for African liberation
movements aimed at ending colonial rule.

The run-up to the 1955 Asian-African Conference at Bandung, Indonesia,
marked the PRC's first serious involvement in Africa. Premier Zhou Enlai led the
Chinese delegation, which met representatives from six African countries—
Egypt, Ethiopia, Liberia, Libya, and soon to be independent Sudan and
Ghana. Zhou Enlai convinced the participants to incorporate the PRC's Five
Principles of Peaceful Coexistence into the Ten Principles of Bandung. The
original five principles remain essential to China's foreign policy. They
include mutual respect for sovereignty and territorial integrity, mutual non-
aggression, non-interference in each other's internal affairs, equality and
mutual benefit, and peaceful coexistence (Shinn and Eisenman 2012: 33).

China used Bandung to open trade talks with Egypt, to speak out against
colonialism and imperialism in Africa, and to support independence movements in Algeria, Morocco, and Tunisia. Zhou Enlai also upheld Egypt's claim
to the Suez Canal as a crisis approached with the United Kingdom and France
over control of the canal. China provided Egypt with a US$5 million loan, a
first for China in Africa, and called on the United Kingdom and France to end
their aggression. Bandung was a watershed for Chinese diplomacy, especially
its relations with Africa (Larkin, 1971: 16–26; Nasser-Eddine, 1972: 60–94,
117–20).

China–Africa trade was primarily an extension of political relations. It served as the foundation for China–Egypt relations. In 1956, China opened a trade office in Cairo, which served as the focus for CPC outreach to African liberation movements and helped expand relations with newly independent Morocco, Algeria, Tunisia, and Sudan. China's purchase of cotton from Egypt played a role in stabilizing Egypt's economy in a time of crisis. In 1960, China's trade with Egypt alone totalled US$69 million, which was more than its trade with all of the rest of Africa.

Following Bandung, China decided to expand its outreach to African and Asian countries. It sent a delegation to the first Afro-Asian People's Solidarity Organization (AAPSO) conference in Cairo which began towards the end of 1957. Afro-Asian solidarity soon became an essential component of China's foreign policy and its engagement with Africa (Ogunsanwo, 1974: 40–4; Neuhauser, 1968). Reflecting the ideology of Mao, China used the forum increasingly to attack US imperialism as a dangerous enemy of African independence. The Cold War loomed large in China's policies towards Africa throughout the 1950s and 1960s.

In 1960, at the second AAPSO conference in Conakry, Guinea, China solidified its ties with an increasing number of independent African nations, but there were also growing signs of friction between China and the Soviet Union. China concluded that the Soviet Union should not be permitted to take part in the organization. AAPSO members were reluctant to take sides in the Sino-Soviet dispute, which in 1963 dominated the third AAPSO conference in Moshi, Tanzania. The PRC portrayed itself as more revolutionary than the Soviet Union; the conflict alarmed many African countries which wanted good relations with both the Soviet Union and China. The Afro-Asian movement never fully recovered from the Sino-Soviet hostility that occurred in 1965 at the fourth AAPSO conference in Winneba, Ghana (Neuhauser, 1968; Ogunsanwo, 1974: 94–8, 165–9). China also occasionally supported left-wing rebel movements that opposed conservative, independent governments in countries such as Niger, Rwanda, and Cameroon (Shinn and Eisenman, 2012: 245, 298, 305–6).

As more African countries became independent and joined the United Nations, an early goal of China was to obtain their support to replace the Republic of China on the UN Security Council. The PRC devoted considerable effort to pursuing diplomatic recognition throughout the continent as this almost always resulted in backing for its UN Security Council bid. In 1956, Egypt was the first African country to recognize the PRC followed two years later by Morocco and Algeria. China's support for African liberation movements began with Algeria's Front de Libération Nationale and quickly expanded to at least one revolutionary group in nearly every country in Africa that was forcibly trying to remove colonialism. Zhou Enlai and other Chinese officials argued that Africa was engulfed in a wave of revolutionary war that deserved China's support (Adie, 1964: 53–4; Larkin, 1971: 38–9).

This was an era when the CPC played an unusually important role in the development of relations with Africa. The party created a series of 'front' organizations that conducted much of China's interaction with African countries. One of the best known was the Chinese-African People's Friendship Association, which was created in 1960 to promote exchanges and cooperation between China and Africa. Other examples were the All-China Students' Federation and China Islamic Association (Larkin, 1971: 213–21; Ogunsanwo, 1974: 97; Eisenman, 2018). The latter continues to function today, as do many country-specific friendship associations. These organizations are relatively inexpensive to operate and emphasize face-to-face contact between Chinese and Africans.

Zhou Enlai's historic ten-country visit to Africa at the end of 1963 and beginning of 1964 marked another important stage in China–Africa relations. It signalled the beginning of a policy emphasizing the importance of regular high-level contact with African leaders. Zhou Enlai used the Africa tour to announce the five principles guiding China's relations with African and Arab countries, principles that remain in effect and have been modified only slightly over the years (China, 2002):

- China supports the African and Arab peoples in their struggle to oppose imperialism and old and new colonialism and to win and safeguard national independence.
- It supports the pursuance of a policy of peace, neutrality and non-alignment by the governments of the African and Arab countries.
- It supports the desire of the African and Arab peoples to achieve unity and solidarity in the manner of their own choice.
- It supports the African and Arab countries in their efforts to settle their disputes through peaceful consultations.
- It holds that the sovereignty of the African and Arab countries should be respected by all other countries.

On the same visit to Africa, Zhou Enlai presented eight principles governing China's foreign aid. They emphasized mutual benefit, national sovereignty, interest-free or low interest loans, self-reliance of recipient countries, quick results, high quality, technology transfer, and modest living conditions for Chinese experts (China, 2002).

China professes that it continues to follow these principles, although arguably not all of them are being fully observed. For example, China's loans have always been tied to Chinese companies, materials, and some labour. This constitutes economic conditionality. African governments have rarely complained about the tying of loans to Chinese companies and materials, but in recent years they have insisted on a reduction in the percentage of Chinese labour allowed on the projects. Complaints in the independent African press regularly appear about the quality of some Chinese projects.

The Great Proletarian Cultural Revolution that began in 1966 marked a new phase in the China–Africa relationship. China called for world revolution and the promotion of wars of national liberation. The harshest phase of the Cultural Revolution lasted through 1969; it continued in a milder form until Mao's death in September 1976 and the purge of the Gang of Four a month later.

The impact of the Cultural Revolution on Africa was significant and coincided with the overthrow of governments in Dahomey (now Benin) and the Central African Republic. The new governments in both countries expelled PRC embassy personnel. In 1966, President Kwame Nkrumah, who had allowed China to train African revolutionaries in Ghana, was removed from power while visiting China. The new government in Accra immediately sent 430 Chinese staff, including thirteen guerrilla warfare instructors, back to China. By the end of the year, Ghana charged that China was supporting an attempt by Nkrumah to return to power; Beijing then closed its embassy. During the Cultural Revolution there was a sharp drop in high-level visits by Africans to China and senior Chinese to Africa. By 1969, four fewer African countries recognized the PRC than in 1965 (Barnouin and Yu, 1998: 47; Ogunsanwo, 1974: 180–240).

By the mid-1960s, the distribution of *The Quotations of Chairman Mao* became one of the highest priorities of China's embassies, including those in Africa. The goal was to demonstrate Maoism's universal applicability and raise Mao to the level of Marx, Engels, Lenin, and Stalin (Eisenman, 2018). While the Little Red Book became ubiquitous throughout Africa, the ideology did not resonate and many Africans treated the campaign with derision.

The independence of a growing number of African nations in the early 1960s provided an opportunity for China to advance its efforts to replace Taiwan at the United Nations. By the early 1970s, China abandoned its support for African revolutionary movements, thus improving its ability to establish relations with more conservative governments. In 1971, the United States made known to the world that it had begun the process of normalizing relations with Beijing, signalling to its allies in Africa that its support for Taiwan was waning.

China began to pursue a more pragmatic policy in Africa and achieved a huge political victory in October 1971—admission to the United Nations and replacement of the Republic of China on the Security Council. Beijing received support from twenty-six African countries; only fifteen voted with Taipei. Ten of the fifteen countries that supported Taipei recognized Beijing in the next few years. China quickly repaired the damage to relations with Africa caused by the Cultural Revolution. It increased significantly the number of friendship, cultural, technical, and governmental delegations visiting Africa. China ended support for revolutionary groups trying to topple established African governments. It began to work closely with African governments irrespective of political ideology, a policy that continues to the present day (Shinn and Eisenman, 2012: 40–1).

While the United States was the primary focus of China's international attacks in the 1960s, the Soviet Union occupied that position in the 1970s. From Beijing's point of view, the Soviet Union replaced the United States as the country working hardest to dominate world power. China believed the world and Africa perceived Moscow in the 1970s as the leader of imperialism. Its criticism of the United States continued, but to a lesser extent than its condemnation of the Soviet Union (Yu, 1977: 104–5). This was in line with Mao's Three Worlds Theory whereby the Soviet Union and United States sought world hegemony. Beijing argued that real power resided in a united Third World that avoids the plunder of its natural resources by the two superpowers (Shinn and Eisenman, 2012: 43).

China has never published bilateral aid numbers, preferring to treat the subject as a state secret. The cumulative total of China's aid to Africa from 1956 through to the end of the Mao era in 1976 is estimated at just over US$2.4 billion, most of it in the form of interest-free loans. The single largest project was the construction of the railway from Tanzania's port of Dar es Salaam to the copper fields of Zambia. This was China's premier effort in Africa and continues to be hailed as one of the best examples of China–Africa cooperation. While clearly a political success, the railway has experienced numerous management problems and a steady decline in both passenger and freight traffic. Other major recipients of China's aid from 1956 to 1976, in descending order, were Somalia, Egypt, Zaire (now Democratic Republic of Congo), Algeria, Ethiopia, Guinea, and Mauritania. Aid levels peaked in the 1970 to 1975 period and then dropped sharply at the end of Mao's reign. The end of funding for the Tanzania–Zambia railway, an internal power struggle, and severe earthquakes in China in 1976 contributed to diminished aid to Africa. Figures are not available for actual loan disbursements or loan repayments by these countries, but China has a track record of rescheduling and even cancelling debt on interest-free loans (Bartke, 1975: 10–11; Iimi et al., 2017: 7; Yu Fai, 1984: 172–4, 182).

One of China's most successful aid programmes has been the sending of medical teams to Africa. The first team from Hubei Province arrived in Algeria in 1963. Algeria has been paired ever since with Hubei Province, which has continued to send teams annually to Algeria and subsequently began sending them to Lesotho. Other provinces began sending teams to paired African countries; since the beginning of the programme, at least forty-four African countries have received the teams (Li, 2011). High-profile sports stadiums, conference halls, and friendship palaces were also a common feature of China's aid programme (OECD, 1987: 13).

From 1961 to 1971, China was only the seventh-largest source of arms exported to Africa after the Soviet Union, France, the United States, United Kingdom, West Germany, and Czechoslovakia. Tanzania received the overwhelming majority while modest quantities went to Algeria, Congo-Brazzaville, and Guinea. There was a significant increase in Chinese military assistance in the early 1970s. The major recipients were Tanzania, Zaire, Congo-Brazzaville, Cameroon, Egypt, Guinea, Sudan, Tunisia, and Zambia. The arms transfers included fighter aircraft, patrol boats, tanks, anti-aircraft guns, small arms, and ammunition. Training African military personnel also became an important part of China's engagement. From 1955 to 1979, China trained almost three thousand African soldiers from at least thirteen countries (Shinn and Eisenman, 2012: 165–6).

By the mid-1960s, Africa's percentage of China's foreign trade had reached about 10 per cent. This reflected the success of China's political outreach, particularly to North Africa. But the commanding role of the colonial powers sharply limited the percentage of Africa's total trade with China, just over 1 per cent in the mid-1960s. While China–Africa trade fell between 1966 and 1969, it still represented 7 to 8 per cent of China's total trade but barely 1 per cent of Africa's total trade. Except for agricultural products, Africa did not have much that China was interested in purchasing. Most of Africa's rich oil and mineral resources had not yet been discovered and, in any event, China's economy was not in a position to use them. China's imports from Africa remained static through the end of the Mao era, although its exports to Africa grew modestly. As a result, Africa experienced a trade deficit with China during the first six years of the 1970s (Shinn and Eisenman, 2012: 106–11).

Mao's hand-picked successor, Hua Guofeng, held power for just over two years and demonstrated little interest in strengthening relations with Africa. He is best known for reviving a grandiose plan known as the Four Modernizations (agriculture, industry, science and technology, and national defence) and the policy of Two Whatevers, i.e. to follow whatever instructions Mao left before his death.

4.3 Deng Xiaoping and the Domestic Reform Era (1978–92)

> African countries should work out strategies and policies for development
> in accordance with actual conditions in each country.
>
> (Comment by Deng Xiaoping to visiting Ugandan
> president Yoweri Museveni in 1989)

Deng Xiaoping became China's general secretary of the CPC Central Committee at the end of 1978 and held the position until late 1989. He is usually considered China's 'paramount leader' until 1992. He formally launched and highlighted the Four Modernizations, which marked the beginning of the reform era and its focus on domestic policy. During the Deng era, China prioritized internal economic modernization. Africa's failure to open itself to international markets further distanced it from China's goals. While China maintained cordial relations with most African countries, trade and aid stagnated. China's foreign direct investment did not become an important factor in the relationship. Beijing's goal was to modernize as quickly as possible; Africa had a minimal role in these plans, especially during the second half of the 1980s (Taylor, 1998: 443–4).

In 1982, the Twelfth National Congress of the CPC shifted China's global policy from 'war and revolution' to 'peace and development'. China also signalled that it would make fewer resources available for aiding other countries. Premier Zhao Ziyang made an eleven-country tour of Africa in 1982 and vice premier Li Peng visited in 1984, but there were otherwise few high-level trips to Africa until after the Tiananmen Square crisis in 1989 when China felt a need to reassure its African partners. The Zhou Ziyang tour resembled Zhou Enlai's famous 1963–64 visit and was an effort to reaffirm China's interest in Africa. He indicated that China was ready to normalize relations with the Soviet Union and that China no longer expected African states to choose between China and the Soviet Union. China had set the stage for a different kind of economic cooperation with Africa (Shinn and Eisenman, 2012: 43–4; Taylor, 1998: 446–7).

Zhao Ziyang announced during his visit a revised foreign aid policy that he called the 'four principles' (Xuetong, 1988: 4):

- Equality, mutual benefit, and non-interference in internal affairs.
- Good economic results with less investment, shorter construction cycles, and quicker results.
- Greater variety of projects that take into account specific local conditions, high quality of work, and a stress on friendship.
- Enhancement of the self-reliant capabilities of both sides and promotion of growth of respective national economies.

These principles constitute a revision of the eight principles announced by Zhou Enlai during his visit to Africa in 1963–64. They emphasize actual results and were designed to counter some of the problems with China's earlier aid projects such as the management failure of the Tanzania–Zambia railway. The emphasis on a variety of projects and mutual cooperation was also new (Yu Fai, 1984: 313).

During the 1980s, China did not develop relations with African countries based on their ideology or who they sided with during the final decade of the Cold War. The number of African countries recognizing Beijing increased from forty-four in the 1970s to forty-eight in the 1980s; fifty-five African presidents visited China from 1981 to 1989. But China's economic modernization left the country short of capital and unable to provide Africa with the same level of economic assistance as previously. China also began to emphasize development cooperation based on commercial contracts, joint ventures, and the provision of technical services. The focus of China's relationship with Africa shifted from the political to the economic arena (He, 2006: 7–8).

Analysts have become increasingly reluctant to estimate the value of China's aid to individual countries, particularly when it became more important to measure the aid against that coming from Western countries. There are problems with the definition of aid used by the OECD countries compared with China's definition. Announcements of China's aid projects often lack details and are not always implemented in the announced amount. They may also be spread over more years than initially stated. On the other hand, interest-free loans are sometimes cancelled, allowing the loan principal to become legitimate aid. The last estimated country breakdown published by the OECD went half-way through the Deng Xiaoping era to 1986. From 1979 to 1985, the OECD put China's aid to Africa at about US$800 million. The major recipients, in descending order, were Sudan, Zimbabwe, Liberia, Madagascar, and Equatorial Guinea (OECD, 1987: 18–19).

Deng Xiaoping changed China's arms transfer policy to one focused on earning hard currency from the sale of arms. As a result, transfers declined to African countries other than Egypt, which was an important buyer of a large selection of military equipment. During the first half of the 1980s, other major African recipients of arms deliveries were Sudan, Somalia, the DRC, Tanzania, and Zimbabwe. Most of the transfers involved low-tech Chinese copies of Soviet systems from the 1950s and 1960s. By the end of the 1980s, China supplied a wide assortment of military equipment to Africa that included fighter aircraft, artillery, patrol craft, and tanks (Shinn and Eisenman, 2012: 167).

The Deng Xiaoping era witnessed static trade levels with Africa, but continuation of a modest trade surplus by China. China's global trade increased from US$37 billion in 1980 to US$117 billion in 1990 while, during the same period, Africa's global trade fell from US$213 billion to US$197 billion. China–Africa trade also fell as a percentage of both sides' world trade. By 1980, China's trade with Africa accounted for only 2.6 per cent of its global trade and this dropped to about 1 per cent by 1988. Africa's trade with China constituted less than 1 per cent of Africa's total trade through the 1980s (Shinn and Eisenman, 2012: 112–13).

4.4 Jiang Zemin Reaches Out to Africa (1992–2002)

> At the turn of the millennium and century, China and Africa are faced with both historical opportunities for greater development and unprecedented challenges.
>
> (Jiang Zemin in his speech at the first Forum on
> China–Africa Cooperation in 2000)

The Jiang Zemin period established the base for the phenomenal expansion of China–Africa relations in the twenty-first century (Shinn and Eisenman 2012: 47, 112–15). Serving as general secretary of the CPC Central Committee from late 1989 until late 2002, Jiang Zemin had to deal immediately with the negative aftermath of Tiananmen Square but was presented with an opportunity following the end of the Cold War. While the West was highly critical of China's handling of Tiananmen Square, the African reaction was muted and, in a few cases, supportive. The presidents of Namibia and Burkina Faso and the foreign minister of Angola all publicly backed China's response (Taylor, 1998: 447–8). The prevailing reaction in North Africa suggested the crackdown was a necessary and understandable response by a legitimate government that felt threatened (Shichor, 1992: 89, 92, 96). China appreciated Africa's silence or support and increased its assistance to the continent. At the same time, the end of the Cold War resulted in less interest in Africa by its traditional donors and allowed China to engage more actively.

There was a sharp increase in high-level visitors from China to Africa. In the three years after Tiananmen Square, foreign minister Qian Qichen visited fourteen African countries and started in 1991 a practice that continues to the present day—China's foreign minister makes his first overseas visit each year to Africa before visiting any other part of the world (Taylor, 1998: 450). President Yang Shangkun visited Cote d'Ivoire in 1992 while Jiang Zemin made state visits in 1996 to Kenya, Egypt, Ethiopia, Mali, Namibia, and Zimbabwe. During this tour, he announced five points that were similar to previous statements on China's Africa policy (He, 2006: 9):

- To foster sincere friendship and become each other's reliable 'all-weather friend'.

- To treat each other as equals, respect each other's sovereignty, and refrain from interfering in each other's internal affairs.

- To seek common development on the basis of mutual benefit.

- To increase consultation and cooperation in international affairs.

- To look into the future and create a more splendid world.

Prime Minister Li Peng visited seven African nations in 1997. Jiang Zemin proposed in 1999 creation of the Forum on China–Africa Cooperation (FOCAC), which signalled a new phase in Sino-African relations (Pham, 2006: 241). In 2000, he visited South Africa in April and in October opened the first FOCAC ministerial conference in Beijing. In the final year of his rule, he went to Libya, Nigeria, and Tunisia. Jiang Zemin made a clear break with the approach of Deng Xiaoping in an effort to expand China's outreach to Africa; the aid and trade figures began to demonstrate this renewed interest in Africa.

China's estimated aid to Africa in 1988 was only US$60 million; it jumped to US$224 million in 1989 and US$375 million in 1990. During the 1990s, more than half of the countries receiving China's aid were African (Taylor, 1998: 450–1). At the end of the Jiang Zemin period in 2002, China's aid to Africa reached about US$600 million, supplemented by about US$200 million in debt relief and US$500 million in concessional loans (Brautigam, 2009: 167). The number of African students studying in China, mostly on government scholarships, also began to rise and exceeded 1,000 at the beginning of the Jiang Zemin era. While the amounts of aid were small compared to larger Western donors, China was sending a message that it had become an increasingly important source of assistance to Africa.

China increased the conventional arms it transferred, mostly sales, to Africa in the 1990s but remained well behind the volume supplied by Russia. Chinese weapons deliveries from 1989 to 1999 totalled US$1.3 billion. Of this total, US$200 million went to North Africa, US$600 million to Central Africa, and US$500 million to Southern Africa. These transfers included ships, anti-ship missiles, tanks, supersonic combat aircraft, surface-to-air missiles, artillery pieces, armoured personnel carriers, and self-propelled guns. China was also a major supplier of small arms and ammunition, but reliable figures are not available. The principal attraction of Chinese weapons is the low price and relative simplicity of the equipment. In 1988, only nine African countries had defence attachés in Beijing; by 1998, the number had increased to thirteen (Shinn and Eisenman, 2012: 167–9).

In 1989, for the first time, China deployed personnel to a UN peacekeeping operation—20 military observers to the UN Transition Assistance Group monitoring elections in Namibia. China subsequently sent small numbers of peacekeepers to the UN mission in the Western Sahara beginning in 1991, Mozambique from 1993 to 1994, Liberia from 1993 to 1997, Sierra Leone from 1998 to 1999, and along the Eritrea–Ethiopia border in 2000. While China did not contribute troops to the two UN missions and the US-led operation in Somalia during the first half of the 1990s, it endorsed all three operations in the Security Council because of their 'exceptional' humanitarian goals (Wu and Taylor, 2011).

In 1993, China became for the first time a net importer of petroleum. During the 1990s, imports of energy and raw materials from Africa were increasingly important to sustaining China's economy and its export of consumer and industrial products. China also sought from Africa iron ore, titanium, cobalt, copper, uranium, bauxite, manganese, and timber. Sino-African trade grew impressively during the Jiang Zemin era, rising from just over US$1 billion in 1989 to more than US$10 billion in 2002. Chinese foreign direct investment in Africa also started to become significant, cumulatively reaching more than US$4 billion in 2002.

4.5 Hu Jintao Rides the Africa Wave (2002–12)

China has formed strategic partnerships and launched strategic dialogue mechanisms with many African countries.

(Hu Jintao in his speech before the fifth FOCAC in 2012)

Hu Jintao, general secretary of the CPC Central Committee from November 2002 until November 2012, inherited a strong relationship with all African countries except for eight that still recognized Taiwan. When Hu Jintao relinquished power in 2012, only four African countries—Eswatini, Burkina Faso, Gambia, and São Tomé and Príncipe—recognized Taiwan. This represented a significant victory for Beijing's 'One China' policy. During his time as general secretary, Hu Jintao made four trips to Africa to underscore the importance China attached to the continent.

The second FOCAC ministerial meeting took place in Addis Ababa in 2003 attended by Premier Wen Jiabao, thirteen African leaders, and more than seventy ministers from Africa and China. In a side session, nearly one hundred Chinese business representatives assembled to meet with their African counterparts. Hu Jintao introduced in the same year the 'peaceful rise' concept, which argued that China's economic rise would not seek external expansion but would uphold peace, mutual cooperation, and common development. In response to concerns by some critics who interpreted 'rise' as threatening, Hu Jintao stopped using it and substituted 'peaceful development' (Glaser and Medeiros, 2007).

In 2005, Hu Jintao introduced the concept of 'harmonious society' and 'harmonious world' at the Asia–Africa Summit. 'Harmonious world' suggested that China is moving to a new stage of development and is more willing to engage in international activities such as UN peacekeeping operations. It assumes that China's economic well-being is its highest priority and this will only be possible in a benign international environment. This concept had important implications for Africa where China supported the status quo and where it depended increasingly on African raw materials to fuel its economy (Zheng and Tok, 2007).

The head of state or government of nearly every African country that recognized Beijing attended the third FOCAC conference in Beijing in 2006.

In advance of the event, China issued its first Africa policy white paper, which contained the following principles (China, 2006):

- China adheres to the Five Principles of Peaceful Coexistence, respects African countries' independent choice of the road to development, and supports African countries' efforts to grow stronger through unity.
- China supports African countries' economic development and nation building and promotes common prosperity in China and Africa.
- China will strengthen cooperation with Africa in the UN and other multilateral systems by supporting each other's just demands and reasonable propositions.
- China and Africa will learn from and draw upon each other's experience in governance and development, strengthen exchange and cooperation in education, science, culture, and health.

These principles are a continuation of China's long-standing policy of non-interference in internal affairs and incorporate the idea that China will not criticize internal African policies and developments. Equally important, African leaders are expected to avoid criticism of China's internal policies such as human rights, Tibet, and its Muslim minority. During the past several decades, not a single head of state of an African country that recognizes Beijing has violated this tacit understanding.

In 2009, Premier Wen Jiabao announced at the fourth FOCAC in Egypt a series of measures for strengthening ties with Africa. While most were previous themes, several suggested a new emphasis in Chinese policy. He called for partnership with Africa on climate change and agreed to increase cooperation in science and technology, including the creation of 100 joint demonstration projects. He announced a loan of US$1 billion for small and medium-sized African businesses and said China would offer zero-tariff treatment to 95 per cent of the products from Africa's least-developed countries with which it had diplomatic relations (He, 2010).

As the Hu Jintao era ended, Beijing hosted in July 2012 the fifth FOCAC conference in Beijing. It resulted in the most comprehensive action plan so far and emphasized a new type of China–Africa strategic partnership. There was a greater focus on supporting African peace and security as Chinese nationals and interests in Africa came under increasing pressure and even occasional attacks. After the fall of Libya's leader in 2011, the evacuation of almost 36,000 Chinese nationals from the country was a wake-up call. China launched the Initiative on China–Africa Cooperative Partnership for Peace and Security. It promised to support African efforts to combat the illegal trade and transfer of small arms and light weapons. It reaffirmed China's participation in the anti-piracy operation in the Gulf of Aden, assistance for the African Union to resolve African conflicts, and support for UN peacekeeping operations in Africa (FOCAC, 2012; Xu, Yu, and Wang, 2015).

China's official development aid to Africa grew modestly during Hu Jintao's rule. One of the best estimates for 2007 puts the amount of aid and debt relief at US$1.4 billion (Brautigam 2009: 168–72). According to the State Council, China provided US$14.4 billion in foreign assistance (grants, interest-free loans, and concessional loans) during the three-year period 2010–2012 to 121 countries, including fifty-one in Africa. About 52 per cent of this aid went to Africa. If you divide the global figure of US$14.4 billion by three years times 52 per cent, Africa received just under US$2.5 billion for each of the three years (China, 2014). This compares with about US$8 billion annually from the United States during the same period.

China continued to be a significant supplier of conventional weapons to Africa. From 2004 to 2011, China delivered US$1.9 billion worth of weapons to North Africa and US$1.8 billion to sub-Saharan Africa, which accounted for 9 per cent and 19 per cent respectively of all weapons delivered to each region. China was the single largest supplier to sub-Saharan Africa but a modest source for North Africa. Most of the weapons were artillery pieces, armoured personnel carriers, minor surface combatants, combat aircraft and other aircraft, and tanks and self-propelled guns (Grimmett and Kerr, 2012: 52–4, 58–9, 68).

China stepped up its training both in China and in Africa for African military personnel. It increased the number of personnel assigned to six UN peacekeeping operations in Africa, reaching 1,520 at the end of the Hu Jintao era. Support for UN peacekeeping operations became a core interest of China, which provided more personnel in Africa than any other permanent member of the UN Security Council. On the other hand, China contributed only about 3 per cent of the UN peacekeeping budget and its contributions to African Union peacekeeping activities were exceedingly small. Beginning in late 2008 in response to Somali pirate attacks on ships and crews, including those from China, the People's Liberation Army Navy (PLAN) began sending a three-ship anti-piracy task force to the Gulf of Aden, a policy that continues to the present day (Shinn and Eisenman, 2012: 179–93).

There was rapid growth from a low base in China's foreign direct investment in Africa during the Hu Jintao years. Even allowing for under-reporting of investment not captured by money entering through tax havens, the amount was modest and below Africa's major Western partners. At the beginning of the Hu Jintao period, FDI was well under US$1 billion annually, reached a high of about US$5 billion in 2008, and fell back to about US$2.5 billion in 2012. On the other hand, there was a sharp increase in contracts won by Chinese companies primarily for infrastructure projects. These contracts totalled about US$3 billion in 2003 and exceeded more than US$40 billion by 2012. International financial institutions, African governments, and

China's Export-Import Bank provided the financing. While China has built much of Africa's infrastructure, there is rarely any investment component; these are contracts won by Chinese companies whose goal is to make a profit (Pairault, 2018).

One of the most impressive developments under Hu Jintao was the growth in China–Africa trade. It increased from about US$10 billion in 2002 to US$180 billion in 2012 and was largely in balance throughout this period. In 2009, China overtook the United States as Africa's largest trading partner. However, most of Africa's exports to China were natural resources, especially oil and minerals, while China's exports to Africa were manufactured and finished goods. The continent-wide trade balance also masked trade deficits that poorer African countries had with China (IMF, 2017: 162–3; Shinn and Eisenman, 2012: 114–21).

The Hu Jintao era witnessed a major increase in China's efforts to increase its soft power in Africa. From 2010 to 2012, China granted almost 19,000 scholarships to students from African countries. By the end of 2012, China had sent more than four hundred young volunteers to sixteen African countries in a programme that resembled the American Peace Corps. Twenty pairs of leading Chinese and African universities began cooperating in a new '20 plus 20' programme. From 2010 to 2012, China sponsored training courses, mostly short-term, for more than 27,000 African officials and technicians in a wide range of fields. By the end of 2012, China had engaged with African countries on 115 joint research and technology projects, and opened thirty-one Confucius Institutes and five Confucius classrooms in twenty-six African countries (China, 2013). China also expanded the activities of Xinhua, China Radio International, and China Central Television (now China Global Television Network) in an effort to improve its image in Africa (Shinn and Eisenman, 2012: 194–210).

4.6 Xi Jinping Becomes More Assertive in Africa (2012–Present)

China–Africa relations have today reached a stage of growth unmatched in history. We should scale the heights, look afar and take bold steps.

(Xi Jinping at the 2015 FOCAC conference in Johannesburg, South Africa)

Xi Jinping took up his position as general secretary of the CPC Central Committee in November 2012. So far, his global policies, including those in Africa, have been marked by a new assertiveness. Following a stop in Russia, Xi Jinping early in 2013 made his first visit outside China to Tanzania, South Africa, and Republic of the Congo. In 2015, he visited Zimbabwe and opened the 6th FOCAC conference in South Africa where he announced an historic US\$60 billion financing package, although some of that programme had not materialized by the end of 2018. Greater attention to risk assessment in Africa, rising concerns about African debt, and a slowing Chinese economy account for the delays in obligating the funds (Eom, Brautigam, and Benabdallah, 2018; Yun, 2018). Xi Jinping returned to South Africa in 2018 for the BRICS summit and included visits to Senegal and Rwanda. The CPC has also continued to encourage party-to-party exchanges with larger numbers of African party leaders coming to China. In Africa, only Eswatini still recognized Taiwan.

In connection with the 6th FOCAC, China released its second Africa policy paper. It emphasized the following themes (China, 2015):

- Enhancing political mutual trust.
- Deepening cooperation in international affairs.
- Deepening economic and trade cooperation.
- Strengthening development cooperation between China and Africa.
- Deepening and expanding cultural and people-to-people exchanges.
- Promoting peace and security in Africa.
- Strengthening exchanges and cooperation in consular, immigration, judicial, and police areas.

Xi Jinping initiated the concept of the Chinese dream. In the case of Africa, he says it connects the development of Africa with that of China and aligns the interests of the Chinese people with those of the African people. Related to this concept is Xi Jinping's 'community of shared future' for reforming and improving the existing international order in a manner more suited to China's interests. The key initiative for achieving this new order is Xi Jinping's Belt and Road Initiative (BRI). Although China has made Africa part of the BRI, it is not clear what this means practically for Africa. China includes in the BRI its infrastructure projects that were conceived and even under construction before the BRI was announced. As China agrees to new projects, they routinely become part of the BRI. The question is what is different. Whatever the significance, this approach is now known as 'Xi Jinping Thought' and intended to propagate his global vision for changing the international order (Rudd, 2018).

During the Xi Jinping era, China's economic interaction with Africa has levelled off and even declined in some cases. This is due largely to a drop in the price of many commodities exported by Africa, a slowdown in China's economy, and China's concerns about Africa's increasing debt burden. According to the International Monetary Fund, five African countries are in debt distress and another eleven are at high risk of debt distress (IMF, 2018).

China's global foreign aid as calculated by the Ministry of Finance increased modestly in 2013 over 2012 and again in 2014, levelled off in 2015 at about US$3 billion, and then declined in 2016 to about US$2.3 billion (China–Africa Research Initiative, 2017). In past years, just over half of China's aid has gone to Africa. Different sourcing of the data accounts for lower Finance Ministry aid figures than those reported by the State Council in 2010–12. In any event, China's aid peaked in 2014–15. At the institutional level, China created in 2018 its first independent international aid agency.

During the period 2012–15, China provided US$900 million in conventional arms to North Africa and US$1.9 billion to sub-Saharan Africa. This amounted to 12 per cent of all arms deliveries to Africa—only 5 per cent to North Africa but a whopping 32 per cent to sub-Saharan Africa (Theohary, 2016: 42–7). China continued to emphasize the security theme in Africa, most notably opening in Djibouti in 2017 its first military base outside China and increasing significantly the number of PLAN ship visits to African port cities. The number of Chinese peacekeepers assigned to UN operations in Africa actually declined slightly due to the end of the mission in Liberia. On the other hand, China sent its first combat battalion ever to a UN mission (UNMISS in South Sudan) and increased its financial contribution to UN peacekeeping operations to 10 per cent of the total budget. By 2018, the number of African countries with defence attaché offices in China rose to thirty-five and China's Ministry of National Defence hosted its first ever Defence and Security Forum for high-ranking military officials from fifty African states.

China's annual flows of foreign direct investment to Africa since 2012 have been largely flat and actually declined to US$2.4 billion in 2016, a decrease of 19 per cent compared to 2015. China accounts for only about 3 per cent of all foreign direct investment in Africa. Contracts completed by Chinese companies have continued to rise since 2012, although they peaked in 2015 at about US$55 billion and fell back in 2016 to about US$53 billion (Pairault, 2018).

China–Africa trade reached a high in 2014 at US$203 billion, fell to US$146 billion in 2015 and then began to recover but reached only US$170 billion by 2017. Throughout this period, China maintained a significant trade surplus (IMF, 2017). It may take several more years before trade returns to the 2014 level. The more important issue is China's large trade surplus, particularly in African countries that have had large deficits throughout this century.

Xi Jinping underscored the need for China to improve its people-to-people outreach in Africa. This resulted in even more scholarships for African students. By 2015, there were almost fifty thousand African students studying in China, more than in either the United States or the United Kingdom but fewer than France. By 2018, there were forty-eight Confucius Institutes and twenty-three Confucius classrooms in thirty-five African countries.

China increased its interaction with African universities, think tanks, and non-governmental organizations. It instructed its embassy personnel to spend more time with ordinary Africans. It also put additional resources into its media activities in Africa. On the downside, it abandoned its young volunteer programme in Africa that was started under Hu Jintao.

4.7 Conclusion

China–Africa interaction has experienced different phases, which correspond roughly to China's changes of leadership (See Appendix: Table A4.1). Support for wars of national liberation and competition with both the West and the Soviet Union, exacerbated by the Cultural Revolution, characterized the first twenty years of the Mao Zedong period. A more pragmatic approach towards Africa began to take hold in the early 1970s. Deng Xiaoping focused on internal domestic reform and pulled back somewhat from engagement in Africa while seeking to maintain cordial relations with as many African countries as possible.

Jiang Zemin, concerned by possible negative fallout from the 1989 Tiananmen Square crisis, early in his rule increased China's outreach to Africa. Near the end of his reign, he created the Forum on China–Africa Cooperation, which permitted a further expansion of relations with the continent. Hu Jintao took advantage of Jiang Zemin's preparatory efforts and a relative decline in Western interest in Africa by increasing significantly China's economic engagement in Africa.

Xi Jinping has extended China's engagement into the security sector and generally taken a more assertive approach globally, which has had important implications for Africa. Chinese and African economic developments have resulted, however, in a recent consolidation, reassessment, and even decrease of China's economic engagement on the continent. A softening in African commodity prices and a modest reduction in China's importation of certain African commodities account for most of this decrease. Worrisome debt in a number of African countries and China's greater focus on minimizing risk contribute to the trend. Although China–Africa trade may have bottomed out since its high point in 2014, it will likely take several more years for China–Africa economic relations to return to their previous high levels.

Looking forward, China will continue to initiate most of the important interaction with African countries primarily because of the inherent asymmetry in the China–Africa relationship and the difficulty of fifty-four countries reaching agreement on most issues. At the same time, China has tried to respond to African concerns about some of its engagement. It has been willing to scale back the percentage of Chinese labour contracted for implementation of infrastructure projects. It has listened to African complaints about the

Appendix: Table A4.1. Evolution and characteristics of China–Africa relations

Phase	Evolution	Characteristics
Pre-nineteenth century until 1949	In the first quarter of the fifteenth century Chinese labourers and traders came to several regions of Africa. After taking power in 1912, Sun Yat Sen and the Republic of China developed official relations, notably with South Africa.	Chinese labour migration to South Africa and Madagascar.
Mao Zedong (1949–76)	The seizure of power by the Communist Party of China (CPC) in 1949 did not result immediately in any significant outreach to Africa. Mao Zedong was preoccupied with consolidating his rule in the early years of the new regime. With the decolonization of African countries, China began to pursue a more pragmatic policy in Africa and achieved a huge political victory in October 1971—admission to the United Nations.	After the Bandung conference of 1955, the PRC's Five Principles of Peaceful Coexistence were established and remain essential to China's foreign policy until today. They include: mutual respect for sovereignty and territorial integrity, mutual nonaggression, non-interference in each other's internal affairs, equality and mutual benefit, and peaceful coexistence.
Deng Xiaoping (1978–92)	The number of African countries recognizing Beijing's 'One China' policy increased from forty-four in the 1970s to forty-eight in the 1980s; fifty-five African presidents visited China from 1981 to 1989.	But China's economic modernization left the country short of capital and unable to provide Africa with the same level of economic assistance.
Jiang Zemin (1992–2002)	This period witnessed an intensification of China–Africa diplomatic relations. For example, Jiang Zemin made state visits in 1996 to Kenya, Egypt, Ethiopia, Mali, Namibia, and Zimbabwe. For the first time, China deployed personnel to a UN peacekeeping operation in 1989.	The main features of China's involvement with Africa are reflected in five areas: development aid; considerable increase in arms export; increased trade; loans for infrastructure; UN peacekeeping.
Hu Jintao (2002–12)	When Hu Jintao relinquished power in 2012, only four African countries—Eswatini, Burkina Faso, Gambia, and São Tomé and Príncipe—recognized Taiwan. This represented a significant victory for Beijing's 'One China' policy.	The second FOCAC ministerial meeting took place in Addis Ababa in 2003 attended by Premier Wen Jiabao, thirteen African leaders, and more than seventy ministers from Africa and China. In a side session, nearly a hundred Chinese business representatives assembled to meet with their African counterparts.
Xi Jinping (2013–)	Xi Jinping oversaw the 6th FOCAC, China released its second Africa policy paper. It emphasized the following themes (China, 2015): • Enhancing political mutual trust. • Deepening cooperation in international affairs. • Deepening economic and trade cooperation. • Deepening and expanding cultural and people-to-people exchanges. • Promoting peace and security in Africa. The key initiative for achieving this new order is Xi Jinping's Belt and Road Initiative (BRI). China agrees to new projects; they routinely become part of BRI.	During the 6th FOCAC, China announced a US$60 billion loan, trade, and aid package to African countries. The package also included debt relief to the least developed African countries. China also announced more scholarships for African students to study in China. By 2015, there were almost fifty thousand African students studying in China.

Source: The author acknowledges inputs from Mohamed Salih and Fantu Cheru in preparing this matrix.

environmental practices of some Chinese companies and published stricter voluntary guidelines. It understands Chinese companies occasionally do not follow local laws and regulations and, in some cases, has not stood in the way of their sanctioning by African governments. China has also responded positively to African requests to support with more vigour industrialization in Africa.

References

Adie, W. A. C. (1964) 'Chinese Policy towards Africa', in S. Hamrell and C. G. Widstrand (eds) *The Soviet Bloc China and Africa*. Uppsala: Nordiska Afrikainstitutet, 43–63.

Barnouin, B. and Yu Changgen (1998) *Chinese Foreign Policy during the Cultural Revolution*. London: Kegan Paul International.

Bartke, W. (1975) *China's Economic Aid*. London: C. Hurst & Company.

Brautigam, D. (2009) *The Dragon's Gift: The Real Story of China in Africa*. Oxford: Oxford University Press.

China (2002) 'China Facts and Figures 2002', http://www.china.org.cn/english/ features/China-Africa/82054.htm.

China (2006) China's African Policy. See at http://www.focac.org/eng/zt/zgdfzzcwj/ t230479.htm.

China (2013) 'China–Africa Economic and Trade Cooperation', http://english.gov.cn/ archive/white_paper/2014/08/23/content_281474982986536.htm.

China (2014) 'China's Foreign Aid', http://english.gov.cn/archive/white_paper/2014/ 08/23/content_281474982986592.htm.

China (2015) 'China's Second Africa Policy Paper', http://www.xinhuanet.com/eng lish/2015-12/04/c_134886545.htm.

China–Africa Research Initiative (2017) 'Chinese Foreign Aid', http://www.sais-cari. org/data-chinese-foreign-aid-to-africa/.

Eisenman, J. (2018) 'Comrades-in-Arms: The Chinese Communist Party's Relations with African Political Organisations in the Mao Era, 1949–76', *Cold War History*, https://www.tandfonline.com/doi/full/10.1080/14682745.2018.1440549.

Eom, J., D. Brautigam, and L. Benabdallah (2018) 'The Path Ahead: The 7th Forum on China–Africa Cooperation', China–Africa Research Initiative, https://static1. squarespace.com/static/5652847de4b033f56d2bdc29/t/5b84311caa4a998051e685e3/ 1535389980283/Briefing+Paper+1+-+August+2018+-+Final.pdf.

FOCAC (2012) 'The Fifth Ministerial Conference of the Forum on China–Africa Cooperation Beijing Action Plan (2013–2015)', Ministry of Foreign Affairs, Peoples Republic of China, Beijing, http://www.focac.org/eng.

Glaser, B. and E. S. Medeiros (2007) 'The Changing Ecology of Foreign Policy-Making in China: The Ascension and Demise of the Theory of Peaceful Rise', *China Quarterly*, 190: 291–310.

Grimmett, R. F. and P. K. Kerr (2012) 'Conventional Arms Transfers to Developing Nations, 2004–2011', Congressional Research Service, https://fas.org/sgp/crs/weapons/ R42678.pdf.

He, W. (2006) 'Moving forward with the Time: The Evolution of China's African Policy', Paper presented at the Hong Kong University of Science and Technology, http://www.cctr.ust.hk/materials/conference/china-africa/papers/He,Wengping.pdf.

He, W. (2010) 'China's Diplomacy in Africa', http://www.african-bulletin.com/wp-content/uploads/2010/02/wenpingc.pdf.

Iimi, A., R. Humphreys, and Y. Mchomvu (2017) 'Rail Transport and Firm Productivity: Evidence from Tanzania', Policy Research Working Paper 8173, World Bank, http://documents.worldbank.org/curated/en/966401504009617940/pdf/WPS8173.pdf.

IMF (2017) *Direction of Trade Statistics*. Washington: IMF.

IMF (2018) List of LIC DSAs for PRGT-Eligible Countries, https://www.imf.org/external/Pubs/ft/dsa/DSAlist.pdf.

Larkin, B. D. (1971) *China and Africa 1949–1970: The Foreign Policy of the People's Republic of China*. Berkeley, CA: University of California Press.

Li, A. (2011) *Chinese Medical Cooperation in Africa*. Uppsala: Nordiska Afrikainstitutet.

Nasser-Eddine, M. (1972) *Arab–Chinese Relations 1950–1971*. Beirut: The Arab Institute for Research & Publishing.

Neuhauser, C. (1968) *Third World Politics: China and the Afro-Asian People's Solidarity Organization, 1957–1967*. Cambridge, MA: Harvard University Press.

OECD (1987) *The Aid Programme of China*. Paris: OECD.

Ogunsanwo, A. (1974) *China's Policy in Africa 1958–1971*. London: Cambridge University Press.

Pairault, T. (2018) 'China in Africa: Goods Supplier, Service Provider Rather Than Investor', *Bridges Africa*, 7(5): 17–22.

Pham, J. P. (2006) 'China's African Strategy and its Implications for U.S. Interests', *American Foreign Policy Interests*, 28: 239–53.

Rudd, K. (2018) 'Xi Jinping's Vision for Global Governance', Project Syndicate, https://www.project-syndicate.org/commentary/xi-jinping-has-a-coherent-global-vision-by-kevin-rudd-2018-07.

Shichor, Y. (1992) 'China and the Middle East since Tiananmen', *The Annals of the American Academy*, 519: 86–100.

Shinn, D. H. and J. Eisenman (2012) *China and Africa: A Century of Engagement*. Philadelphia, PA: University of Pennsylvania Press.

Snow, P. (1988) *The Star Raft: China's Encounter with Africa*. New York: Weidenfeld & Nicolson.

Taylor, I. (1998) 'China's Foreign Policy towards Africa in the 1990s', *The Journal of Modern African Studies*, 36(3): 443–60.

Theohary, C. A. (2016) 'Conventional Arms Transfers to Developing Nations, 2008–2015'. Congressional Research Service. See at https://fas.org/sgp/crs/weapons/R44716.pdf.

Wu, Z. and I. Taylor (2011) 'From Refusal to Engagement: Chinese Contributions to Peacekeeping in Africa', *Journal of Contemporary African Studies*, 29(2): 137–54.

Xu, W., W. Yu, and L. Wang (2015) 'An Analysis of the Security Situation in Africa', in Institute for Strategic Studies (ed.) *International Strategic Relations and China's National Security*. Singapore: World Scientific, pp. 263–85.

Xuetong, Y. (1988) 'Sino-African Relations in the 1990s', CSIS Africa Notes, https://csis-prod.s3.amazonaws.com/s3fs-public/legacy_files/files/publication/anotes_0488.pdf.

Yap, M. and D. L. Man (1996) *Colour, Confusion and Concessions: The History of the Chinese in South Africa*. Hong Kong: Hong Kong University Press.

Yu Fai, L. (1984) *Chinese Foreign Aid: A Study of its Nature and Goals with Particular Reference to the Foreign Policy and World View of the People's Republic of China, 1950–1982*. Saarbrücken: Verlag Breitenbach.

Yu, G. (1977) 'China's Role in Africa', *The Annals of the American Academy*, 432: 96–109.

Yun, S. (2018) 'Foresight Africa Viewpoint—China's Engagement in Africa: What Can We Learn in 2018 from the $60 Billion Commitment?' Brookings, https://www.brookings.edu/blog/africa-in-focus/2018/01/30/foresight-africa-viewpoint-chinas-engagement-in-africa-what-can-we-learn-in-2018-from-the-60-billion-commitment/.

Zheng, Y. and S. K. Tok (2007) 'Harmonious Society and Harmonious World: China's Policy Discourse under Hu Jintao', University of Nottingham Briefing Series 26, https://www.nottingham.ac.uk/iaps/documents/cpi/briefings/briefing-26-harmonious-society-and-harmonious-world.pdf.

5
Evolving Debates and Outlooks on China–Africa Economic Ties

Chris Alden

China and Africa's economic relations have evolved over time, from the tentative commercial engagements characteristic of the early 1980s to the comprehensive infrastructure loans and increased foreign direct investment being pursued across all sectors today. Expanding economic ties have been accompanied by changing debates as to the nature of China–Africa engagement and its significance for their respective development aspirations. South–South cooperation, for instance, framed the approach in this first phase of intensifying economic relations and reflected the combination of technical assistance, grant aid, and concessional loans negotiated by Chinese and Africans in exchange for access to the continent's abundant resources. As African economies came to demonstrate sustained patterns of higher rates of growth and two-way trade with China grew proportionally, the debates shifted decidedly towards one that focused on economic complementarities between them and Africa's integration into global value chains. In the aftermath of the global financial crisis and China's ascendency to become the world's second-largest economy, scholars like Justin Yifu Lin articulated a vision of a new structural economics for development based on strategic state-led policy planning, calibrated to infrastructure expansion, and mediating the allocation of resources through market forces. Furthermore, as the African industrialization process intensifies in economies like Ethiopia, China's key role in global development finance and its sectoral experiences put it in a crucial position to promote this new phase of development on the continent.

In this respect, China–Africa economic relations have evolved considerably from the mid-1950s to the present day in ways that track the patterns of domestic change in the political economy of China itself and follow larger changes to the international political economy wrought by globalization and accompanying policy responses to these changes. Concurrently, as China's rapid growth translated into an increasingly prominent economic position on the global stage, the recognition of these achievements inspired the promulgation of 'models' for regions like Africa that aimed to encourage learning from China's development experiences. Marking those changes and how they have manifested in the context of changing debates on development, as well as identifying the accompanying evolution in development policies, is critical to understanding the content of China–Africa economic relations.

This chapter will examine how interpretations of China's role in African development have evolved over time from one dominated by solidarity politics to a discourse based on economic complementarities and, in its most recent iteration, positioning China as a leader in fostering industrialization on the continent. Secondly, it will throw a spotlight on the distillation of Chinese experiences in development and how, through the mechanism of 'models' promoted in Africa, this serves as a way of encouraging policy transfer and peer learning. Finally, the chapter will reflect upon future trends and how these might shape the next phase of China–Africa economic relations.

5.1 South–South Cooperation: from Solidarity Politics to Economic Engagement

To understand China's economic engagement in Africa, one necessarily starts with the Cold War and the concurrent debates that arose out of prevailing conditions found in the newly established People's Republic of China and in post-independence Africa. Critiques of capitalism articulated by dependency theorists and revolutionary movements alike led these new governments to pursue state-led development strategies, ranging from mixed-market approaches and import substitution to state-mandated collectivism and even autarky (Gray and Gills, 2016: 557–8). With delivering development to their overwhelmingly rural populations an imperative for both, the initial decades were marked by a time of experimentation, growing South–South economic cooperation, and an embrace of Third-World solidarity. Declarations at mini-laterals such as successive summits of the Non-Aligned Movement (NAM) and regional organizations like the Organisation of African Unity (OAU) endorsed technical assistance and economic cooperation in the broadest possible terms as developing countries began to embark on bilateral exchanges and projects (Lopez Cabana, 2014).

Specific to China and Africa economic relations, the diplomatic support provided by China for the anti-colonial struggle on the continent paved the way for its technical assistance in the independence era. During Foreign Minister Zhou Enlai's tour of Africa in 1963–4, he outlined the eight principles of cooperation that were to shape Beijing's aid policy towards the continent during this period, including commitments to equality and mutual benefit, the transfer of knowledge through training of Africans, and the maintenance of the same standard of living commensurate with African host countries (Shinn and Eisenmann, 2012: 130). China–Africa economic engagement that featured around the continent during this period was focused on the agriculture and health sectors, where China's own evolving experiences were seen to be especially appropriate for Africa's rural economies (Brautigam, 1998: 61–100). Largely forgotten today is the intense diplomatic contestation between Beijing and Taipei as a structural feature of Chinese engagement on the continent, shaping, in particular, forms of economic engagement where countries switched recognition, with Beijing determined to make good on projects abandoned by Taipei.

Without a doubt, the iconic project of this ideologically tinged solidarity period of China–Africa economic cooperation remains the Chinese-sponsored railway between Zambia's copper belt and the Tanzanian port of Dar es Salaam. The Tazara railway, as it came to be called, grew out of discussions between the leaders of Tanzania and Zambia and Mao Zedong when they asked for support to build a rail link that would enable Zambian copper to be exported abroad without having to rely upon the transport networks of the white settler states of Rhodesia and South Africa (Monson, 2008: 197–219). From the outset, the Chinese government provided virtually all the finance, management, labour, technical assistance, training, and materials to build the 1,060-mile-long Tazara railway from Ndola on the Zambian copper belt to the Tanzanian port of Dar es Salaam (Liu and Monson, 2011; Monson, 2009: 3). Completed a decade later in 1976, the US$400 million project was China's largest and most comprehensive at the time. The Tazara railway was immediately hailed as a success by African governments (Monson, 2009: 3–4; Katzenellenbogen, 1974). Interestingly, in many respects the key features of China's more contemporary economic engagement with the continent were already on display in this project: the African request for Chinese assistance in pursuing a development project spurned by Western governments; the Chinese role in designing, managing, and financing that project; the use of Chinese labour and supplies in constructing the project; and finally the post-project debate on handing over management to the host government and addressing the issue of recurrent costs.

The onset of the 'reform and opening' policies in late 1978 of the new Chinese leader, Deng Xiaoping, ushered in a new period of gradualist domestic economic reform coupled to export-oriented strategies in China, which in turn precipitated changes to aspects of its economic engagement with Africa. This reflected growing recognition within Chinese policy circles of the development successes of newly industrialized economies like Singapore, Taiwan, and South Korea, which had pursued integration into global markets rather than spurning them. The impact on Chinese policy towards Africa was not long in coming. During Premier Zhao Ziyang's tour of the continent in 1982, he informed African counterparts that China's solidarity-based support for African development would henceforth be reoriented towards market-based criteria that would assess projects in terms of their commercial value to both parties rather than solidarity ties (Shinn and Eisenmann, 2012: 130). Beijing's 'Four Principles for Sino-African Economic and Technical Cooperation' that would guide its future cooperation with the continent, re-affirmed the commitment to mutual benefit, the maintenance of cost efficiency in delivery of its projects, and equivalency with African standards of living. This policy shift towards Africa, initially framed in terms of the familiar language of 'mutual benefit' but later rephrased as 'win–win', refracted the ongoing market-led reforms in China's domestic productive sectors and the growing confidence in that approach felt by policymakers in Beijing. Extended negotiations with the World Trade Organization (WTO) culminated in China's membership in 2001 which spurred on deeper integration into global markets and, concurrently, an unprecedented drive by Beijing to encourage its newly consolidated state-owned enterprises (SOEs) to expand their activities abroad (Alden and Davies, 2006).

As China's domestic economy grew dramatically over the next two and a half decades, the search for resources, markets, and investments did indeed come to occupy a larger part of economic engagement with the continent. From the mid-1990s onwards China's ExIm Bank provided large-scale loans to support the Chinese National Petroleum Company (CNPC)'s drive to develop and expand production in Sudan's nascent oil industry (Junbo, 2017; Patey, 2014). In early 2004, following a refusal by Western-led donors to pledge financial support for post-war reconstruction in Angola (citing widespread corruption of oil revenues by the ruling party), Luanda and Beijing signed the first in a series of loans worth US$2 billion to support infrastructure development in that country (Alves, 2012: 106–11). China's large-scale debt financing of infrastructure backed by African resources and mostly tied to use of Chinese factors of production in countries like Sudan and Angola fed assumptions about China and its impact on development, especially as conceived by the West, and the challenges that it posed to OECD donor conventions (Naim, 2009).

It was in the context of Chinese involvement in Sudan and Angola that many of the now 'classic' debates on China–Africa development took root, highlighting the role of popular and elite discourses in formulating perceptions that remain relevant today. The central question that seemed to drive debates at this stage—'Is China going to change Africa?'—was one focused on fear of the Chinese impact on Western-inspired norms, practices, interests, and institutions in Africa, in short, of its challenging Western dominance over the continent (Alden, 2008; Gaye, 2008). At play in shaping these ideas, at least in part, was an active Western media and in its wake many Western academics, often mirroring concerns held by development agencies and financial institutions. This outlook was in reaction to the wholehearted praise offered by African governing elites and many academics, who saw in China's 'no political conditionalities' an alternative to nearly two decades of imposition of neoliberalism through structural adjustment programmes and democratization promotion.

African perspectives on development were, however, not unreservedly positive, nor were they exclusively negative. For instance, Dambisa Moyo's influential publication damned the Western aid industry for both its self-serving 'altruism' and patent failure to deliver development in Africa despite decades of effort and hundreds of billions of dollars (Moyo, 2010). She openly called upon African governments to look to the 'Chinese model of development' as an alternative (Moyo, 2012). African leaders echoed this sentiment, with Nigeria's President Olusegun Obasanjo amongst others calling for closer economic ties with Beijing to foster development (*Daily Trust*, 2003). Always acutely sensitive to power projection, other African elites began to voice some concerns about the newly leading position that China occupied as the top trading partner in their respective economies and its growing interests in African economies (Alden, 2007: 120). As African statesman and longstanding friend of China, Julius Nyerere, expressed it as far back as 1968, the continent's relationship with China was 'the most unequal of equals' (Bailey, 1976: 80). An overlooked but critically important source of African perceptions that found its way in various forms into the national and continental debates was the role of popular discourses about China and the Chinese. Ordinary Africans' observations about Chinese labourers ('they must be prisoners'), however absurd or misguided, nevertheless influenced the relationship and policy choices pursued by politicians (Sheridan, 2018). At the same time, periodic surveys of African public opinion on China scored it consistently high but nonetheless reflected this bifurcation between admiration and concern (Afrobarometer, 2016).

Heady enthusiasm during the new millennium's first decade, which saw influential international financial analysts shift their highest growth forecasts towards emerging markets, mirrored the changing role of emerging economies as sources of concessional loans, investment capital, and grant aid to other developing countries (O'Neil, 2001). In the aftermath of the global financial crisis of 2008, which China and other emerging powers weathered without the immediate damage seen in the industrialized North, African expectations of China rose still further. By 2013, at the tail end of the global commodity boom, China had reportedly invested US$26 billion in Africa and had become the leading source of concessional finance in much of Africa (Chen, Dollar, and Teng, 2015). It was in this context that Justin Yifu Lin's work on structural transformation of the Chinese economy and the opportunities it offers Africa came to the fore of debates (Lin, 2012). Lin points to the ongoing shift towards greater domestic consumption in China and the drive to off-shore some industry as factor costs like labour rise (Lin and Wang, 2015). His call was for a new structural economics for development based on strategic state-led policy planning, calibrated to infrastructure expansion, and mediating the allocation of resources through market forces.

African expectations for development began to reflect the prospects inherent in the emerging international environment and, in particular, the role that China could play in facilitating industrialization. The emergence of buoyancy in policy circles around Africa's sustained growth, captured by the phrase 'Africa rising', recast the possibilities for Africa as an investment destination with growing consumer markets bolstered by intra-regional trade. Beyond the growing optimism reflected in publications by the African Development Bank and UNECA, Arkebe Oqubay's work both widened and deepened ambitions for the continent by focusing on the requisite political and industrial policy frameworks needed to pursue industrialization in Ethiopia (Oqubay, 2015). His theoretical and practical insights were given further significance due to his role as a key policymaker in government.

In the case of the Forum on China–Africa Cooperation (FOCAC), which the South African government hosted in 2015, this 'new thinking' by African economists and policymakers translated into a greater focus on 'beneficiation' in resource sectors such that spillover occurs in the form of job creation, training, and provisions for services. Premier Li Keqiang, on a state visit in May 2014 that took him to Ethiopia, Nigeria, Angola, and Kenya, launched two initiatives—the '461 China–Africa Cooperation Framework' and the 'Three Networks and Industrialization Projects'—which responded to these concerns. Events like the China–Africa Poverty Reduction and Development Conference, involving leading figures in the Chinese development community along with AU counterparts and held in Addis Ababa in November 2014, aimed to provide further insights into the industrialization experiences of China and its possible transfer to the continent (IPRCC/AU/Government of Ethiopia/UNDP, 2014).

Moving to the particulars of development policy proposals put forward by Beijing, the '461 China–Africa Cooperation Framework' was a short-hand description of a new policy framework based on four principles (equality and mutual respect, solidarity, inclusive development, innovation on practical cooperation), six projects (industrial cooperation, financial cooperation, poverty reduction projects, ecological/environment protection projects, cultural and people-to-people exchanges, peace and security) and one platform

(FOCAC) (Li, 2014). The 'Three Networks and Industrialization Projects' included provision for the construction of high-speed rail networks, the building of road transportation networks, and the expansion of airports and aviation networks. The underlying idea, following from proponents of structural development, is that vital infrastructure provides the foundation for the rational siting of industrial clusters which create opportunities for economies of scale, linkages with supply chains, investment hubs, knowledge transfer, pooling labour, and other positive spillover effects on the local economy (Immarino and McCann, 2006). Three projects in particular, the Addis Ababa Light Rail System, the Addis Ababa to Djibouti standard gauge railway, and the Mombasa to Nairobi standard gauge railway, were seen as emblematic of this approach. Moreover, they cohered closely with one of the key 'flagship' programmes, namely the 'world-class infrastructure criss-crossing Africa' identified by AU officials as part of Agenda 2063's first phase. Taken together, these initiatives represented the Chinese vision of a 'new deal' with Africa, one which sought to intensify economic ties around a series of capstone infrastructure and industrialization projects which would involve Chinese firms in collaboration with Africans and underwritten by Chinese finance. FOCAC VII, convened in September 2018, reinforced this orientation towards infrastructure-led development as the capstone of China–Africa engagement in this period.

5.2 Models in Motion: Chinese Experience and African Development

At the heart of changing emphases and debates on China–Africa economic ties is a set of transformative policies that highlight the development success achieved by China and the tantalizing possibilities this holds for African development aspirations. These successes are given expression through the promulgation of 'models' which provide a distilled form of the Chinese experience in achieving significant gains in areas such as industrialization and agricultural production, and are realized as a battery of concrete policy prescriptions to animate local development. Their changing structure and orientation reflect the different stages and paths of development that China and Africa were engaged in over time.

The fascination with Chinese development dates back to the 1960s and 1970s. Fed largely by African idealism, revolutionary fervour, and a dose (befitting that era) of Chinese propaganda at its model farms in Dazhai, Tanzanian leader Julius Nyerere was convinced to adapt Mao's rural collectivization strategies to his promulgation of the 'ujaama villages' scheme in 1968 (Alden, 2018). Liberation movements such as Frelimo (Frente para Libertacao de Mocambique) operating out of bases in Tanzania and flush with the heady success of occupying a patchwork of territory in the northern reaches of the Portuguese colony, turned to Maoist precepts on revolutionary warfare in constructing the micro-economies of their liberation zones.

Notwithstanding these early examples from the heyday of the revolutionary epoch, the focus in the near-contemporary period reflected African interests in the evident successes of China's 'reform and opening' policy and the transferability of its programme of industrialization and agricultural production to African soil. While Deng Xiaoping had famously demurred back in the 1980s when asked about the transferability of the Chinese experience to Africa, this change in Beijing's approach was underscored by the formal launching of 'three to five' Economic Cooperation and Trade Zones (ECTZs) and 'ten' (later extended to 20) Agricultural Technical Demonstration Centres at the Forum on China–Africa Cooperation (FOCAC) Summit held in Beijing in November 2006 (FOCAC, 2006). The former was derived from the successful experience of the Chinese special economic zones which were launched in late 1978 in coastal South-East China, while the latter were the product of the cumulative experiences of agricultural reform starting in the early 1980s.

With *industrial policy/special economic zones*, China's salutary experience of developing an export-oriented manufacturing sector built on FDI and technology transfer from the industrialized countries was to be replicated through its Economic Cooperation and Trade Zones (ECTZs) initiative which promised to combine Chinese state funding with public–private investment to 'hothouse' a site for job creation, skills transfer, and possible outsourcing of increasingly costly Chinese industrial production and to nurture a nascent African manufacturing sector (Howell, 1993). According to Brautigam and Tang, the 'principles of profitability reign' at all levels of Chinese engagement in this process, from the conceptualization by Chinese provincial authorities, enterprises, and developers to their financing by Chinese banks and the decisions to invest in local markets (Brautigam and Tang, 2011: 49–51). Interestingly, the ECTZ initiative—contrary to perceptions held by many academics and policymakers in Africa—is actually global in its scope and has resulted in the establishment of ECTZs in Southeast Asia and beyond.

In the *agricultural sector*, the Chinese government established over twenty Agricultural Technical Demonstration Centres (ATDCs), including provision for financing and technical expertise, whose primary purpose is aimed at raising agricultural productivity for local markets and, with that, improvements in rural incomes, bolstered by a range of technical cooperation programmes in agriculture. A phased-in 'public–private partnership' approach is used, commencing with Chinese-designated provincial authorities partnering with a local host government to set up the infrastructure of the centre in the first year, provision for training and experimental farms in the second year, and the handing over of the local government to manage in the third year.

According to Jiang, one of the longer-term purposes is to create a platform for Chinese agricultural enterprises to obtain exposure to the local market in that African country, and to gain position and experience in globalizing their production (Jiang, 2015: 16–17). Notably, despite their inclusion in the model, 'public–private partnerships' were not a feature of the original Chinese experience in agricultural reform domestically but rather reflect later developments in that sector.

Collectively, it is clear that these Chinese initiatives being promoted in Africa are drawn in the main from the transformative policy approaches and implementation strategies that were behind the rapid development of the modern Chinese economy over the last four decades. They are grounded in the interest-based form of cooperation that has prevailed in China–Africa relations manifested in the solid commercial component devised for the support and involvement of Chinese firms and their African counterparts. While perspectives differ as to the role of the state and the private sector as catalysts in this process, they reflect an emerging consensus within the development community as to the importance of linkages between growth and poverty reduction in the case of China. As such, these initiatives are central to the effort to bring a distinctive Chinese experience of development to the task of catalyzing African development.

While these Chinese-led initiatives in Africa are still very much in the process of being rolled out, there are some indicators that not all of them are fully meeting expectations as catalysts for development. For instance, despite the publicity associated with the launch, a decade later a number of ECTZs remain relatively undeveloped sites (Mauritius, Lekki) with limited Chinese investment or spillovers to local economies, while others are little more than the 'rebranding' of existing Chinese investments as an ECTZ (Zambia) (Alves, 2011). In this regard, the Ethiopian ECTZ outside Addis Ababa stands apart and, concurrently, highlights the significant role that African host governments operating in conjunction with Chinese private capital have in fostering this process. Led by a focused Ethiopian leadership and anchored by the investment by Chinese company Huajian, the Eastern Industrial Zone has become a magnet for foreign direct investment into manufacturing (including firms from both emerging economies and established economies of the North) and has even inspired the expansion of a broad-based policy of creating industrial parks clustered by sector across different regions in the country and aligned with Chinese-built infrastructure projects like the Addis Ababa to Djibouti railway line. Other governments including those of Rwanda, Senegal, and South Africa have created ECTZs modelled in part on the Chinese–Ethiopian experience aimed at benefiting from the same coterie of factors.

The take-up of Agricultural Technical Demonstration Centres was much higher across the continent, with over twenty being established by 2011, though actual FDI attributed to the initiative was a fairly modest US$400 million, representing just 12 per cent of China's total agricultural investment in the continent (Jiang, 2015: 7). Experiences have varied depending on a number of contingencies, including local provisions for necessary infrastructure and the degree of integration with local agricultural training and extension services, as have differing expectations on the part of Chinese and the local end users. For instance, the flagship Agricultural Technical Demonstration Centre in Mozambique, considered by Beijing to be the most successful of the demonstration centres, initially had difficulty even in the hands of private Chinese companies in finding a local market that would sustain production at a cost-effective level, a situation that was compounded by a series of disputes with local employees and local communities over labour conditions and property rights (Chichava, Duran, and Jiang, 2014). These teething pains are, in their own way, reflections of the experimental character of China's own historical domestic development experience as it sought out the most effective combination of resources and policy frameworks to delivery success.

The attraction that the Chinese development experience holds in African policy circles continues to grow, measured in part by the proliferation of 'Look East' policies by African governments and their efforts to integrate these through a variety of regional and international forums such as FOCAC. Xi Jinping's forthright declaratory expressions of China's leadership role in global development at the 19th Party Congress in October 2017, backed by the considerable financial resources on offer as announced at FOCAC VI in December 2015 and FOCAC VII in September 2018, points to the continuation of creative thinking and expanded means to foster new modalities of delivery of transferable policy lessons to Africa (*Straits Times*, 2017).

5.3 Debating the Future: Towards Greater Diversification or Rising Dependency?

Commensurate with the changing dynamics of China–Africa economic relations into the present day, debates around the necessity of diversification away from resource-based economies and technology transfer are intensifying as Africans become more aware of Chinese (and other emerging economies') development experiences. Reflecting upon these possibilities, Mzukisi Qoba and Garth Le Pere contend that Africans must further broaden their aims:

> There is a need to rethink the terms of Africa's future growth and development not only in terms of industrialization—often conceived narrowly as manufacturing—since there are fewer possibilities for the continent to undertake industrial development along a trajectory similar to earlier industrializers. Rather, going forward a

strategic trade and industrial policy perspective should be the thrust of China–Africa relations in order to take advantage of the calculus of opportunity that currently exists. Thinking in terms of value-addition and value chains broadens the sectoral focus to encompass aspects of manufacturing, services and innovation in agriculture. (Qoba and Le Pere, 2018: 209)

Running in parallel to this, however, there is a critical discourse that like its predecessors questions the structural form of the relationship and its impact on African development. For some critics, the dominance of African primary products in exchange for Chinese finished goods in merchandise trade, coupled to the growing Chinese position in services like the financial sectors, suggested that the relationship was still in need of further recalibration (Le Pere, 2007). This concurs with the sharpening of the debate on improving market access into China which is beginning to take shape, with calls for a 'Chinese AGOA' featuring amongst South African policymakers (Altman, 2018). Given China's leading position in the relationship, the creation of market opportunities aimed specifically at African imports—especially value-added products, manufactured goods, and even services—is an important step to enhancing the integration of their respective economies. Bolstering these concerns is a revival of debates around the debt burden being taken on by African governments, especially in the aftermath of the dramatic fall in commodity prices in 2014.

Finally, in March 2018, China announced the creation of a new agency to coordinate foreign aid and overseas development projects: the State International Development Cooperation Agency (SIDICA). Fitted within the Belt and Road Initiative (BRI) framework, its principal aim is to support existing and future development projects in Africa and Asia including facilitating better oversight and coordination of Chinese development projects. The prospect that FOCAC initiatives would be aligned to the BRI, as indicated at FOCAC VII, holds out the possibilities of further infrastructure financing that could ultimately contribute to Africa's integration into global value chains (China Ministry of Foreign Affairs, 2018). Chinese financial resources based within the BRI framework, such as the Asian Infrastructure Investment Bank (AIIB) and the BRICS New Development Bank, can now be leveraged alongside the China–Africa Development Fund, the newly formed China–Africa Fund for Industrial Cooperation, and the Special Loan Facility for African SMEs. Beyond the attention given over to development financing, it is notable that FOCAC VII builds on the inclusion of environmental and socio-cultural considerations, once remote from China's economic engagement with the continent, and signalling again the alignment with parallel concerns in China.

5.4 Conclusion

China–Africa economic relations have evolved enormously over the past five decades, echoing in many respects the patterns of domestic change in the political economy of China itself. If debates about African industrialization and fitting local economies into Chinese global value chains are now prevalent, this marks yet another stage in the progressive development of economic relations between China and Africa. Beijing's role as a leader in promoting the international liberal trading regime implies that it will recognize the need to respond to the next challenge in the changing economic relationship, namely specialized provision for greater access to the Chinese market, and work together with African policymakers on sustainable development financing. The relentless dynamism of Chinese economic prowess which has powered changing economic ties is now being coupled to Africa's own rapid development, promising, it would seem, a new cycle of growth and change in both their economic relations.

References

Afrobarometer (2016) 'Here's What Africans Think about China's Influence in their Countries' http://afrobarometer.org/blogs/heres-what-africans-think-about-chinas-influence-their-countries.

Alden, C. (2007) *China in Africa*. London: Zed Books.

Alden, C. (2008) 'Is Africa Changing China?', South African Institute of International Affairs, 21 August, http://www.saiia.org.za/opinion-analysis/is-africa-changing-china.

Alden, C. (2018) 'A Chinese Model for Africa', in C. Alden and D. Large (eds) *New Directions in Africa-China Studies*. London: Routledge.

Alden, C. and M. Davies (2006) 'A Profile of Chinese MNCs Operating in Africa', *South African Journal of International Affairs*, 13(1): 83–96.

Altman, M. (2018) National Planning Commission, presentation at the Shanghai Forum, Shanghai, 26 May 2018.

Alves, A. C. (2011) 'The Zambia–China Cooperation Zone at Crossroads: What Now?' SAIIA Policy Briefing 41, South African Institute of International Affairs, Braamfontein.

Alves, A. C. (2012) 'Chinese Economic and Trade Cooperation Zones in Africa: The Case of Mauritius', SAIIA Policy Briefing 51, South African Institute of International Affairs, Braamfontein.

Bailey, M. (1976) *Freedom Railway: China and the Tanzania–Zambia Link*. London: Collings.

Brautigam, D. (1998) *Chinese Aid and African Development: Exporting Green Revolution*. Basingstoke: Palgrave, pp. 61–100.

Brautigam, D. and X. Tang (2011) 'African Shenzen: China's Special Economic Zones in Africa', *African Affairs*, 49(1) pp. 49–51.

Chen, W., D. Dollar, and H. Teng (2015) 'Why Is China Investing in Africa? Evidence from the Firm Level', *Brookings Papers*, August.

Chichava, S., J. Duran, and L. Jiang (2014) 'The Chinese Agricultural Technology Demonstration Centre in Mozambique: A Story of a Gift', in C. Alden and S. Chichava (eds) *China and Mozambique: From Comrades to Capitalists*. Auckland Park: Jacana, pp. 107–19.

Chinese Ministry of Foreign Affairs (2018) 'Forum on China-Africa Cooperation Beijing Action Plan (2019–2022)' https://www.fmprc.gov.cn/mfa_eng/zxxx_662805/t1593683.shtml.

Daily Trust (2003) 'Nigeria: Obasanjo Calls for Closer Ties with China', 17 December 2003, https://allafrica.com/stories/200312170136.html.

FOCAC, 'Forum on China-Africa Cooperation Beijing Action Plan (2007–2009)' 2006/11/16, https://www.fmprc.gov.cn/zflt/eng/zxxx/t280369.htm.

Gaye, A. (2008) 'China in Africa: After the Gun and the Bible . . . a West African Perspective', in Chris Alden, Dan Large, and Ricardo Soares De Oliveira (eds) *China Returns to Africa: An Emerging Power and a Continent Embrace*. London: Hurst, pp. 129–41.

Gray, K. and B. Gills (2016) 'South–South Cooperation and the Rise of the Global South', *Third World Quarterly*, 37(4): 557–8.

Howell, J. (1993) *China Opens its Doors: The Politics of Economic Transition*. Boulder, CO: Lynne Rienner.

Immarino, S. and P. McCann (2006) 'The Structure and Evolution of Industrial Clusters: Transactions, Technologies and Knowledge Spillovers', *Research Policy*, 35, pp. 1018–36.

IPRCC/AU/Government of Ethiopia/UNDP (2014) 'Africa-China Poverty Reduction and Development Conference: Industrial Development—Cross-Perspectives from China and Africa', sponsored by the IPRCC, AU, UNDP, and Government of Ethiopia, Addis Ababa, 18–20 November.

Jiang, L. (2015) 'Chinese Agricultural Investment in Africa: Motives, Actors and Modalities', *Occasional Paper* 223, South African Institute of International Affairs, October, pp. 16–17.

Junbo, J. (2017) 'China in International Conflict Management', in C. Alden, A. Alao, C. Zhang, and L. Barber (eds) *China and Africa: Building Peace and Security Cooperation on the Continent*. Basingstoke: Palgrave, pp. 147–62.

Katzenellenbogen, S. (1974) 'Zambia and Rhodesia: Prisoners of the Past: A Note on the History of Railway Politics in Central Africa', *African Affairs*, 73, p. 290.

Le Pere, G. (ed.) (2007) *China in Africa: Mercantilist Predator or Partner in Development?* Midrand: Institute for Global Dialogue.

Lin, J. Y. (2012) *New Structural Economics: A Framework for Rethinking Development and Policy*. Washington, DC: World Bank.

Lin, J. Y. and Y. Wang (2015) 'China's Contribution to Development Cooperation: Ideas, Opportunities, and Finances', Working Paper, FERDI.

Liu, H. and Jamy Monson (2011) 'Railway Time: Technology Transfer and the Role of Chinese Experts in the History of TAZARA', in T. Dietz, K. Havnevik, M. Kaag, and T. Oestigaard (eds) *African Engagements—Africa Negotiating an Emerging Multipolar World*. Leiden: Brill, pp. 226–51.

Lopez Cabana, S. (2014) 'Chronology and History of South–South Cooperation', Working Document 5, Ibero-American Program for Strengthening South-South Cooperation.

Monson, J. (2008) 'Liberating Labour? Constructing Anti-Hegemony on the TAZARA Railway, 1965–1976', in C. Alden, D. Large, and R. Soares De Oliveira (eds) *China Returns to Africa: An Emerging Power and a Continent Embrace*. London: Hurst, pp. 197–219.

Monson, J. (2009) *Africa's Freedom Railway*. Bloomington, IN: Indiana University Press.

Moyo, D. (2010) *Dead Aid: Why Aid Is Not Working and How There Is Another Way*. London: Penguin.

Moyo, D. (2012) *Winner Takes All: China's Race for Resources and What It Means for Us*. New York: Basic Books.

Naim, M. (2009) 'Rogue Aid', *Foreign Policy*, 15 October.

O'Neil, J. (2001) 'Building Better Global Economic BRICS', Global Economics Paper 66, 30 November.

Oqubay, A. (2015) *Made in Africa: Industrial Policy in Ethiopia*. Oxford: Oxford University Press.

Patey, L. (2014) *The New Kings of Crude: China, India and the Global Struggle for Oil in Sudan and South Sudan*. London: Hurst.

Qoba, M. and G. Le Pere (2018) 'The Role of China in Africa's Industrialization: The Challenge of Building Global Value Chains', *Journal of Contemporary China*, 27(110), p. 209.

Sheridan, D. (2018) 'Chinese Peanuts and Chinese *Machinga*: The Use and Abuse of a Rumour in Dar es Salaam (and Ethnographic Writing)', in C. Alden and D. Large (eds) *New Directions in Africa-China Studies*. London: Routledge.

Shinn, D. and J. Eisenmann (2012) *China and Africa: A Century of Engagement*. Philadephia, PA: University of Pennsylvania Press.

Straits Times (2017) '19th Party Congress: 7 Key Themes from President Xi Jinping's Work Report', 18 October 2017.

6

The Institutional Framework of Sino-African Relations

Ian Taylor

The increase in China's economic and political involvement in Africa is arguably the most momentous development on the continent since the end of the Cold War. The People's Republic of China (PRC) is now Africa's most important bilateral trading partner and since the upsurge of interest in Africa (*circa* post 2000), the Chinese leadership has been enthusiastic in showcasing its country's engagement with Africa and publicizing what it habitually describes as a relationship based on mutual benefits and 'win–win' situations (see Chapters 4 and 5). However, the institutional framework that supposedly guides Sino-African relations is confusing and at times contradictory—what has been termed 'harmony and discord' (Alden and Hughes, 2009). Its effectiveness is also problematic, although there are clear efforts by the Xi Jinping administration to rectify matters. At the moment, however, policy coherence is fragmentary at best and in fact often contradictory in practice as policies are arbitrated by numerous Chinese actors.

6.1 The Effects of Liberalization

The first step in attempting to understand the institutional structures is to acknowledge that we must always keep in mind that there are many Chinas and equally, many Africas. It is absolutely true that there are official policy frameworks, most notably the White Papers on China–Africa Economic and Trade Cooperation, China's Foreign Aid, China–Africa Economic and Trade, and China's Second Africa Policy Paper (Information Office of the State Council, 2010, 2011, 2013, 2014, 2015). However these are much less interesting than what is actually happening on the ground and in any case, it would be a mistake to argue that Chinese foreign policy in Africa neatly follows an overarching grand strategy dictated by Beijing. Rather, it is at best acceptable to state that Beijing's policymakers have certain aspirations for specific facets of Sino-African ties (as mentioned above) and that these are then refracted through an array of different actors and institutions. As one commentary put it when speaking more generally about Chinese policy-making, 'The Chinese state is often viewed as a machine whose parts all mesh smoothly... Closer to the mark is Kenneth Lieberthal's use of the term "fragmented authoritarianism" to characterize the regime' (Wang Shaoguang, 2003: 39). Indeed, factionalized bureaucratic interests related to foreign relations are an important influence on policy formulation in China (Bell and Feng Hui, 2007: 52; Zhao Quansheng, 1992). Such problems are only growing as China deepens its engagement with the global economy under the conditions of de facto liberal capitalism.

This latter point needs development. Huang Yasheng (2011) recaps that for much of the post-Mao period, the emphasis has been on the introduction of the market rather than its suppression (Hsueh, 2014: 3–4). What we have seen in fact is a fusing of macroliberalization with a selective continuation of state discretion and sectoral regulation. Indeed, 'on questions of trade, FDI and regulation, China's actual reform experience is pretty much in line with the policy prescriptions attributed to the Washington Consensus' (Karp, 2009: 204), albeit that 'the functioning of neoliberalism is largely concealed beneath the edifice of China's specific conditions' (Wu Fulong, 2010: 629). Quite clearly, the basis for the current Chinese mode of accumulation is to be found in the project initiated under the leadership of Deng Xiaoping and then (unevenly) advanced since his death in 1997 (see Chossudovsky, 1986; Hinton, 1991, 2006; Weil, 1996; and Sharma, 2007). Deng and his successors have instrumentalized the Chinese state to reorganize social relations, corresponding with the restoration of capitalism (Hart-Landsberg and Burkett, 2004: 26). China itself has been moving 'unmistakably toward the market doctrines of neoclassical economics, with an emphasis on prudent fiscal policy, economic openness, privatization, market liberalization and the protection of private property' (Yang Yao, 2010). A particular form of capitalism has developed in China, one that has strong propensities to aspects of the policy paradigm of neoliberalism (Hart-Landsberg and Burkett, 2004: 26). This move towards the norms of the market has led to a proliferation of actors *and* the relative weakening of the central state's ability to control matters.

Rivalries among and between different ministries, provinces, cities, municipalities, and/or individuals play themselves out on a daily basis in Africa and lay bare the myth of a monolithic China relentlessly pushing forward on some sort of 'trade safari'. Complexities have in fact rapidly developed as the wall between domestic and foreign policies has been eroded (Alden and Hughes, 2009). As Thomas Christensen (2001: 27) says of Chinese foreign policy in general, 'many of the means to reach the regime's domestic and international security goals are so fraught with complexity, and sometimes contradiction, that a single, integrated grand plan is almost certainly lacking, even in the innermost circles of the Chinese leadership compound'. How much more so as China continues to liberalize?

6.2 The Key Drivers of Policy

It should be noted that the opaqueness of Beijing's foreign policy processes has long been recognized (Brautigam, 2009; Jakobsen and Knox, 2010). Indeed, 'rather than foreign policy being formulated and implemented through a clear hierarchy, it is evident that there are several influential figures to report to who are embedded within overlapping institutions that can at times blur the chain of command, particularly if competing policy implementation bodies are of equal rank' (Corkin, 2011: 65). Thus any commentary on how policy is made and implemented can be at best tentative.

It first needs to be pointed out that Africa remains a relatively low priority in terms of Beijing's general foreign policy. Consequently, precise policymaking vis-à-vis the continent is diffused throughout the policy system and is neither concentrated nor synchronized. While the highest-level policymakers may proclaim broad strategic directions, it is the working-level institutions that are expected to implement these goals through appropriate policy actions. Economic and political interests have been the key drivers of Chinese attention in Africa, and thus the Ministry of Commerce (MOFCOM) and the Ministry of Foreign Affairs (MFA) have so far operated as the important state institutions implementing Beijing's policy towards the continent. Additional institutions may be turned to if and when the need arises.

In general terms, the Politburo Standing Committee (PBSC) is the paramount decision-making body with regard to foreign policy. Xi Jinping is the PBSC's delegated individual for foreign policy, and 'since 2012, Xi Jinping has taken charge of all foreign policy related decision-making bodies in what appears to be an attempt to improve coordination of interest groups' (Jakobsen and Manuel, 2016: 101). Xi is aided by the director of the Foreign Affairs Office (FAO) of the Central Committee of the Communist Party of China (CCP). This individual is effectively the highest official of the Chinese foreign service, occupying a post analogous to the United States National Security Advisor.

On a day-to-day basis, the MFA administers regular relations with foreign states. Depending on how important an issue may be, policy processes are dealt with at different levels. Significant matters that need to be sorted out at the highest level go to the FAO; only such matters as cannot be sorted out at that level go up to Xi Jinping. Aside from this process, broader affairs, such as the presentation of the latest major policies, are elaborated and then determined by the Politburo. The Foreign Affairs Leading Small Group (FALSG), made up of important government and CCP actors, formerly presented analyses from their agencies to the FAO and suggested recommendations. The FALSG included the MFA, MOFCOM, Ministry of Public Security, Ministry of State Security, Office of Taiwan Affairs, Office of Hong Kong and Macao Affairs, Office of Overseas Chinese Affairs, Information Office, Department of Propaganda, International Department, Ministry of Defence, and the General Staff Department. Recently, the FALSG became a permanent foreign affairs commission under a new name, the Central Foreign Affairs Commission. Xi Jinping heads this body, with Premier Li Keqiang as deputy head (Manuel, 2018).

Within the broader foreign policymaking apparatus:

> Line agencies are the primary source of daily information on foreign policy affairs. Each line agency involved, such as the MFA, the Ministry of Commerce and the People's Liberation Army (PLA), provides regular reports that reflect work and concerns specific to the agency's focus. Other line agencies also bear responsibility for information collection and analysis used in the national security decision making process, especially in their respective fields...Externally, the decision making system also relies on governmental and semi-governmental think-tanks for information and policy analysis. These think-tanks are affiliated with government agencies and act as additional research arms. (Yun Sun, 2014: 18)

The rest of the chapter will discuss the more day-to-day operations of the different institutions involved in Sino-African affairs.

6.2.1 *The Ministry of Foreign Affairs (MFA)*

It might be assumed that the MFA would be central to foreign policy in China. After all, 'The MFA has always had great prestige within the Chinese political system dating back to its close association with Premier Zhou Enlai' (Paltiel, 2010: 5). However, as Paltiel (2010) notes, 'Its great prestige...is not matched by bureaucratic clout. Within China's domestic system it serves mainly to communicate with foreign governments and to uphold and maintain China's international image.' Indeed, the MFA has been a weak actor in the institutional framework of China's foreign relations and has had an insubstantial presence in China's State Council, despite the fact that at the organizational level, Beijing has regularly defined the MFA as the country's top ministry (Fijałkowski, 2011).

Historically, the MFA has been starved of resources and it has been unable to construct an influential system or *xitong* within China's institutional structures that might engender durable economic assets—unlike other ministries. Consequently, it has been traditionally marginalized and is the poor relation vis-à-vis policymaking. This has led to a rather pathetic situation, as recounts Jing Sun (2017: 430). Apparently, members of the Chinese public have taken to posting calcium pills to the MFA as a deliberate insult implying that the ministry staff have no backbones. Equally, the MFA is known colloquially by Chinese netizens as the 'Ministry of Protests' as it has developed a reputation for issuing diplomatic phrases such as 'strongly denounce' or 'strongly protest' (and the classic 'hurt the feelings of a billion Chinese people') over relatively trivial issues. Chinese netizens now routinely, jokingly 'strongly denounce' things, ridiculing the MFA's intemperate language. As one Chinese commentator notes, China's diplomats 'come across as silent, passive, isolated, and boring, except when they are coming across as aggressive (often without meaning to)' (Qiu Zhibo, 2017).

However, officially, through its Africa Desk, the MFA is in control of executing foreign policy and it 'implement[s] the state's diplomatic principles and policies and related laws and regulations' (MFA, 2018). China has an extensive diplomatic presence across Africa and is present in all African countries with the exception of eSwatini, due to that country having diplomatic relations with Taiwan, and Burkina Faso (which only recently switched relations). China has the most embassies of any foreign country in Africa and the MFA is charged with operating these.

It should be pointed out that recent developments *may* suggest an improvement in the MFA's fate. At the National People's Congress (NPC) in 2018, the MFA received an important boost through a budget increase of 15 per cent, taking it to circa US$9.5 billion for 2018 (roughly 40 per cent higher than the 2013 budget) (*Financial Times*, 6 March 2018). This reflects a wider trend under Xi Jinping which has seen a much more assertive role for China in global politics, notably Xi's expressed wish to turn China into a global power by 2049. The need to help manage the ambitious Belt and Road Initiative (BRI) also no doubt helps explain a developing greater role for the MFA. As part of the reforms announced at the NPC, minister of foreign affairs Wang Yi kept his position but was also promoted to be one of China's five state councillors. This is important as state councillors are more senior than ministers. To date, it has been unusual (though not unprecedented) for an individual to hold both positions and it is expected the consolidation of the two posts under Wang Yi will lead to a more effective foreign policy. Equally, as part of other reforms, Beijing granted the MFA more authority over embassy personnel decisions. This will change the current situation where the MFA has no control over staff posted to embassies by other ministries or agencies.

Although the official face of China in Africa, the embassies are limited in their scope. Interviews with Chinese diplomatic personnel across Africa reveal a somewhat demoralized staff, with limited knowledge of what is actually happening vis-à-vis other Chinese actors' activities. Although mandated to look after consular affairs, often embassy staff do not actually know how many Chinese citizens are in the country. Equally, the activities of other actors, outside the control of the MFA or embassy staff, have meant that Chinese embassies have habitually been compelled to figuratively clean up the mess after activities by another Chinese actor have caused reputational damage. In China itself, companies habitually dodge environmental and labour regulations liable to impede the profitability of any given venture, either by colluding with local state officials interested in encouraging economic growth or by graft (Sun Yan, 2004). Either way, violations of environmental law and hazardous conditions for workers are the norm in much of China. It can therefore be no surprise that similar circumstances develop overseas. Since the central state cannot control such problems within China, it is doubly unlikely to regulate what myriad Chinese actors do in Africa. The MFA then has, in certain circumstances, been relegated to the role of fixing the damage. This is likely to deepen given that economics is very much in charge with regard to Sino-African ties and MOFCOM has increasingly played a critical role in the interpretation and rolling out of policy towards the African continent. It is MOFCOM that manages Chinese aid to Africa and as one commentary put it, the 'MFA is being relegated to greasing the cogs of diplomacy while MOFCOM officials engage in the implementation of policy' (Corkin, 2011: 68). It is to MOFCOM that we now turn.

6.2.2 Ministry of Commerce (MOFCOM)

The MOFCOM's Department of West Asian and African Affairs is in charge of coordinating economic relations with Africa and provides advice on Africa to key policymakers, as well as promoting investment and trade. As part of this, it collects intelligence on local African economic, political, and social trends, and provides this to Chinese companies interested in the continent. MOFCOM also dispatches the officials that serve in China's trade offices in Africa, as well as sending officials on trade missions. Officially, the office of the Economic and Commercial Counsellor (ECC) is regarded as the local MOFCOM representative in African countries. Located inside Chinese embassies or consulates, the ECC is technically subject to the embassy's managerial authority. In practice, this seems less clear-cut, and relations between the ECC and the in-situ ambassador tends to be personality driven and the locus of any rivalry between the MFA and MOFCOM. The result is that:

Diplomacy and politics is in fact in competition with economics, it would seem. This is played out in the African countries themselves. Whereas the Chinese Embassy reports directly to the MFA, the Economic Counsellor's Office, nominally under the embassy's umbrella structure . . . actually reports to the MOFCOM, serving as the MOFCOM's 'eyes and ears on the ground'. This can readily cause confusion, as it is apparent in some countries that the two offices do not exchange information, as they work for separate ministries that may be competing for influence in Beijing. (Corkin, 2011: 67)

It should be noted here that it is only in *some* countries that the ECC and the embassy do not exchange information. Nevertheless, as one analysis admitted, 'in extreme cases ambassadors may learn of new aid projects for the first time in the local newspaper' (Zhang Denghua and Smith, 2017: 2336).

MOFCOM's ability to monitor Chinese economic activity is relatively limited. The ECC in a Chinese embassy is often unable to provide dependable data on, for instance, how many Chinese businesses are really functioning in the country they supposedly have oversight over—and often ask (foreign) researchers for additional information. Capacity in managing Sino-African relations is a serious issue not only for both the MOFCOM and the MFA but also for *all* Chinese actors involved in the institutional framework managing relations. With regard to the ECC:

[S]taffing limitations—and often lack of interest—hamper their ability to monitor and evaluate aid projects, let alone to develop coherent in-country aid programmes. Compared with their western counterparts, the Economic and Commercial Counsellors' offices have little autonomy. As a Chinese aid official said, 'they have to report almost all the aid related issues back to MOFCOM and MFA for approval'. (Zhang Denghua and Smith, 2017: 2333)

A further issue is the role of MOFCOM in the provisioning of Chinese aid to Africa. This has been a contentious issue. In broader terms, much of what China claims to be 'aid' does not fit standard definitional norms and is often more akin to commercial activities. Beijing's foreign aid (*duiwai yuanzhu*) differs considerably from what the Organisation for Economic Cooperation and Development's (OECD) Development Assistance Committee (DAC) calls official development assistance. China's ostensible 'aid' to Africa includes things such as football stadiums, political party headquarters, and training and assistance given by the Peoples' Liberation Army (PLA). None of these are classified as foreign aid by the OECD-DAC. Equally, while many aid donors only deliver grant aid, China's 'aid' is dominated by concessional loans, invariably based on commercial rates and aimed at making a profit for the Chinese agency that disburses such finance (see Chapters 7 and 8). The result is that there has been massive confusion and contestation between what China claims to give as aid and what is accepted as actual development finance by the majority of the global donor community. Accumulating accurate data on how much actual aid China gives to Africa has proven in any case, at least thus far, impossible.

6.2.3 *Institutional Rivalry between the MFA and MOFCOM*

Within the institutional framework, while MOFCOM's concentration is on China's commercial interests, it has been the primary agency in charge of what China defines as its bilateral aid projects. 'This dual role results in internal differences between its overarching commercial mandate, the increasing interest in aid sustainability, and effectiveness within the development-focused areas' (Varrall, 2016: 24). In terms of policy alignment in Africa, the tensions between the MFA and MOFCOM play out with regard to the role of the Export-Import Bank of China (Exim Bank). This is a policy bank responsible for delivering concessional loans, subsidized by MOFCOM. Its function as a policy bank, in other words answerable directly to the State Council and often relying on directives from the State Council to determine operating principles and priorities, would suggest that it should be chiefly related to Beijing's wider foreign policy. However, the way it actually functions demonstrates that profitability and commercial concerns are more important to the institution. The result has been that 'the commercial focus of Exim Bank and some parts of MOFCOM causes tensions with the diplomatic goals of the MFA. This is the case in areas where MOFCOM is encroaching on what would traditionally be considered as MFA territory' (Varrall, 2016: 25). Consequently:

> The MFA and the MOFCOM do not see eye to eye on the purpose of concessional loans or indeed the 'correct' role for China Exim Bank to play in terms of African foreign policy. While the MFA sees these loans as primarily a mechanism for fulfilling its mandate of improving diplomatic relations between China and other developing countries through foreign aid, the MOFCOM sees them as principally a market entry tool for Chinese companies' goods and services. (Corkin, 2011: 73)

This has had an impact on the effectiveness of China's institutional arrangements for managing Sino-African affairs. Although MOFCOM and the MFA are formally equal in status, MOFCOM has engaged in mission creep and has eroded the MFA's authority abroad. In its pursuit of commercial opportunities and in prompting Chinese business interests, MOFCOM has at times contradicted what the local Chinese embassies have wanted to achieve within specific countries. In contrast to MOFCOM, for the MFA, 'political relations trump short-term economic gains, because it is not possible to develop good economic relations without excellent political relations' (Zhang Denghua and Smith, 2017: 2335).

Equally, given that capacity is an issue, some of the policy advice emanating from the ECC can surely be of questionable value. The involvement of the Exim Bank has further complicated matters and added an additional dimension to the institutional management of Beijing's relations with the continent. Unity of purpose is not something that may be said to characterize the working relationship between the MFA and MOFCOM. How Chinese aid is institutionalized is what we turn to next.

6.3 China's Aid Framework

MOFCOM is the administrative ministry authorized by the State Council to oversee foreign aid, along with the Executive Bureau of International Economic Cooperation, the China International Centre for Economic and Technical Exchanges, and the Academy of International Business Officials. With regard to the planning of China's aid, authority over decision-making has always resided in the hands of the central state. Today, MOFCOM, the Ministry of Finance, and the MFA lead twenty-one central and provincial institutions in a joint participation planning arrangement. Through the planning process, MOFCOM is primarily concerned with the economic aspects of foreign aid and mainly deals with the establishment of policies, the drafting of country-specific plans, and the coordination of implementations. The MFA, on the other hand, is responsible for the political aspects of foreign aid. The Ministry of Finance controls the distribution of China's annual foreign aid budget.

Aside from these larger aid-planning responsibilities, there are other institutions that take part according to their specialities. For example, the Ministry of Agriculture arranges agricultural experts to transfer the required technologies to Chinese agricultural aid sites, while the Ministry of Health allocates medical personnel, medicines, and medical equipment to dispatch medical teams. In addition to these responsibilities, the management of these specialized projects is also passed to these institutions. In 2008, the implementation management of China's primary foreign aid methods (namely complete project aid, goods and materials aid, and human resource development cooperation) were assigned to subsidiary institutions of MOFCOM. Altogether within MOFCOM, there are seven departments and institutions associated with the policymaking and management process.

6.3.1 *The Department of Western Asian and African Affairs*

This department liaises with all of the Economic and Commercial Counsellor's Offices stationed in the West Asian and African region, collects and researches country-specific data, and provides policy suggestions. In addition to collating information, it files other reports investigating the recipient country's trade, economic cooperation, and political situation.

6.3.2 Department of Aid to Foreign Countries

The Department of Aid to Foreign Countries is the central administrative division of China's foreign aid. In planning for China's annual aid, this department develops agreements by negotiation with recipient-country governments. Domestically, it supervises the institutions managing aid, and develops and enforces policies and codes of practices.

6.3.3 Chinese Academy of International Trade and Economic Cooperation (CAITEC)

CAITEC responds to research initiated by MOFCOM and publishes internally circulated journals and statistics. CAITEC also edits and releases China's official publications on aid.

6.3.4 The Executive Bureau of International Economic Cooperation

Established in 2003, this bureau is appointed and commissioned by MOFCOM to manage the implementation of complete project aid initiatives and support Chinese enterprises abroad. It organizes project bidding, verification of tendering enterprises, supervision and inspection of contract execution, and construction of aid expert teams and databases. In addition, this executive bureau also currently manages the implementation of technical aid.

6.3.5 China International Centre for Economic and Technical Exchanges (CICETE)

The CICETE was founded in 1983 as a subsidiary public institution of the then Ministry of Foreign Economics and Trade. It was first assigned the role of managing cooperative projects between China and United Nations organizations, primarily the United Nations Development Programme (UNDP) and the United Nations Industrial Development Organization (UNIDO). This was to promote human resources exchanges and to increase economic and trade cooperation, initially in support of the modernization of China. CICETE subsequently became responsible for providing training courses for Chinese foreign aid personnel and procuring China's supplies for humanitarian aid. In 2008, CICETE was additionally assigned the implementation management of goods and materials aid.

6.3.6 *Academy for International Business Officials (AIBO)*

As the only associated training centre of MOFCOM, the AIBO is one of the first State Council-approved Foreign Aid Training Centres. When AIBO began to engage in human resource programmes in 1998, it was initially tasked with organizing seminars for commercial officials. Subsequently, it became the principal coordinator of China's human resource development cooperation programmes. In addition to preparing training courses for high-level officials, the AIBO is also in charge of arranging specialized training courses and associated training centres.

6.3.7 *Economic and Commercial Counsellor's Office*

Since China established its first Economic and Commercial Counsellor's Office in Vietnam in 1956, these offices have become the frontline communication and management institutions for China's foreign aid. They are principally focused on local environment research, contract negotiation, aid personnel protection, and implementation supervision. The offices not only assist in the planning of China's aid but also supervise projects and programme deliveries, as well as monitoring effectiveness and sustainability after project completion. Their relationship with the MFA and the embassies in which they are sited abroad has been discussed above.

It should be here noted that in March 2018, at the 13th National People's Congress, it was announced that Beijing was to establish an international development cooperation agency, part of broader plans to reform the institutions of the State Council. The new agency, the State International Development Cooperation Agency (SIDCA), will take over the foreign assistance duties of MOFCOM and the MFA. On 4 April 2018, Wang Xiaotao, former Deputy Director of the National Development and Reform Commission (NDRC), was appointed Director of SIDCA. At the NDRC Wang had been in charge of foreign capital, overseas investment, and trade, and been involved in the BRI, negotiating with India, Pakistan, and Thailand on transport projects. Tentatively, it might be said that Wang's appointment as head of SIDCA demonstrates that development and infrastructure will remain the focus of China's international aid. As one analyst noted, 'MOFCOM and the Ministry of Foreign Affairs have been competing for control of Chinese foreign aid for decades. Appointing a new director from a third party or a third agency could bypass this conflict—and could make the process of establishing the new agency as easier' (quoted in Cornish, 2018). Equally, the fact that an important figure from the NDRC was appointed indicates that Beijing has ambitions for SIDCA.

The new agency will be directly under the State Council and will have responsibility for the drafting of strategic guidelines, formulating and implementing foreign aid policies, and offering advice on overseas assistance. 'The agency is intended to give full play to the role of foreign aid as a key instrument of China's diplomacy as a major country' according to the reform plan (*China Daily*, 14 March 2018). This significant development is likely to have a major impact on the institutional framework of Chinese aid policies towards Africa.

6.4 Chinese Policy Banks

The two key policy banks are the China Development Bank (CDB) and the Export-Import Bank of China (Exim Bank). In the energy sector, these two banks have provided roughly US$225.8 billion since 2000 (China Global Energy Finance database, 2018). To put things into perspective, US$68.7 billion or 30.4 per cent was invested in Europe and Central Asia, US$61.9 billion (27.4 per cent) went to Latin America, and US$60.3 billion (26.7 per cent) went into Asia. Only US$34.8 billion (15.4 per cent) went into Africa. This reiterates the comments made earlier about the relative importance of Africa to overall Chinese foreign policy.

The CDB operates the China–Africa Development Fund, more commonly known as the CAD Fund. This is a Chinese private equity fund aimed at promoting investment in Africa by Chinese companies in power generation, transportation infrastructure, natural resources, manufacturing, and so on. The CAD Fund was announced at the Forum on China–Africa Cooperation (FOCAC) summit in 2006 and was established in June 2007 with an initial funding of US$1 billion by the CDB. In December 2017, Chi Jianxin, chairman of the CAD Fund, told *Xinhua* that the fund has US$4.5 billion to invest in 91 projects in 36 countries, with more than US$3.2 billion having already been invested (*Xinhua*, 24 December 2017). Of note, at the FOCAC Summit in South Africa in 2015, President Xi Jinping proposed an additional US$5 billion, bringing the total funding to US$10 billion. According to Chi Jianxin, after completion of the current investments, the CAD Fund projects will have produced 11,000 trucks, 300,000 air conditioners, 540,000 refrigerators, 390,000 televisions, and 1.6 million tonnes of cement each year. This was claimed to raise Africa's exports by US$2 billion and taxation income by US$1 billion dollars every year (*Xinhua*, 24 December 2017).

The CAD Fund invests in Chinese companies that have economic and trade activities in Africa, as well as Chinese firms that have invested in African businesses and projects. The guiding principle of the fund is the promotion of investment by Chinese entities in Africa. The fund invests through equity investments, quasi-equity investments (such as preference shares and convertible bonds), and fund investments.

The Exim Bank gives out concessional loans and is administered and subsidized by MOFCOM; thus it is owned by the central government. The Exim Bank was set up in 1994 and in 1995 started distributing concessional loans as Beijing's solitary lender. It reports to the State Council. Dependable statistics on Exim Bank's concessional loans are unavailable and most studies on the bank can only arrive at estimates (such as the China Global Energy Finance database). The most reliable estimate, given by the China–Africa Research Initiative (2018) is that between 2000 and 2015, the Chinese government, banks, and contractors gave US$94.4 billion in loans to African states and state-owned enterprises (SOEs).

The internal procedures and apparatuses that the Exim Bank and CDB follow when deciding on loan practice are problematic to follow, as a wide variety of agents take part and the processes do not always follow the official policy framework. As Corkin notes, the Ministry of Finance is *theoretically* 'responsible for formulating policies and plans, drawing up the framework agreement to be signed, and determining the interest rate of the loan' (Corkin, 2011a: 71). However, in reality MOFCOM and Exim Bank, for instance, shoulder the greater part of these tasks, and the Ministry of Finance's role appears to be to merely approve the financial plan and cover the difference between the commercial and concessional interest rates in the Exim Bank's concessional loans.

With regard to the policy banks, it should be pointed out that as China has emerged as the world's largest exporter of capital, it has become increasingly exposed to potentially perilous situations in those states that are the recipients of Chinese loans. There has thus been, in the last few years, an attempt to tighten up the loan process so as to maximize the effect of the capital disbursed and try to make sure that the loans will produce relatively good returns. Both the Exim Bank and the China Development Bank now concentrate on 'bankable' projects and evaluate potential loans against a viable and profitable set of standards (Brautigam, 2009). Certainly, the CDB has been converted 'from a bank created for the explicit purpose of undertaking policy-driven lending into one of the most dynamic and successful financial institutions' (Downs, 2011: 2).

Concessional loans, including preferential buyer's credits, and all other Exim Bank-operated funding methods deviate from the foreign aid norm, given that they are now provided only if the proposed project is profitable. According to the loan regulations for concessional loans, concessional loan-funded aid projects must now have the ability to repay capital and interest. Concessional loans are no longer applicable to social charitable projects, unless they have economic benefits (see Zhangxi Cheng and Taylor, 2017). The policy banks have increasingly become less concessional and much more commercial in their loan disbursement behaviour.

6.5 The International Department of the Communist Party of China

A key actor in China's relations with Africa beyond the government ministries is the International Department of the Chinese Communist Party (ID) (see Shambaugh, 2007). This body manages party-to-party relations. The predecessor of the ID, the International Liaison Department, played a major role during the Maoist period in developing ties with sympathetic political parties abroad and with those liberation movements in Africa that supported China, as opposed to the Soviet Union, during the Cold War. Today, the ID develops links not only with communist parties and other left-wing organizations, but also what are classed 'national democratic parties of the developing countries' and 'political parties and statesmen of various ideologies and natures such as socialist, labour and conservative parties in the developed countries' (CPC Encyclopedia, 2018). The ID is an important institution for promoting Beijing's policy, analyzing the contemporary international situation, and nurturing relations with significant foreigners. As one commentary has noted:

> [T]he department has been more active than ever in recent years, dispatching and receiving several hundred delegations annually. Department officials have assessed that its activities will continue to expand along with China's state-to-state relations. The CPC/ID also distinguishes its diplomatic role from that of the Ministry of Foreign Affairs as being more long-term oriented, more flexible, and especially focused on helping rectify foreigners' "incorrect ideas" on the Party and country. (Gitter and Fang, 2016)

Party-to-party relations are considered vital by Beijing as a means to promote state-to-state relations and have become integral to some aspects of Sino-African relations. For example, with regard to FOCAC, inter-party relations have played a distinctive role in dialogue on governance issues and also for the advancement of trade relations. Critically, the ID played a crucial role in getting the heads of state of five African countries to attend the China–Africa Summit in Beijing in 2006, despite the fact that these heads of state governed countries which did not actually have diplomatic relations with China at the time. As part of Beijing's policy of denying any notion of Taiwan as a legitimate state entity, ID liaises with political parties in states that may lack diplomatic ties with China, but which acknowledge Beijing's 'One China' policy. In Africa, for instance, the ID cultivated ties with São Tomé and Príncipe's Movimento de Libertação de São Tomé e Príncipe/Partido Social Democrata. As the country's second-largest political party, this organization helped move the debate forwards until São Tomé and Príncipe formally recognized Beijing in 2016.

The ID maintains connections with about 400 political parties in over 140 countries, with regional bureaus coordinating the process. Notably, in November 2017 the ID hosted a four-day meeting between the Communist Party of China and representatives from 300 foreign political parties and organizations. This Dialogue with World Political Parties High-level Meeting, the Communist Party's first ever high-level meeting with assorted political parties from across the world, attracted over 600 representatives from 120 countries (*People's Daily*, 30 November 2017). As has been noted, no other ruling party devotes so much attention and effort to maintaining ties with political parties in other countries as does the CPC (Shambaugh, 2007). Indeed, 'The party-to-party relationship plays a critical role in strengthening the political foundation for China-Africa new strategic partnership [sic]' (China Radio International, 2012).

6.6 China's IR Think Tanks and Africa

It has long been recognized that think tanks have been exercising a growing influence on policy formulation in China (Jakobsen and Knox, 2010; Lai, 2010; Tanner, 2002). Think tanks are now playing a much larger role than in the past with regard to providing advice (Abb, 2015; Glaser and Saunders, 2002; Tanner, 2002) and foreign policy is no exception (Liao Xuanli, 2006; Shambaugh, 2002). However, these organizations are obviously not independent by Western standards and it is a veritable understatement to assert that 'under the current system, think tank scholars are required to "endorse" (*beishu*) government policies rather than critically evaluate policy initiatives and political dissent' (Cheng Li, 2017: 7).

Furthermore, the capacity for providing high-quality research is extremely limited. In the area of African analysis, it is rare for think tank researchers to travel to Africa to do actual research (attending forums and conferences to pronounce on the official Chinese policy line is a different matter). As a consequence, Chinese policy research institutions have 'a bad reputation for the quality of their policy recommendations, especially when compared with their Western counterparts' (Menegazzi, 2014).

Indicative of the capacity problem is the Chinese Academy of Social Sciences (CASS), which is ostensibly the leading social science think tank in China. Analysis of Africa is run out of the Institute of West Asian and African Studies and within this, the Africa Research Office handles the continent, concentrating on political change and democratization, economic development, security issues, the African Union and regional integration, as well as Sino-African political, diplomatic, and economic relations. The Africa Research Center describes itself as 'one of the major academic centres for African studies' in China, but emblematic of the low priority actually given to Africa within CASS, the Research Office only consists of three 'senior professional' positions, three 'associate senior' positions, and two assistant researchers (CASS, 2018). This makes a grand total of eight researchers working on the whole of Africa.

The China Institutes of Contemporary International Relations (CICIR) is no better in the capacity regard, despite being among China's largest, oldest, and most influential research institutes for international studies and affiliated to the Ministry of State Security, with oversight by the Central Committee of the CPC. Indeed, CICIR has a total of three research staff in its Institute of African Studies: two associate research professors and one full research professor (CICIR, 2018).

The China Institute of International Studies (CIIS) is the think tank of China's Ministry of Foreign Affairs and publishes the famous CIIS *Blue Book on International Situation and China's Foreign Affairs*, which documents important trends for the previous year. However, it has no research centres devoted to Africa and CIIS's website only has four researchers working on the continent (CIIS has a staff complement of approximately one hundred people). Indicatively, within CIIS the executive director of the China-Asia Africa Cooperation Centre, which was founded at Xi Jinping's behest, is actually a Latin American expert. The Shanghai Institutes for International Studies (SIIS) is another government-affiliated think tank and has a Centre for West Asia and Africa Studies. Like all other think tanks in China, however, SIIS has minimal interest in Africa: it has four people working on the continent (SIIS, 2018).

Mirroring the developments between the MFA and MOFCOM, one of the more effective Chinese think tanks working on Africa is the Chinese Academy of International Trade and Economic Cooperation (CAITEC), which is affiliated to MOFCOM. CAITEC specifically focuses on providing consulting services to government departments and businesses and undertakes market investigations and policy analyses for these. CAITEC does have an Institute of Asian and African Studies, although Africa is subsumed within the Department of West Asian and African Studies. A dedicated China–Africa Research Centre was established in 2010 but has thus far produced little. Nonetheless, in 2013, CAITEC officials developed concrete proposals for developing foreign aid country strategies specifically for Africa. Equally, CAITEC and MOFCOM approached UNDP China for advice and feedback on a draft of the second aid White Paper. And despite China not being a development assistance committee (OECD-DAC) member, MOFCOM and CAITEC officials also actively took part in the ChinaDAC Study Group in which questions around the quality of aid were deliberated (Varrall, 2016: 30). Overall, however, China's think tanks are currently lacking with regard to Africa.

6.7 State-Owned Enterprises

The state-owned enterprises (SOEs) may also be considered noteworthy agents of Chinese foreign policy, given that the SOEs participate in the broad agenda of overseas economic policy and since 2000 have been actively encouraged to 'go out' (*zou chuqu*) (Hong and Sun, 2006). They are important actors in China's domestic milieu and have a growing role abroad. It should be noted that, according to Xu Yi-Chong (2014: 824), a distinction needs to be made between large and smaller SOEs:

Large SOEs may dominate China's investment in Africa, but their activities often constitute only a small proportion of their global activities. To compete in mature economies, their reputation is important and depends on their adoption of internationally acceptable behaviour. A large group of small SOEs and private enterprises, however, have brought into Africa fierce and unregulated competition and practices which are not acceptable in Western democracies and African countries. Tension therefore often arises between local people and these poorly regulated small enterprises.

Within the Chinese system, the directors of large SOEs are the same as high-ranking officials, in that they are routinely moved into senior political positions, such as governorships of provinces or ministerial office. Notably, the current governor of Guangdong, which is China's richest province, was formerly general manager of China Aerospace Science and Technology Corporation (CASC), an SOE and the main contractor for the Chinese space programme. As a result, intense personal connections link the large SOEs to the Party-state. The large SOEs are the key players in actual implementation of China's aid in Africa; not only are they state companies and thus produce income for Beijing, but they also possess the resources and political support to finish the projects, most of which require contracting in SOEs.

The SOEs operating abroad, by their nature, start out with huge initial advantages, having access to hard assets, capital, and intellectual property. With the reform of the Chinese economy, 'beyond these initial endowments, and once they have been restructured or partly privatized, SOEs are [now] run less as pure arms of the state and more as complex, hybrid organisations' (Zeng and Williamson, 2007). Today, they are profit driven and act as powerful interest groups that try to inform the policy agenda in Beijing.

Yet, the problem for Beijing and SOEs vis-à-vis Sino-African policy is that many (most?) SOEs do not actually see their activities or functions as being involved in some ostensible broader geopolitical stance by Beijing. Rather, they perceive their role (and duty) as being to maximize profits, as well as accumulate capital for either honest or dishonest reasons. There are thus numerous contradictions between the behaviour of SOEs and wider Chinese foreign policy.

In general, Chinese SOEs in Africa are concentrated in two key economic areas: energy and natural resources, and infrastructure construction (see Chapter 8). Both of these are capital intensive. 'Given the simple fact that SOEs predominate in the resource and energy industries (not only in China but also in many other countries), it is hardly surprising that they are leading the charge' (Chintu and Williamson, 2013). Critically, extractive industries in Africa had been plagued by numerous questions related to corruption, exploitation, human rights, and environmental damage long before China came on the scene.

Interestingly, the activities of the large Chinese SOEs in Africa encourage a variety of smaller SOEs and private players, mainly in light manufacturing, the retail sector or as sub-contractors to the large SOEs (see Chapter 13). The activities and tribulations of these actors mirror those in China where economic liberalization has not been harmonized with the elaboration of regulation.

The State-owned Assets Supervision and Administration Commission of the State Council (SASAC) is either the owner of, or maintains a controlling share in, over a hundred of the largest SOEs directly under the State Council. SASAC appoints the boards of directors and is concerned in any investment decision abroad which may have implications for ownership. As of 2017, its companies had a combined revenue of more than US$3.6 trillion and an estimated stock value of US$7.6 trillion, making it the largest economic organ in the entire world (*South China Morning Post*, 17 June 2017). It is led by the former head of the Aluminium Corporation of China, who has vice-premier rank, thus outranking line ministries such as MOFCOM and the MFA.

SASAC 'has a clear incentive to maximize value and profit in China's SOEs, even if these companies' pursuit of profits ends up damaging China's broader diplomatic or strategic interests in Africa' (Gill and Reilly, 2007: 42). SOEs have provincial and city as well as national offices, each with their own often-divergent interests (Oi and Walder, 1999). Given that provincial SOEs make up the majority of all Chinese SOEs investing overseas, centre–province tensions—long a problem within the domestic polity (Breslin, 1996; Goodman, 1997; Goodman and Segal, 1994)—clearly have the potential to play out abroad, further complicating policy coherence.

Given that the SOEs play a large role in China's aid towards Africa, it is important to note that there is evidence that SOEs actively seek to influence/distort China's aid by proposing projects to the ECC at the Chinese embassy in an African country or lobbying MOFCOM and the Exim Bank through personal connections back in China. Once an SOE has become established in an African country, staff from it actively cultivate good ties to the embassy, local government offices, and local elites. As Zhang Denghua and Smith (2017: 2339) note:

> They [SOEs] are familiar with China's aid policies, often tailoring their commercial strategies to work around policies designed to limit their influence on China's aid programme. One example is the restriction on the number of concessional loan projects that can be undertaken by a single Chinese contractor in a given country. While the limit is set at three, companies subvert this by subcontracting the projects among themselves, typically charging a 10 per cent fee for projects that they outsource to other firms, with the side benefit of avoiding host country duty on the importation of construction materials.

Given the generally corrupt nature of many African states (and many Chinese SOEs), it is no surprise that personnel from the SOEs enter into informal cooperation with local policymakers to ensure that the African government asks for a new aid project from Beijing (see Zhangxi Cheng and Taylor, 2017). A mutually agreed side payment will be made to the African officials involved in this scam. A correlation between Chinese aid in Africa and corruption has in fact been demonstrated (see Isaksson and Kotsadam, 2018).

The large number of SOEs operating in Africa and the aggressive competition among and between them for contracts has generated profound challenges for Beijing. Additionally, while the SOEs have grown and spread out, Beijing's ability to manage, supervise, and control their behaviour has been weakened by the ongoing effects of liberalization and the rival interests and power struggles among official state agencies tasked with policy implementation. These aspects of state–SOE dealings have seriously complicated an important aspect of the institutions involved in Sino-African relations.

6.8 China's Provinces

Many of China's provinces are enormously wealthy: if Nigeria (Africa's largest economy) was a Chinese province, its GDP would mean that it would only rank twelfth in a list of the richest Chinese provinces. While provinces have no official ability to formulate or implement foreign policy, they do have a role in twinning relationships[1] and in promoting economic relations, given that each local government in China is required to take a leading role in

---

[1] In the PRC, the more advanced provinces (or municipalities) have aided the less developed provinces to grow, a scheme known as *duikou zhiyuan* ('twinning assistance'). A comparable programme has been pursued by China abroad, initially most notably in Beijing's aid programmes and specifically in the medical teams, begun in 1963, which have been sent abroad. Medical teams from individual provinces and municipalities were sent to their twin and each Chinese province was allocated at least one African country as their twin. Examples would include,

developing its own economy. Since many of these entities are middle-income economies in their own right, a refined foreign affairs management system at the provincial level, invariably managed by a small leading group dealing with foreign affairs headed by either the provincial governor or Party secretary, operates.

After 1994, there was a restructuring of the central government–provincial relationship into a pattern of 'strong localities and strong centre' (Chen Zhimin and Jian Junbo, 2009). Under provincial leadership, the provincial Foreign Affairs Office (FAO) and the Foreign Trade and Economic Cooperation Commission (FTEC) are the two key agency organs engaging with local foreign relations for the individual provinces. The FAO, which operates under the provincial leadership in collaboration with the MFA, manages general local foreign relations for the province. The FAO has the duty of implementing Beijing's foreign interests locally through, inter alia, organizing the reception of important foreign visitors and the visits of provincial delegations abroad. The FAO also organizes and promotes activities with the sister cities and provinces of foreign countries, and guides the foreign-related activities of other provincial and local government departments.

The FTEC (in some provinces this has been reorganized as the Department of Commerce), is primarily concerned with provincial foreign economic relations. A standard provincial FTEC is in charge of executing Beijing's policies regarding external trade. FTEC takes an active role in scrutinizing and then supporting a foreign investment decision by a provincial SOE, but also conducts market exploration research abroad and also engages in trade promotion strategies. In summary, provinces act as 'not just agents of the central government in Africa, but also its partners' (Chen Zhimin and Jian Junbo, 2009: 15). While constrained by the institutional framework of Chinese diplomacy, many provinces have carved out niches for themselves in Africa and influence local manifestations of the China–Africa relationship. 'The central government remains as the dominating actor in China's foreign relations; nevertheless, the provinces have raised their profile on the international stage, and made themselves important foreign policy players in low-politics areas' (Chen Zhimin, Jian Junbo, and Chen Diyuc, 2010: 335).

6.9 The Forum on China–Africa Cooperation (FOCAC)

FOCAC, established in 2000, is a platform established in collaboration with African countries for collective consultation and dialogue. FOCAC ministerial

---

inter alia, Zhejiang being twinned with Mali, Tianjin with Congo-Brazzaville and Gabon, and Fujian with Botswana and Senegal.

summits take place every three years, alternately in China and Africa. The existence of FOCAC might be best seen as the formal institutionalization of Sino-African relations (Taylor, 2011). The first Forum met in October 2000 in Beijing and was attended by nearly eighty ministers from forty-four African countries. The second Ministerial Conference was held in Addis Ababa, Ethiopia, in December 2003 and passed the Addis Ababa Action Plan (2004–6). The FOCAC Summit and the third Ministerial Conference were held in Beijing from November 2006, whilst FOCAC IV met in Sharm el-Sheikh, Egypt, in November 2009. The fifth Ministerial Conference was held in July 2012 in Beijing, while the second FOCAC Summit and sixth Ministerial Conference were held in December 2015 in Johannesburg, South Africa. At the time of writing, a summit is planned for September 2018 in Beijing.

Chinese sources claim that it was African leaders who initiated and asked for a summit. He Wenping (2007: 147) asserts that: 'At the end of the 1990s, some African countries proposed that as the US, Britain, France, Japan and Europe had established mechanisms for contact with Africa, it was necessary for China and Africa to establish a similar mechanism to fit in with the need to strengthen relations. After earnest study, China decided to echo the suggestions of African countries, and proposed to hold the Forum in 2000'. However, it was China that publicly initiated the move: in October 1999, then President Jiang Zemin wrote to all heads of African states, as well as the Secretary-General of the Organisation of African Unity, to formally propose the convening of a Sino-African forum. In his letter he outlined principles for carrying out consultation on an equal footing, enhancing understanding, increasing consensus, promoting friendship, and furthering cooperation. When this was greeted with a favourable reception, the Chinese established a preparatory committee consisting of eighteen ministries. FOCAC has quickly proved to be a major feature in Africa's international relations. Whatever the origins, FOCAC has developed as a very public manifestation of formalized Sino-African relations.

What is notable about FOCAC is its emphasis on trade and commerce. The formation of the China–Africa Joint Business Council and the China–Africa Products Exhibition Centre are emblematic of this. As Alves notes:

> The strong commitment of the Chinese central government in the creation of the Forum clearly illustrates the growing importance of economic affairs in China's relations with Africa at the beginning of the 21st century . . . Economic matters . . . have been the strongest component of the Forum since its founding.   (2008: 72)

Another notable element of FOCAC is its strong emphasis on results. FOCAC consists of various mechanisms for future dialogue on China–Africa ties and a Follow-up Committee of FOCAC coordinates follow-up actions of all Chinese departments. The procedures state that the ministerial meeting of the Forum will be held every three years in China and an African country by turns, and that a senior officials' meeting will be held twice, one year before and several days before the main FOCAC ministerial meeting. In addition, the Beijing-based African diplomatic corps and the Secretariat of the Chinese Follow-up Committee of FOCAC hold regular sessions. A formal strategic dialogue mechanism has also been established between China and the African Union.

A chief problem with FOCAC, however, is that China is very much in control of the whole process and it is Beijing that sets the agenda, and the declarations and outcomes. Africa plays a bit-part at best, largely because of the obvious asymmetry but also because of the lack of any coherent African voice to shape the relationships. In these circumstances, even if China's policymakers wanted to make FOCAC more 'Africa centric', it would be difficult for Beijing policymakers to engage with any unified voice beyond platitudes from the African Union or the regional bodies. In fact, there is rarely any unified African voice on anything and so it is perhaps understandable that FOCAC has played out as it has. As *The Economist* noted:

> Africa's leaders could also play their hands rather better. They should talk to each other as well as their hosts in Beijing. If they negotiated as a block, they could drive a harder bargain. Just as China insists that foreigners enter into joint ventures with its companies, so Africans should make sure they get China's know-how, not just its money. (*The Economist*, 26 October 2006)

This indeed is a serious problem. Africa's leadership has, in general, promoted and fostered dependent relationships with the Western capitalist powers and there is a danger that FOCAC may simply reproduce this dependency. An Africa where external actors consume the continent's resources and add little to African self-development is something which has staked out much of post-colonial Africa's trajectory. In these circumstances, African elites attending forums such as FOCAC can, from a particular perspective, be seen as characters reduced to beggars angling for some Chinese largesse, rather than development-conscious participants and certainly not 'partners'.

6.10 Summarizing Sino-African Ties: Coordination and Friction

If the question of the institutions that manage Sino-African relations could be reduced to its essence, a key point stands out: China is not a unitary actor. This may seem elemental, but judging from much of the literature on Sino-African relations, it seems to have been overlooked. As the Chinese leadership has pursued its (admittedly uneven) post-Mao economic liberalization policies, they have encountered increasing difficulties in controlling—or even keeping abreast of—the diverse activities in which various Chinese corporations and actors are engaged overseas. Although major oil and other energy-based companies are probably under constant supervision (which rivalries may however complicate; see Chapter 9), the huge proliferation of small-scale traders operating in Africa, very often private individuals or families, is all but impossible to manage. Weak rule of law, endemic corruption, and bureaucratic tendencies at every level of government means that the central leadership is in a perpetual and losing struggle to keep up with a surging economy, whether domestic or when it is projected overseas. While there is evidence that Xi Jinping is seeking to re-centralize power, the ability to do so at home is debateable and when extended to far-flung activities in Africa or elsewhere, unlikely.

Integral to the shift within China towards capitalism has been the abundance of new actors alongside the relative decline in Beijing's capacity to manage and regulate developments. Chinese relations with Africa have thus become, in many ways, 'normalized', which is to say diverse, and involving multiple actors, rather than state directed and state controlled, which was the case before the reform period. Tracing the institutional networks that may inform this relationship is increasingly complicated and often opaque. This may be why so many analyses reduce relations between 'China' and 'Africa' to an almost bilateral level.

Another key point is that Chinese policy towards Africa is evolving and its institutions are often behind the curve in managing this evolution. Although the Chinese have considered their approach to Africa to be benign, they are beginning to feel exposed by the intricacies of Africa's politics. Kidnappings in Nigeria, the murders of Chinese workers in Ethiopia, anti-Chinese riots in Zambia, a high-profile campaign against the Beijing Olympics over China's role in Darfur—all of these have provided a steep learning curve. Chinese institutions have necessarily had to adapt and learn as the relationship deepens and matures.

However, a perennial problem for Beijing is that the Chinese state obviously has no wish to broadcast the reality of its power being diffused or that foreign policy is mediated, refracted—and at times distorted—by the myriad of actors and institutions outlined above. Bodies such as FOCAC, but also the MFA and MOFCOM, in this sense compound the problem, as no Chinese official is going to publicly admit that China's Africa policies are in fact not necessarily under the firm control of Beijing. Yet when one examines even SOEs, *actual* state control and direction is often nominal and even the largest Chinese companies, which remain under direct government control, are motivated by competition and the profit margin, and behave relatively autonomously. None of this is acknowledged by the sort of rhetoric that emanates from official Chinese sources.

In fact, just as Beijing has long had difficulty controlling what companies, domestic or foreign, do in China, what Chinese actors do abroad has amplified the problem. Control over external investment has already been relaxed, and ongoing reforms progressively make it easier for companies to act alone. Although Beijing has made concerted efforts to educate Chinese traders operating in Africa about local labour laws and safety standards and made patriotic appeals to protect the image of China abroad, there is the distinct possibility it has failed on both counts (see Chapter 12). In these circumstances, 'The conception of a rich and powerful China that can ... have a significant impact on policymakers across the world sits rather uneasily with analyses of serious domestic problems' (Breslin, 2007: 27). This is problematic for Beijing policymakers if and when Chinese companies do not deliver or they misbehave, as official Chinese pronouncements have been carefully crafted to give the impression that the central state is indeed in charge of operations.

Ultimately, neither Beijing nor Africa's leaders are 'in charge' of Sino-African relations. Africa has no credible China policy and in any case each individual country manages and directs (more or less) relations with Beijing and the myriad Chinese actors engaged with the continent. Only a handful of African states, those with serious governments and with developmental visions, seem to grasp the need to engage and negotiate mutually beneficial relationships. Elsewhere it seems that some regimes take what they can get *today*, with no thought of the future and no credible China policy in place. In turn, China's official African policy and the institutions involved are to a degree compromised by the nature of the Chinese state and the increasingly liberalized economy in the way they can—or cannot direct—the multitude of Chinese actors engaging with the continent. In short, China's relations with the continent are ever more complicated, increasingly like other external actors involved in Africa. The institutional framework of Sino-African relations reflects this.

References

Abb, P. (2015) 'China's Foreign Policy Think-Tanks: Institutional Evolution and Changing Roles', *Journal of Contemporary China*, 24(93): 531–53.

Alden, C. and C. Hughes (2009) 'Harmony and Discord in China's Africa Strategy: Some Implications for Foreign Policy', *China Quarterly*, 199: 563–84.

Alves, C. (2008) 'Chinese Economic Diplomacy in Africa: The Lusophone Strategy', in C. Alden, R. Soares de Oliveira, and D. Large (eds) *China Returns to Africa: A Rising Power and a Continent Embrace*. Cambridge: Cambridge University Press, pp. 69–82.

Bell, S. and Feng Hui (2007) 'Made in China: IT Infrastructure Policy and the Politics of Trade Opening in Post-WTO China', *Review of International Political Economy*, 14(1): 49–76.

Bell, S. and Feng Hui (2013) *The Rise of the People's Bank of China: The Politics of Institutional Change*. Cambridge, MA: Harvard University Press.

Brautigam, D. (2009) *The Dragon's Gift: The Real Story of China in Africa*. Oxford: Oxford University Press.

Breslin, S. (1996) *China in the 1980s: Centre-Province Relations in a Reforming Socialist State*. Basingstoke: Macmillan.

Breslin, S. (2007) *China and the Global Political Economy*. Basingstoke: Palgrave.

CASS (2018) 'Africa Research Office', http://iwaas.cssn.cn/jgsz_70110/fzyjs/.

Chen Zhimin and Jian Junbo (2009) 'Chinese Provinces as Foreign Policy Actors in Africa', Occasional Paper no. 22, South African Institute of International Affairs, Braamfontein.

Chen Zhimin, Jian Junbo, and Chen Diyuc (2010) 'The Provinces and China's Multi-Layered Diplomacy: The Cases of GMS and Africa', *The Hague Journal of Diplomacy*, 5: 331–56.

Cheng Li (2017) *The Power of Ideas and Ideas of Power: Chinese Think-Tanks in Search of Prominence*. Singapore: World Scientific Publishing Company.

China–Africa Research Initiative (2018) 'Chinese Foreign Aid', http://www.sais-cari.org/data-chinese-loans-and-aid-to-africa.

China Global Energy Finance database (2018) 'Locations', https://www.bu.edu/cgef/#/all/Country.

China Radio International (2012) 'IDCPC: China-Africa Party-to-Party Relations Entering a New Developmental Stage', 20 November.

Chintu, N. and P. Williamson (2013) 'Chinese State-Owned Enterprises in Africa: Myths and Realities', *Ivey Business Journal*, March/April, https://iveybusinessjournal.com/publication/chinese-state-owned-enterprises-in-africa-myths-and-realities/.

Chossudovsky, M. (1986) *Towards Capitalist Restoration: Chinese Socialism after Mao*. New York: St Martin's Press.

Christensen, T. (2001) 'China,' in R. Ellings and A. Friedberg (eds), *Strategic Asia 2001–02: Power and Purpose*. Seattle: National Bureau of Asian Research, pp. 27–69.

CICIR (2018) 'Institute of African Studies', http://www.cicir.ac.cn/NEW/html/organization.html?id=b755a395-055f-e711-957e-60eb69e86223&type=region&subtype=Africa.

Corkin, L. (2011) 'Redefining Foreign Policy Impulses toward Africa: The Roles of the MFA, the MOFCOM and China Exim Bank', *Journal of Current Chinese Affairs*, 40(4): 61–90.

Cornish, L. (2018) 'China's New Aid Agency: What We Know', https://www.devex.com/news/china-s-new-aid-agency-what-we-know-92553.

CPC Encyclopaedia (2018) 'International Department of the Communist Party of China Central Committee', http://cpcchina.chinadaily.com.cn/2011-10/27/content_13985845.htm.

Downs, E. (2011) *Inside China, Inc.: China Development Bank's Cross-Border Energy Deals* John L. Thornton China Centre Monograph Series, No. 3. Washington, DC: Brookings Institution.

Fijałkowski, Ł. (2011) 'China's "Soft Power" in Africa?', *Journal of Contemporary African Studies*, 29(2): 223–32.

Gill, B. and J. Reilly (2007) 'The Tenuous Hold of China Inc. in Africa', *Washington Quarterly*, 30(3): 37–52.

Gitter, D. and L. Fang (2016) 'The Chinese Communist Party International Department: Overlooked Yet Ever Present', *The Diplomat*, 8 August.

Glaser, B. and P. Saunders (2002) 'Chinese Civilian Foreign Policy Research Institutes: Evolving Roles and Increasing Influence,' *China Quarterly*, (171): 601–20.

Goodman, D. (1997) *China's Provinces in Reform: Class, Community and Political Culture*. London: Routledge.

Goodman, D. and G. Segal (eds) (1994) *China Deconstructs: Politics, Trade and Regionalism*. London: Routledge.

Hart-Landsberg, M. and P. Burkett (2004) 'China's Economic Transformation', *Monthly Review*, 56(3): 26–54.

He, Wenping (2007) 'China's Perspective on Contemporary China–Africa Relations', in Wenping He, C. Alden, R. Soares de Oliveira, and D. Large (eds) *China Returns to Africa: A Rising Power and a Continent Embrace*. Cambridge: Cambridge University Press, pp. 143–66.

Hinton, W. (1991) *The Privatisation of China: The Great Reversal*. London: Earthscan.

Hinton, W. (2006) *Through a Glass Darkly: US Views of the Chinese Revolution*. New York: Monthly Review Press.

Hong, E. and L. Sun (2006) 'Dynamics of Internationalization and Outward Investment: Chinese Corporations' Strategies', *China Quarterly*, (187): 610–34.

Hsueh, R. (2014) *China's Regulatory State: A New Strategy for Globalization*. Ithaca, NY: Cornell University Press.

Huang Yasheng (2011) 'Rethinking the Beijing Consensus', *Asia Policy*, 11: 1–26.

Information Office of the State Council (2010) 'China–Africa Economic and Trade Cooperation', http://www.gov.cn/english/official/2010-12/23/content_1771603.htm.

Information Office of the State Council (2011) 'China's Foreign Aid', http://english.gov.cn/archive/white_paper/2014/09/09/content_281474986284620.htm.

Information Office of the State Council (2013) 'China–Africa Economic and Trade Cooperation', http://en.people.cn/90883/8382239.html.

Information Office of the State Council (2014) 'China's Foreign Aid', http://english.gov.cn/archive/white_paper/2014/08/23/content_281474982986592.htm.

Information Office of the State Council (2015) 'China's Second Africa Policy Paper', http://www.china.org.cn/world/2015-12/05/content_37241677.htm.

Isaksson, A. and A. Kotsadam (2018) 'Chinese Aid and Local Corruption', *Journal of Public Economics*, 159: 146–59.

Jakobsen, L. and D. Knox (2010) 'New Foreign Policy Actors in China', Policy Paper, SIPRI, 26 September.

Jakobsen, L. and R. Manuel (2016) 'How Are Foreign Policy Decisions Made in China?', *Asia and the Pacific Policy Studies*, 3(1): 101–10.

Jing Sun (2017) 'Growing Diplomacy, Retreating Diplomats: How the Chinese Foreign Ministry Has Been Marginalized in Foreign Policymaking', *Journal of Contemporary China*, 26(105): 419–33.

Karp, P. (2009) 'China's Development Experience: Key Lessons for Other Developing Countries' in Beijing Forum Organizing Committee (eds) *The Global Financial Crisis: International Impacts and Responses*. Beijing: Beijing Forum.

Lai Hongyi (2010) *The Domestic Sources of China's Foreign Policy: Regimes, Leadership, Priorities and Process*. New York: Routledge.

Liao Xuanli (2006) *Chinese Foreign Policy Think-Tanks and China's Policy toward Japan*. Hong Kong: Chinese University Press.

Manuel, R. (2018) 'Foreign Policy Is China's New Guiding Light', *China Policy Institute: Analysis*, https://cpianalysis.org/

Menegazzi, S. (2014) 'Building Think-Tanks with Chinese Characteristics: Current Debates and Changing Trends', *China Brief*, 14(24), https://jamestown.org/program/building-think-tanks-with-chinese-characteristics-current-debates-and-changing-trends/.

MFA (2018) 'Main Responsibilities of the Ministry of Foreign Affairs of the People's Republic of China', http://www.fmprc.gov.cn/mfa_eng/wjb_663304/zyzz_663306/.

Oi, J. and A. Walder (eds) (1999) *Property Rights and Economic Reform in China*. Stanford, CA: Stanford University Press.

Paltiel, J. (2010) *Structure and Process in Chinese Foreign Policy: Implications for Canada*. Toronto: Canadian International Council.

Qiu Zhibo (2017) 'China's Outdated Foreign Service Needs Rebooting for the Age of Trump', *Foreign Policy*, 27 January, http://foreignpolicy.com/2017/01/23/reboot-chinas-foreign-service-for-the-age-of-trump/.

Shambaugh, D. (2002) 'China's International Relations Think-Tanks: Evolving Structure and Process', *China Quarterly*, 171: 575–86.

Shambaugh, D. (2007) 'China's "Quiet Diplomacy": The International Department of the Chinese Communist Party', *China: An International Journal*, 5(1): 26–54.

Sharma, R. (2007) *Paradoxes of Chinese Socialism*. New Delhi: Manaak Publications.

SIIS (2018) 'Center for West Asian and African Studies', http://en.siis.org.cn/En/Center/4.

Sun Yan (2004) *Corruption and Market in Contemporary China*. Ithaca, NY: Cornell University Press.

Tanner, M. (2002) 'Changing Windows on a Changing China: The Evolving "Think-Tank" System and the Case of the Public Security Sector', *China Quarterly*, 171: 559–74.

Taylor, I. (2011) *The Forum on China–Africa Cooperation (FOCAC)*. London: Routledge.

Varrall, M. (2016) 'Domestic Actors and Agendas in Chinese Aid Policy', *Pacific Review*, 29(1): 21–44.

Wang Shaoguang (2003) 'The Problem of State Weakness', *Journal of Democracy*, 14(1): 36–42.

Weil, R. (1996) *Red Cat, White Cat: China and the Contradictions of 'Market Socialism'*. New York: Monthly Review Press.

Wu Fulong (2010) 'How Neoliberal Is China's Reform? The Origins of Change During Transition', *Eurasian Geography and Economics*, 51(5): 619–31.

Xu Yi-Chong (2014) 'Chinese State-Owned Enterprises in Africa: Ambassadors or Freebooters?', *Journal of Contemporary China*, 23(89): 822–40.

Yang Yao, 'The End of the Beijing Consensus', *Foreign Affairs Snapshot*, 2 February 2010, http://www.foreignaffairs.com/articles/65947/the-end-of-the-beijing-consensus?page=2.

Yun Sun (2014) 'Chinese National Security Decision-Making: Processes and Challenges', Brookings Institution, Washington, DC.

Zeng, M. and P. Williamson (2007) *Dragons at Your Door: How Chinese Cost Innovation Is Disrupting the Rules of Global Competition.* Boston, MA: Harvard Business School Press.

Zhang Denghua and Graeme Smith (2017) 'China's Foreign Aid System: Structure, Agencies, and Identities', *Third World Quarterly*, 38(10): 2330–46.

Zhangxi Cheng and Ian Taylor (2017) *China's Aid to Africa: Does Friendship Really Matter?* London: Routledge.

Zhao Quansheng (1992) 'Domestic Factors of Chinese Foreign Policy: From Vertical to Horizontal Authoritarianism', *Annals of the American Academy of Political and Social Science*, 519: 158–75.

Part III
The Dynamics of China–Africa Economic Ties

7

Chinese Loans and African Structural Transformation

Deborah Brautigam

7.1 Introduction

Guinea was China's first African borrower. In 1960, Beijing offered Guinea a line of credit worth about US$25 million. The government of Sekou Toure used this finance to construct a cigarette and match factory employing 1,800 workers, a tea plantation and factory, a conference centre, and a small hydro-electric station in the Kavendou mountain area. This engagement went largely unnoticed by others. In 2017, fifty-seven years later, numerous media reported that Guinea's minister of mining had announced that his government was negotiating with Chinese companies for a resource-secured line of credit worth US$20 billion that would be used for infrastructure in Guinea. Although this latter report turned out to be wishful thinking rather than factual, the comparison tells us quite a bit about how China's loan programme has changed over time. It also shows how Chinese loans have supported Africa's infrastructure and structural transformation for a very long time.

This chapter explores the relationship between Chinese loans and structural transformation in Africa. It draws on earlier research by the author (Brautigam, 1998, 2009) and on an original database of Chinese lending between 2000 and 2017 collected and curated by the China–Africa Research Initiative at Johns Hopkins University's School of Advanced International Studies (Brautigam and Hwang, 2016).

Viewing Chinese loans historically and across Africa, the chapter begins by outlining the changing actors involved in lending and the rise of different kinds of loan instrument. It then discusses recent trends in loan finance, the regional distribution of loans, and the sectors financed by Chinese loans.

Drawing on this information, it examines the degree to which African borrowers use these loans directly or indirectly to support structural transformation projects in industrialization and agro-finance, and related infrastructure.

Although China's loan programme in Africa was 58 years old at the time this chapter was being written, it has only recently begun to receive considerable media attention. Not surprisingly, Chinese lending is not well understood by the media and casual observers. In recent years, one might read that China provides loans to Africa primarily to facilitate Chinese access to the continent's abundant resources, or that China provides loans to Africa primarily to meet Chinese strategic intentions. Multiple reports surfaced in 2017 and 2018 voicing fears about the terms of Chinese loans and the securities required by Chinese banks. This chapter will also shed light on those issues.

The chapter will pay special attention to the modalities of structuring loan finance and providing guarantees of repayment in risky environments, with many countries having only recently emerged from a long debt crisis. It will consider concern over rising debt levels in a number of African countries. Finally, it will provide case studies of several particularly interesting loan-financed arrangements in countries that are still to be determined, but potentially including Angola, Ethiopia, Zimbabwe, Chad, Ghana, South Africa, and the DRC.

7.2 A Historical Framework for Chinese Loans

The line of credit offered by Beijing to Guinea in 1960 was interest free, and denominated in Chinese renminbi. Other lines of credit followed. By 1970, Guinea had borrowed about US$70 million from China (Bartke, 1989). At that time, China's Ministry of Commerce and its various predecessors were the only Chinese entities providing loans overseas. All lines of credit were zero interest and carried a term of either fifteen or twenty years, with a five- or ten-year grace period before principal payments began.

Cash from these loans was never actually delivered to Guinea, but Guinea could use these lines of credit to pay—in China—for Guinea's imports of Chinese goods, technical expertise, and other Chinese services, including engineering and construction projects. These credits could also pay for local project expenses such as the local labour teams that worked on the projects.

Monthly accounts were kept and reconciled by the People's Bank of China on the Chinese side and by Guinea's Ministry of Finance, specifying disbursements of the credit to other Guinean ministries: Public Works, Agriculture, Energy and Power, Social Welfare, and so on. When Guinea decided which projects they wanted to fund with these credits, the Chinese would arrange for a Chinese team of skilled personnel to arrive and conduct feasibility studies (the costs of this were shared by the two sides). If the project appeared feasible—and in Chinese eyes of the Mao era and even later, this was generally limited to technically, not economically, feasible—the Chinese and their counterparts in the particular Guinean ministry would proceed to build a bridge, develop an agricultural project, and so on.

In the first decades after independence, foreign exchange shortages were common in Africa and the Chinese yuan was not a convertible currency, that is, it could not be directly used overseas. Therefore, these zero-interest loan agreements always specified that repayment could be made in the form of convertible currencies (i.e. dollars, pounds, francs, etc.) or through the export of goods from the African country to China.

Likewise, in order for projects not to be delayed because African governments were often unable themselves to finance the local expenses such as payments to local workers, local transport, and food and housing for the Chinese experts, the Chinese structured the system so that their loans could also pay for these. This was done through the export of goods from China that were then sold locally, generating local currency. Each side would develop a list of commodities that could be part of this process. From African countries like Guinea, these would typically include all that Guinea was able to export: agricultural commodities, locally manufactured food, and mineral ores. From China, the list was more varied and would include textiles, rice, building materials, and so on.

The repayment period for many of these early loans coincided with the start of a long and contentious period of economic crisis in Africa. During the 1970s, an excess of petrodollars from the first oil price shocks cycled through the global economy and into the accounts of eager borrowers in the developing world. At the same time, the wealthy countries of the north sank into prolonged stagnation combined with inflation. The election of Margaret Thatcher in the United Kingdom and Ronald Reagan in the United States led to a sharp rise in global interest rates. Led by Mexico in August 1982, countries that had been borrowing at a variable rate, based on the low interest rates of the 1970s, defaulted on their loans from Western commercial banks.

This ushered in a long period of what is often called neoliberalism, with an emphasis on markets, privatization, and austerity. With very few exceptions, African countries fell deeply into debt to private markets, wealthy creditor-country governments, and the international financial institutions (IFIs)—the World Bank and the International Monetary Fund. They also owed more modest amounts of money to China's central bank, the People's Bank of China, which repeatedly requested that countries remit the payments due on their loans. However, as one West African government lamented in 1979, 'due to the inavailability [sic] of foreign exchange we have not been able to meet their requests'.

During the 1980s, while countries in Africa struggled with controversial neoliberal structural adjustment programmes negotiated with their creditors in the West, China embarked on its own march towards the market. China continued providing zero-interest loans to African countries during this period, with new economic and technical cooperation agreements penned in forty-five countries between 1980 and 1999 (Brautigam, 2008).

In 1994, in an institutional reform designed to make China's economic statecraft compliant with the World Trade Organization, China established two new credit-issuing institutions that by 2018 had become the dominant face of Chinese loans in Africa: the China Export Import Bank (China Eximbank) and the China Development Bank (CDB). The zero-interest loan programme would continue, and would continue to be administered by the Ministry of Commerce. As Chinese firms began to expand their commercial business in Africa after 1978, they began to draw on their own financing sources to offer supplier's credits to African borrowers. We see the first of these company-financed credits emerging in the late 1990s. Finally, the first Chinese commercial banks began operating in Africa at the turn of the new millennium, around 2000.

Thus, as the twentieth century drew to a close, Chinese lending in Africa was changing, with new instruments of engagement, but the overarching goals of this lending did not change. In 1960, Chinese loans supported China's economic diplomacy, and its then very limited commercial aspirations. In those decades, the primary goal of economic diplomacy was to encourage countries to recognize the People's Republic of China (Beijing) as the 'One China' instead of its political rival the Republic of China (Taiwan). At the same time, these loans also provided opportunities to boost China's limited overseas business—which in the 1960s consisted only of a small quantity of exports. When China began to turn towards the market in late 1978, those goals remained in place, although the diplomacy aspect was far and away the most dominant. And though the order has been reversed, with commerce taking the lion's share, the data suggest that these goals are still in place today.

7.3 China's Overseas Lending Institutions in the Twenty-First Century

Between 1994 and 2017, as we can see in Table 7.1, Chinese lenders proliferated in Africa. This was in keeping with the much larger Chinese economic engagement with all world regions, including the rest of Asia, North America, Europe, and Latin America, where trade, outbound foreign direct investment, and contracting all expanded along with the expansion and maturation of the Chinese economy.

Table 7.1. Chinese lending to African governments

Chinese lender	Year lender provided first loan in Africa	No. of loans provided 2000–16 (how many)	Gross value of loans 2000–16 (in US$ billion)
Chinese government (ZIL)	1960	117	1.34
China Eximbank	1995	559	75.72
Suppliers' credits from Chinese firms	2000	46	8.22
China Development Bank	2007	152	30.47
Chinese commercial banks	2002	33	8.4
Syndicated loans involving Chinese banks	2015	6	3.08

Source: China–Africa Research Institute, Chinese Loans Database

Beginning in 2000, as other contributions to this volume have noted, African countries and China established the Forum on China–Africa Cooperation (FOCAC). With its regular summits and ministerial meetings, FOCAC over time has institutionalized and simplified the Chinese government's economic cooperation and assistance pledges for African development. Since 2006, loan pledges have become a regular part of the FOCAC summits and ministerial meetings, but in each FOCAC the wording has been different, making the pledges hard to compare. In 2006, for example, Beijing pledged to provide US$5 billion (in concessional loans and preferential export credits) and to 'double' official aid by 2009 (this we can take to be interest-free loans and grants). By 2015, the pledge had mounted to US$35 billion (concessional loans, preferential export credits, lines of credit) plus US$5 billion in zero-interest loans and grants. In 2018, the Chinese pledge combined the grants, interest-free loans, and concessional loans (US$15 billion) and added US$20 billion in lines of credit.

Table 7.1 and Figure 7.1 provide overviews of the quantity of Chinese lending in Africa since 2000. More details on these lenders can be found below.

7.3.1 *Ministry of Commerce (MOFCOM)*

As of 2016, the Ministry of Commerce remained actively in charge of China's economic diplomacy, and the zero-interest loan programme continued to provide at least symbolic support to China–Africa relations. These agreements are difficult to track. They are usually signed during diplomatic events (generally during visits by Chinese officials to an African country) and they take the form of an 'economic and technical cooperation agreement' which will usually include a specific amount of funding made up of zero-interest loans and grants. These have become relatively small, compared with the larger

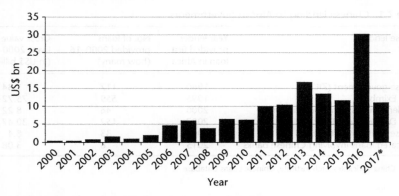

Figure 7.1. Chinese loans to Africa, 2000 to 2017 (US$bn)

Note: * 2017 figures are provisional. Only includes Chinese loans to African governments and their state-owned enterprises.

Source: China Africa Research Initiative

loans available from newer lenders, and they generally fund government buildings, including stadiums. We do not track grant funding, but our database shows at least 117 separate zero-interest loan and economic and technical cooperation agreements signed by Chinese and African governments between 2000 and 2016.

7.3.2 *China Export Import Bank (Eximbank)*

As noted above, in 1994, China Eximbank became China's official export credit agency. As with other export credit agencies, its primary mission is to bolster opportunities for national companies seeking business opportunities overseas. To do this, China Eximbank provides three basic kinds of loans. Export seller's credits are loans to Chinese companies or 'export sellers' who need funds to boost their business abroad. Export buyer's credits are loans to buyers of exported Chinese goods and services. These two are provided at negotiated commercial rates based on the market. However, China Eximbank also operates a third category that it calls 'preferential loans'—preferential export buyer's credits (*youhui maifan xindai*) and concessional foreign aid loans (*youhui daikuan*). Both loan instruments have interest rates that are subsidized by annual appropriations from the Chinese budget. They are only provided to other developing-country governments or their state-owned firms. Only the concessional loans are considered Chinese official development assistance (ODA). Finally, the Eximbank also provides guarantees for Chinese companies who are not borrowing from this bank but need to reduce their risks.

Because the Chinese foreign aid budget—which supports the interest-rate subsidies for the concessional loans—is relatively small, the number of concessional loans that China Eximbank can fund each year is limited. Interest-rate subsidies for the preferential export buyer's credits, which are supported from a separate budget for economic cooperation, are also limited. China Eximbank raises capital for its other loan instruments through bond issues and various other means, but they are not supported directly by appropriations from the state budget.

China Eximbank issued its first eight overseas concessional foreign aid loans in 1995, including at least one US$5.75 million loan in Africa, for Equatorial Guinea. Over the next two decades, China Eximbank opened branch offices in Morocco (to serve West and North Africa) and in South Africa (for Southern and East Africa). By 2017, according to our data, China Eximbank had signed off on at least 559 loans with a total value of US$75.7 billion in forty-four African countries (this includes separate projects emerging from a single line of credit). From the evidence we have seen, China Eximbank appears to be in charge of fulfilling the FOCAC commitments relating to concessional and preferential loans and other lines of credit. Between 2012 and 2016, this bank averaged US$9 billion annually in loan commitments.

7.3.3 *China Development Bank*

Like China Eximbank, China Development Bank is a state-owned policy arm of the Chinese government, much like the Overseas Private Investment Corporation (OPIC) in the United States, or the Commonwealth Development Corporation (CDC) in the United Kingdom. China Development Bank's main mission is, as its name suggests, the development of China. Most of CDB's loans have been provided to various borrowers within Chinese territory, to build infrastructure or otherwise boost economic transformation in China itself.

In 2005, CDB began providing support for Chinese overseas investment projects (Downs, 2011). In 2009, CDB established a branch in Cairo, and this remains its only African office. CDB is in charge of one of the FOCAC loan pledges: support for African small and medium enterprises. By the end of 2017 (provisional figures) CDB had committed around US$30.5 billion in loan finance to governments and their SOEs in Africa, according to our figures.

7.3.4 *Chinese Commercial Supplier's Credits*

Chinese companies also offer supplier's credits to African borrowers, often through export seller's loans that the Chinese company has obtained from China Eximbank (or another Chinese bank). This means that the African borrower needs to repay the Chinese firm, which in turn will repay the Chinese bank—a practice that reduces risks and lowers costs for the Chinese banks. Chinese companies have been offering these supplier's credits for nearly two decades. In 2000, for example, we can see the China International Water and Electric Corporation (CWE) using its access to export seller's finance to secure a contract for a rural electrification project in Ghana, while a commercial supplier's credit from Chinese Harbin Power and Electricity Company helped finance a gas-fired power plant in Sudan. In order to safeguard against non-payment or default by African governments or their state-owned firms, Chinese suppliers using official export seller's credits were required to purchase export credit insurance from China Eximbank, and later, Sinosure (see Section 7.3.6). Our data show that by 2017, at least twenty-three different Chinese companies had provided project finance to African governments using supplier's credits, for a total of at least US$8.22 billion.

7.3.5 Chinese Commercial Banks

The first Chinese commercial bank to arrive in Africa, Bank of China (not to be confused with China's central bank, the People's Bank of China), set up an office in Zambia in 1997. However, loans from Bank of China were primarily targeted to Chinese construction companies who needed financial guarantees to support their contracting bids, and other instruments like short-term letters of credit issued to support China–Africa trade finance. Bank of China rarely appears in our database as a sole lender to African governments, although they have joined other Africa-based banks in some syndicated loans. In 2008, Industrial and Commercial Bank of China, the world's largest commercial bank, purchased around 20 per cent of South Africa's Standard Bank. Since then, ICBC has expanded its Africa portfolio and by 2018, ICBC had been involved in thirty large projects in Africa (Eom, Brautigam, and Benabdallah, 2018). Much of this involved ICBC as lead arranger for, or participant in, syndicated loans.

Beginning as early as 2002, we start to see Chinese commercial banks—sometimes joined by the policy banks—participating in syndicated loans and other novel (for China) kinds of credit instruments in Africa. In the earliest example in our data, we see China Construction Bank and Bank of China participating as arrangers in several three- and five-year-term syndicated loans to boost the foreign exchange position of South Africa's Reserve Bank. The largest syndicated loan in our database is US$4.1 billion in support of the massive 2170MW Caculo Cabaca hydropower project in Angola. Here, ICBC brought together a number of China-based banks, Bank of China's Beijing Branch, China Construction Bank's Beijing Branch, China Minsheng Bank, Ping An Bank, and China Shanghai Pilot Free Trade Zone Branch.

The involvement of Chinese banks and foreign banks continues to expand. For example, a consortium of banks, including ICBC, Deutsche Bank, and

Goldman Sachs, led Angola's Eurobond issue in 2015. Finally, as the newest lending instruments, we see that in 2017, the Johannesburg branch of the Bank of China issued the first renminbi-denominated bond offered in Africa, with a yield of 4.88 per cent (Dai, 2017).

7.3.6 Sinosure

While Sinosure does not directly offer loan finance to Africa, it is an important actor in the lending and risk mitigation system. Sinosure was established in late 2001, and took over much of the credit insurance business from China Eximbank. As its website states, Sinosure provides a number of export credit insurance products, including short-, medium-, and long-term export credit insurance, overseas investment insurance for Chinese companies operating in riskier environments, and bonds and guarantees that might be required by an African government or multilateral financial institution to allow Chinese firms to participate in engineering, procurement, and construction (EPC) projects.

Sinosure also provides accounts receivable management assistance to help Chinese companies manage the process of collecting money owed to them, and information consultation and risk analysis services including its proprietary SinoRating. Sinosure releases an annual *Handbook of Country Risk,* and country and sovereign credit risk analysis reports that evaluate political risk, economic risk, business risk, and legal risks for firms.

In Africa, we begin to see Sinosure in the picture as a guarantor as early as 2002, when Chinese companies began to offer their own financing. Sinosure also began to accompany representatives of China Eximbank and China Development Bank as countries discussed borrowing arrangements and restructuring or arrears on some of their current Chinese loans. In 2004, when Zimbabwe had fallen behind on a US$35 million loan borrowed from China Eximbank in 1997 to refurbish blast furnace 4 of the Zimbabwe Iron and Steel Corporation, Sinosure had to make a payment to China Eximbank. In 2008, three countries dominated Sinosure's payouts for medium- and long-term export credit insurance claims by Chinese financiers: Cuba (84.3 per cent), Benin (9.8 per cent), and Zimbabwe (5.9 per cent) (Sinosure, 2008). African claims are normally only about 5 per cent of Sinosure's claims. In 2011, however, after the crisis in Libya, African claims jumped to 32 per cent, of which 29 per cent was for claims related to Libya.

7.4 Chinese Loans and Structural Transformation

When Ngozi Okonjo-Iweala, a vice president of the World Bank and former finance minister for Nigeria, asked the Chinese how Nigeria could achieve

10 per cent growth like China's, they answered: 'Infrastructure—infrastructure and discipline' (Downs, 2011). By all accounts, improved infrastructure is not simply a by-product of social and economic development; it is also an essential precondition. Improved roads and transport options not only enable low-income families to reduce costs when moving their products to market, they also save lives when people living in remote areas are able to reach medical care during emergencies such as difficult births and on-farm accidents. Debates exist over just how to establish the benefits of a particular infrastructure investment and over what kind of time period. To some, the construction of a large public building like a new airport can be seen as an expensive white elephant requiring care and maintenance; to others, the same building can be a symbol of national pride and a step into the future.

It is clear from our data that African governments have borrowed from China largely to fund infrastructure, but also to fund productive projects that aim to add value to Africa's natural resources, including its agriculture. These dual emphases have a long history. In the 1960s, the government of Sekou Toure used its first zero-interest loan from China to construct a cigarette and match factory to substitute for imports, and also a 3.2kW hydroelectric station at Kinkon with high-voltage lines that would electrify Guinea's Kavendou mountain area. Several subsequent rounds of loans from China funded a tea plantation and factory, a vegetable oil-pressing mill, and a second hydropower station at Tinkisso (Bartke, 1989; Brautigam, 2015). Let us turn first to infrastructure.

7.4.1 *Chinese Loans and African Infrastructure*

It was also in Guinea that the Chinese began their first discussions about financing a railway in Africa. It is generally known that one of the flagship projects financed by Chinese loans during the Mao period was the Tazara Railway, built between 1970 and 1975, which allowed Zambia to export its copper to Europe through Tanzania without using the railway built by the British and controlled by then white-ruled South Africa. However, few remember that during the 1960s, China, Guinea, and Mali began to plan a 360km railway that would give Mali a more direct outlet to the ocean by extending the French colonial railway from Mali's capital Bamako to the Guinean town of Kankan, where it would join Guinea's railway system.

The three countries concluded an agreement to build the railway in 1968, and Chinese surveyors arrived to begin work in August that year. When the French government had earlier studied the same project while ruling Guinea as its colony, it had rejected the project as uneconomical. But Senegal, which at the time did not have official diplomatic relations with Beijing, refused to grant the project the right to use the Dakar–Bamako railway line. As one analyst concluded: 'The railway line is of no economic importance whatever, as there is no goods exchange between Guinea and Mali nor will there be any in the near future. Obviously the plans for this line were made for political considerations on the part of both Sekou Toure and Modiba Keita. After Keita's fall, the project was, accordingly, never heard from again' (Bartke, 1989).

Throughout the ensuing decades, Chinese loans continued to fund African infrastructure. For example, in addition to the hydropower plants in Guinea and the well-known Tazara Railway project completed in 1976, China funded hydropower plants in the Congo (1980) and Sierra Leone (1986). Water supply projects were financed in metropolitan areas of Mauritania (1987) and the Republic of the Congo (1990). Ethiopia borrowed to build a road between Werota and Woldia (1983), while Zambia built the 2.5-kilometre-long Luapula Bridge with a Chinese loan (1983). In Mauritius, a Chinese loan funded the construction of a terminal at Plaisance Airport (1983), while the Central African Republic built a public broadcasting station with a Chinese loan. While there were not many projects in these sectors during this period, Chinese companies were gaining experience and adding to their portfolios, something that stood them in good stead when China joined the World Trade Organization (in 2001) and began accelerating its push for state-owned companies to 'go global'.

During the 1980s and 1990s, Chinese companies in Africa were finding that construction was an attractive business. As early as 1979, they began to bid on projects financed by others: bilateral and multilateral donors, African governments, and the private sector. In Mali, for example, a Chinese company won the contract to build the King Fahd Bridge in Mali's capital Bamako between 1990 and 1992; this was financed by Saudi Arabia.

In 2000, Chinese EPC companies reported gross revenues of US$1.1 billion from their African projects, and Africa made up just 13 per cent of their global revenues. By 2016, their annual revenues had climbed to US$50 billion, and Africa was providing over a third of global EPC revenues. Loans from China's export credit agency China Eximbank were intended to stimulate African business for Chinese exporters of goods and services. Yet our data show that only about 20 per cent of these projects were financed by Chinese loans. Chinese companies were getting increasingly good at marketing themselves and competing with others to win tenders.

Between 2000 and 2016, African governments and their state-owned enterprises borrowed approximately US$130 billion from Chinese lenders, including all of the institutions profiled above. The majority of Chinese loans to Africa go towards transportation. During this period, at least US$40.6 billion (31 per cent of loans) financed the building or upgrading of roads, railways, ports, airports, and harbours. Although railway projects have attracted considerable attention in the media, as far as we can tell, China has actually only financed four greenfield railway projects: a new standard-gauge railway (SGR) in Sudan, several new sections of the Lagos–Kano railway in Nigeria, several sections of a new SGR in Kenya, and a new line from Ethiopia through Djibouti giving land-locked Ethiopia access to the sea. Since 2000, the Chinese have also provided loan finance for the renovation of several previously existing railways, including Tazara (Tanzania–Zambia) and Benguela in Angola.

The changing nature of Chinese loan funding in Africa's railway sector is well illustrated by the contrast between the 1970s-era Tazara project and South Africa's Transnet. Given its diplomatic importance, all Chinese loans for Tazara were, and continue to be, zero-interest foreign aid loans. However, South Africa's state-owned railway corporation has financed purchases of rolling stock from China, first by borrowing from China Development Bank and then through several syndicated commercial loans involving Chinese participants (Bank of China and China Construction Bank) as well as South African financiers (ABSA, Nedbank, Future-growth Asset Managers, and Old Mutual Specialised Finance).

African governments have also borrowed heavily from China to build new roads and repair existing roads. Our database shows Chinese loans for the road sector totalling US$18 billion between 2000 and 2016. Angola has borrowed more than other African countries for roads and bridges, which is not surprising given that Angola's civil war (1975–2002) destroyed much of the country's transport infrastructure. The other top borrowers for roads and bridges include the Republic of Congo, Zambia, Mozambique, and Ethiopia. In these countries, Chinese loans have funded the construction of major roads. For example, in the Republic of Congo, loans from China helped rebuild National Road No. 2, the country's major north-south, colonial-era transport corridor. Ethiopia used loans from China to build a ring road around the capital, Addis Ababa, and to construct a toll road extending out from the capital, among other road projects. Finally, Chinese loans have financed air transport infrastructure—mainly adding more modern terminals at Africa's existing airports. We see very few examples of greenfield airport finance.

The second infrastructure sector where African governments borrow most heavily from China for their development goals is electric power. Our database contains over 160 loans for electric power production and distribution totalling nearly US$33 billion between 2000 and 2016. Most of these projects are for renewable energy. Within the power sector, African governments have borrowed US$24 billion from China for hydropower projects and associated distribution lines and just US$2.5 billion for coal- and oil-fired power plants.

Other important sectors for infrastructure loans from China include telecommunications and water. African governments have borrowed over US$7 billion for telecoms projects, particularly for the installation of broadband fibre-optic lines that are connecting more remote areas to the internet. Urban and rural water projects make up about US$4.5 billion.

7.4.2 Chinese Loans for Manufacturing, Agro-Industry, and Other Value-Added Production

As with infrastructure, China has a long history of providing African governments with loans for manufacturing, agro-industry, and other value-added productive sectors. In the first decades of the zero-interest loan programme, African governments were far more statist in orientation, and many established state-owned farms and state-owned factories. China provided financial assistance for some of these. During the era of structural adjustment, many African countries privatized their state-owned companies. Some established joint ventures with Chinese participation. For example, the Friendship Textile Factory in Tanzania, built between 1966 and 1968, was partially privatized and is currently a joint venture between the Tanzanian government and a company owned by a provincial government in China. In Mali, a large sugar project continues to operate as a joint venture between the Mali government and a Chinese company.

However, given the strong trend towards moving governments out of the running of productive enterprises, between 1995 and the present, we do not see many African governments borrowing for the setting up of new agro-industries or manufacturing. There are some exceptions to this. The most notable are probably the establishment of petroleum refineries in Sudan, Chad, and in Niger. The Chinese government provided loan finance for all three projects. As oil producers, these three countries decided to eschew the trend across Africa of sending their raw crude out to be refined in Europe, and importing petroleum products. Questions have been raised about the cost-effectiveness of establishing these local refineries.

Chad, Eritrea, Ethiopia, and the Republic of Congo have borrowed from China to set up modern cement factories. Several countries, including Ethiopia and Sudan, have used Chinese loans to build sugar refineries. As noted above, in 1997, Zimbabwe borrowed US$35 million from China Eximbank to refurbish its state-owned steel company. Several countries have borrowed to finance agro-industrial grain-milling projects, including Zambia and Mozambique. The country that has borrowed the most from China for production-oriented projects is Angola. In particular, Angola has countered the trend of privatization by borrowing money and Chinese expertise to set up state-owned farms that the government hopes will help end Angola's high dependency on imported grains (Brautigam, 2015).

7.4.3 *Special Economic Zones and Industrial Zones*

The first African country to request Chinese assistance in setting up a special economic zone or industrial zone was Egypt in 1997 (Brautigam and Tang, 2011). Others followed, and today there are zones with Chinese involvement as investors in a number of African countries. However, we do not see much in the way of African government borrowing for the construction of these industrial zones. Most have been co-financed by Chinese investors (some of whom have themselves borrowed from Chinese banks) and African governments. An exception is an industrial park focused on machinery that is being co-developed in Adama, Ethiopia by the Ethiopian Industrial Parks Development Corporation (IPDC) and Changsha Economic and Technical Development Group Corporation, a state-owned company located in Hunan, China. The Ethiopian government borrowed US$262.3 million for its share of this park.

7.4.4 *Risky Business*

Around 1980, nearly two decades after independence, many African countries began falling into a prolonged period of debt crisis. In 1996, after many years of contentious structural adjustment programmes and the continued inability of countries to repay their loans, the international financial institutions (IFIs) launched what was called the Highly Indebted Poor Countries (HIPC) Initiative. The HIPC Initiative allowed low-income African countries that were able to meet its conditions a pathway to have all their IMF and World Bank debts cancelled. Some countries, including Zimbabwe, were deemed not eligible for HIPC. Others, including Somalia, Sudan, and Eritrea, were unable to start the HIPC process. These four remained in a debt distress that dated back to the 1980s.

As we can see, during the period when the IFIs were developing the HIPC process, the Chinese were just beginning to expand their lending to Africa, moving for the first time away from zero-interest loans to interest-bearing instruments. Their response to the first African debt crisis was two-fold. First, they developed their own debt relief programme for the zero-interest debt that countries were unable to repay. And second, they developed a number of ways in which they thought the risks of lending in African countries might be reduced.

7.4.4.1 DEBT RELIEF
At the start of the debt crisis, the Chinese first responded by providing debt relief: rescheduling payment terms for debts. For example, repayment for Zambia and Tanzania's Tazara Railway was postponed for ten years. Ghana

and Niger were granted another five years for repayment. China's debt cancellation programme was first announced in 2000 at the first summit of the FOCAC in Beijing. China pledged to reduce or cancel RMB10 billion of debt (about US$1.2 billion at the time) owed by highly indebted poor countries and least-developed countries in Africa. Given that Eximbank's concessional loans normally had a five-year grace period, this would have been before any countries had begun to make payments on their concessional loans, and so all of this debt was due to zero-interest loans.

At the United Nations in New York in 2005, the Chinese pledge became both more specific and cross-regional. China would cancel 'or forgive in other ways all the overdue parts as of the end of 2004 of the interest-free and low-interest governmental loans owed by all the HIPCs having diplomatic relations with China'. Unlike the IMF and the World Bank, China cancelled debts without requiring any programme of reforms, after a brief review of the country's economy and actual need, and after a reconciliation of Chinese figures with those held by the local ministry of finance. Somalia's, Eritrea's, and Sudan's zero-interest loan debts were among those cancelled (Brautigam, 2009). In almost all of the FOCAC triennial summits, new pledges were made about cancelling overdue zero-interest debt. By the end of 2012, the Chinese announced that they had cancelled African overdue zero-interest loan debt worth Chinese ¥20.38 billion in renminbi (approximately US$3.27 billion) at the 2012 exchange rate (State Council of China Information Office, 2014). There have been no announcements of totals of debt cancellation since that date.

7.4.4.2 REDUCING RISKS FOR AFRICAN LENDING

Keenly aware that Africa was a risky lending environment, China Eximbank used several methods to reduce risks on its loans. Some low-income, crisis-prone countries like Liberia were provided only with modest grants for many, many years. But with riskier countries like Zimbabwe, Angola, or Ghana, that had high income potential but had already proven unable to pay back their loans, China Eximbank commonly negotiated further security for some (but not all) loans. These were based on future profit streams or future income and were built into the lending agreements. These future-flow receivable transactions were complex, as they involved multiple actors: China Eximbank, the African country's ministry of finance, usually another ministry or African state-owned company in charge of some kind of production that could be sold to earn foreign exchange, and a buyer, nearly always a Chinese buyer.

For example, in Ghana, a Chinese loan to support construction of the Bui Dam was secured through an arrangement whereby the Ghanaian marketing board for cocoa, Cocobod, arranged to export cocoa beans to a Chinese buyer (Brautigam, Hwang, and Wang, 2015). Bui Dam was financed by Ghana's government and by four Chinese loans. The first two were negotiated successively: first, a commercial-rate export buyer's credit of US$292 million signed in September 2007 with a seventeen-year maturity, five-year grace period, and a rate of CIRR plus a margin of 0.75 per cent; and second, a concessional foreign aid loan of RMB 2.1 billion (about US$306 million at the time) signed in September 2008 with a twenty-year maturity, seven-year grace period, and a fixed interest rate of 2 per cent. Two additional loans were later negotiated in 2012 to pay for cost overruns on the dam: a US$75.4 million loan at an interest rate of 2 per cent for twenty years, with a five-year grace period, and a US$76.2 million loan at a zero interest rate, for fourteen years, with a two-year grace period.

The Chinese funding is secured through 'off-take' arrangements that involve future flows of income: one based on cocoa, and a second based on future electricity revenues expected from the dam. The cocoa security was arranged through a sales agreement between Genertec Corporation of China and the Ghana Cocoa Board (Cocobod) for up to 40,000 metric tons (Mt) of cocoa beans (30,000 main crop, 10,000 light crop) annually for the first five years of the loan. The cocoa beans will be sold at the prevailing market price, and the proceeds placed in an escrow account with China Eximbank.

The off-take arrangement requires Bui Hydropower to have a power purchase agreement with the Electricity Company of Ghana: 85 per cent of energy sales from Bui will be deposited into an escrow account to help repay the loan. The excess funds in the account can be withdrawn by Ghana, or they can stay in the account and earn interest. The price for the future electricity was tentatively negotiated to be in a range between US$0.035 and US$0.055 cents/kWh. According to the World Bank, the average electricity tariff in Africa was effectively much higher than Ghana's at US$0.13 per kWh. It is possible that Ghana will face pressure to raise its electricity tariffs from the China Eximbank, a role the World Bank and IMF have played in the past.

This chapter has gone into some detail on the Bui Dam arrangement because it has been one of the most transparent. However, in our experience, perhaps surprisingly to many, these arrangements are rather uncommon. We find that most of the large lines of credit in Angola (the most well-known examples) take this form. The Chinese have also used this future-flow security for large lines of credit in the DRC, Equatorial Guinea, Sudan, and the Republic of Congo. In several other countries, the model was proposed and sometimes an agreement was even signed (Niger, Nigeria, Gabon) but for various reasons the arrangement did not progress beyond that point and the agreements expired. In Ethiopia a similar arrangement was put in place when the first large line of credit was signed, but in this case, repayments came from an escrow account filled with receipts from all of Ethiopia's then exports to China, which were nearly all sesame seeds (Brautigam and Hwang, 2016).

7.4.4.3 CONCERNS OVER CHINESE LENDING AND AFRICAN DEBT MANAGEMENT CAPACITY

Our CARI loans database tracks Chinese loans through 2017. It shows that Chinese loan commitments to Africa increased significantly after the December 2015 FOCAC summit in Johannesburg. In 2015, China committed US$13 billion; in 2016, China committed over US$30 billion, the highest annual commitment to date. Preliminary figures for 2017 show a more 'normal' year (see Figure 7.1). There are two points to note here. First, our loan figures should not be viewed as fitting neatly into the categories announced at various FOCAC summits. China Eximbank is usually in charge of FOCAC pledges of general loans, export credits, and credit lines, although China Development Bank manages the Special Fund for SME loans. Second, we also track loans made by a number of other Chinese banks, including China Development Bank, as well as Chinese supplier's credits which, as noted above, involve commercial loans at negotiated market rates. Angola has had a large appetite for these loans, particularly in 2016, which explains that year's anomalous figure.

As of 2018, worries about Africa's debt situation had risen to very high levels. As of July 2018, a third of the forty-five countries in Africa had overreached in external and internal borrowing, according to a statement by Abebe Aemro Selassie, director of the IMF's Africa Department. At the same time, he noted, 'most African countries have debt levels that are manageable'.

What is the role of Chinese lending in this debt distress? Our analysis updates the July cases to add an additional two considered to be in debt distress. In August 2018, our team analyzed seventeen countries at risk of, or already in, debt distress, using IMF criteria (Eom, Brautigam, and Benabdallah, 2018). In Group 1, comprising eight countries—Burundi, Cape Verde, Central African Republic, Chad, The Gambia, Mauritania, São Tomé and Príncipe, and South Sudan—Chinese loans were a relatively small share of debt. In most of these cases, the major factor behind the debt distress was conflict-related economic collapse, commodity price collapse, or other economic management factors internal to the country. In Group 2—Cameroon, Ethiopia, Ghana, Mozambique, Sudan, and Zimbabwe—China was a more important creditor but each country in this group had also borrowed significantly from other sources. Chinese loans (which are not the same as debt, since countries have made some payments on these loans) ranged from a quarter to just under half of total debt in each case. Finally, Chinese loans at that point were the major factor in only three countries (Group 3): Zambia, Republic of the Congo, and Djibouti.

While history tells us that in Africa, debt has, along with economic growth, gone through several cycles of high and low, the China factor should neither be exaggerated nor ignored. Given the lower pledges of loans in the 2018

FOCAC, it is clear that Chinese policy banks have a similar analysis. What is not clear is whether the other commercial lenders and exporting companies will exercise the same restraint.

References

Bartke, Wolfgang (1989) *The Economic Aid of the PR China to Developing and Socialist Countries.* 2nd edition. London: K. G. Saur.

Brautigam, Deborah (1998) *Chinese Aid and African Development: Exporting Green Revolution.* London: MacMillan Press.

Brautigam, Deborah (2008) 'China's African Aid: Transatlantic Challenges', German Marshall Fund of the United States, Washington, DC.

Brautigam, Deborah (2009) *The Dragon's Gift: The Real Story of China in Africa.* Oxford: Oxford University Press.

Brautigam, Deborah (2015) *Will Africa Feed China?* New York: Oxford University Press.

Brautigam, Deborah, and Jyhjong Hwang (2016) *China–Africa Loan Database Research Guidebook.* Washington, DC: China Africa Research Initiative, Johns Hopkins University.

Brautigam, Deborah, Jyhjong Hwang, and Nancy Wang (2015) 'Chinese Engagement in Hydropower Infrastructure in Africa', Working Paper 2015/1, School of Advanced International Studies, China Africa Research Initiative, Johns Hopkins University School of Advanced International Studies, Washington, DC.

Brautigam, Deborah, and Xiaoyang Tang (2011) 'African Shenzhen: China's Special Economic Zones in Africa', *Journal of Modern African Studies*, 49(1): 27–54.

Dai, Tian (2017) *China Daily*, 20 April, http://www.chinadaily.com.cn/business/2017-04/20/content_29010547.htm.

Downs, Erica (2011) *Inside China, Inc: China Development Bank's Cross-Border Energy Deals.* Washington, DC: Brookings Institute.

Eom, Janet, Deborah Brautigam, and Lina Benabdallah (2018) 'The Path Ahead: The 7th Forum on China–Africa Cooperation', SAIS-CARI.org, http://www.sais-cari.org/s/Briefing-Paper-1-August-2018-Final.pdf.

Eom, Janet, Jyhjong Hwang, Ying Xia, and Deborah Brautigam (2016) 'Looking back and Moving forward: An Analysis of China–Africa Economic Trends and the Outcomes of the 2015 Forum on China Africa Cooperation', Policy Brief No. 9, School of Advanced International Studies, China Africa Research Initiative, Johns Hopkins University, Washington, DC.

Sinosure (2008) *Annual Report 2008*. Beijing: Sinosure.

State Council of China Information Office (2014) 'China's Foreign Aid (2014)', English Chinese Government Document Archive. http://english.gov.cn/archive/white_paper/2014/08/23/content_281474982986592.htm.

8

China's Development Finance and African Infrastructure Development

Jing Gu and Richard Carey

8.1 New Models, New Rivalries, New Cooperation?

China has written a new story in global development finance over the last two decades, based on domestic institutions built to fund its own development and then adapted to finance its 'Going Out' policy. Its two key policy banks, the China Development Bank (CDB) and the China Exim Bank (China Exim) are now two of the major development finance institutions in the world (Dollar, 2018); their combined outstanding loans to developing countries compare with the same aggregate for all of the established multilateral development banks. Further, China has emerged more recently as architect of a new set of multilateral development financial institutions based around the large geo-economic visions embodied in its Belt and Road Initiative (NDRC, 2015). The supply of Chinese development finance to Africa has reflected this evolution of institutions and policies—and the 2018 triennial Forum for China–Africa Cooperation (FOCAC) now explicitly brings Africa into the global Belt and Road Initiative (BRI) frame, while establishing several new platforms for China–Africa cooperation, including not least a China–Africa Infrastructure Plan, a China–Africa Developmental Financing Forum, and a China–Africa Financial Cooperation Consortium (Ministry of Foreign Affairs PRC, 2018).

In this chapter we argue that Chinese entrepreneurialism in the field of development finance has stirred up the established development finance system, generating constructive new rivalries alongside new cooperative learning processes that will need to be taken further (Dollar, 2018; Xu and Carey, 2015). China's development finance history has been instrumental in its unprecedented development success and its ongoing innovation processes. The China Development Bank has a balance sheet of more than US$2.4 trillion and China Exim US$560bn, with international loanbooks of US$262bn and US$169bn, respectively, at the end of 2017 (these numbers compare with the combined loanbooks of the established MDBs $500bn). China's five main commercial banks are among the largest corporations in the world, a reflection of the scale of the financial effort involved in a development process that has lifted China to its present development level. Even as its burgeoning financial sector is today the subject of a set of critical reforms focused on sustainability, efficiency, and integrity, there are important lessons to be learned from China's development finance history for international development finance now and looking ahead (Xu and Carey, 2016).

In this chapter we look at the factors behind the significant increase in China's 'market share' in African infrastructure development and the issues and opportunities this presents for wider development cooperation in infrastructure sectors across Africa.

We use a global political-economy approach to put this question into its wider global context. The rise of China has impacted dramatically on the growth patterns and distributional features of the global economy. And China has a different position on the states–market spectrum of organizing its economy from Western norms. We address a series of research questions: (i) Why has China been so competitive in this domain over the last two decades? (ii) How do China's concepts, institutions, and policies differ from those of established sources of official development finance? (iii) What are the impacts on development concepts, vocabulary, and practice at the level of the G20 and the multilateral development banks? (iv) What is the impact on infrastructure development cooperation and finance scenery in Africa, where there are many actors and coordination initiatives and where the September 2018 FOCAC Beijing Summit (Ministry of Foreign Affairs PRC, 2018) has produced some major new platforms and initiatives for China–Africa cooperation, reaching out to work with international multilateral development finance institutions?

We then look at how China is playing into the economic transformation scene through its role in two infrastructure sectors, electrification and digitalization of Africa's economy. The chapter concludes by looking at how the FOCAC proposals for the creation of shared platforms for African connectivity infrastructure planning and investment could advance African governance and capacities on these frontiers, drawing on China's new policies and programmes for green infrastructure in its own economy (Okonjo-Iweala, 2018).

8.2 A Global, Political Economy Lens on China's International Development Finance

This study investigates China's role in African infrastructure development using a global political economy (GPE) approach. It is, therefore, interested in the intersection between economics and politics, examining the interplay of policy and practice and adapting to the international arena the 'who gets what, when, and how' definition of the political process in Harold Lasswell's famous phrase (Lasswell, 1936).

The emergence of China has changed fundamentally for Africa the economic and political configuration of the global economy and its macroeconomic transmission mechanisms, including commodity prices. In the field of infrastructure, because of China's emergence, the 'who gets what, when, and how' is radically different from just two decades ago. We explain the supply side of the Chinese infrastructure finance and construction industries in the following sections of this chapter.

There are many possible avenues for a GPE approach. The specific strand chosen for the present analysis utilizes the work of the late Susan Strange and particularly the framework she advanced in her renowned work *States and Markets* (Strange, 1994). Strange's political-economy perspective focuses on the structures, processes, and agencies of power in the world economy and the inherently complex dynamics of change involved. Strange's framework consists of a matrix of four inter-related structures: security, production structures, finance, and knowledge. As the title of her book suggests, this lens is used to examine the effects of any kind of political authority (including states) on markets, and, conversely, of market forces on states, thus drawing attention to the political facets of markets and the impact of market forces on states themselves.

This framework is particularly salient for the analysis of the diachronic relationship between states and markets in the context of China–Africa relations and the wider changing relationships between the structures, processes, institutions, and the public and private enterprises of the 'traditional' donor system and those of China. For instance, the four elements of the matrix developed by Strange—security, production structures, finance, and knowledge—all appear as the subjects of significant programmes in the September 2018 FOCAC Beijing Action plan.

We argue that China's particular state–market relations configuration creates a 'public entrepreneurship' system, combining vision, action, and learning. China's governance structure consists of a vertical component in the form of national narratives and accountability, and a horizontal component in the form of radical decentralization via provinces and cities, combined with a dynamic enterprise sector including both state-owned enterprises (SOEs) and private companies (Xiao et al., 2015). This system is manifest in the way in which China maps out and carries through its own development programmes. It is now embraced and articulated in the Belt and Road Initiative, with the creation of new economic landscapes at the heart of the BRI vision. It also accounts for the combination of the two policy banks with the wide range of national and provincial SOEs in the engineering and construction industries, who engage at the project implementation level as an entrepreneurial system with the financial, corporate, and human resources, and the orientations and incentives to tackle major infrastructure investment programmes that most other agents on the international investment scene find too hard in terms of decision processes or political complexity.[1]

The fact that China recognizes serious imbalances in its economy and is now seeking to contain associated financial system vulnerabilities serves as evidence that China advances through 'directed improvisation' and entrepreneurial institutions rather than through a Leninist-style 'state capitalism', a characterization which until recently has led many commentators to miss the dynamics of China's development process and its emergence as a dynamic, globally engaged economic power (Ang, 2016; Xu and Carey, 2016). China's role and methods in its involvement in infrastructure development in Africa and associated policy and cooperation arrangements, as set out in this chapter, are a manifestation of this public entrepreneurship (Gu et al., 2016), shaping the African infrastructure investment scene through the interaction of four key vectors: the policy banks, the BRI, FOCAC, and the BRICS. The interaction of these vectors explains why China has been taking an increasing share of the African infrastructure investment and construction market—a competitive advantage manifested in the form of scope, scale, and speed.

8.2.1 *China's Policy Banks*

The primary vector has been the creation in 1994 of China's two major 'policy banks'—the China Exim Bank and the China Development Bank—reporting directly to the State Council, in a rationalization of China's financial system to separate 'policy banking' from 'commercial banking' (Xu, 2016). China brings to African infrastructure development an approach in which its policy banks are lenders of first resort, and with its construction industry provide integrated investment packages that cut project-cycle time frames and supply scarce management capacity.

---

[1] For a list of the major Chinese construction firms active in Africa and their role in individual loan projects, see CARI database (China Africa Research Centre, 2018).

The Exim Bank was designed to provide loans to support the trade orientation of China's economic strategy, using standard short-term export credit financing as well as mega-project finance, but its instruments also include financing outward foreign direct investment and providing credits which Chinese firms can lend to their customers (buyers' credits). Further, it is the only Chinese bank authorized to provide concessional development loans, which are approved and subsidized by the Ministry of Commerce.[2]

At the same time, China Exim Bank also plays a major role in China's national development strategies via a large domestic loans portfolio, upgrading and helping to shape the industrial and hi-tech sectors in China, and lends to China's SMEs with a view to enhancing their international competitiveness. It also intermediates development loans to China from other countries and from multilateral development banks to Chinese provinces and cities, and has introduced a green growth financing programme in China (China Exim Bank, 2016).

The China Development Bank, for its part, and in the context of fiscal reforms in 1994 that recentralized tax revenues and forbade borrowing by local authorities, filled a huge gap in China's own financing needs by inventing the off-balance sheet local government financing vehicles (LGFVs) that essentially financed the rapid urbanization process and associated infrastructure needs across China, as well as special economic zones (Sanderson and Forsythe, 2013; Xu, 2016). The CDB then became incorporated into China's fiscal policy as a vehicle for combating the recessionary impact of the financial crisis that enveloped US and European banks in 2008. A massive expansion of lending to local governments and their SOEs, spearheaded by the CDB, generated new momentum to China's growth, with global impact, particularly via global commodity markets, cushioning the impact of the 2008 Great Recession on developing countries. CDB lending to support local authority infrastructure investment continues to be an instrument of China's fiscal policy even as the central authorities work to rebalance the Chinese economy from investment to consumption and to deleverage the financial system, including through reforming local authority finances.[3]

China's 'Going Out' policy, announced in 2000, provided a springboard for the two policy banks to go on to create major investment projects and programmes internationally. The statistics are impressive. The capital of the policy banks was increased in 2015 and the China Development Bank was

---

[2] A recent estimate puts the Exim Bank's concessional lending in 2015 at US$2.6bn, higher than China's grants and interest-free loans at US$2.2bn and its multilateral grants at US$0.6bn, making a total of ODA-like finance of US$6.1bn. China Exim's preferential buyer's credits at US$7.3bn, treated by some partner countries as ODA, have thus been larger than the amount that could be considered as ODA-like in DAC terms (Kitano, 2017).

[3] It has been argued that development banks, such as the KfW and the EIB in Europe, should become major agents of fiscal policy in a reformed international monetary system.

officially designated by the State Council a development finance institution (DFI), in name as well as in substance equivalent to Germany's KfW which also serves these hybrid functions. (As noted above, China Exim is also a hybrid, lending domestically as well as internationally.) Subsequently, the CDB has established a CDB Institute of Development Finance, with a research and outreach programme. It seeks to promote development finance as a special branch of the finance industry.

Funding for the policy banks is provided by capital injections from the Chinese state budget and from the now very large RMB bond market in which the policy banks played a pioneering role. In other words the policy banks are playing the same role as traditional MDBs in intermediating between bond markets and their borrowers, including developing countries. The policy banks borrow in the Chinese bond market at the prime sovereign interest rate and they have access to a 'pledged supplementary lending facility' from the PBOC (Peoples Bank of China) which in effect provides a subsidy for their development lending. The leverage ratios of the policy banks (and of China's emerging system of international development banks and funds) have been much higher than the corresponding ruling limits in the established MDB system, helping to explain their financing power (UNCTAD, 2018). However, the Chinese Banking Regulation Commission has now brought the policy banks within its jurisdiction, issuing regulations to clarify their business positions and enhance oversight of their risk control with external supervisory boards (Wu and Jia, 2017). The extent to which this may impact on their lending capacities and business models has yet to be seen.

8.2.2 Belt and Road Initiative

Reinforcing the capacity building evident in the creation and development of the policy banks and their subsequent global expansion has been the initiation of the Belt and Road Initiative (BRI), launched in 2013 by President Xi Jinping. The BRI's essential parameters are set out under the authority of the State Council in the 2015 'Visions and Actions' statement of principles and cooperation (NDRC, 2015), further developed at the inaugural Belt and Road Forum for International Cooperation established in 2017 (Xi Jinping, 2017). The BRI draws upon the underlying economic powerhouse that is contemporary China. It seeks to harness the accumulated financing, engineering, and project management capacities of an economy now larger than the US economy measured at purchasing power parity. As described above, China utilizes the capacities of the two policy banks as a platform to project this power into the BRI as its flagship international project. Funding and institutional modalities and programme agreements and project implementation have followed apace, to make the BRI the largest international development financing initiative in history, with widely recognized geo-economic and geopolitical impact.[4]

8.2.3 FOCAC

Since its founding in 2000, FOCAC has evolved into an institutionally grounded, multi-track process shaped at heads-of-state summits as a 'comprehensive strategic partnership' (Li and Carey, 2016). The 2018 FOCAC Summit in Beijing has carried this evolution to a new level. Infrastructure and its financing play an integral role in the manifold new programmes spanning the states–markets matrix developed by Susan Strange with its four interactive elements—security, production structures, finance, and knowledge (see also Chapter 6).

FOCAC summits have traditionally had an important focus on African infrastructure needs. In 2014, at the African Union (AU), Prime Minister Li Keqiang advanced a proposal to 'connect up' Africa via regional roads and aviation, and high-speed rail networks (State Council, 2014). This speech was followed up by Chinese financing for a Growing Together Fund established at the African Development Bank, providing US$2bn over ten years, and by an invitation for other partners to join in this endeavour to build a 'trilateral cooperation platform' for working on connectivity in Africa.

The FOCAC 2018 Beijing summit establishes, jointly with the AU, a new China–Africa Infrastructure Cooperation Plan as the centrepiece of a FOCAC Infrastructure Connectivity Initiative, with a focus on enhanced cooperation in energy, transport, telecommunications, and cross-border water resources. The Chinese public entrepreneurship model with integrated investment, construction, and operation is explicitly cited in Section 8.3.2 below, but other models are also explicitly envisaged and a number of 'key connectivity projects' are to be included (Ministry of Foreign Affairs PRC, 2018).

Alongside this new Infrastructure Connectivity Plan, the Beijing Action Plan establishes a new China–Africa Developmental Financing Forum and an Africa–China Financial Cooperation Consortium to provide 'more diversified financing packages', stepping up cooperation between the policy banks and other sources of finance, including MDBs ('on the basis of following multilateral rules and procedures') and institutional investors.

These new FOCAC platforms for infrastructure and finance and the openness to adjusting the Chinese model are significant moves towards the 'trilateral cooperation platform' which is an integral part of the vision of the Chinese government. We come back to this opening in our conclusion to this chapter.

---

[4] For a comprehensive review of the Belt and Road Initiative and its larger economic and geopolitical dimensions, see the 2018 OECD Business and Finance Outlook (OECD, 2018b).

8.2.4 *The BRICS*

The BRICS New Development Bank (NDB), launched in 2016 and headquartered in Shanghai, has a regional office in Johannesburg. It is initially focusing on green energy projects and has made its first loan in Africa. No doubt this 'African window' of the NDB will evolve further. Less well known is the BRICS Inter-bank Co-operation Mechanism which brings together the heads of the main development finance institutions of the five BRICS countries plus the president of the NDB. While there have been meetings of BRICS development cooperation officials, this area of public policy has not so far been a prominent

---

Box 8.1. HOW SIGNIFICANT IS CHINA IN AFRICAN INFRASTRUCTURE FINANCING AND CONSTRUCTION?

According to the Infrastructure Consortium for Africa (ICA), China committed an average of US$13bn per year to African infrastructure projects over the seven years 2011–17, a period covered by FOCAC V which provided US$20bn in concessional/preferential financial credits from China Exim for the three years 2013–15 (ICA, 2018). Additional loans have been committed by the China Development Bank, which as at mid-2017 had lent US$50bn to African countries, with an outstanding loan book of US$37bn (CDB News, 2017) and by other Chinese commercial banks, such as the ICBC.

To put these Chinese loans into perspective, over the 2012–17 period, average total commitments for African infrastructure investment from all sources amounted to US$77bn. The largest contribution came from African countries themselves, at over US$30bn per year (partly financed by significant eurodollar bond issues by some African countries in this period). Some US$20bn came from other members of the ICA (essentially OECD countries). China's contribution of $13bn per year was thus less than 20 per cent of the total, but China was clearly the largest single financing source, bilateral or multilateral (ICA, 2018). The US$35bn concessional financial credits announced in the 2015 FOCAC three-year Johannesburg Action Plan, essentially from China Exim, clearly have lifted China's infrastructure financing significantly since 2016. Indeed the CARI database on Chinese loans commitments to Africa shows a sudden peak to US$30bn in 2016, with a return to a more normal US$10bn in 2017 (China Africa Research Centre, 2018). The two Chinese policy banks are the most significant investors in large-scale projects in Africa, with China Exim ready to finance undertakings such as the standard-gauge rail links joining Addis Ababa to Dijbouti, and Mombasa with Nairobi (to eventually link to Uganda, Rwanda, and South Sudan), the urban light rail systems in Addis Ababa and Abuja, and the Abuja–Kaduna fast train service. Chinese financing has also underwritten recently completed major bridges in Dar es Salaam and Maputo, both with large connectivity dimensions, and over twenty hydro projects and 20,000 kms of power transmission and distribution lines, with more under construction.

As contractors to other project sponsors, the Chinese construction industry is conspicuously engaged in building a much greater proportion of African infrastructure, drawing on the scale and capabilities accumulated in building Chinese infrastructure. According to a recent estimate, Chinese construction companies' revenues from completed projects in Africa averaged over US$50bn annually in 2013–16 (Pairault, 2018). This number gives an indication of the size of China's footprint in African infrastructure investment activity as a construction services provider.

part of the BRICS process, and the drivers of development cooperation policies and programming vary widely among the BRICS countries (Gu et al., 2016b).

8.3 China's Impact on Global and African Infrastructure Investment Frameworks

8.3.1 *The Evolving Discourse on Infrastructure as a Development Priority*

While China invested heavily in infrastructure as part of its economic reform programme from 1978, orthodox development policies and financing saw infrastructure spending fall drastically as a share of development financing among OECD donors and MDBs. For example, in the 1950s and 1960s, infrastructure represented 70 per cent of World Bank allocations, but this fell to 30 per cent in the 1980s and 1990s. With few exceptions, this shift in priorities was paralleled in developed-country domestic budgets and in their aid programmes (Dollar, 2008). Infrastructure has now re-entered economic thinking and public policy at the level of the G20 and in the MDBs, recognized as multidimensional interactive networks of public goods with critical geospatial contributions to the functioning of their economies and societies. An extensive set of policy prescriptions and frameworks has emerged in the G20 context.

Recent accounts of infrastructure provision and issues in the Africa context have been published by the World Bank in its biannual Economic Pulse reports (World Bank Group, 2017, 2018). And the Infrastructure Consortium for Africa provides an annual review of financing trends. Its most recent report reviews estimates of the 'infrastructure gap' in Africa, still based on 2010 World Bank estimates. Noting some more recent estimates, the ICA report has called for a complete rethinking of the methodology and costings in the light of new conditions, notably the advent of the digital economy (ICA, 2017).

As concern with infrastructure in Africa revived, the 2005 G8 Summit in Gleneagles saw the major undertaking to double aid to Africa and the founding of the Infrastructure Consortium for Africa, to be housed at the African Development Bank (G8 Summit, 1985). Yet, the donor community singularly failed to realize the political goals and specific targets intrinsic to the commitment to double aid to Africa; objectives, design, and means of delivery became mired in gridlock. Beyond this stasis, however, were strong sub-currents of change. China at this point remained outside the global policy fora built around the G8. The literature in the field provided new insights into new perspectives and fresh delivery approaches. Further empirically grounded research challenged the then widely held perception of Chinese investment in Africa as simply large state-owned enterprises in search of natural resources, documenting the growing importance of Chinese private enterprises in Africa and a shift to manufacturing and service sectors (Gu, 2011).

There was early institutional engagement with these emerging themes. For example, in 2010, the China–DAC Study Group held a special meeting in Beijing on infrastructure as the foundation for growth and poverty reduction in Beijing, underlining the importance of Chinese experience and drawing lessons for both Chinese and DAC development policymakers (China–DAC Study Group, 2011). In 2010 the G20 Seoul Development Agenda included, as its first item, a major work programme on infrastructure questions and instigated a High-Level Panel on Infrastructure (G20 Summit, 2010).

Among the High-Level Panel's recommendations was a request for debt sustainability analysis to take account of the impact of the infrastructure–growth nexus, and in particular, the transformative impact of regional infrastructure. In an associated list of 'exemplary regional infrastructure projects', five were in Africa. Transformation and connectivity had become part of the lexicon of G20 work on debt sustainability and growth, alongside private-sector financing for infrastructure.

While the direction of G20 work has thus been to attempt to find consensus around these issues, divisions remain, at both conceptual and practical levels. The South–South principle of 'mutual benefit' (or 'win–win' in Chinese terminology) and non-interference, and the OECD/DAC principle of development contributions that are independent of direct trade and political benefits but require good governance, have yet to coalesce. The 2011 Busan High-Level Forum on Development Effectiveness aimed to bring these two approaches into a voluntary and complementary framework, but the follow-up process has failed to engage China so far. And at the level of Africa, dialogue is fragmented, with China, Japan, the United States, and the European Union each having its own Africa dialogue and planning forum, and the question of African membership of the G20 remains unresolved. In addition, China has not joined the G7 Infrastructure Consortium for Africa (ICA) or the AU/NEPAD Partnership for Infrastructure Development in Africa (PIDA) promoting regional infrastructure projects (African Development Bank, 2018), although it does interact with these bodies.

8.3.2 *Areas of Difference*

Thus Chinese approaches, capacities, and practices still differ in a number of critical ways from the ongoing mainstream of policies and frameworks. The approach is grounded in China's own history of semi-colonization, revolution, and reconstruction. Importantly, it is significantly informed by its commitment to principles, values, and practices of peaceful coexistence, mutuality, and reciprocity elaborated as far back as the mid-1950s by the Chinese government and in the Bandung Declaration. In terms of the international institutional architecture, at the heart of this distinctive approach is avoidance of the conditionality perceived to be intrinsic to established development approaches grounded in Western political and economic culture, and state interests. The approach of China detaches economic and political interests by focusing on practical, achievable projects. This is evident in a number of key aspects.

8.3.2.1 INFRASTRUCTURE AND STRUCTURAL TRANSFORMATION

China builds infrastructure ahead of time as a leading sector in structural transformation, creating new economic landscapes in the form of special economic zones, and national and regional connectivity (Lin and Wang, 2015, 2017). The externalities involved are considered to be large and, to a large extent, intrinsically unforeseeable, while costs of early construction are significantly lower than in the case of demand-led approaches to investment decisions. Implicitly, mistakes in the form of over-capacity or under-capacity and the purely political dimensions of some major infrastructure projects are compensated by the returns to the whole investment effort. In this analysis, developed in their book *Going beyond Aid: Development Cooperation and Structural Adjustment*, Lin and Wang thus argue that traditional aid frameworks are ineffective for stimulating structural transformation. The apparatus of cost–benefit analysis is not able to handle the growth dynamics of structural transformation. Hence the lack of success in Africa and the need to look beyond current aid concepts and practices to finance infrastructure that foments structural transformation across the African continent, drawing on Chinese experience and the scope for interaction with China's own ongoing transformation, in which real wages are forcing the export of labour-intensive industries to low-income countries.

8.3.2.2 CONTRACTING AND PROCUREMENT

Chinese infrastructure projects take the form of engineering, procurement, and construction (EPC) packages. Financing moves from the Chinese policy bank direct to the Chinese contractor. There are no transactions through the home-country public finance systems. This approach has the advantage for the host country of getting around serious capacity gaps in project formulation and financial management while speeding up project completion. Transparency and governance issues associated with this approach are for the developing country alone to resolve. Economic, social, and governance standards are those of the developing country itself (Dollar, 2018). Building local public project and financial management capacities in African countries has not been a significant concern in this context, although there are now moves to remedy this gap, notably in the establishment of a new China–IMF

Capacity Development Centre, anchored in Beijing and sponsored by China's central bank, focusing on macro policy issues (IMF, 2017) and now complemented by China's 2018 FOCAC initiative to construct an Institute for Capacity Development, alongside the African Capacity-Building Foundation (ACBF) in Harare, reflecting Chinese assessments of how to tackle governance deficits in Africa by fostering a broad range of policy and operational skills for delivering public goods.

8.3.2.3 PUBLIC INVESTMENT VERSUS PRIVATE INVESTMENT

A third divide is the Chinese public-investment-led approach to infrastructure investment versus the search for private-sector solutions and financing underlying much of the World Bank and G20 policy guidelines. The World Bank Group (WBG) adopted a 'cascade' concept, where private-sector solutions are first investigated and WBG financing is only forthcoming when a private-sector solution cannot be found or incubated. However this concept is now being rearticulated as a 'maximizing finance for development' approach (World Bank Group, 2017). And the IFC is now looking to identify projects on a prospective basis, moving from a retrospective scoring system to a forward-looking Anticipated Impact Measurement and Monitoring (AIMM) system, seeking to sharply increase investments with high leverage on private-sector investments in fragile states. Such advance reporting on transformation potential and impact should work to focus programme and project managers on transformational rather than incremental approaches (OECD, 2018b; Xu and Carey, 2015).

The objectives of the G20/OECD Task Force on Long-term Investment and the OECD/DAC Blended Finance project aim to pull in commercial finance from pension funds and from investment companies via infrastructure asset market development and risk reduction processes While seeking to build capacity and avoid crowding out in the private sector, these approaches are inherently more complex and time-consuming. In Chinese experience, private-sector development is ignited by upstream public-sector action in the context of a broad vision which provides information about future connectivity and capacities. This is the philosophy of the BRI and FOCAC, which rely on strong flows of foreign direct investment and rising public revenues to carry forward a sustainable transformation process, as happened in China and other emerging countries.

At the same time, there is a new move in China to rebalance from public-sector to private-sector enterprises and to promote public–private sector partnerships (PPPs), including in the BRI and FOCAC contexts, where funding requirements are large and diverse. Hence there is scope for some fusion of approaches; current shifts in vocabulary and tools on all sides suggest this may be underway.

8.3.2.4 INTERNATIONAL DISCIPLINES ON EXPORT CREDITS AND TIED AID

A fourth divide is that China does not participate in the export credit and tied aid disciplines established in the late 1980s among OECD countries to avoid aid and trade distortions associated with tied aid. These disciplines are applied to prevent trade competition via export credit subsidies and the use of aid to win contracts rather than promote development. Thus neither the China Exim Bank nor the China Development Bank is constrained by these disciplines and the transparency and contestation processes through which they are applied. The Chinese policy banks, while retaining an implicit sovereign status, apply international business norms regarding the confidentiality of commercial transactions.

Following an agreement between Presidents Xi and Obama in 2012, an International Working Group (IWG) on Export Credits with China, the OECD, and other countries as members was created to establish a set of international guidelines by 2014 (Ministry of Foreign Affairs, PRC, 2015). The IWG (chaired on a rotating basis by the United States, China, European Union, and Brazil) has been meeting regularly and now has a secretary general. It provides a forum for information sharing, to which the OECD secretariat contributes, but remains a long way from reaching an agreement that would replace the discipline and transparency of the established Arrangement on Guidelines for Officially Supported Export Credits or the DAC's tied aid measures (OECD, 2018b).

8.3.2.5 MANAGING OFFICIAL DEBT PROBLEM CASES

China has not so far joined the Paris Club of creditor countries, which has been the forum for collective restructuring of distressed official debt. Nevertheless, China has restructured or forgiven significant amounts of low-income country debt, including in parallel with the heavily indebted poor countries (HIPC) process (Dollar, 2018). With Chinese debt now becoming a larger part of the overall official bilateral creditor position, and signs of possible debt distress beginning to appear, discussions are in process with China on whether it might join the Paris Club. The context is changing as Chinese financing of the BRI increases. Possible IMF rescue packages in BRI countries might involve conflict between China and the United States.

8.3.2.6 HUMAN AND CORPORATE CAPACITIES AND COMPETITIVENESS

A sixth differentiating factor is that China has, over the course of the last forty years, developed massive human resources and corporate capacities in building infrastructure, helped along the way by the World Bank and OECD partners (Bottelier, 2007). At this point, these capacities are available for deployment in developing countries. Indeed, as described earlier in this chapter, large Chinese engineering and construction companies, mainly SOEs at the national and provincial or municipal levels, provide the possibility and the capacity for China to build power, transport, and ICT infrastructure across Africa with wide impacts, and to conceive and prosecute the Belt and Road Initiative, increasingly a global project. Indeed, it is difficult to imagine where this capacity to contribute to Africa's huge infrastructure needs could have come from, were it not for China's infrastructure build on a massive scale over the last three to four decades, creating in the process these human and corporate capacities. In that sense, China's development has been a prerequisite for meeting Africa's unprecedented infrastructure backlog and future needs. Engineering education system investment in China has produced a flow of skilled graduates with salaries still way below developed-country levels for comparable expertise. Thus the Chinese engineering, construction, and telecoms industries win a significant share of international contracts, including from the multilateral development banks. The main competitors are other emerging-country corporations and large OECD engineering firms such as Bechtel of the United States, currently in the final stages of negotiations to build an expressway between Nairobi and Mombasa. US has legislated to establish an International Development Finance Corporation designed to support US companies in expanding their business in developing countries (US Congress, 2018).

8.3.2.7 STANDARDS

Finally, China has not signed on to the environmental, social, and governance (ESG) standards for development banks that have progressively been specified through intensive discussion processes in their governance fora which also involve national and international civil society organizations. This remains a point of conflict with international civil society organizations, some of whom (such as Global Witness) keep a close eye on Chinese projects from this perspective. Others have worked closely with the Chinese policy banks to assist in the evolution of China's own lending standards (for example, the World Wildlife Fund for Nature). A series of regulations and guidance notes to Chinese enterprises has emerged over the years. The most recent set of Regulations on Outbound Investment and Business Activities, issued in December 2017 requires businesses to respect local laws, cultures, and standards and to work actively to improve their performance on five specific fronts, including corporate social responsibility and resources, and environmental protection, as well as to refrain from illegal activities and financial transfers. The two policy banks have their own standards and compliance and risk management functions which align with the regulations in force, and they participate in international work on responsible business conduct in the OECD context (OECD, 2018a). The China Development Bank is a member of the International Development Finance Club, which brings together twenty-three multilateral and bilateral development banks in a learning network, currently chaired by the Agence Française de Développement (AfD),with a work programme focused on green finance (AfD, 2018).

In his assessment of whether China is undermining the international order in the area of development financing, Dollar takes the view that the extensive and detailed processes for applying standards that now apply in project preparation in established MDBs have gone beyond what is functional, and indeed constitute a serious problem of dysfunctionality in the traditional MDB system, which has seen its role in infrastructure financing reduced to a very small percentage of total infrastructure finance. The approach to standards adopted by the Asian Infrastucture Investment Bank represents a step towards sanity in this view (Dollar, 2018).

Nevertheless, leaving in the hands of partner governments standards and programming in sensitive areas such as resettlement, especially troublesome in hydro projects where Chinese construction firms have extensive operations, runs major reputational and disruption risks, so that the Chinese authorities and businesses have strong incentives to assist in local capacity development in this area. Chinese migrant participation in illegal mining activities is another neuralgic point for China's relations with African countries, as in Ghana. The indication in the 2018 FOCAC Action Plan that China is ready to work with the MDBs in Africa, following multilateral rules and procedures, is thus highly significant.

8.3.3 *China's New Activism on Architecture and Concepts in the International Development Finance System*

The issues above have made it difficult for China and other partners to work together at the project level. A World Bank–China Exim Bank Memorandum of Understanding on Cooperation signed in 2007 proved impossible to execute because of the very different approaches to project cycles and standards. This impasse arose despite the very close relationship built between China and the World Bank on China's reform and capacity-building process, as described by a former director of the World Bank's Beijing Office (Bottelier, 2007).

Most spectacularly, China launched the Asian International Investment Bank (AIIB) in 2015, linked to its BRI, with a response in terms of membership uptake from G7 and G20 countries that went beyond expectations. This was a shock to the MDB system, though the AIIB is now de facto part of a larger MDB cooperative system that includes also the BRICS New Development Bank (NDB). Essentially, Chinese ambitions could no longer be pursued within the World Bank where the US Congress and the US Treasury effectively hold a US golden share (Xu, 2016). The emergence of a Chinese development finance architecture of banks and special funds with risk appetites and leverage ratios beyond the established norm has been explored in a recent study by UNCTAD (UNCTAD, 2018).

More recently China and the World Bank have been able to co-operate at the level of knowledge partnerships:

- An Investing in Africa Forum (IAF) was originated by the China Development Bank in 2015 with the Africa Department of the World Bank joining as a co-convener. The third IAF, held in Senegal in 2017, saw a joint CDB/WB publication, 'Leapfrogging: The Key to Africa's Development—from Constraints to Investment Opportunities', with a comprehensive historical and future-oriented assessment of the infrastucture–growth nexus, identifying innovation and new technologies as the new source of Africa's sectoral and infrastructure dynamics (CBD News, 2017).

- An initiative emerging from the G20 Hangzhou Summit in 2016, the Global Infrastructure Connectivity Alliance (GICA) is headquartered at the World Bank office in Singapore, with China as a leading member and with a first plenary meeting held at the OECD in January 2018. The GICA provides a comprehensive mapping of infrastructure network construction around the world, including in Africa, with the objective of consolidating information and promoting interaction at the level of concepts and practice (Global Infrastructure Connectivity Alliance, n.d.)

These two recent initiatives introduce two strands of thinking that constitute a shock to established frameworks of thinking about African infrastructure.

First is the proposition that innovation and technology will be the source of development dynamics in Africa. This view, now rapidly gaining ground, holds that the fourth industrial revolution is already changing Africa's development prospects by radically lowering transaction costs, creating and disseminating information in real time, and generating an inclusive financial system based on the latest that global financial technology (or FinTech) can offer, boosting entrepreneurial activity in Africa. As the report 'Leapfrogging as the Key to Africa's Development' illustrates, the ramifications across the development agenda will be transformational. While education and governance progress will remain even more essential in this context, even here the ICT revolution promises to radically improve access and accountability vectors and public management systems. The impact on discourse on development prospects and processes is already evident in the Bretton Woods context, the UN, and the OECD. The Commission on the Economy and Climate is producing a series of papers on how China–Africa technology and infrastructure cooperation can generate clean growth paths with very major employment creation impacts (Commission on the Economy and Climate, 2018). China's leading role in the hardware and software of the new ICTs is covered below.

A second shock is the recognition that the discussion of infrastructure development in international fora has indeed, with few exceptions, left out the essential connectivity/ geospatial dimension. This has been a shock even though the 'new economic geography' had been established by Krugman in the early 1990s (Krugman, 2011). By now, it turns out that economic geography is central to current domestic and geopolitics in all countries and to development processes in a global economy. The Global Infrastructure Connectivity Alliance is the only piece of global economic architecture that is built around the new economic geography, the economics and performance of connectivity networks as public goods, and the impact of the digital economy on these questions (GICA, 2018b). In the African context, the stark fact of the political and economic fragmentation of the continent emerging from the Berlin Conference of 1884, means that network economics stretch across boundaries, requiring a re-imagining of the African economy as it enters a Continental Free Trade Agreement. How costs and externalities are shared in this context and how system-wide infrastructure interdependencies are factored into this context remains largely outside the development finance system in Africa and beyond debt sustainability analytics.

These two Chinese initiatives may help to unlock the standard rigidities in thinking about African development, which is otherwise taking a pessimistic turn. Currently, there remains an institutional and intellectual divide between the G7/G20 processes described above, on the one hand, and the FOCAC thinking and processes on the other hand. The FOCAC triennial action plans are more comprehensive, more investment intensive, and more 'hands on' than the G7/G20 policy-intensive documents. At the same time, the ICA and PIDA work is based around detailed connectivity programmes, and the ICA discussion process has now begun to focus on the radical changes that come with the new digital economy revolution (ICA, 2017b).

There may now be an opportunity to pull together a shared umbrella framework for the ICA/PIDA and FOCAC, drawing on the toolkit of the GICA for linking visions, programmes, and projects (GICA, n.d.). This prospect is developed in the conclusions below.

The BRI is also in play in this context, since the inclusion of Africa and other regions beyond Asia as a constituent part of its vision of a reshaping global economy has added geopolitical dimensions. Japan's decision to join the BRI is particularly significant in this context, since it also plays a key role in African connectivity programmes, with a longstanding focus on economic corridors and on broader approaches to African development via the triennial TICAD conferences. As president of the 2019 G20 Summit, Japan is bringing forward an initiative on 'quality infrastructure', while also considering the idea of an 'open Indo-Pacific initiative' for infrastructure development in Africa, with the objective of positioning Japan as an active player on both the industrial and diplomatic fronts (Sano, 2018).

The BRI introduces critical questions about the environmental and social governance and safeguards we have noted above. International organizations including the World Bank, OECD, and European Union as well as civil society organizations have argued that the huge infrastructure projects involved in the BRI carry serious potential environmental, social, and corruption risks. Such risks include biodiversity loss, environmental degradation, and elite capture. One observer argues that such risks 'may be especially significant in countries involved in the BRI, which tend to have relatively weak governance. These risks will need to be identified and safeguards put in place to minimise their potential negative effects' (Ruta, 2018).

8.4 Electrification and Digitalization as Transformative Vectors in Africa–China's Contributions

8.4.1 *Transformation, Electrification, and Demography*

The prospects that economic transformation in Africa will be of sufficient magnitude and character to absorb the massive increase in Africa's labour force in the coming decades is perhaps the single most dramatic question of the twenty-first century. It ranks alongside and will interact with climate change. By 2050, the population of Western Africa will exceed the population of Europe. Associated risks for security and identity are already playing out in European politics.

How economic transformation might play out in Africa is explored in a recent IMF working paper (Fox et al., 2017). The IMF study finds that the demographic headwinds in Africa are such that a large proportion of the labour force will continue to be employed in low-productivity agriculture and that transfers of labour out of agriculture will be heterogeneous, to manufacturing and to services, some in high-productivity jobs but many in low-productivity employment. Fertility rates remain high with the failure to generate a decisive move out of low-productivity agriculture. This pessimism is matched by recent studies on the impact of infrastructure investment on growth due to quality problems associated with poor public management systems (Barhoumi et al., 2018). In turn these findings create pessimism about debt sustainability in many African countries and concern about the rising share of China in African debt stocks (IMF, 2018).

Is there a way in which these dynamics can be tamed? The remarkably high proportion of populations still in agriculture with strikingly high fertility rates and the extremely low rate of electrification in rural Africa suggest that here is a critical intervention point. Universal access to electricity at the household level is now within reach, given the dramatic fall in the costs of solar PV systems and the spread of FinTech systems that make them affordable. Evidence from demographic work in Indonesia shows that rural electrification has a significant impact on fertility rates. It also suggests that the greatest impact is access to television. The researchers conclude that their findings may have important application in sub-Saharan Africa (Grimm, Sparrow, and Tasciotti, 2015). The undertaking in FOCAC VI to provide television in ten thousand African villages must have been formulated with just this development impact in mind.

Putting these elements together suggests that rural electrification bringing lower fertility rates should become an even more strategic priority in African countries. Its association with the expansion of the digital economy would also bring multidimensional impacts, such as the expansion of agri-business supply chains, rising agricultural productivity, and improved educational opportunities and learning outcomes.

Rural electrification based on household solar systems and mini-grids is already gathering pace across Africa, with evolving system integration issues that will need to be addressed, but where solutions can be devised. Fast-tracking this process will address the demographic drama with the urgency it needs. In this context the World Bank has launched a major initiative to spur radical advances in battery storage technologies.

In terms of debt sustainability prospects, rising savings rates and tax-to-GDP ratios are likely to be the key frontiers. Both are low in Africa, but the prospects for lifting them will increase, with rural electrification promoting rising agricultural productivity and agribusiness supply chains which create jobs. Alongside that, a focus on generating virtuous circles between investment in urban infrastructure and increasing land values would create a public revenue base that has always been central to economic transformation processes. Interaction between cities and regions in Africa via investment in connectivity infrastructure as the core of FOCAC action plans would be part of a dynamic African transformation process. Domestic fiscal and financial systems would be the fundamental sources of financing. The Debt Sustainability Framework employed by the IMF/World Bank, now in its latest incarnation (World Bank, 2018a), needs to be much more closely related to such strategic development issues, as indeed is argued in another recent IMF research report on the causes of economic growth (Cherif et al., 2018).

8.4.2 Transformation, the Digital Economy, and Leapfrogging

China's large private ICT firms are driving the country's digital revolution at home and internationally, including a growing commitment to, and in, Africa. Huawei located in Kenya in 1998, and together with ZTE has since put in place a large proportion of Africa's backbone digital infrastructure in close association with African governments and private telecoms operators (Institute of Developing Economies, 2009), maintaining a number of R&D centres in Africa. It has also provided extensive training programmes for engineering staff (Tsui, 2016).

A perceptive McKinsey Global Institute analysis in 2017 argued that:

> A rising number of Chinese digital companies are developing a global presence through M&A, by expanding their business models, and as providers of technology to partner companies. These developments could mean that China sets the world's digital frontier in coming years. China's increasing prominence on the world's digital stage also means that China can contribute, and even lead, broader debates on global governance issues such as barriers to foreign competition, reciprocity, and digital sovereignty. (Woetzel et al., 2017)

What, then, does this mean for Africa? A recent study has detailed the digital journey being taken by African economies, highlighting the leading role played by what the study terms the 'KINGS' of Africa's digital economy, namely, Kenya, Ivory Coast, Nigeria, Ghana, and South Africa (Osiakwan, 2017). In addition to extensive bilateral ICT collaboration with African states, the cumulative body of declaratory policy agreements and action plans of the three primary multilateral fora—FOCAC, BRICS, and BRI—demonstrates a consensus for helping to promote and facilitate Africa's digital economy. This is exemplified, for example, in the May 2016 'Joint Communiqué of the Leaders Roundtable of the Belt and Road Forum for International Cooperation', committing the BRI to smart economic growth:

> Strengthening cooperation on innovation, by supporting innovation action plans for e-commerce, digital economy, smart cities and science and technology parks, and by encouraging greater exchanges on innovation and business startup models in the Internet age in respect of intellectual property rights.
> (Ministry of Foreign Affairs PRC, 2017)

While widely portrayed as another 'win–win' of China–Africa collaboration, questions have been raised as to the implications of China's deepening involvement. The recent assessment by Iginio Gagliardone (Gagliardone, 2018) explored the question of whether China is imposing its information society model on the continent. Gagliardone's evaluation is that, Chinese involvement is essentially determined by the framework dictated by host states and directly or indirectly gives succour to them whether they be authoritarian or democratic in character. Nevertheless, this important caveat notwithstanding, at the core of this issue remains Africa's need and Africa's potential.

8.5 Conclusions: Towards Shared Platforms for African Connectivity Infrastructure

Working at scale on the frontiers of infrastructure development explored above on a continent with pervasive fragility is challenging but essential. China's engagement, drawing on its own development experiences and the capacities created in that process, holds the promise of helping Africa move onto a transformation path that captures its demographic dividend via rural development and urbanization dynamics, and regional and global integration. China's vision of a reshaped world economy based on new connectivities, technologies, and networks of peoples, within a cooperative global governance system, is injecting fresh ambition and hopes for Africa in a context of heightened geopolitical competition, identity politics, and crisis-prone geo-economic faultlines. The use of night-time satellite images to reveal how Chinese aid projects have contributed to connecting up isolated communities through the construction of road, energy, and digital capacities and networks in Africa and elsewhere provides a timely injection of confidence that China's development cooperation priorities and methods are having an impact on poverty reduction and inequality. At the same time, African agency in shaping its own development process at national, regional, and continental levels will be crucial to ensuring that Chinese development finance yields inclusive and sustainable development and helps to build public management capacities and integrity.

Africa's challenges in managing the one billion plus increase in its population over the coming three decades require a 'Lewis-type' transformative development process on a scale to which only China in the recent past and India now provide comparators. As in China and India, the resources for this transformation will emerge from the transformation process itself, in the form of higher domestic savings rates and public revenues in Africa, and human capital increasing exponentially with urbanization, electrification, and digitalization (Glaeser and Lu, 2018). China's contribution to Africa's growth drivers in terms of leapfrogging change in technologies and business models, connectivity infrastructure investments, and linking aid, trade, and investment in the 'Asian' style brings a structural approach that goes beyond regulatory reform and standard good governance agendas.

Scope, scale, and speed are qualities that China brings in ways that others cannot. At the same time China's non-interference principle will need to continue to adjust as the success of its partner countries becomes vital to the viability and reputation of the whole BRI, and thus of China's global vision itself. There are African agents who have exploited the non-interference principle, undermining the integrity and creditworthiness of their countries, not least in the context of infrastructure financing (Corkin, 2016). The risk assessment systems of the policy banks, including reputational risk, are being reinforced along with their systems for assuring social and environmental standards (CDB, 2018; China Exim Bank, 2017).

With China taking on an increasing market share of development finance across the now global reach of the BRI, including Africa, it also assumes an increasing part of official debt exposure and reputational risk in terms of performance, standards, and integrity. But China cannot succeed in its BRI without major parallel and connected efforts from others. The creation of joint approaches and systemic processes at the policy and operational levels will be essential. New proposals on the reform of the WTO touch upon important parts of the 'China model', including the role and governance of SOEs (European Commission, 2018). Meanwhile there are indications that the US administration may resist China's emerging leadership role with the African Union. And the United States has legislated for a new US International Development Finance Corporation (US Congress, 2018). How the new FOCAC platforms can help to generate cooperative endeavours, synergies, and accommodation on these fronts in the African context is the principal challenge in the near future.

An experts report written for the G7-founded ICA calls for a holistic reassessment of Africa's infrastructure needs (ICA, 2017). This may be the opportunity to bring a shared trilateral platform into being, under the AU umbrella and supported by the African Development Bank and the UN Economic Commission for Africa. Alongside this, the new Institute for Capacity Development, to be constructed by China as an integral part of the African Capacity Building Foundation (ACBF), will help underpin Africa's public management capacities for the critical transformation process and the one billion more Africans to be alive in the three decades ahead.

References

AfD (2018) IFDC Website, https://www.idfc.org/.

African Development Bank (2018) 'Programme for Infrastructure Development in Africa (PIDA)', African Development Bank, https://www.afdb.org/en/topics-and-sectors/initiatives-partnerships/programme-for-infrastructure-development-in-africa-pida/.

Ang, Y. Y. (2016) *How China Escaped the Poverty Trap*. Cornell Studies in Political Economy. Ithaca, NY: Cornell University Press.

Barhoumi et al. (2018) 'Public Investment Efficiency in Sub-Saharan African Countries', https://www.imf.org/en/Publications/Departmental-Papers-Policy-Papers/Issues/2018/07/06/Public-Investment-Efficiency-in-Sub-Saharan-African-Countries-45953.

Bottelier, P. (2007) China and the World Bank: How a Partnership Was Built', *Journal of Contemporary China*, 16(51): 239–58.

CDB (2018) 'China Development Bank Annual Report 2017', http://www.cdb.com.cn/ English/bgxz/ndbg/ndbg2017/.

CDB News (2017) *'The 3rd Investing in Africa Forum Wrapping up in Dakar—CDB Investing and Financing More than USD 50 billion in Africa'*, 27 September 2017, China Development Bank, http://www.cdb.com.cn/English/xwzx_715/khdt/201803/t20180309_4998.html.

Cherif et al. (2018) 'Sharp Instrument: A Stab at Identifying the Causes of Economic Growth', https://www.imf.org/en/Publications/WP/Issues/2018/05/21/Sharp-Instrument-A-Stab-at-Identifying-the-Causes-of-Economic-Growth-45879.

China Africa Research Centre (2018) *Chinese Loans and Aid to Africa: Data*, China Africa Research Initiative, http://www.sais-cari.org/data-chinese-loans-and-aid-to-africa/.

China-DAC Study Group (2011) *Economic Transformation and Poverty Reduction Vol. 1 & 2.*, China-DAC Study Group.

China Exim Bank (2016) 'White Pater On Green Finance', http://english.eximbank.gov.cn/tm/en-TCN/index_1154.html.

China Exim Bank (2017) 'The Export-Import Bank of China Annual Report for 2016', http://english.eximbank.gov.cn/tm/en-AR/index_634_30016.html.

Commission on the Economy and Climate (2018) 'New Climate Economy', https://newclimateeconomy.net/.

Corkin, L. (2016) *Uncovering African Agency: Angola's Management of China's Credit Lines*. London: Routledge.

Dollar, D. (2008) 'Supply Meets Demand: Chinese Infrastructure Financing in Africa', *East Asia & Pacific on the Rise*, http://blogs.worldbank.org/eastasiapacific/supply-meets-demand-chinese-infrastructure-financing-in-africa.

Dollar, D. (2018) 'Is China's Development Finance a Challenge to the International Order?' *Asian Economic Policy Review*, 13(2): 283–98.

European Commission (2018) 'European Commission Proposals for the Modernisation of the World Trade Organisation', http://europa.eu/rapid/press-release_IP-18-5786_en.htm.

Fox et al. (2017) 'Structural Transformation in Employment and Productivity: What Can Africa Hope for?' https://www.imf.org/en/Publications/Departmental-Papers-Policy-Papers/Issues/2017/04/07/Structural-Transformation-in-Employment-and-Productivity-What-Can-Africa-Hope-For-44710.

G8 Summit (1985) '2005 G8 Gleneagles Documents', http://www.g8.utoronto.ca/summit/2005gleneagles/index.html.

G20 Summit (2010) 'G20 Seoul Summit', http://www.g20.utoronto.ca/summits/2010seoul.html.

Gagliardone, I. (2018) Is China Changing Information Societies in Africa? *Bridges Africa*, 7 (5), https://www.ictsd.org/bridges-news/bridges-africa/news/is-china-changing-information-societies-in-africa.

GICA (n.d.) 'Vision to Program to Projects (V2P2P)', https://www.gica.global/activity/vision-program-projects-v2p2p.

Glaeser, Edward and Lu, Ming (2018) 'Human Capital Externalities in China', https://voxeu.org/taxonomy/term/137.

Grimm, M., R. Sparrow, and L. Tasciotti (2015) 'Does Electrification Spur the Fertility Transition? Evidence from Indonesia', *Demography*, 52(5): 1773–96.

Gu, J. (2011) 'The Last Golden Land? Chinese Private Companies Go to Africa', http://www.ids.ac.uk/go/idspublication/the-last-golden-land-chinese-private-companies-go-to-africa-wp.

Gu, Jing, Alex Shankland, and Anuradha Chenoy (eds) (2016) *The BRICS in International Development*, International Political Economy Series. Basingstoke: Palgrave Macmillan.

Gu, J., C. Zhang, A, Vaz, and L. Mukwereza (2016) 'Chinese State Capitalism? Rethinking the Role of the State and Business in Chinese Development Cooperation in Africa', *World Development*, 81: 24–34.

ICA (2018) 'Infrastructure Financing Trends in Africa—2017', https://www.icafrica.org/fileadmin/documents/IFT_2016/Infrastructure_Financing_Trends_2017.pdf.

ICA (2017) 'Toward Smart and Integrated Infrastructure for Africa: An Agenda for Digitilisation, Decarbonisation and Mobility', https://www.icafrica.org/fileadmin/documents/Annual_Meeting/2017/2017_Annual_Meeting_-_background_paper_FULL.pdf.

IMF (2017) 'IMF and the People's Bank of China Establish a New Center for Modernizing Economic Policies and Institutions', 14 May 2017, https://www.imf.org/en/News/Articles/2017/05/14/pr17167-imf-and-china-establish-a-new-center-for-modernizing-economic-policies-and-institutions.

IMF (2018) 'Macroeconomic Developments and Prospects in Low-Income Developing Countries', https://www.imf.org/en/Publications/Policy-Papers/Issues/2018/03/22/pp021518macroeconomic-developments-and-prospects-in-lidcs.

Institute of Developing Economies (2009) 'China's Telecommunications Footprint in Africa', Chapter 9, http://www.ide.go.jp/English/Data/Africa_file/Manualreport/cia_09.html.

Kitano, N. (2017) 'A Note on Estimating China's Foreign Aid Using New Data: 2015 Preliminary Figures', https://www.jica.go.jp/jica-ri/publication/other/20170526_01.html.

Krugman, P. (2011) 'The New Economic Geography, Now Middle-Aged', *Regional Studies*, 45(1): 1–7.

Lasswell, H. D. (1936) *Politics: Who Gets What, When, How*. New York; London: Whittlesey House; McGraw-Hill.

Li, X. and R. Carey (2016) 'China's Comprehensive Strategic and Cooperative Partnership with Africa', http://www.ids.ac.uk/publication/china-s-comprehensive-strategic-and-cooperative-partnership-with-africa.

Lin, J. Y. and Y. Wang (2015) 'China–Africa Cooperation in Structural Transformation', in C. Monga and J. Y. Lin (eds) *The Oxford Handbook of Africa and Economics, Vol. 2: Policies and Practices*. Oxford: Oxford University Press, pp. 792–812.

Lin, J. Y. and Y. Wang (2017) *Going Beyond Aid: Development Cooperation for Structural Transformation*. Cambridge: Cambridge University Press.

Ministry of Foreign Affairs PRC (2017) 'Joint Communiqué of the Leaders Roundtable of the Belt and Road Forum for International Cooperation', https://www.fmprc.gov.cn/mfa_eng/zxxx_662805/t1462012.shtml.

Ministry of Foreign Affairs PRC (2018) 'Forum on China–Africa Cooperation: Beijing Action Plan (2019–2021)', https://www.fmprc.gov.cn/mfa_eng/zxxx_662805/t1593683.shtml.

NDRC (2015) 'Vision and Actions on Jointly Building Silk Road Economic Belt and 21st-Century Maritime Silk Road', http://en.ndrc.gov.cn/newsrelease/201503/t20150330_669367.html.

OECD (2018a) 'Export Credits Work at the OECD: Co-operating on Smart Rules for Fair Trade', https://www.oecd.org/tad/policynotes/export-credits-OECD.pdf.

OECD (2018b) 'OECD Business and Finance Outlook', http://www.oecd.org/daf/oecd-business-and-finance-outlook-26172577.htm.

Okonjo-Iweala, N. (2018) 'Africa Needs China's Help to Embrace a Low-Carbon Future', *Financial Times*, 21 September, https://www.ft.com/content/5854f9b6-bdc3-11e8-8274-55b72926558f.

Osiakwan, E. M. K. (2017) 'The KINGS of Africa's Digital Economy', in Bitange Ndemo and Tim Weiss (eds) *Digital Kenya: An Entrepreneurial Revolution in the Making*, Palgrave Studies of Entrepreneurship in Africa. London: Palgrave Macmillan, pp. 55–92.

Pairault, Thierry (2018) 'China in Africa: Goods Supplier, Service Provider rather than Investor', International Centre for Trade and Sustainable Development, https://www.ictsd.org/bridges-news/bridges-africa/news/china-in-africa-goods-supplier-service-provider-rather-than.

Ruta, M. (2018) 'Three Opportunities and Three Risks of the Belt and Road Initiative', *The Trade Post*, http://blogs.worldbank.org/trade/three-opportunities-and-three-risks-belt-and-road-initiative.

Sanderson, H. and M. Forsythe (2013) *China's Superbank: Debt, Oil and Influence—How China Development Bank Is Rewriting the Rules of Finance*. 1st edition. Singapore: John Wiley & Sons.

Sano, S. (2018) 'Japan's Potential Engagement in China's Belt and Road Initiative—AIIA', 23 February, Australian Institute of International Affairs, https://www.internationalaffairs.org.au/australianoutlook/japan-one-belt-one-road/.

State Council (2014) 'Bring about a Better Future for China–Africa Cooperation', text of Li Keqiang's speech at Africa Union, The State Council—The People's Republic of China, 5 May, http://english.gov.cn/premier/speeches/2014/08/23/content_281474983012932.htm.

Strange, S. (1994) *States and Markets*. 2nd edition. London; New York: Pinter Publishers; St. Martin's Press.

Tsui, B. (2016) 'Do Huawei's Training Programs and Centers Transfer Skills to Africa?', Policy Brief 14/2016, China Africa Research Initiative.

UNCTAD (2018) 'Keep an Eye on China's Innovations in Development Finance, 26 February, http://unctad.org/en/pages/newsdetails.aspx?OriginalVersionID=1671.

US Congress (2018) 'BUILD Act of 2018 115th Congress (2017–2018)', https://www.congress.gov/bill/115th-congress/senate-bill/2463.

Woetzel, J. et al. (2017) 'China's Digital Economy: A Leading Global Force', https://www.mckinsey.com/featured-insights/china/chinas-digital-economy-a-leading-global-force.

World Bank Group (2017) 'Africa's Pulse 15', https://openknowledge.worldbank.org/handle/10986/26485.

World Bank Group (2018) 'Africa's Pulse 17', https://openknowledge.worldbank.org/handle/10986/29667.

Wu, X. and D. Jia (2017) 'New Rules Released on Policy Banks to Enhance Risk Control', *Caixin Global*, 15 November, https://www.caixinglobal.com/2017-11-16/new-rules-released-on-policy-banks-to-enhance-risk-control-101171390.html.

Xi Jinping (2017) 'Work Together to Build the Silk Road Economic Belt and the Twenty-First-Century Martime Silk Road', *Chinadaily.com.cn*, 14 May, http://www.chinadaily.com.cn/beltandroadinitiative/2017-05/14/content_29341195.htm.

Xiao, G., Y. Zhang, C. Law, and D. Meagher (2015) 'China's Evolving Growth Model: The Foshan Story',. Fung Global Institute, http://www.asiaglobalinstitute.hku.hk/en/chinas-evolving-growth-model-foshan-story/.

Xu, J. and R. Carey (2015) 'Post-2015 Global Governance of Official Development Finance: Harnessing the Renaissance of Public Entrepreneurship', *Journal of International Development*, 27(6): 856–80.

Xu, J. and R. Carey (2016) 'China's International Development Finance: Past, Present and Future', https://www.wider.unu.edu/publication/china%E2%80%99s-international-development-finance.

Xu, Q. (2016) 'CDB: Born Bankrupt, Born Shaper', Institute of World Economics and Politics, CASS, http://policydialogue.org/files/events/Future_of_National_Development_Banks-_Presentation_-_CDB.pdf.

9

The Changing Dynamics of Chinese Oil and Gas Engagements in Africa

Cyril Obi

9.1 Introduction

Although Chinese state oil corporations (SOCs), most of which had their roots in the 1980s and 1990s, have gained a foothold in the African oil and gas sector, they are latecomers to globally integrated oil and gas operations. The history of the oil and gas industry in Africa has been largely dominated by investments by Western oil multinational corporations (OMNCs). The entry of Chinese SOCs—China Petroleum and Chemical Corporation (Sinopec), China National Offshore Oil Corporation (CNOOC), and China National Petroleum Corporation (CNPC/PetroChina)—into Africa's oil fields in the late 1990s has therefore raised serious questions, both about the drivers of China's search for oil in Africa, the tactics of, and structural challenges facing Chinese SOC investments in the oil and gas sector on the continent, and the implications of their investments both for the corporations and for the development of African petro-states.

In a context where Africa accounts for an estimated 22 per cent of China's oil imports, its second-largest source of oil supplies after the Middle East (Obi, 2010: 181–2), and China has surpassed the United States as Africa's largest trading partner (based mostly on oil trade and investments), the place of oil in China–Africa relations cannot be overlooked (Zhenxing, 2013). The analysis of the changing dynamics of China's oil engagements in Africa is framed within the broader narratives of Sino-African relations and its implications for the continent's development.

Table 9.1 shows China's oil imports from various African oil exporting countries in percentage terms. It identifies the main providers of China's African oil supplies, and the export receipts that accrue from the oil trade

Table 9.1. Value of China's crude oil imports from African countries (in percentage terms)

Name of Country	2007	2008	2009	2010	2011	2012	2013	2014	2015	2016
Angola	16	17	16	17	12	15	14	13	12	12
Republic of the Congo	3.3	2.6	1.9	2.1	2.1	1.9	2.4	2.2	1.7	1.9
Sudan	5.2	5.9	6.6	N/A	4.1	0.64	0.87	0.6	2.4	0.3
South Africa	1.7	0.083	0.17	N/A	N/A	0.17	N/A	N/A	0.11	0.075
Equatorial Guinea	2	1.6	1.1	0.37	0.71	0.75	0.87	1.1	0.64	0.32
Libya	1.7	1.7	3.8	3	1	2.8	0.91	0.31	0.7	0.3
Nigeria	0.66	0.2	0.78	0.62	0.41	0.41	0.45	0.67	0.22	0.25
Gabon	0.49	0.65	0.11	0.18	0.064	0.12	0.17	0.5	0.45	0.92
Chad	0.096	N/A	0.066	0.38	0.12	0.088	0.044	0.045	0.065	0.099
Egypt	0.044	N/A	N/A	N/A	0.4	0.28	0.43	0.28	0.44	0.25
South Sudan	N/A	N/A	N/A	N/A	N/A	0.23	1.1	1.9	N/A	1.3
DRC	N/A	N/A	N/A	N/A	0.15	0.32	N/A	0.34	0.042	0.092
Ghana	N/A	N/A	N/A	N/A	0.061	0.18	0.14	0.29	0.71	0.79
Cameroon	N/A	0.25	0.27	0.15	0.18	0.21	0.4	0.22	0.29	0.12
Algeria	1.4	0.33	1.1	0.97	1.1	1.3	0.74	0.23	0.097	N/A
Mauritania	N/A	N/A	0.2	0.061	0.1	0.09	0.047	N/A	N/A	N/A

Source: Compiled from various sources by Kelly Mu
https://atlas.media.mit.edu/en/visualize/tree_map/hs92/import/chn/show/2709/2008/

with the continent. The trends in Chinese oil engagements with African petro-states, particularly the countries shown in the table, reveal some of the changing dynamics in Africa–China oil trade. In this regard, Angola, Republic of Congo, Sudan, Equatorial Guinea, and Nigeria can be considered as accounting for the bulk of China's African oil imports. It would appear that Chinese SOCs have sought investments in those countries, but the extent to which these trends are the result of China's strategic energy security calculations, or corporate profit interests, remains unclear.

Many commentators on the implications of China's expanding relations with African petro-states operate within a larger narrative based on opposing views (Cheru and Obi, 2011: 91–110; Zhao, 2014; Zondi, 2017). The first frames China as a natural partner that will catalyze Afro-centric development in the context of South–South solidarity (Wenping, 2007: 23–40), and help put an end to Western domination of the continent (Campbell, 2008: 89–105), while the second is rather suspicious and critical of what is perceived as China's intention to exploit and dominate Africa (French, 2014; Maasho, 2018; Sanusi, 2013; Tiffen, 2014). Cheru aptly captures the various contending perspectives on the impact of emerging global powers such as China on Africa's development as ranging from the 'alarmists, the critics of "new imperialism", to the pragmatic cheerleaders' (Cheru, 2016). He describes the alarmists as those that see China's growing engagement with Africa through the lens of threats to the United States and its Western allies, and to national security (Pillsbury, 2015), and the sceptics as including 'aid bureaucrats' that are wary of 'new donors whose practices fragment and undermine aid, including OECD/DAC best practices of aid effectiveness'.

In his view, the critics of the 'new imperialism' are of the view that emerging powers like China mainly seek to extract Africa's vast natural resources while cozying up to the continent's corrupt and despotic leaders within the context of an East–West scramble for Africa's resources and markets. The 'pragmatic cheerleaders' are described as those who see the engagement of Southern powers with Africa more as an opportunity, and less as a threat, with the opportunity being defined in relation to the expansion of the 'policy space' to enable the continent to pursue alternative developmental models (Cheru, 2016). He then makes a case for transcending the preceding perspectives, agreeing with Mohan and Lampert's (2013) position on the primacy of 'African agency', rooted in the nature of the state, and the roles of leadership and institutions in influencing the impact of the continent's engagement with external and emerging powers.

Four caveats need to be observed when seeking to explain the nature and ramifications of China–Africa relations. The first is to avoid any hasty conclusions on the basis of so-called 'facts' about Chinese domination of Africa, but to actually interrogate them—whether they are generalizations based on a few examples or cases, or data that do not capture certain realities. Second is to pay attention to changes and responses that may have taken place over time, either in response to contextual shifts, or due to lessons learnt. Third is to pay attention to the diverse, sometimes competing or contradictory interests embedded within China and Africa, and not confuse the trees for the forest.

While it may be easier to assume the image of an undifferentiated China or Africa, it is useful to always note that several sets of 'Chinese' actors engage with Africa, which in itself in made up of fifty-four states, each with different histories, capacities, and interests. This suggests that Sino-African relations or engagements cannot be uniform across the board or yield the same results/outcomes. Fourth, and related to the preceding point, is the need to pay close attention to the 'increasing fragmentation, decentralization and internation-alization of states', including China, where 'many agencies, regulatory bodies and subnational units have developed their own international policies and relationships' (Hameiri and Jones, 2016: 73).

It is important to be reminded of a related point made by Hameiri and Jones about (2016: 74) 'how disaggregated state apparatuses and quasi-independent, market-facing actors are increasingly acting overseas in ways not effectively coordinated in Beijing'. What this suggests is that there are subtle differences in how Chinese SOCs act in Africa, depending on a set of factors, including the level of the state (provincial/regional or national) or economic sector (oil and gas) that they are affiliated to, or their relationship to the ruling party/government. The point is that Chinese behaviour may not be driven by a 'grand strategy', but rather reflects a mix of 'commercial considerations that are often fragmented and incoherent' (Hameiri and Jones, 2016: 86). Also the point has been made elsewhere about some of the limitations of Chinese SOCs in the highly competitive international oil sector largely dominated by American and European oil multinationals (Patey, 2017: 759). It is equally important to recognize the importance of Africa's agency vis-à-vis its relations with China (Corkin, 2015: 171).

This chapter explores the changing dynamics of China's engagements with some of the African oil-producing and exporting countries. It intervenes in debates about the nature and implications of the investments by Chinese SOCs in the oil sectors of established and new African oil producers such as Nigeria, Angola, Equatorial Guinea, Sudan, Chad, Gabon, and Ghana. It interrogates some of the claims about the impact of the Chinese SOCs on development in oil-rich African states, by arguing that engagements and relations respond to, and are shaped by, global and national contextual factors, and lessons learnt on both sides, including the actions/agency of ruling elites in African petro-states. Patey (2014: 4–5) goes further to demonstrate how African petro-states, particularly Sudan, shaped China's oil investments on the continent and beyond.

In exploring the changing dynamics of Chinese oil engagements with Africa, the first section of this chapter provides an overview of the issues, while the second involves a conceptual framing of the China–oil–Africa nexus, including how it can facilitate a better reading of the nature and impact of oil, which is of immense strategic and economic value to Africa's development. The third section provides an analysis of the changing dynamics and impact of Chinese SOC engagements with select African petro-states. In the fourth and concluding section, the chapter sums up the arguments and examines the prospects for African development on the basis of a nuanced and more balanced reading of the evolving China–Africa oil nexus.

9.2 A Conceptual Framing of China–Africa Oil Relations

Studies of relations between China and Africa have often been framed in historical, structural, economic, and political terms. In most cases, relations have been explained in terms of inter-state relations, sometimes from opposing perspectives of dependency/neocolonialism, or the rhetoric of 'win–win' development. This state-centric approach to China–Africa relations is undermined by a dichotomy of views. Those critical of investments by Chinese SOCs argue that unlike Western oil MNCs that possess sophisticated technology and management skills, and are guided by the principles of transparency, human rights, and environmental best practices, including corporate social responsibility, the Chinese SOCs are out to dominate and plunder Africa's oil and gas resources. They also argue that Chinese SOCs back African petro-states/leaders that unleash violence on their people to pave the way for oil exploitation, and refer to the adoption of sub-standard environmental and labour practices by Chinese oil companies as neo-imperialism or a new form of colonialism of the continent.

Such analyses also seek to implicate Chinese SOCs into the perpetration of the so-called African oil curse—constructed on the view that oil wealth paradoxically fuels corruption and violent conflict, and subverts development (Obi, 2013). The debate on the oil curse has been discussed elsewhere and will not be repeated here. It suffices to note that the notion of the oil curse has been critiqued and found wanting both in terms of its empirical basis and analytical value which renders it unhelpful in understanding China–Africa oil relations. Such narrow deterministic perspectives also serve to reinforce concerns that growing Chinese SOC investments pose a threat to Western strategic and economic interests in Africa—which represents the last frontier in the global oil and gas sector.

On the other hand, the 'win–win' school of thought argues that Chinese SOCs represent a better alternative to the Western oil MNCs that have dominated and plundered Africa's oil and gas sectors, leading to the impoverishment and pollution of oil-producing communities. They see Chinese SOCs backed by the Chinese state as representing an opportunity for investments in oil infrastructure, transfer of skills and technology, and new oil revenues capable of catalyzing national economic growth. As will be later shown, the changing dynamics of Chinese investments in Africa's oil and gas sector demand a more nuanced approach that exposes the limitations of existing claims about what Chinese NOC investments mean for China's engagements with African petro-states. It is in this regard that we shift attention to an alternate conceptual framing that opens up the space for a more flexible reading of the changing dynamics of China–Africa engagements.

This alternate conceptual approach focuses on the agency of state and non-state actors in the context of China–Africa relations (Mohan and Lampert, 2013: 92–3; Cheru, 2016; Corkin, 2015: 163–72). This is useful both in explaining the nature of, and drivers of, changes in relations as well as challenging the view that China is the dominant partner, while Africa is subservient or weak. Increasing empirical evidence is being produced to show that far from being caught in a neocolonial relationship with, or powerless in the face of, China's economic might, some African states have been able to turn the opportunities and resources provided by Chinese engagement to their own advantage. Corkin (2015: 171) argues that 'African agency should be the key tenet in analyzing Africa's international relations'.

What flows logically from the foregoing is the need to go beyond a stylized reading of relations as inter-state engagement (where states are assumed to be coherent, undifferentiated entities), or as Mohan and Lampert (2013: 94) note, with reference to the works of Carmody and Taylor (2010: 497), transcend the 'tendency to acknowledge African agency but then focus on the flexibility of the Chinese' or 'flexigemony', whereby Chinese actors 'adapt their strategies to suit the particular histories and geographies of the African states with which they engage'. They underline China's capacity to flexibly engage, largely based on 'soft power' and respond to the realities within diverse African countries. Such state-centric analyses also bring to the fore the role of domestic elites in shaping state behaviour, echoing some of the views and aspirations of Chinese and African state elites. While knowledge of Chinese elite perceptions of Africa is rather sketchy, some African state elites seem to have developed a fairly good grasp of how engagement with China can advance their class and national interests. The Chinese are also learning how to flexibly and pragmatically respond to the opportunities and challenges that come with their engagements with African countries.

Another relevant issue is the interplay between state and elite agency. Either way, issues of motivation, context, and roles shape relations and matters in terms of 'who gets what, when and how'. In a critique of Wight's perspective to state agency, Mohan and Lampert (2013: 96–7) point to the heterogeneous nature of Chinese capital in Africa, and the ways in which class interests are embedded in social and political agency. They note the importance of transcending inter-state relations, bringing in the role of non-state actors, and fractions of capital, including how various levels and 'textures' of state feature in the emerging relations. Given the attention to the agency of African states and elites, this chapter recognizes the need to go beyond assumptions that present China as taking advantage of passive or pliant African states. The challenge is identified as seeking empirical support for African agency to show that the relations are more complex, and contingent on the interaction between a diverse set of interests on both sides.

The foregoing facilitates the interrogation of the emerging relationship between China and Africa's petro-states. Most of the earlier analysis on this subject has either been framed in the context of an East–West scramble for Africa's oil, and its attendant political, strategic, economic, and environmental risks, or the contribution of China to the 'African oil curse' (Cheru and Obi, 2011; Obi, 2010; Taylor, 2014). A lot has been made of the entry of the Chinese SOCs from an emergent and energy-hungry Asian power into Africa's established and new oil states, and the effects of Chinese petro-dollars and resource diplomacy on these countries. This has also provoked debates around a set of questions such as: in which ways are Chinese SOCs different from the Western multinationals that have dominated the oil industry in Africa over the past six decades, without much to show in terms of development in the oil-endowed countries of the continent? What factors influence relations between the Chinese state and African petro-states? What is the relationship between the Chinese state and Chinese SOCs and how is this reflected in engagements with African petro-states and oil regulatory agencies? Do Chinese SOCs represent an alternate oil-based developmental model (to Western MNCs), to African petro-states?

A focus on the agency of African petro-states and elites vis-à-vis relations with China is more likely to move the debate in a different and more productive direction. Apart from enabling a critical engagement with some of the questions raised in the foregoing paragraph, it also offers a framework for analyzing some of the empirical evidence emerging from African petro-states where Chinese SOCs have made inroads, or suffered losses in relation to oil investments on the continent. Although China still remains a largely marginal player based on the size of its investments both in Africa's and global oilfields, its role on the continent and the impact of the political economy of oil can no longer be ignored. Oil remains an important aspect of China–Africa relations, and a point from which to glean how African agency plays out and helps us transcend rather limited perspectives to the diverse dynamics, possibilities, and outcomes that such may portend for Africa's development.

9.3 Chinese SOCs and African Petro-States: Evidence from Three Cases

Chinese SOCs are the new kids on the block in the global oil industry. Within the space of two decades, two Chinese SOCs, Sinopec and PetroChina, are now among the world's top ten oil companies with estimated market values of US$89.9 billion and US$203.8 billion (Coleman, 2017; Poole, 2018). Although, the rather 'peaceful rise' of Chinese SOCs in the global oil market is yet to attract much attention; it is significant in three regards. First is how Chinese SOC oil investments and trade in Africa may have contributed to their growing global profiles, and second, how skills, experiences, investments, and managing risks in African oil fields informed SOC's global oil policies and operations. Third, Chinese SOCs are increasingly becoming formidable as global oil actors vis-à-vis the African petro-states.

It is against this background that Chinese SOCs should be seen as recent entrants into Africa's oil fields, long the preserve of Western oil MNCs, state oil corporations, and independents. Africa has emerged as the second-largest source of Chinese oil imports (the largest source being the Middle East), accounting for 1.3 million barrels of oil per day or 22 to 23 per cent (Alessi and Xu, 2015). While Africa increasingly features prominently in Beijing's global energy security calculations, care should be taken not to limit the role of Chinese SOCs to national energy security alone, but to factor in their emergence as global energy corporations seeking to maximize returns from oil investments like their Western oil MNC counterparts.

As suggested in Section 9.2, early studies of the relationship between Chinese SOCs (often presented as agents of the Chinese state) and African petro-states were usually framed either as being asymmetrical and exploitative of, or beneficial to, Africans. Accounts abound of how Chinese SOCs were backing the Sudanese government accused of violating human rights in Darfur, deploying scorched-earth tactics to clear villagers out of their lands preparatory to oil exploration activities, and backing corrupt governments in oil-rich Angola and Equatorial Guinea. The narrative of an energy-hungry Asian giant using resource diplomacy to corner Africa's oil reserves, offering sweetened oil deals and loans for infrastructure development aid packages, or turning a blind eye to corruption or human rights violations under the guise of its policy of 'non-interference' is gradually giving way to more nuanced analysis. This new approach is on the basis of increased acknowledge of the agency of African states and elites that are pushing back against Chinese practices or projects they consider inimical to their interests, as well as lessons learnt by Chinese actors operating in African 'petrolized' contexts.

Another important issue is that of the existence of zero-sum competition between Chinese SOCs and Western oil MNCs over Africa's oil and gas resources. New information is gradually emerging showing that while there is competition, there is also cooperation between Chinese SOCs and Western MNCs in oil operations in Nigeria, Angola, and other African petro-states. Several scholars go as far as to suggest that Chinese SOCs are relatively autonomous of the Chinese state and operate like regular oil multinationals defining their corporate missions as seeking maximum returns/profits on oil investments (Patey, 2017; Manero, 2017; Zhenxing, 2013).

In the light of the foregoing, the oil sector is a useful context for understanding the evolving nature of China–Africa relations. It is also a point from which to glean empirical evidence supporting the thesis of African agency as an influencer and shaper of such relations, and how the lessons Chinese 'latecomer' SOCs are learning in the course of investing in African oil-producing countries shapes relations. This will enable us to transcend the cul-de-sac of pre-determined outcomes, based on assumptions of Chinese neo-imperialism, African dependence or vulnerability. By analyzing China–Africa interactions in relation to a strategic commodity, oil, using three case studies, this chapter explores the factors that influence Chinese SOC behaviour towards African petro-states, including their broader ramifications for changes in China–Africa relations, particularly the development of the continent.

9.4 China and Nigeria: How is the 'Sweet Crude' Tilting the Balance?

China's SOCs entered the Nigerian oil sector in the quest to expand access to global oil investments when Petro-China signed a contract in 2004, valued at US$800 million, with the Nigerian National Petroleum Corporation (NNPC), the Nigerian state oil corporation, to supply 30,000 barrels of crude oil per day to China (Mbachu, cited in Cheru and Obi, 2011: 185). This coincided with the signing of 'an agreement between Chinese NOC, Sinopec and the NNPC to develop five exploration wells' (Obi, 2010: 185). In 2005, the China National Offshore Oil Corporation (CNOOC), the largest offshore oil and gas SOC in China, bought a 45 per cent stake in the Apo oil-for-gas field in Nigeria, valued at US$3 billion, regarded as CNOOC's largest acquisition in the world at the time. Following a visit by the Chinese president to Nigeria in 2006, Chinese SOCs were granted the right of first refusal for four oil blocks by the NNPC in exchange for the rehabilitation of the Kaduna refinery and several infrastructure development deals.

However, a year later, most of the oil-for-infrastructure deals involving Chinese SOCs were either cancelled by the Nigerian government or simply petered out. The government was clearly asserting its power over oil and expressing its autonomy in decision-making relating to getting the best deal for its oil. Another example of this was in 2009, when the 'Nigerian government rejected CNOOC's offer of interest in twenty-three oil fields for which leases to Western oil interests were about to expire after news of the offer was leaked to the press' (Cheru and Obi, 2011: 102).

According to Umejei (2013), two explanations could be advanced for the collapse of the oil-for-infrastructure deals. He identifies the first as 'the interest of Nigerian elites, who felt implementing the deal would cut them off from crude oil sales on the international market', and the second as 'the influence of IOCs, who contributed in developing the Nigerian oil industry and their influential home countries'. Either way, Nigerian elite perceptions of the value of Chinese oil engagement were decisive in the decision not to proceed with the oil deals. There is no doubt that the Chinese did learn some lessons from the experience and became more cautious about engaging in oil investments in Nigeria. This contributed to a shift away from oil-for-infrastructure deals and towards getting direct access to Nigeria's oil fields through global acquisitions and mergers.

In August 2009, Sinopec's acquisition of Addax, a Geneva-based oil company, gave it control of two offshore oil fields owned by the Nigerian subsidiary of the company. As a result, Sinopec struck oil at Addax's UDELE 3 oil well in the Niger Delta in July 2010, giving it direct access to some of Nigeria's oil. Given the recent trends in the Nigerian oil industry, the combination of prolonged insecurity, uncertainties related to the non-passage of the Petroleum Industry Bill (PIB) in its original form (a Petroleum Industry Governance Bill (PIGB) was passed by the House of Representatives in 2018) by the National Assembly, and allegations of corruption levelled against the NNPC, the nature of oil investments have been affected. This atmosphere of uncertainty around oil industry regulation, and changes in the global oil market is leading some Western oil MNCs to sell to onshore oil blocs in Nigeria; thus the way has been opened for those willing to take on risks in the oil sector.

In 2012, Sinopec bought a minority stake (20 per cent) in a Nigerian oil field from Total of France for the sum of US$2.5 billion (Hu, Wu, and Patel 2012; Kavanagh, 2012), increasing the level of its direct access to Nigeria's oil. Analyzing this development, Quigley (2014), makes the point that 'almost all the investments by Chinese companies are in buying shares in blocks, not sole control, so that the Chinese often rely on their IOC partners to do most of the actual production work for them, releasing them from the technological demands that come with offshore drilling'. What is not clearly mentioned, but implied, is that Chinese NOCs have learnt from their previous experience with oil-for-infrastructure deals, just as the Nigerian elite continues to straddle scepticism and acceptance of Chinese investments and aid. It is also important to note that Chinese SOCs are partnering with Western IOCs and service companies (rather than competing) in oil investments in Nigeria.

This shows SOC integration into transnational petrolized oil capital in the search for access to Nigeria's oil reserves and profits. It is not all too clear what the response of the Nigerian ruling elite is to this trend. So far, while oil is a prominent commodity in the trade between both countries, it is not the only one. The view of a 'scramble' for Nigeria's oil between the United States and China has also been laid to rest (Taylor, 2014: 403), in the context of decreased demand for Nigeria's oil by the United States (partly due to rising levels of domestic oil production in the United States) and the general recent slump in the global oil market. It is also not clear that China has been able to snap up the difference, as most of Nigeria's oil exports still end up in Europe. If recent developments are anything to go by, some Chinese SOCs may be rethinking their oil investments in Nigeria. For example, a Reuters report late in 2017 speculated that Sinopec 'had hired BNP' to sell its oil assets in Nigeria, in the face of declining global oil prices, insecurity in the Niger Delta, and reports in sections of the global media about an investigation in the United States into the alleged bribing of Nigerian officials by Addax (acquired by Sinopec) to resolve a business dispute (Miller and Schoenberg, 2017; Reuters, 2017). Although the contents of the reports have been denied by Sinopec, it does partly confirm the point that the SOC operates purely by the profit logic, and is ready to move investments from high-risk areas to places where it is more likely to get optimal returns.

There is no real evidence to show that Chinese SOCs have been able to leverage their quest for oil at the expense of their Nigerian partners. However, there is evidence of two broad developments. First is the acquisition of oil assets in Nigeria through the takeovers of global oil companies seeking to offload their oil assets in the global South, or acquisition of shares in Nigerian subsidiaries of Western oil MNCs, and the expansion into non-oil sectors of the economy, particularly trade, construction, and infrastructure. Earlier this year it was reported that two Chinese companies, COOEC (a subsidiary of CNOOC) and China Harbour Engineering Company, had won a contract to build oil pipelines for the Dangote Group (XinhuaNet, 2018), a Nigerian conglomerate, showing the flexibility of Chinese SOCs in relation to investments in Nigeria's oil and gas sector. Also, Harbour Engineering and Sinopec signed a deal to build a modular refinery in Edo state, Nigeria (Vanguard, 2018). Nigeria's petro-elite continues to exert great influence over 'who gets what', and determine how the country engages Chinese SOCs.

To echo the thoughts of Cheru (2016), 'transforming the new relationship with Chinese SOCs to a "win–win" situation will ultimately depend on African agency'. Also important is Taylor's observation that the reality of Nigeria's political economy, including its unpredictability, ensures that neither the

United States nor China can avoid the vulnerabilities associated with Nigeria's rather raucous petro-politics (Taylor, 2014). Time will tell where the pendulum will swing—towards greater engagement of a Nigerian petro-elite by Chinese SOCs or a continued preference for ad hoc short-term bids for acquisitions and deals that can deliver optimal returns from oil investments without any coherent long-term strategic/economic vision in mind. Either way, the evidence clearly suggests that the Chinese SOCs are not displacing Western oil MNCs (which are giving up onshore oil fields of their own volition), nor are the SOCs taking over oil blocs given up by the oil MNCs. There are also no signs of an agenda for the takeover of Nigeria's oilfields by the Chinese state, or steps by Chinese SOCs towards dominating Nigeria's oil fields. If anything, the Chinese SOCs have literally burnt their fingers several times in the course of learning how to better navigate Nigeria's complex oil business landscape.

9.5 Angola: Petro-Nationalism or Transnationalized Engagements?

Angola offers a similar, though more deliberate form of engagement with Chinese SOCs (Burgos and Ear, 2012: 351–67, Corkin, 2011), particularly Sinopec which entered Angola's oil fields in 2004 when it bought a 50 per cent stake in Block 18, operated by BP and sold by Shell. Sinopec later formed a joint venture with the Angolan state oil corporation Sonangol (Alves, 2012: 100; Corkin, 2011). Angola, Africa's second-largest oil exporter, remains the largest source of China's oil imports from the continent, followed by the Republic of Congo (following the decline in Sudan's and later, South Sudan's oil production). Although some pundits argue that Chinese SOCs entered Angola on the heels of oil-backed credit lines from the Chinese Exim bank, the initial euphoria that came with Sinopec's successes in acquiring shares in oil Blocks 18, and 3/80 in 2005, turned out to be rather short-lived. There is no doubt that the entry of Chinese SOCs may have initially benefited from a large-scale effort in the direction of oil-for-infrastructure deals and oil-backed loans, buoyed by the quest of Angola's governing elite to fund post-civil-war reconstruction efforts.

Sinopec initially 'benefited' from Sonangol's rejection of the deal that Shell signed with India's ONGC Videsh for 50 per cent of Block 18 in 2004, after which the Angolan oil corporation handed the shares over to the Chinese SOC. Although Sinopec similarly benefited in the following year, 2005, when it also 'acquired Block 3/80 previously owned by Total, after Sonangol refused to renew the French oil company's contract' (Corkin, 2011), their partnership was not altogether unproblematic. Alves (2012: 100–1) notes that tensions developed in the partnership between Sinopec and Sonangol in 2006 and 2007. In 2006, the disagreement was over the payment of a specific amount considered high by Sinopec as payment for signature bonus to Sonangol, following its successful bid for oil blocks in Angola.

The 'commercial disagreement' in 2007 was reportedly rooted in an aspect of the joint venture agreement between Sinopec and Sonangol for building an oil refinery in Angola. According to Alves (2012: 101), 'whereas Beijing wanted to supply the Chinese market, Luanda envisaged supply to its domestic and Western markets (US and Europe)', leading to Sonangol's decision to terminate the Sonaref project with Sinopec, and award the contract for the building of the refinery to an American firm. This was a clear example of the Angolan petro-elite's decision to act in line with what it considered to be its interest. Following the disagreement, Sinopec suffered some other reversals in its bid to acquire additional oil interests in Angola. Of note was its attempt in 2009 to partner with CNOOC to acquire 20 per cent shares of oil Block 32 put up for sale by Marathon Oil, which was blocked by Sonangol (Alves, 2013: 102). This again underscores the point about the agency of Angola's petro-elite and how they did not hesitate to leverage their ownership of oil over Chinese SOCs. In this regard, China's inroads into the country and its use of credit lines recorded more success in other economic sectors, particularly construction, rather than oil which remains largely dominated by Western oil MNCs such as 'Marathon, Total, Chevron, Texaco, Exxon and BP' (Quigley, 2014; Zhao, 2011).

The evidence suggests that China's presence in the oil and other sectors of the Angolan economy has had to contend with Angolan ministries, the 'strong' Angolan SOC Sonangol, and other institutional arrangements, including the Reconstruction Office (controlled by the president) that ensure that loans and deals offered to China are used in ways that reflect national priorities (Mohan and Lampert, 2013). While there are those who raise issues about the lack of transparency in most of Chinese engagement with Angola, the point remains that the Angolan state and petro-elite play a key role in the engagement with Chinese SOCs. What can be gleaned goes beyond 'a particular form of African political agency' (Mohan and Lampert, 2013: 99), to the integration of the Angolan elite and the NOCs into a transnationalized form of capitalist oil relations based on mutual gains, but decisively mediated by the Angolan state. Most recent figures about oil imports from the continent continue to place Angola as the leading African oil exporter to China, and the third global supplier of China's oil imports. In spite of this, the experience of Chinese SOCs seeking a foothold in Angola's oil fields has been mixed. What is clear is that as is the case in Nigeria, the governing elite is not surrendering its autonomy to decide who gains access to its strategic oil fields, even as Chinese SOCs are learning important lessons and becoming more pragmatic and realistic in the ways they engage the Angolan petro-state.

9.6 The Two Sudans: SOC Success and Losses Wedded to African Agency?

The cases of Sudan, and after the breakaway and independence in 2011, South Sudan, are particularly instructive for understanding the changing dynamics of Chinese SOC engagement with African petro-states. There are several reasons for this. In the first place, Sudan was the first African state where Chinese SOCs struck oil and fully built an integrated oil industry from scratch. The country also hosted China's largest oil investments. At the time the Chinese National Petroleum Corporation (CNPC) arrived in Sudan in the mid-1990s following the retreat of Western oil MNCs, Chinese SOCs were largely unknown outside their country—minnows in the global oil scene (Patey, 2014). Chinese SOCs recorded their first major breakthrough into Africa's oil scene in Sudan in 1996, when CNPC, in partnership with Petronas, Sudapet, Talisman, and India's Oil and Natural Gas Corporation Videsh (OVL), formed the Greater Nile Petroleum Corporation (GNPC) and commenced oil production in southern Sudan, followed by oil exports in 1999 (Obi, 2010: 184). The GNPC was followed by Petrodar Operating Oil Company (PDOC), made up of consortia of China's CNPC, Nilepet, Malaysia's Petronas, Sinopec, and Tri-Ocean Energy of Kuwait also operating in southern Sudan. This process transformed Sudan (before 2011) into the third-largest oil producer in Africa, and one of Africa's top oil suppliers to China. It also afforded Chinese SOCs—in the absence of Western oil multinationals forced out by domestic pressures from human rights groups, Western governments, and insecurity occasioned by civil war (Patey, 2017: 760–1)—the opportunity to develop their capacity and gain valuable experience investing in and building the Sudanese oil industry (Patey, 2014: 111–20).

In spite of the success story of Chinese SOCs in Sudan, there has been a noticeable decline in their fortunes since the independence of South Sudan in 2011. As Patey notes, 'until South Sudan's separation in 2011, which stripped away three-quarters of Sudan's oil resources, Sudan was the third largest oil producer in sub-Saharan Africa after Nigeria and Angola' (2017: 760). The split adversely affected CNPC's fortunes as the SOC could do little but seek to adapt to the new situation in the two Sudans. This case affirms the earlier point of the agency of African petro-states and elites vis-à-vis Chinese SOCs, including the ways in which the former have leverage over the latter. As Patey (2014: 4) notes, 'the violent and unstable politics of oil in Sudan and South Sudan' have restricted Chinese SOCs, which underscores the point about how African petro-states and elites influence China.

Given the geography of oil endowment in the Sudan, the independence of the South where most of the oil is located exposed China, which had long-term relations with Khartoum, to the vagaries of Sudanese politics, which was further complicated first by bickering between the North and South over oil, then by the outbreak of civil war in the South shortly after its independence. Although the CNPC and the Chinese government tried hard to build cordial relations with South Sudan, without necessarily alienating the North, this did not insulate them from the testy relations between both countries. The shutting down of oil fields by the government of South Sudan in 2012 over a disagreement with the North over pipelines through which all the oil was piped for export led to severe losses to Chinese SOCs and brought home the lesson of their vulnerability in rather painful ways. The high-risk nature of Chinese SOC investments in Sudan and South Sudan, and the losses suffered, also show the limits of China's so-called resource diplomacy in Africa.

As it turned out, Chinese SOCs have little or no leverage over either side, and there is very little the Chinese state can do about the situation except to engage in bilateral and multilateral efforts aimed at bringing peace to the Sudans, including the deployment of Chinese UN peacekeepers to both countries. This also reflects the point made earlier in this chapter and affirmed by Patey (2014, 2017; Walker, 2014), relating to the relative autonomy of Chinese SOCs, which are not executing a state-directed agenda, but are clearly driven by a 'corporate agenda to ensure survival and wellbeing by acquiring new oil reserves and production' (Patey, 2014: 82), which translate into profit. With time it is becoming more obvious that Chinese SOCs will have to balance their investment decision-making against the risk factors inherent in African petro-states, not least the political terrain and the interests of competing political elites. At this point the dichotomies that underpin mainstream narratives of China–Africa relations are of limited analytical value. Chinese SOC engagements are primarily driven by the quest for profit, including minimizing risks, while maximizing returns on investments. What we see are changes in the behaviour of SOCs as they seek to pragmatically adjust to or respond to Africa's petro-states and elites. Part of the lessons learnt by Chinese SOCs is not just about developing strategies for cutting their losses in South Sudan after a good run up till 2011, but prioritizing the diversification of its international oil investments away from the emerging high-risk Sudans to other African countries, and other parts of the world.

9.7 Conclusion

China–Africa relations are more complex than is often presented (Corkin, 2015; Wang and Elliot, 2014: 1012–32). In spite of the official rhetoric on both sides, both still have a lot to learn from, and about each other. However, the three case studies in this chapter suggest that a more accurate reading of the trends and prospects of relations partly lie in unravelling some of the 'fictions' embedded in the 'truths' that are often accepted and deployed in some official and media circles or scholarly debates. In the past two decades, Chinese SOCs have gradually established themselves across a growing number of established and emerging African oil-producing countries. With the exception of Sudan, and later South Sudan, Chinese SOCs are fast learning about oil operations on the continent, and also using some of the experiences from the continent to strengthen their international operations elsewhere across the world (Patey, 2017). The success of oil-for-infrastructure in opening up Africa's oil fields to Chinese SOC investments has been somewhat mixed, if not disappointing, following the initial euphoria generated by pundits of a 'looking East' moment in Africa's international development cooperation options.

The changing dynamics of Chinese oil engagements with African petro-states over the past two decades reflects a learning curve at several levels: the accumulation of experiences both in terms of the technologies, management, and risks associated with the complex operations of the oil industry, growing pragmatism in terms of diversifying operations across established and emerging African oil producers, while realizing the limitations of oil-for-development as a strategy for gaining access to Africa's oil and gas fields, and collaborating with Western and non-Western oil companies in tapping into lucrative oil operations in Africa. Perhaps more significant is the observation that rather than being the new 'oil colonizers', Chinese SOCs have had to contend with Africa's governing elites who are acutely aware of the leverage, choices, and autonomy that oil power confers on them and do not hesitate to use it to their advantage either by blocking Chinese SOCs based on strategic calculations, or playing them against other foreign and Western oil companies. This is a further challenge to the SOCs seeking a foothold in an African oil sector that is still dominated by more experienced and sophisticated Western oil companies.

China's evolving relation with Africa continues to reflect a mix of opportunities and challenges. It is mediated by the relative autonomy of Chinese SOCs from the Chinese state, the high premium placed by the governing elites of Africa's petro-states on controlling access to the oil within their countries, including the limitations this places on the capacity of Chinese SOCs to pursue their goals vis-à-vis the agency of African elites. Ultimately, the outcome of China's engagement with Africa will depend on how effectively African states, leaders, and governing elites can purposely use the opportunities presented by the current conjuncture in its ties with emerging Southern powers such as China to strategically advance a holistic developmental project.

Perhaps the building of partnerships between Africa and Asian SOCs alongside strategic engagements of Western 'oil majors' will help catalyze oil and gas production capacities in terms of technological innovation and managerial skills and facilitate the transformation of the continent. The changing dynamics of Chinese engagements with African oil-producing states can either open the space for connecting African agency to a transformative project, or close it. This requires an African agency that is both strategic and transformative, which goes beyond usual rhetoric of 'win–win' partnerships. This project of transformation must be participatory and people oriented, based on the will and desire of a visionary African leadership to integrate a developmental ethos into state–society relations in re-directing the purpose of strategic and productive economic engagements to serve the interests of the African people.

References

Alessi, Christopher and Beina Xu (2015) 'China in Africa', USC US–China Institute, 27 April, https://china.usc.edu/council-foreign-relations-cfr-backgrounders-china-africa-april-27-2015.

Alves, A. C. (2012), 'Taming the Dragon: China's Oil Interests in Angola', in M. Power and A. C. Alves (eds) *China and Angola: A Marriage of Convenience*? Nairobi: Pambazuka, pp. 106–11.

Burgos, Sigfrido and Sophal Ear (2012) 'China's Oil Hunger in Angola: History and Perspectives', *Journal of Contemporary China*, 21(74): 351–67.

Campbell, Horace (2008) 'China in Africa: Challenging US Global Hegemony', *Third World Quarterly*, 29(1): 89–105.

Carmody, Pádraig and Ian Taylor (2010) 'Flexigemony and Force in China's Resource Diplomacy in Africa: Sudan and Zambia Compared', *Geopolitics*, 15(3): 496–515.

Cheru, Fantu (2016) 'Emerging Southern Powers and New Forms of South-South Cooperation: Ethiopia's Strategic Engagement with China and India', *Third World Quarterly*, 37(4): 592–610.

Cheru, Fantu and Cyril Obi (2011) 'Chinese and Indian Engagement in Africa: Competitive or Mutually Reinforcing Strategies', *Journal of International Affairs*, 64(2): 91–110.

Coleman, Polly (2017) 'Top10 Oil and Gas Companies in the World', *Energy Digital Magazine*, 17 March, https://www.energydigital.com/utilities/top-10-oil-and-gas-companies-world.

Corkin, Lucy (2011) 'Uneasy allies: China's evolving relations with Angola', *Journal of Contemporary African Studies*, 29(2): 169–80.

Corkin, Lucy (2015) 'Forum: African Agency in the Context of China in African Relations', *African East-Asian Affairs*, Issue 1 and Issue 2, Forum, June.

French, Howard (2014) *China's Second Continent: How a Million Migrants Are Building a New Empire in Africa*. New York: Alfred A. Knopf.

Hameiri, Shahar and Lee Jones (2016) 'Rising Powers and State Transformation: The Case of China', *European Journal of International Relations*, 22(1), https://journals.sagepub.com/doi/10.1177/1354066115578952.

Hu, Fox, Zijing Wu, and Tara Patel (2012) 'Sinopec Said to Buy Nigeria Oil Blocks from French Total', *Bloomberg*, 7 November. https://www.bloomberg.com/news/articles/2012-11-06/sinopec-said-to-buy-nigeria-oil-blocks-from-french-total.

Kavanagh, Michael (2012) 'Total and Sinopec Agree Nigeria Oil Deal', *Financial Times*, 19 November, https://www.ft.com/content/0f070cfa-3268-11e2-ae2f-00144feabdc0.

Maasho, Aaron (2018) 'Africa Should Avoid Forfeiting Sovereignty to China over Loans: Tillerson', *Reuters*, 8 March, https://www.reuters.com/article/us-usa-africa/africa-should-avoid-forfeiting-sovereignty-to-china-over-loans-tillerson-idUSKCN1GK114.

Manero, Elizabeth (2017) 'China's Investment in Africa: The New Colonialism?' *Harvard Political Review*, 3 February, http://harvardpolitics.com/world/chinas-investment-in-africa-the-new-colonialism/.

Miller, Hugo and Tom Schoenberg (2017) 'Chinese Oil Giant Sinopec Probed by US over Nigeria Bribery Allegations', *Bloomberg*, 30 August https://www.bloomberg.com/news/articles/2017-08-30/sinopec-is-said-to-be-probed-by-u-s-over-nigeria-payments.

Mohan, Giles and Ben Lampert (2013) 'Negotiating China: Inserting African Agency in China–Africa Relations', *African Affairs*, 122: 446.

Obi, Cyril (2010) 'African Oil in the Security Calculations of China in India', in Fantu Cheru and Cyril Obi (eds) *The Rise of China and India in Africa: Challenges, Opportunities and Critical Interventions*. London and Uppsala: Zed Books and the Nordic Africa Institute.

Obi, Cyril (2013) 'Oiling Neocolonialism and Conflict? The Implications of China's Engagement with African Petro-States for Peace and Development', SSRC Think Piece, Social Science Research Council.

Patey, Luke (2014) *The New Kings of Crude: China, India and the Global Struggle for Oil in Sudan and South Sudan*. London: Hurst.

Patey, Luke (2017) 'Learning in Africa: China's Overseas Oil Investments in Sudan and South Sudan', *Journal of Contemporary China*, 26(107): 756–68.

Pillsbury, Michael (2015) *The Hundred Year Marathon: China's Secret Strategy to Replace America's Global Power*. New York: Henry Holt.

Poole, Claire (2018) 'The World's Largest Oil and Gas Companies: Royal Dutch Shell Surpasses Exxon as Top Dog', *Forbes*, 6 June 2018: https://www.forbes.com/sites/clairepoole/2018/06/06/global-2000-oil-gas/#6ac6b4111d1b.

Quigley, Sam (2014) 'Chinese Oil Acquisitions in Nigeria and Angola', American University in Cairo, 1 June, http://schools.aucegypt.edu/huss/pols/Khamasin/Pages/article.aspx?eid=14.

Reuters (2017) 'Exclusive: China's Sinopec Looking to Sell Nigerian Business—Sources', https://www.reuters.com/article/us-china-sinopec-divestiture-exclusive/exclusive-chinas-sinopec-looking-to-sell-nigeria-business-sources-idUSKBN1E01LN.

Sanusi, Lamido (2013) 'Africa Must Get Real about Chinese Ties', *Financial Times*, 11 March, https://www.ft.com/content/562692b0-898c-11e2-ad3f-00144feabdc0.

Taylor, Ian (2014) 'Dependency Redux: Why Africa Is Not Rising', *Review of African Political Economy*, 43(147): 8–24.

Tiffen, Adam (2014) 'The New Neo-Colonialism of Africa', http://blogs.lse.ac.uk/africaatlse/2014/09/26/the-new-neo-colonialism-in-africa/.

Umejei, Emeka (2013) 'Why Did China's Infrastructure for Resources Deal Fail in Nigeria?', *African Arguments*, 2 September, http://africanarguments.org/2013/09/02/why-did-chinas-infrastructure-for-resources-deal-fail-in-nigeria-by-emeka-umejei/.

Vanguard (2018) 'Obaseki, China SINOPEC Sign 5,500 bpd Edo Modular Refinery Deal', 1 January, https://www.vanguardngr.com/2018/01/obaseki-china-sinopec-sign-5500bpd-edo-modular-refinery-deal/.

Walker, Beth (2014) 'How Africa Is Changing Chinese Oil Companies', 10 December, https://www.chinadialogue.net/article/show/single/en/7583-How-Africa-is-changing-Chinese-oil-companies.

Wang, Fei-Ling and Esi A. Elliot (2014) 'China in Africa: Presence, Perceptions and Prospects', *Journal of Contemporary China*, 23(90): 1012–32.

Wenping, He (2007) 'China Policy Balancing', *China Security*, 1(3): 33–9.

XinhuaNet (2018) 'Chinese Firms to Start Building Sub-Sea Pipeline Installation in Nigeria', 13 January, http://www.xinhuanet.com/english/2018-01/13/c_136893514.htm.

Zhao, Shelly (2011) 'The China-Angola Partnership: A Case Study of China's Oil Relations in Africa', *China Briefing*, 25 May, http://www.china-briefing.com/news/2011/05/25/the-china-angola-partnership-a-case-study-of-chinas-oil-relationships-with-african-nations.html.

Zhao, Suisheng (2014) 'A Neo-Colonialist Predator or Development Partner? China's Engagement and Rebalance in Africa', *Journal of Contemporary China*, 23(90): 1033–52.

Zhenxing, Luo (2013) 'A Trilateral Dialogue on the United States, Africa and China: Conference Paper 4', Brookings Institute, Washington DC, https://www.brookings.edu/wp-content/uploads/2016/07/All-China-Oil-Papers-2.pdf.

Zondi, Sikhumbuzo (2017) 'Potential Seen in African Oil, Gas Sector', *China Daily*, 8 August, http://www.chinadaily.com.cn/kindle/2017-10/08/content_32983898.htm.

10

The Political Economy of China's Investment in Nigeria

Prometheus or Leviathan?

Omolade Adunbi and Howard Stein

10.1 Introduction

There has been a growing influence of China globally in the last two decades. One of the major changes shaping China's growing economic and political impact is its 'Going Out' policy which has led to negotiations and the signing of multilateral and bilateral trade agreements across the globe. These agreements have been brokered through the organization of groups such as the Forum on China–Africa Cooperation (FOCAC), established in 2000 as a meeting point to discuss trade between China and Africa. These kinds of interactions have facilitated the growth of economic linkages between China and Africa which, as we have seen in other chapters, have rapidly expanded in the past decade and a half. One way to deal with the massive trade deficit in manufacturing goods which has characterized China–Africa economic relationships is to attract Chinese manufacturing capital. Closely linked to this is to establish special economic zones (SEZs)[1] in African countries.

Proponents of SEZs argue it could draw on Chinese expertise on managing zones, which have been very successful in China in contrast to sub-Saharan Africa where they have generally done poorly for a variety of reasons (Stein,

[1] There is a rather imprecise usage of language in the names associated with zones in Nigeria and elsewhere. They tend to be spatially defined and separated from the broader political territory and often have incentives to operate and produce within these zones with easier access to the international economy for trade and investment purposes. In this chapter terms like export processing zones, free trade zones, and special economic zones are used interchangeably. A more detailed investigation of the taxonomy of zone terminology can be found in Stein (2012).

2012). This could propel sub-Saharan Africa onto the path of industrialization and move the continent away from aid dependency. At the First Ministerial Conference of the Forum on China–Africa Cooperation in 2000, China pledged to share its experience with Africa on investment promotion through SEZs. In 2006, China's president Hu Jintao announced the establishment of three to five SEZs in African countries (FOCAC, 2006). Starting in 2007 Chinese SEZs were established in Zambia, Egypt, Nigeria, Ethiopia, and Mauritius (UNDP, 2015). Zone construction tenders were set in 2006 and 2007.

By February 2015, there were eight to thirty-eight companies operating in all but the Mauritius zone which was partly held up due to disputes over compensation for evicted farmers (Cowaloosur, 2014; Tang, 2016). Since then some zones have continued to attract Chinese companies. In Ethiopia, by 2018 the Chinese-run Eastern Industrial Zone had completely leased or sold all the land in its 233-hectare first phase. There were seventy-nine mostly Chinese companies in the zone, with fifty-six starting operations. The zone produced a wide variety of items including textiles and garments, motor assembly, chemical and soap production, pharmaceuticals, building materials including cement and steel products, shoes, aluminum products, and foodstuffs for both the domestic and export markets. Employment was estimated at 14,700 workers including 1,500 Chinese nationals. However they were having considerable difficult securing the 167 hectares for Phase two from the local government, partly due to protests from evicted farmers and the price that was demanded for the new land (interview with administration office, Eastern Industrial Zone, 25 August 2018).

Nigeria had two Chinese zones established, one in Lekki in Lagos State and another in Ogun State just north of Lagos. The remainder of this chapter maps out the history of Nigerian and Chinese relationships including their economic linkages before turning to a discussion of free trade zones (FTZ) in Nigeria with a specific focus on the two Chinese-run zones. A key focal point will be to present the nature and impact of the Chinese SEZs in Nigeria and determine if China's economic relationship and presence can be seen as a Leviathan, the all-powerful giant monster that devours everything in its path, or should be seen in the spirit of the Greek God Prometheus who brought to humanity the gifts to dramatically improve their livelihoods.

10.2 Nigerian and Chinese Linkages: An Overview

Beijing established diplomatic relations with Lagos in 1971, overcoming the hostility that was associated with Chinese support for Biafra during the Nigerian civil war of 1967–70. A delegation visited Beijing in 1972 and signed an open-ended agreement on trade and technical cooperation. Despite the close relations of the 1970s, Nigeria asserted its foreign policy independence. For example, Nigeria not only became a member of the frontline state but also supported materially and otherwise groups fighting for independence in many Southern African countries. For instance, following the 1975 civil war in Angola, Nigeria supported the Soviet-backed MPLA, while China aligned itself with the FNLA, which was also supported by the United States and CIA. During the Abacha dictatorship years of 1993–8 when Western aid was again cut off because of the abysmal human rights record of the regime, Nigeria adopted a 'Look East' policy, which strengthened the Beijing–Abuja alliance and built trust between the two nations.

Cooperation has continued to the present (see Chapter 4 documenting this historical cooperation for the rest of Africa and Nigeria). Since 1999 when democratic elections started, every Nigerian president has visited China. In 2005, China and Nigeria published a joint communiqué with China announcing Taiwan as an inalienable part of the territory of China. In 2015, China endorsed Nigeria's attempt to become a permanent member of the UN Security Council, while Nigeria supported China's position in territorial disputes in the Pacific region. China has also provided military support in counter-insurgency efforts in the Niger Delta (Ramani, 2016; Umejei, 2015).

Good political relations have spilled over into economics (and vice versa). Historically, there were a number of Hong Kong-based companies that invested in Nigeria after independence. Some originated in mainland China but moved to Hong Kong after the Communist takeover. Two are still operating in Nigeria. The Lee Group produces shoes, bread, plastic bags, steel, and ceramics. The second, Western Metal Products Company Limited (WEMPCO), which is controlled by the Tung family, is in ceramics, building materials, and the hospitality sector, and opened the largest cold-rolled steel mill in Africa in 2015 (Chen et al., 2016.)

In 2006, China and Nigeria signed a memorandum of understanding (MOU) on the establishment of a strategic partnership, which was the first for an African country. The partnership led to an oil-for-infrastructure arrangement, under which Chinese companies were offered first access to oil-processing licences. Presidential visits have led to large Chinese loans. President Jonathan's visit to Beijing in 2013 led to a US$3 billion loan for infrastructure which included expansion of the airports in Lagos, Kano, Abuja, and Port Harcourt. Following President Buhari's visit in 2016, Nigeria was offered an infrastructural loan of US$6 billion.

Chinese companies have increasingly been locating[2] to Nigeria. As of 2013, according to the local investment agency, there were 208 registered Chinese

[2] In May 2018 Nigeria signed a US$6.68 billion contract for the new rail line with the China Civil Engineering Construction Corporation (CCECC).

companies in Nigeria focusing on oil and gas, construction, and telecommunications (Umejei, 2015). By 2016, the number registered with the investment agency had grown to 308 though the numbers could be considerably higher (Sun et al., 2017). Chen et al. (2016) surveyed two sources—the Nigerian Investment Promotion Council (NIPC) and the Chinese Ministry of Commerce (MOFCOM)—for the number of Chinese companies approved to invest in Nigeria and found 221 and 297 respectively though there was no guarantee they actually invested. 141 listed with MOFCOM and ninety-two with NIPC were in manufacturing. Only twenty-one to thirty were overlapping in manufacturing.

Nigeria has also been one of the largest recipients of loans from China (Chapter 7 details many of the Chinese loans contracted by Nigeria and other African countries). Between 2010 and 2015, Nigeria received the fourth-highest amount of loans in Africa from China and the sixth highest over the longer period of 2000–15 (SAIS-CARI, 2018). However, that is likely to have gone up in the wake of the US$7.5 billion dollar loan from China in 2017 for the Lagos to Kano and Lagos to Ibadan railways (Adamu, 2017). As of 2011, they were the second-highest recipient of FDI after South Africa (Umejei, 2015). Between 1995 and 2017, Nigeria has been the second-largest importer of Chinese goods after South Africa. Exports to China have also been in the top five in most years over the same period (UNCTAD, 2018).

10.3 Nigerian–Chinese Trade Relations and Textiles

The Chinese trade relationship with Nigeria has been severely criticized both in the press and in academic writings. Sansui, the former governor of the Central Bank of Nigeria, stated in 2013: 'China takes from us primary goods and sells us manufactured ones. This was also the essence of colonialism.' Others have been equally scathing. Agubamah (2014) writes: 'The relationship between Nigeria and China is not a Win-Win situation as being claimed by China but rather Win-Lose situation as reality shows . . . Nigeria should be wary of being used as a dumping ground for cheap Chinese exports.'

Particularly heavy criticism has focused on the claims that Chinese imports have completely undermined the textile sector. Both China and Nigeria have long histories of textile production dating back to hand weaving in the eighteenth century in the Yangtze valley in China under the Qing dynasty and the city of Kano under the Sokoto Caliphate, which began in 1804. Both were affected by colonialism, foreign ownership, and mechanization in the twentieth century. In China, cotton textiles rapidly expanded after the nationalization following World War II. In Nigeria, the modern history of textiles began in the 1940s and 1950s as part of the textile development scheme centred in Kano and Kaduna with support from overseas capital. The first indigenous factory was commissioned in Kano in 1952. Later the Emir of Kano, with the financial support of Lebanese businessmen, opened a number of factories. Other factories were opened in the 1960s with capital from Britain, Sudan, and the Hong Kong-based CHA group which provided financial support for United Nigeria Textiles Ltd (UNT).

In the 1980s Nigeria had 175 textile plants employing 250,000 people with many more employed as traders and suppliers of cotton and other inputs including thousands of cotton farmers. It accounted for around 25 per cent of manufactured value added with roughly 35 per cent exported to West African countries. However, by the end of the 1980s and early 1990s, production began to decline, while production in China led by FDI in the SEZs dramatically increased.

By 2007, Nigeria had only twenty-six companies still operating in textiles, employing roughly 24,000 people. Closures included early plants like United Nigeria Textiles Ltd. (UNT). Growth of Chinese imports was facilitated by the massive influx of Chinese company representatives to Nigeria and Nigerian traders flocking to China. The numbers by 2008 had reached 50,000 Chinese representatives in Nigeria and 20,000 Nigerians in China (Muhammad et al., 2017; Renne, 2015; Umejei, 2015). Muhammad et al. (2017) go as far as to call this 'Chinese textile imperialism' and blame the decline on the Chinese: 'From this healthy state the textile industry began to decline steadily. This was largely due to cheap imports from China' (p. 676).

Renne (2015) takes a more nuanced view. Nigerian textile production fell apart in the 1980s and 1990s due largely to internal problems though illegal cheap Chinese imports might have been present from the 1970s. The main source of the decline was poor and unstable leadership which failed to provide consistent supporting industrial policy, decline of infrastructure, including the failure to maintain the power grid, and the impact of structural adjustment after 1986 which among other things devalued the currency and made spare parts and modern weaving equipment prohibitively costly.

While Nigerian production declined, the Chinese industry began to prosper after the mid-1980s. The initial success of the four SEZs led to their expansion and the development of SEZ industrial clusters focusing on textile production in cities in Zhejiang and Hebei provinces. They started importing state-of-the-art equipment and producing high-quality textiles in an efficient manner. In 1980, China was the tenth-largest producer of textiles. By 1995, the improved equipment, large low-wage labour force, and modernized infrastructure propelled China to become the largest producer and exporter of textiles in the world. By the late 1990s and early 2000s Chinese textile companies and their representatives had institutionalized new trading practices in Nigeria while fostering the presence of Nigerian trading representatives in China.

What does the data actually show on this and other issues? Data on the general trends in the structure of Nigerian trade with the rest of the world can be used as a basis of comparison with the China–Nigeria trade relationship. The structure of trade is very important from a development perspective. At least since the work of Prebisch (1950) and Singer (1950), development economists have been aware of the need to increase manufacturing exports and the problems with continuing to rely heavily on unprocessed resource exports. Among other things, manufacturing, is subject to increasing returns, is a conduit for the transfer of technology, has higher income elasticities compared with other activities, generates employment, is very tradable, is more heterogeneous which can allow for better market segmentation which helps avoid the price volatility of homogeneous commodities, and can stimulate extensive backward, forward, and demand linkages (Stein, 2013).

What is apparent is the continued problematic dependence of Nigeria on fuel exports and its apparent inability to increase manufacturing exports. Between 1995 and 2017, fuel accounted between 91 an 97 percent of total exports. In 2017 it was above 96 per cent, the highest level since 2006.

The percentage of manufactured goods, except for one year, stayed below 2.5 per cent of the total achieved in 1995. More worrisome is the dramatic decline in absolute dollar terms, with manufacturing exports in 2016 falling by nearly 80 per cent compared to 2014, to a level below 2005 (UNCTAD, 2018).

The import side shows a continued heavy reliance on manufactured goods which averaged 70.5 per cent in 2005–11, dropping slightly to 65.1 per cent from 2012–17. The other significant import is fuel which is quite extraordinary for a major oil exporter and comprises over 20 per cent of imports in 2016 and 2017. This reflects the very low refinery capacity and the need for Nigeria to import massive amounts of petrol and petrol products. In 2017, for example, it was estimated that the country's refining capacity was only 17 per cent of its domestic needs with the rest imported (Reuters, 2017).

Nigeria generated large positive trade balances from 2005 to 2014 that contributed to very healthy reserves as high as US$53 billion in 2008 but still above US$45 billion in 2014 (World Bank, 2018). During the period crude petroleum was on average more than three times the 2000 price level but fell to less than half the 2014 price from 2015–17, leading to the rapid deterioration in the trade balance into negative numbers (UNCTAD, 2018). How do the general trade accounts for Nigeria compare to the trading relationship with China? Tables 10.1 and 10.2 provide data over the same period of 1995 to 2017.

We can see that fuels dominate exports to China though the numbers are not as high in recent years. Chapter 9 also shows the dynamism of China's

Table 10.1. Nigeria–China exports 1995–2017 in US$m, except ratios

Year	Exports of manufactured goods	Manufactured goods/Total	Exports of fuels	Fuels/Total	Total Exports
1995	0.3	0.005455	53	0.963636	55
2000	0.07	0.000348	177	0.880597	201
2005	16	0.030361	491	0.931689	527
2006	11	0.034483	285	0.893417	319
2007	39	0.058824	603	0.909502	663
2008	52	0.095941	433	0.798893	542
2009	63	0.059943	932	0.886775	1,051
2010	239	0.180106	958	0.721929	1,327
2011	270	0.12987	1,497	0.720058	2,079
2012	62	0.032074	1,599	0.827212	1,933
2013	62	0.032856	1,623	0.860095	1,887
2014	48	0.014674	2,703	0.826353	3,271
2015	52	0.037901	959	0.69898	1,372
2016	31	0.034368	588	0.651885	902
2017	87	0.049014	1,300	0.732394	1,775

Source: UNCTAD, 2018

Table 10.2. Nigeria–China imports 1995–2017 and trade balance in US$m, except ratios

Year	Imports of manufactured goods	Manufactured goods/Total	Imports of fuels	Fuels/Total	Total imports	Balance
1995	235	0.975104	0.1	0.000415	241	−186
2000	472	0.936508	8	0.015873	504	−303
2005	1,807	0.913549	16	0.008089	1,978	−1,451
2006	2,989	0.919975	40	0.012311	3,249	−2,930
2007	3,848	0.931268	9	0.002178	4,132	−3,469
2008	6,605	0.930282	18	0.002535	7,100	−6,558
2009	4,721	0.92189	10	0.001953	5,121	−4,070
2010	6,329	0.930051	7	0.001029	6,805	−5,478
2011	7,312	0.874432	53	0.006338	8,362	−6,283
2012	9,019	0.892617	5	0.000495	10,104	−8,171
2013	11,295	0.908981	6	0.000483	12,426	−10,539
2014	14,212	0.928828	75	0.004902	15,301	−12,030
2015	10,873	0.91593	18	0.001516	11,871	−10,499
2016	8,841	0.935061	7	0.00074	9,455	−8,553
2017	10,507	0.909539	49	0.004242	11,552	−9,777

Source: UNCTAD, 2018

oil interest in countries such as Sudan, Nigeria, and other oil-producing countries in Africa. Generally, manufacturing exports have been very low, in the range of 1–3 per cent of total exports, with the exception of 2010 and 2011 when there is likely to have been some re-export of equipment originally manufactured in China. The absolute exports seem to have actually fallen by half in 2016 compared to 2012–13. Overall, primary commodities completely dominate exports to China and in most years exceed 95 per cent of the total (UNCTAD, 2018).

Table 10.2 looks at the import side of the trade relationship with China. What is striking is the very high dominance of manufacturing which is above 90 per cent of total imports over most of the period and well above the figures of Nigerian imports from the rest of the world. What is also striking is the huge trade imbalance in favour of China that is present in every year in the table. The imbalance has been extremely high since 2006 and has fallen in the range of 75–92 per cent of total trade. The contrast with the world figures is striking since Nigeria has been running a trade surplus with most of the rest of the world over most years.

Table 10.3 provides a detailed representation of the structure of imports with China. What is interesting is that the largest import category is machinery, which has the potential for technology transfer and the expansion of manufacturing production for the export and domestic markets. Chen et al. (2016) in their survey of Chinese companies and Chinese-linked companies in Nigeria report that cost is the major factor in purchasing Chinese machinery though they tend to be less durable. There was some evidence of technology transfer in the servicing and maintenance support provided by Chinese suppliers.

As discussed above, a good deal has been written on the negative impact of the dumping of Chinese textile and clothing exports in Nigeria. What is evident is that clothing and textile imports, even when footwear is included, have not been the dominant manufacturing import falling into a range of between 10 and 17 per cent after 2012. However, there has still been a significant increase both in absolute dollar imports of textiles and clothing and in the percentage of total manufacturing imports from China. A key question is: how do the imports of Chinese textile and clothing compare to overall imports of this group from all countries? At what point, if at all, does it become dominant? Data on the trends in manufacturing production from the CBN annual report indicate that by 2002 the volume of the production of synthetic-fibre-based textiles was down by 56 per cent and cotton by 24.1 per cent compared to 1990 (CBN, 2006). By the fourth quarter of 2007 synthetic-based textiles fell an astonishing 77.1 per cent below their level of 1990 and cotton textiles were down 27 per cent. In both cases this is prima facie evidence of significant de-industrialization in the sector in line with the claims above. The figures in the CBN annual report for 2011 show continued problems in the sector, with production falling to only 69.1 per cent of the 1990 level in cotton textiles. Synthetic fibres recovered to 41.2 per cent in the first quarter of 2011 compared to the 1990 base year.[3]

---

[3] The figures in the latest CBN annual reports available (2014 and 2015) combine footwear and textiles; hence it is difficult to identify the trends in textiles only.

Table 10.3. Nigeria–China detailed structure of imports of manufactured goods 1995–2017 in US$m, except ratios

Year	Imports of manufactured goods	Machinery	Machinery/Total manufactured goods	Textiles and clothing	Textiles, clothing and footwear	Textiles, clothing, and footwear/Total manufactured goods
1995	235	59	0.251064	9	16	0.068085
2000	472	133.3	0.282415	53	72	0.152542
2005	1,807	590	0.326508	187	235	0.13005
2006	2,989	1,062	0.355303	168	178	0.059552
2007	3,848	1,315	0.341736	157	177	0.045998
2008	6,605	2,748	0.416048	215	263	0.039818
2009	4,721	1,891	0.400551	194	231	0.04893
2010	6,329	2,600	0.410807	296	361	0.057039
2011	7,312	2,990	0.408917	530	613	0.083835
2012	9,019	3,085	0.342056	813	925	0.102561
2013	11,295	3,628	0.321204	984	1,198	0.106065
2014	14,212	4,789	0.336969	1,745	2,045	0.143892
2015	10,873	3,644	0.335142	1,151	1,370	0.126
2016	8,841	3,090	0.349508	1,356	1,588	0.179618
2017	10,507	4,748	0.451889	598	720	0.068526

Source: UNCTAD, 2018 (machinery = machinery and transport-road vehicles and other transport)

We can draw some comparisons on the role that China played relative to the declines cited in the CBN data. From 1995 to 2002, Chinese imports were a very small portion of textile and clothing imports, averaging 9.8 per cent. Between 2003 and 2007, when domestic production fell further, total world imports rose by more than 50 per cent on average. The Chinese share significantly increased to 27.5 per cent of the total. During 2008–11 imports more than doubled compared to the 2003 period. The Chinese share rose slightly to 28.5 per cent. In the latest period, 2012–17, imports again soared by 50 per cent on average per year. During the period Chinese imports dominated and averaged 62.4 per cent of the total (UNCTAD, 2018).

How do we interpret this data relative to the claims above of the harmful role of Chinese imports? Clearly the period of the greatest de-industrialization in the textile sector occurred prior to the large surge in imports from China. To suggest as Muhammed et al. (2017) do that Nigerian textile production was in a healthy state until the Chinese came along is simply untrue. Clearly the Renne (2015) argument which points to the severe decline in the sector prior to the surge of Chinese imports is accurate. However, it is also clear that Chinese imports have become dominant, particularly since 2011. As pointed out above, Chinese and Nigerian trading networks have become entrenched in the textile trade.

Renne (2015) argues that one way forward is to get the Chinese to relocate their production to Nigeria. In her view, one possibility is in the Chinese-run SEZs, including the Lekki Free Trade Zone which has plans to expand into textile production and could become a model for a new trade zone focused on textiles in Kano. However she also warns:

> Nonetheless, those seeking to establish export trade zone projects in Nigeria face many challenges. In the case of the Lekki Free Trade Zone in Lagos, there have been delays due to financing constraints and a lack of clarity over partnership terms within the Chinese consortium, misunderstandings between Nigerian partners and the Chinese consortium over funding and infrastructure responsibilities, and local Lekki community members' protests over terms of resettlement . . . These problems exemplify more general problems with the implementation of Chinese-Nigerian Free Trade Zones, which include miscommunication and a lack of transparency on both sides, as well as distrust by Nigerians about the possibility that economic zones will become Chinese enclaves and be used to bring Chinese goods for resale in Nigeria. (Renne, 2015: 228)

On the latter point, Shin and Eisenman (2012) reported that the Chinese Zhejiang company Yuemei, which used to export textiles to Nigeria, decided in 2008 to build a textile-focused industrial park and by 2013 had attracted twenty companies undertaking complementary activities such as spinning, dyeing, weaving, sewing, knitting, and embroidery, However, Chen et al.

(2016) visited the site and contested the claims in Shin's World Bank working paper. In fact Yuemei was renting space in the Calabar Free Trade Zone. Only two Chinese companies had located there. One company embroidering cloth closed after a year in 2011 and the other involved with dyeing textiles ceased operation in 2014. Both stayed through 2014 and were evicted on suspicion that they were more interested in trans-shipping products from China without paying duties.

One positive sign is that the contribution of manufacturing to GDP has been rising in recent years. In 1980 manufacturing GDP was 9.1 per cent of total GDP. By 2005–10 it had fallen to the range 6.2–6.5 per cent. However, by 2014 it reached nearly 10 per cent of GDP before falling back in 2016 to 9.2 per cent (UNCTAD, 2018). Textile, apparel, and footwear production has increased its contribution to manufacturing from 9.9 per cent in 2010 to 22.8 per cent in 2016. In nominal value-added terms, this sector was responsible for nearly a third of the rise in manufactured GDP and was the second-highest contributor to the increase after food, beverages, and tobacco (CBN, 2016). What role did the EPZs or Chinese capital play, if any, in this expansion of this sector? How much is this a reflection of changing government priorities, and what role is China playing in this?

10.4 New Government Measures in Support of Industry

In 2010 Nigeria undertook a renewed effort to support industry. Nigeria adopted an ambitious long-term development plan, Vision 2020, which focused on propelling the country into the list of the top twenty economies of the world by 2020. The Industrial Sector-Specific Action Plan focused on the technologically driven and globally competitive manufacturing sector, with a high level of local content and a higher contribution to GDP. Five sub-sectors were prioritized, including chemicals and pharmaceuticals, basic metal, iron and steel and fabricated metal, food, beverages and tobacco, textiles and apparel and leather footwear, along with non-metallic mineral products. Priorities were set based on ease of development relative to the country's comparative advantage and because they had the highest potential to provide raw materials for other key industries (Jereome, 2013).

The government also took steps to stem the bottlenecks associated with the importation of industrial inputs, including the establishment of a task force on trade facilitation to encourage compliance with multilateral and regional decisions, reduce the numerous check points in border areas, and better harmonize the activities of all government agencies involved in foreign trade. In addition to some efforts to involve the private sector in power generation, the federal government inaugurated several financing schemes in support of industry. In 2010, the federal government, through its agencies and parastatals, inaugurated several financing schemes to unlock the potential of the industrial sub-sector. Packages included a 100 billion naira Textile Intervention Fund (150 naira/US$) and other funds to support power rehabilitation, small and medium-sized enterprises, and a restructuring facility for manufacturing with the 200 billion naira Commercial Agriculture Credit Scheme, the 300 billion naira Power and Aviation Intervention Fund, the 200 billion naira Refinancing/Restructuring Facility for the manufacturing sector, and the 200 billion naira Small and Medium-Scale Enterprises Credit Guarantee Scheme. By the end of December 2010, the restructuring/refinancing facility had been fully used and the textile fund had facilitated the re-opening of two textile firms in Kaduna and Kano states. The first recipient was UNT, which was reopened in December 2010 after being closed for four years (Madushir, 2010).

In 2014, the National Industrial Revolution Plan (NIRP) was launched. Its aim was to expand the country's industrial capacity through agricultural-related industries, metal and mineral processing, oil and gas, construction, and light manufacturing. The federal government also initiated the National Cotton, Textile, and Garment Policy under the NIRP. The policy was aimed at reducing the US$2 billion bill on imported textiles and garments. It was also targeted at increasing export earnings of at least US$3 billion annually, attracting FDI, and expanding the country's seed cotton production capacity from 300,000 MT in 2013 to 500,000 MT in 2015. Policies used in support of the goals were two-year duty and VAT waivers for textile manufacturing between 2015 and 2019, as well as a three-year tax holiday.

The textile sector gained further support in 2015 with the constitution of a special committee to help the country's ailing cotton and textile industry. The Nigeria Investment Promotion Commission (NIPC) partnered with the National Cotton Textile and Garment (CTG) Policy Committee to promote 'made-in-Nigeria' products. The Central Bank of Nigeria committed to providing a concessionary loan under the Real Sector Support Facility (RSSF) to operators in the sub-sector (CBN, 2014, 2015). Jereome (2013) wrote:

> A country's industrial policy is the dynamic tool for stimulating and regulating its industrial development process. It is a blueprint detailing the objectives and strategies for optimally attaining the goals of non-primary production, particularly manufacturing, taking into consideration the resource endowment of the country in terms of labour, land, capital, entrepreneurship, international goodwill ... Nigeria currently has no coherent national industrialization strategy. Rather, what exist are sectoral plans for sugar, cement and automobiles. (Jereome 2013: 4)

While clearly Nigerian support for industry has now gone beyond these sectors into new areas including textiles, there are still questions about the coherency of Nigeria's industrial strategy, including the nature and role of Chinese investment. One other area neglected in Nigeria and other countries has been the integration of export-processing zone policy into a broader industrial policy strategy (Stein, 2012). The CBN's industrial policy and institutional support section of their annual report (2010–15) does not mention zones anywhere. In line with Renne's (2015) suggestion, can free trade/export-processing zones become a centre for attracting Chinese capital into textiles and other manufacturing areas? In the remainder of this chapter we turn to the issue of zones, with a focus on the two Chinese-run entities in Lekki and Ogun.

10.5 Export Processing Zones in Nigeria

Nigeria has a history of free trade zones that dates back to the 1990s. In 1989, the administration of General Ibrahim Babangida introduced a Structural Adjustment Programme (SAP) as part of his economic and political reform. SAP as an economic policy has as part of its objectives the establishment of export processing zones (EPZs) as a way to attract FDI. Thus, in 1992, a Nigeria Export Processing Zone Authority Act No. 63 was enacted as a continuation of the economic liberalization policy of the Babangida administration. The Nigeria Export Processing Zone Authority (NEPZA) was given the responsibility to establish, regulate, licence, and monitor EPZs and in 1992, Calabar EPZ was created, followed by Onne oil- and gas-free zone in 1997. In 2001, due to the poor performance of the zones (there were only two operating in the country then), Nigeria altered their export focus in the zones to become free trade zones focused on logistics, tourism, commerce, agriculture, and ICT. They no longer needed to export 75 per cent of their production but could sell to the domestic market without restriction though customs duties on imported raw material needed to be paid. With the new arrangement, public, private, and jointly owned zones became possible.

More importantly, with the expansion of the responsibilities of NEPZA, new regulatory practices in the establishment of EPZs were put in place. These included a new regime of incentives that guarantees: 'complete holiday from all federal, state and local government taxes, rates, and levies; duty free importation of capital goods, machinery/components, spare parts, raw materials and consumable items in the zones; 100 per cent foreign ownership of investments; 100 per cent repatriation of capital, profits and dividends; waiver of all imports and export licenses; waiver on all expatriate quotas; one-stop approvals for permits, operating licenses and incorporation papers; and permission to sell 100 per cent of goods into the domestic market . . . However, when selling into the domestic market, applicable customs duty on imported raw material shall apply. For prohibited items in the custom territory, free zone goods are allowed for sale provided such goods meet the requirement of up to 35 per cent domestic value addition.' In addition the zones guaranteed to 'minimize delays in the movement of goods and services' and rent free land during the first six months of construction for government-owned zones (NEPZA, 2013).

By 2018, NEPZA lists a dozen active free zones in seven states and twenty-one which are inactive for various reasons. More than half were established before 2009 but are yet to operate. Five others come under the authority of the Oil and Gas Free Zones Authority of Nigeria (NEPZA, 2018; OGFZA, 2018) which was set up in 2000. Some are converted ports like Warri, which became a zone in 2011. The oldest is Onne which started in 1997 (first under NEPZA) and now boasts that it has licensed more than two hundred companies to operate in the zone.

Though the literature is fairly limited, it points to a generally underwhelming performance in the zones in Nigeria. Farole (2011) found that EPZ had no real effect on the export structure of the country with only a tiny contribution to non-oil exports (4 per cent). Only 25 per cent of production was destined for exports. The employment generated was lower than all but one of the five African countries surveyed. Only 29 per cent of inputs were locally sourced and only 46 per cent of managers were Nigerian nationals, which was the lowest of all countries surveyed. Stein (2012) focused on the Onne Oil and Gas Free Trade Zone and found that through 2007, ten years after it started, Onne was mostly being used as a warehouse for oil and gas companies. While there were roughly 7,000 jobs generated there was little or no evidence of any processing beyond a cement plant, a pre-cast panel factory, and a pipe-coating and machine shop.

More recently, Harry (2016, 2018) surveyed fifty-four randomly selected enterprises in four zones in 2015—Calabar, Onne, Snake Island, and Lagos—and found minimal local sourcing of materials or technological inputs with an overwhelming focus on labour and assembly. While respondents knew there was a value-added policy, 'the level of variation in the participants' views concerning the minimum value addition policy at the zones suggests that some of them may not be familiar with the actual value addition requirements of their zones' (Harry, 2018: 169). There were few products exported out of the zone. Nearly 70 per cent of the respondents indicated they exported less than 20 per cent of their production (Harry, 2016).

10.6 Chinese Sezs in Nigeria

10.6.1 *Lekki Zone*

The Lekki Free Zone (LFZ) is located in the Ibeju-Lekki area of Lagos, about 60 km to the east of central Lagos, and covers a total area of 16,500 hectares. The governor of Lagos State, Bola Tinubu, first conceived of the idea of a free trade zone in Lekki in 2004 and allocated an initial 1,000 hectares for the project. In 2006, the Lagos state government, in partnership with a Chinese consortium, established the LFTZ. The partnership is being managed by the Lekki Free Zone Development Company. In the partnership, China–Africa Lekki Investment Company owns 60 per cent, the Lagos state government 20 per cent, and the Lekki Worldwide Investment Ltd., a local private investment group, owns 20 per cent. The members of the Chinese group are the China Railway Construction Corporation, China Civil Engineering Construction Company, Nanjing Jiangning Economic and Technology Development Company, which developed a zone in China, and Nanjing Beyond International Investment and Development Company (a private equity firm), along with the China–Africa Development Fund. The 20 per cent ownership by the China–Africa Development Fund (CADF) highlights the importance that the Chinese government attaches to the Lekki Free Trade Zone.

Construction for Phase I began in 2007 though there was a delay due to disagreement between the Chinese and Nigerians on financing and operations. In March 2007 an MOU, negotiated by the Lagos-based Social Economic Rights Action Center, SERAC, was signed with nine communities that were displaced by the project. A few communities frowned at the MOU, claiming that where they were to be relocated belonged to another community. In an interview conducted in July 2018, a leader of a youth group in the community stated that 'we are not happy with how we are being displaced by this project. They promised us jobs but we have not seen the jobs'.[4] Evictions began in 2009 and are still continuing. Promises made to the communities, many informants said, have not been fulfilled.

The Master Land Use Plan was developed in 2010 in China by the Shanghai Tongji Urban Planning and Design Institute with little or no input from Nigerians. Phase 1 (South-West Quadrant), made up of general mixed industries, was completed first while construction of the Phase 2 (South-East Quadrant) petroleum refinery commenced in 2014. Phase 3 (North-West Quadrant) is proposed for workers' housing, while Phase 4 (North-East Quadrant) is proposed as a new town providing employment, and commercial, residential, community, and recreational activities. The master plan was

---

[4] Interview conducted at the LFTZ, July 2018.

completed three years after construction began which was contrary to Nigerian law.

In 2010 the China Civil Engineering Construction Company was given the clear leadership in the project. The Chinese head of the project was experienced and first came to Africa to work on the Tazara Railroad in the 1970s. The deputy director is Nigerian. The approach taken, 'one axis, six parks', is aimed at light manufacturing, textile production, warehousing, logistics, car assembly, and real-estate development facilities. In the initial phase, the Chinese consortium committed US$200 million to the zone and the local public and private investors, US$65 million (Lawanson and Agunblade, 2018; UNDP, 2015).

A report by UNDP (2015) indicates that the Chinese government continues to put a high priority on making Lekki successful and there are frequent visits by the Chinese embassy and frequent exchanges between Nigerian representatives and stakeholders from the headquarters in Beijing.

It is seen by Chinese companies as a gateway to West African countries, which will attract interest. A key element is the construction of the long-delayed Lekki deep-sea port in the zone which finally began construction in March 2018. The aim is to complete the US$1.5 billion project by 2020 and to build it to a depth of 16 metres which would dramatically exceed the current maximum of 13 metres in existing Nigerian ports and make it competitive with most other ports in West Africa (LFTZ, 2018).

As of April, 2015, there were twenty-one companies operating with a total investment of US$12.4 million in areas that include construction, manufacturing, trading, and assembling. Another seventy-nine companies were registered and expected to commence within a year. However, as of August, 2018, the website only listed twenty-six operating enterprises. From interviews in July 2018, we learned that only twenty-two were operational. All but three were Chinese owned. As we can see in Table 10.4, of the twenty companies listed as operating in 2015 only eight were listed on the website in 2018, which is an extraordinarily high turnover rate. Table 10.4 also provides a list of the eighteen new firms. What is quite evident is the absence of a critical mass of companies in any one area which precludes clustering and its potential positive effects. What is also evident is that the number of companies listed is well below the expectations expressed to the UNDP investigators in 2015 when they interviewed key people operating the zone.

The zone's website claims there are 116 companies in the zone, though it would appear that these are mostly still companies that have expressed an interest and registered with the zone. One of the advantages of the zone is that it has its own power generation (gas-fired power plant started in 2015) and along with the Ogun zone it is the only free trade zone that can provide power 24/7 (Tang, 2016). In an interview in July 2018, an executive of one of the

Table 10.4. Companies listed as operating in Lekki FTZ in UNDP, 2015 and new companies 2018

Companies	Year started	Type of operation	Listed August 2018?
Wanhao Doors	2013	Manufacturing	No
MC Lighting	2013	Assembling	No
H & Y FZE	2013	Trading (human wigs)	Yes
Sinotruck FZE	2013	Assembling (trucks)	Yes
Loving Homes	2013	Assembling (furniture)	Yes
Crown Nature	2013	Manufacturing (clothing)	Yes
CCECC	2010	Construction	Yes
CRCC	2010	Construction	No
Rainfield	2013	Manufacturing	No
Candel	2013	Manufacturing (pesticides)	Yes
Cosmos	2013	Manufacturing	No
Rungas	2014	Manufacturing	No
Greengrapes	2014	Manufacturing	No
KKL	2012	Manufacturing	No
Dabu Pump	2013	Assembling	No
Hannover Boton	2015	Assembling (sockets and switches)	Yes
Ruyat Oil	2015	Manufacturing	No
New Energy	2015	Manufacturing	No
St. Nicholas	2014	Services (hospital)	Yes
Engee Pet	2014	Manufacturing	No

New Companies

Zhi Jiang Nigeria	Construction
Datang International	Furniture
Huachang Steel and Engineering	Steel structures
ZCC Construction	Construction
Bollore Transport & Logistics	Telecomms products
Golden Dream	Baby diapers and insecticides
Aslan Nigeria	Furniture
Asia Africa International	Assembling (trucks)
Yulong Steel Pipe	Steel pipes
Hidier Power	Assembling generators
Coral Beach	Real estate
RWE Africa LPA	LPG containers
CNSS	Assembling (mobile phones)
Jiangsu Geology and Engineering	Construction
PCCM	Spraying accessories
Longrich	Cosmetics
Sunshine Commodity	Houseware
Henan	Building materials

Source: UNDP, 2015; LFTZ, 2018

companies in the zone confirmed that one of the major attractions of the zone is the level of security obtainable in the area. The executive, whose company started in the zone in 2017, projects a sense of optimism about the zone. When asked if he had started making a profit, he proudly responded with a 'yes' while also acknowledging that there are some hiccups. Overall, he is happy with the performance of his company and his Nigerian staff. The zone is a gated community with areas earmarked as living quarters. While some apartments are still under construction, the Chinese expatriates occupied some of the completed housing units.[5]

However for Nigerian workers there was no local housing or transportation to the zone, which was a huge impediment to accessing labour. Companies had to bus labour in or provide dormitories, dramatically increasing the expenses. There were also no training facilities nearby and no linkages to any vocational training schools anywhere. There were also serious communication issues. The first teams appointed by the Chinese needed translators, had no experience building FTZs and 'were overwhelmed, with weather conditions, with the working environment and working attitude of the locals and they simply did not understand how to deal with the Ibeju-Lekki community' (UNDP, 2015: 30). Other problems included port delays, difficulties in repatriation of capital gains by companies, and inconsistencies in policy and decision-making which have caused companies to cancel their investments.

Disputes with the local community have also overshadowed the project, with violent outbreaks and demonstrations that led to the killing of the director of the project in October 2015. Through 2015 more than 50 per cent of the community had not been compensated for loss of land and crop production, contrary to the 2009 agreement. Rates of compensation were ridiculously low. Almost half of those who were compensated received less than US$67. An initial 750 hectares that were to go to the evicted villagers was land already occupied by others, leading to tension in the community. Another 375 hectares were allocated in 2014, but as of 2015 none had been occupied by the evicted villagers (Lawanson and Agunblade, 2018).

In 2015, total employment created was listed as 551 for the companies surveyed (UNDP, 2015). By July 2018, the workforce had risen to above a thousand. Roughly eighty-six were non-Nigerian (LFTZ, 2018).

10.6.2 *Ogun-Guangdong Zone, Igbesa*

The Ogun-Guangdong Free Trade Zone is located in Igbesa, Ogun State, 30 km from Lagos's Murtala Muhhamed International Airport and 31 km from Nigeria's main seaport located in Apapa, Lagos. Igbesa is a farming community noted for its proximity to Agbara Industrial Estate—a private industrial estate established by a businessman, Chief Adeyemi Lawson, but later acquired by the Ogun state government in 1976. Chief Lawson had wanted to create an industrial and residential estate that was not only very close to

---

[5] Interview conducted at the LFTZ, July 2018.

Lagos but also accessible to countries such as the Republic of Benin, Togo, and Ghana in the West African sub-region. The proximity of Agbara town to Badagry, the border town with Cotonou in the Republic of Benin, made economic sense considering that the Economic Community of West African States, (ECOWAS) had been introduced in 1973 to facilitate easy business access for West Africans. The industrial estate thrived for a while until it was devastated by the economic liberalization policies of the 1980s and 1990s that saw the introduction of the Structural Adjustment Programme. While Agbara Industrial Estate thrived, the Igbesa community prospered in its farming activities while also providing support services to those who worked in the industrial estate. Thus, it was not surprising when the Ogun state government, in collaboration with a Chinese consortium, decided to locate a free trade zone in Igbesa.

The original feasibility study of the zone was undertaken in China and used successfully in a bid by the Xinguang International Group consortium in 2006. The original suggestion was to locate the zone in Imo State near the Niger Delta. However, for security reasons, after some Chinese were kidnapped in Imo State, and political reasons (former President Obasanjo was from Ogun State and the former governor of the state was staunchly pro-Chinese) the zone was relocated to Ogun. This delayed the start of the project with construction only beginning in the first half of 2009. Delays were also caused by the failure of the Ogun state government to provide promised infrastructure.

A total of 100 km^2 were promised for the zone including 40 km^2 allocated for displaced people. The start-up area consisted only of 250 hectares (2.5 km^2), though Phase 1 was to cover 20 km^2 in total. By June 2013, there were thirty-four enterprises registered in the zone, coming from Nigeria, China, Lebanon, and India (Brautigam and Teng, 2013; Chen et al., 2016).

Ogun-Guangdong Free Trade Zone was issued with a Certificate of Occupancy for 20 km^2 in January 2008, and the start-up area was nearly exhausted by the end of 2017. In 2017, the erection of a perimeter fence for the second phase was completed. The most recent data indicates that there were fifty registered enterprises, twenty-six of which have started operation, with another twelve under construction. Around four thousand Nigerians were employed in the zone. The cumulative investment is US\$325.3 million. Main enterprises included Hewang Packing & Printing FZE, Goodwin Ceramic FZE, China (Nigeria) Glass FZE, Sun Ceramic FZE, Winhan Industry FZE, Panda Industry FZE, and Green Power Utility FZE. The industries involved included ceramics, packaging, glass, furniture, electricity generation, electrical appliances, steel structures, wigs, and hardware (Economic and Commercial Counselor's Office, 2018).

10.7 Evaluation of the Operation of Chinese Companies in the Zones

A key element of the zones is their potential to attract Chinese manufacturing companies. Chinese FDI has the potential not only to provide employment, expand manufactured exports, and increase demand linkages but also to contribute more broadly to the structural transformation of the country through technology transfer and spillovers to domestic companies. They are a potential source of labour skills development and training, entrepreneurship, and management upgrading, and have the potential to dramatically increase value added. FDI can develop forward and backward linkages which will allow domestic companies to be better integrated into global supply chains. The clustering of firms around a particular industry is a way to concentrate many of these effects.

There have been few studies of the impact of Chinese manufacturing companies in Nigeria either inside or outside zones. Chen et al. (2016) undertook interviews in July 2014 with a sample of twenty firms, including six in the Ogun-Guangdong FTZ and two of the four or five firms that are in Lekki. Chinese firms in Ogun-Guangdong FTZ were mostly in light industry including furniture manufacturing, ceramics, and paper and packaging. There were also two steel and construction firms in the zone. Two Chinese companies in Lekki were in furniture and light bulbs. There was no evidence of clustering among the Chinese firms in either of the zones or for that matter anywhere in the country. In fact one of the main reasons for the Chinese to come to Nigeria was the absence of competition. Clustering was one thing they directly wanted to avoid because it was seen as a source of potential competition.

One key way that spillovers into the local economy can occur is through joint ownership arrangements with local companies. However, there were very few examples of joint ventures in the study. There were cases where Chinese firms provided a small minority share to local government officials but this was seen as a quid pro quo for political reasons or to access land at favourable rates. There were virtually no examples of true partnerships with an equitable division of investment, responsibilities, and profits, nor were Chinese companies seriously sourcing local suppliers for inputs; hence there was little evidence of backward linkages.

Upholstered furniture was banned from being imported in 2004. There was a 35 per cent local requirement content for furniture produced in FTZs to be sold to the local market. This was being met with low-value bulk items like wood. However, higher-quality and higher value-added items like leather were still being imported from China. Steel producers simply used local scrap. In general, when used, the relationship 'seemed shallow'. Companies complained of the poor local quality of inputs. However no Chinese businessperson interviewed in the Chen et al. study had actively invested in upgrading the technology or skills of their local suppliers.

Total employment in the seven companies surveyed in the zones for which data is presented is 1,496, or an average of 214 people per firm. However only two firms employed above the average number. In all the companies, 84 per cent of employees on average were from the local population and 16 per cent Chinese.

10.8 Conclusions

The chapter has examined the nature of the Chinese and Nigerian economic relationship with a focus on the new Chinese SEZs created in 2006. We began with the debates in the literature on the characterization and impact of the growing Chinese presence in Africa and the associated expansion in financial and trade relationships. Among other things, there is little doubt that Chinese loans have dramatically expanded infrastructure on the continent. However the price is the growth of indebtedness.

There is also some question of the nature of trade relations in which China has overwhelmingly exported manufactured goods and imported mostly oil and other primary commodities which are raw and unprocessed. Nigerian relations with China have followed a similar pattern, though with worse trade deficits and even higher levels of manufactured goods compared to the rest of sub-Saharan Africa.

The chapter finally turns to the issue of SEZs which have been very successful in attracting FDI to China and have been centres for the manufacturing-focused transformation of the country. In general Nigerian zones which were organized in 1992 have performed poorly. Two new zones were created in 2006/7 with great fanfare and in the hope that they would draw on Chinese expertise in running zones and attract Chinese manufacturing capital which would have the potential to generate jobs, foreign exchange through exports, technological spillovers, management and labour training, and forward, backward, and demand linkages.

To date, neither the image of Leviathan or Prometheus seems to capture the impact of China. The zones have been disappointing, attracting a small number of Chinese firms, while generating little employment, and few of the other desired effects. Nigerian manufacturing exports have not expanded. There has been a rise in the manufacturing portion of GDP which is probably largely the result of government intervention to rehabilitate closed companies.

The government of Nigeria is keen on diversifying its economy and expanding the manufacturing sector, and has improved some of its industrial policies. However, to date they have done a poor job of integrating their export-processing zone strategy into their approach to industrialization. To some degree, handing management and control of some zones over to the Chinese might look good politically (for China and Nigeria) but is far less important from an economic perspective compared to putting policies in place to attract FDI and domestic investors and to ensure their activities are developmentally enhancing.

References

Adamu, A. (2017) 'Nigeria Secures $7.5 Billion Loan from China for Rail Project', *Amaechi Premium Times*, 6 February, https://www.premiumtimesng.com/news/headlines/222767-update-nigeria-secures-7-5-billion-loan-china-rail-project-amaechi.html.

Agubamah, E. (2014) 'Bilateral Relations: Periscoping Nigeria and China Relations', *European Scientific Journal*, 10(14), https://eujournal.org/index.php/esj/article/view/3392.

Brautigam, D. and T. Xiaoyang (2013) '"Going Global in Groups": Structural Transformation and China's Special Economic Zones Overseas', *World Development* 63: 78–91.

Central Bank of Nigeria (CBN) (2006) 'Annual Report'. Lagos: CBN.

Central Bank of Nigeria (CBN) (2014) 'Annual Report'. Lagos: CBN.

Central Bank of Nigeria (CBN) (2015) 'Annual Report'. Lagos: CBN.

Central Bank of Nigeria (CBN) (2016) 'Statistical Bulletin', http://www.cbn.gov.ng/documents/statbulletin.asp.

Chen, Y. et al. (2016) 'Learning from China? Manufacturing, Investment, and Technology Transfer in Nigeria', Working Paper 2, January, SAIS-CARI.

Cowaloosur, H. (2014) 'Land Grab in New Garb: Chinese Special Economic Zones in Africa', *African Identities*, 12(1): 94–109.

Economic and Commercial Counselor's Office in Nigeria, Ministry of Commerce, People's Republic of China (2018) 'Ogun-Guangdong Free Trade Zone', 12 July, http://english.mofcom.gov.cn/article/newsrelease/counselorsoffice/westernasiaandafricareport/201807/20180702765135.shtml.

Farole, T. (2011) *Special Economic Zones in Africa: Comparing Performance and Learning from Global Experience*. Washington, DC: World Bank.

FOCAC (2006) 'Forum on China–Africa Cooperation: Beijing Action Plan (2007–2009)', FOCAC Secretariat, Ministry of Foreign Affairs of China, Beijing.

Harry, D. (2016) 'Export Processing Zones and Economic Diversification in Nigeria, 2001–2013', *Journal of Political Science and Leadership Research*, 2(2), https://iiardpub.org/get/JPSLR/VOL.%202%20NO.%202%202016/EXPORT%20PROCESSING%20ZONES.pdf.

Harry, D. (2018) 'Value Addition Policy in Nigeria's Export Processing Zones: Lessons from the Asian Economies', *Mediterranean Journal of Social Sciences*, 9(3): 165–72.

Jereome, A. (2013) 'Industrial Policy, Institutions and Mechanisms in Africa: The Case of Nigeria: Synthesis Report'. Background Paper, UNECA, Annual Report.

Lawanson, T. and M. Agunblade (2018) 'Land Governance and Megacity Projects in Lagos, Nigeria: The Case of Lekki Free Trade Zone', *Area Development and Policy*, 3(1): 114–31.

Lekki Free Trade Zone (LFTZ) (2018) http://lfzdc.org/.

Madushir, I. (2010) 'Hopeful Ex-Workers Besiege UNTL, Kaduna for a New Lease of Life', *Sunday Trust*, 19 December.

Muhammed, M., M. Mukhtar, and G. Lola (2017) 'The Impact of Chinese Textile Imperialism on Nigeria's Textile Industry and Trade: 1960–2015' *Review of African Political Economy*, 44(154): 673–82.

Nigeria Export Processing Zone Authority (NEPZA) (2013) 'Investment Opportunities in the Nigeria Free Zones Presented by: Nigeria Export Processing Zones Authority for the Polish Trade Delegation' 11 April, http://www.goafrica.ecms.pl/files/?id_plik=47.

Nigeria Export Processing Zone Authority (NEPZA) (2018) website, http://www.nepza.gov.ng/.

Oil and Gas Free Trade Zone Authority of Nigeria (OGFZA) (2018) https://www.ogfza.gov.ng/.

Prebisch, Raul (1950) 'The Economic Development of Latin America and its Principle Problem' UN ECLA.

SAIS-CARI (2018) 'Data' http://www.sais-cari.org/data/.

Ramani, S. (2016) 'China-Nigeria Relations: A Success Story for Beijing's Soft Power', *The Diplomat*, 12 July, https:/thediplomat.com/2016/07/china-nigeria-relations-a-success-story-for-beiings-soft-power/.

Renne, E. (2015) 'The Changing Contexts of Chinese-Nigerian Textile Production and Trade 1900–2015', *Textile*, 13(3): 212–33.

Reuters (2017) 'Nigeria Refining Capacity Is One-Sixth of Needs, Says Oil Minister', Reuters, 8 June, https://www.reuters.com/article/nigeria-oil/nigeria-refining-capacity-is-one-sixth-of-needs-says-oil-minister-idUSL8N1J55PS.

Shinn, D. H. and J. Eisenman (2012) *China and Africa: A Century of Engagement*. Philadelphia, PA: University of Pennsylvania Press.

Singer, Hans (1950) 'The Distribution of Gains between Investing and Borrowing Countries', *American Economic Review* 40: 473–85.

Stein, H. (2012) 'Africa, Industrial Policy and Export Processing Zones: Lessons from Asia', in A. Noman et al. (eds) *Good Growth and Governance in Africa: Rethinking Development Strategies*. Oxford: Oxford University Press, pp. 322–44.

Stein, H. (2013) 'Africa and the Perversities of International Capital Flows', in Philip Arestis and Malcolm Sawyer (eds) *Economic Policies, Governance and the New Economics (International Papers in Political Economy)*. Basingstoke: Palgrave Macmillan, pp. 165–208.

Sun, I. Y., K. Jayaram, and O. Kassiri (2017) 'Dance with the Lions and the Dragons: How Are Africa and China Engaging and How Will the Partnership Evolve?' McKinsey and Company Report, June, https://www.mckinsey.com/featured-insights/middle-east-and-africa/the-closest-look-yet-at-chinese-economic-engagement-in-africa.

Tang, X. (2016) 'Does Chinese Employment Benefit Africans? Investigating Chinese Enterprises and their Operations in Africa', *African Studies Quarterly*, 16(3/4): 107–28.

Umejei, E. (2015) 'China's Engagement with Nigeria: Opportunity or Opportunist?' *African East Asian Affairs: The China Monitor* Issue 3 and Issue 4 December.

UNCTAD (2018) 'On-Line Stats', http://unctad.org/en/Pages/Statistics.aspx.

UNDP (2015) 'If Africa Builds Nests, Will the Birds Come? Comparative Study on Special Economic Zones in Africa and China', Working Paper Series, No. 6.

World Bank (2018) 'International Debt Statistics: Nigeria', http://datatopics. worldbank.org/debt/ids/country/NGA.

11

Agreements and Dispute Settlement in China–Africa Economic Ties

Won L. Kidane

11.1 Introduction

Unencumbered by a history of an intrinsically hierarchical relationship,[1] contemporary China–Africa economic ties appear to have the benefit of being on balance politically horizontal,[2] economically reciprocal,[3] and systemically transactional.[4] A corpus of credible evidence now demonstrates

---

[1] See Philip Snow (1987) *The Star Raft: China's Encounter with Africa*, xiii–xiv. Africa's historical relationship with the now developed world of the North has either been colonial or post-colonial aid dependency. The nature of the historical relationship has never permitted purely reciprocal and mutual beneficial commercial interactions to flourish.

[2] See Ian Taylor (2006) *China and Africa, Engagement and Compromise*, 30–1.

[3] See Deborah Brautigam (2009) *The Dragon's Gift: The Real Story of China in Africa*, 308 ('China does not claim to know what Africa must do to develop.')

[4] Although the overwhelming majority of Western media coverage continues to pursue a narrative of exploitation and neo-colonialism akin to Africa's past relations with the West, more than a decade of data now shows measurable advantages to Africa's economy. Ironically, it is not unusual to see reports containing evidence of progress in a creatively negative light. Consider David Pilling's *Financial Times* article entitled 'Chinese Investment in Africa: Beijing's Testing Ground' (13 July 2017). He reports on the one hand that: 'A few numbers illustrate the shift. In 2000, China–Africa trade was a mere $10bn. By 2014, that had risen more than twenty-fold to $220bn according to the China–Africa Research Initiative at Johns Hopkins School of Advanced International Studies in Washington, though it has fallen back because of lower commodity prices. Over that period, China's foreign direct investment stocks have risen from just 2 per cent of US levels to 55 per cent, with billions of dollars of new investments being made each year. China contributes about one-sixth of all lending to Africa, according to a study by the John L Thornton China Center at the Brookings Institution.' The article goes on to cite Jeffrey Sachs, director of the Earth Institute at Columbia University, as describing Chinese investment in Africa as 'the most important single development for Africa in this generation.' But the overall message of the article is that China is using Africa as a testing ground. The article reads in relevant part: 'Beijing's engagement with Africa is more multi-layered than is often recognised. China, Ms Jing says, has used Africa almost as a testing ground for its growing international ambitions, whether through peacekeeping missions or construction of the roads, ports and railways intended to bind much of the developing world, via a new Silk Road, to the Middle Kingdom.' The article is available at https://www.ft.com/content/0f534aa4-4549-11e7-8519-9f94ee97d996 (accessed 13 February 2018).

that overall the economic ties of the last couple of decades have been remarkably successful in the areas of trade,[5] investment,[6] and other types of commercial relations.[7] The trajectories also appear optimistic.[8]

Beginning from ancient times, political boundaries notwithstanding, commercial relations have always been ordered by law albeit customary law in Africa,[9] *Li* and *Fa* in China,[10] Sharia in the Islamic world,[11] *lex mercatoria*,[12] Common Law or Civil Law[13] in Europe. The existing post-colonial modern world order is, however, largely formalistic and moderately harmonized. It

[5] The Johns Hopkins University School of Advanced International Studies China–Africa Research Initiative (CARI) keeps useful compilation of data. It shows a rapid growth since 2002 with few occasions of slowing down. The data shows that the volume of trade between China and Africa has comfortably been around US$200 billion since around 2015. See data on China–Africa Trade at http://www.sais-cari.org/data-china-africa-trade/

[6] Although the estimates of Chinese investment in Africa tend to defer, almost every source acknowledges that it is considerable. For example, David Dollar of Brookings Institute suggests that in 2014 China had about as much ODI in Africa (US$32 billion) as in the United States (US$38 billion). David Dollar (2016) *China's Engagement with Africa: From Natural Resources to Human Resources*, 34. CARI estimates Chinese investment between 2003 and 2014 at approximately US$124 billion. See CARI, Excel spreadsheet at http://www.sais-cari.org/data-chinese-and-american-fdi-to-africa (last visited 7 October 2016). The American Enterprise Institute and the Heritage Foundation's China Global Investment Tracker estimates China's total investment in sub-Saharan Africa to be US$241.75 billion (Scissors 2018). See China Global Investment Tracker's Data at https://www.aei.org/china-global-investment-tracker/. CARI further estimates that China has loaned approximately US$86 billion to African states during the same time period for various projects (2001 to 2014). See http://www.sais-cari.org/data-chinese-loans-and-aid-to-africa. Chinese-financed projects include railways (see *The Guardian*, 'Next Stop the Red Sea: Ethiopia Opens Chinese-Built Railway to Djibouti' at https://www.theguardian.com/world/2016/oct/06/next-stop-the-red-sea-ethiopia-opens-chinese-built-railway-to-djibouti (5 October 2016)), power plant transmissions (see e.g. Modern Power Systems, 'The Chinese in Africa: An Electrifying Story: A New International Energy Agency Report Shows that Chinese Companies Are Leading the Way in the Electrification of Sub-Saharan Africa' at http://www.modernpowersystems.com/features/featurethe-chinese-in-africa-an-electrifying-story-4991516/ (26 August 2016)), ports (see D. Smith (2015) 'China Denies Building Empire in Africa' at https://www.theguardian.com/global-development/2015/jan/12/china-denies-building-empire-africa-colonialism (Chinese firms are carrying out a US$653m (£430m) expansion of the main airport in the capital, Nairobi), and various other projects.

[7] Chinese companies' construction contracts have now exceeded US$50 billion. See CARI data at http://www.sais-cari.org/data-chinese-contracts-in-africa. Moreover, CARI data shows that from 2000 to 2015, Chinese loans to African interests amounts to US$94.4 billion. See http://www.sais-cari.org/data-chinese-loans-and-aid-to-africa.

[8] A 2015 report sponsored by Baker and McKenzie projects that China will invest up to US$1 trillion in Africa in the next decade or so: see H. Warren (2015) 'Spanning Africa's Infrastructure Gap: How Is Development Capital Transforming Africa's Project Build-Out'.

[9] For a comprehensive treatment of this subject, see generally, T.Olawale Elias, *The Nature of African Customary Law* (1956).

[10] See John W. Head and Yanping Wang (2005) *Law Codes in Dynastic China: A Synopsis of Chinese Legal History in the Thirty Centuries from Zhou to Qing*, 35–50.

[11] For a comprehensive treatment see Raj Bhala (2011) *Understanding Islamic Law* (Sharia).

[12] For definition see Bloomberg Law at https://definitions.uslegal.com/l/lex-mercatoria/ ('Lex mercatoria refers to a body of oral, customary mercantile law which developed in medieval Europe and was administered quite uniformly across Europe by merchant judges, adjudicating disputes between merchants.')

[13] For a comprehensive treatment see generally, René David and John E. C. Brierley, *Major Legal Traditions of the World Today* (1985).

expects formal rules and institutions for the ordering of economic affairs of the scale and complexity represented by China's contemporary relations with Africa.

This chapter identifies and critically appraises China's use of agreements to order its economic relations with its African counterparts, and the mechanisms of dispute settlement that these agreements envision. The term 'agreements' is used in its broadest sense to include not only state-to-state international treaties but also transnational commercial and infrastructure contracts concluded between Chinese state-owned enterprises and African governments or other African-owned interests.

This chapter is divided into four further sections. Section 11.2 offers a cultural note on China and Africa's understandings of law and legal institutions in light of Western notions that each has experienced in its own ways. We then delineate the contemporary substantive rules contained in China–Africa trade, investment, and commercial agreements, followed by description and evaluation of the dispute settlement provisions contained in each category of agreements (with profiles of some recent cases for purposes of demonstration). The final section offers a brief recap of the discussions and concludes with a few recommendations for improvement.

11.2 Agreements in China–Africa Economic Ties: A Cultural Note

No matter what form they take, legally enforceable agreements are essentially exchanges of promises. The meaning that various societies attach to them could be different. In Western societies, cultural proverbs such as 'promises must be kept though the heavens fall' are enforced through legal principles such as the parol evidence rule. The parol evidence rule, an elementary legal notion as it were, considers written contracts as the entirety of the parties' understandings and excludes all exogenous evidence to prove the nature and content of the contract in question.[14] Scholars who have had sufficient opportunity to study the cultural nuances involved in agreements between Western and Eastern interests note the differing understandings that each side assigns to agreements or contracts with a degree of amusement. For example,

---

[14] Wex Legal Dictionary/Encyclopedia describes it thus: 'The parol evidence rule governs the extent to which parties to a case may introduce into court evidence of a prior or contemporaneous agreement in order to modify, explain, or supplement the contract at issue. The rule excludes the admission of parol evidence. This means that when the parties to a contract have made and signed a completely integrated written contract, evidence of antecedent negotiations (called "parol evidence") will not be admissible for the purpose of varying or contradicting what is written into the contract.' Available at https://www.law.cornell.edu/wex/parol_evidence_rule.

Dean Philip McConnaughay, who spent ten years as the head of a major US firm in Tokyo and several years as dean of the Peking University's School of Transnational Law in Shenzhen writes: 'Asian and Western parties to a commercial transaction may both understand clearly the terms of their agreements but still hold [entirely] differing conceptions of the [meaning and effect of their] contract.'[15] He further notes that Asians regard contracts as ' "relational" in the same sense that Western commercial relationships are "legal" '.[16] And as such, for Asian culture 'situational and circumstantial considerations prevail . . . over contractual terms and expectations, conflict avoidance and negotiation or conciliations prevail over all-or-nothing adjudication, and custom and usage (along with the rest of these values) prevail over written law'.[17]

Former International Court of Justice president T. O. Elias had a similar observation vis-à-vis African and European understandings of legal rules and disputes. He notes in particular: 'The ultimate purpose of law in a society, be it African or European, is to secure order and regularity in the conduct of human affairs and ensure the stability of the body politic. Where there is a divergence in the approach is that whereas African law strives consciously to reconcile the disputants in a lawsuit, English law often tends to limit itself to the bare resolution of the conflict by stopping at the mere apportionment of blame as between the disputants.'[18] The fundamental difference is therefore, '[The African judgement] is a judgment by agreement intended to resort and preserve the social balance, and differed materially in principle from a judgment in European courts, which is a judgment by decree intended to enforce the legal rights of one party to the complete and permanent exclusion of the other, whatever the effect on the social equilibrium may be.'[19]

The existing conceptions of agreements, laws, and legal institutions in Africa and China may be deeply rooted in tradition but are not purely traditional. They have undergone centuries of transformation through interactions with the Western world, both voluntarily and involuntarily, but they are by no means totally Westernized. As the renowned French comparatist, René David, opines, the superimposition of colonial law in Africa has

---

[15] Philip J. McConnaughay (2001) 'Rethinking the Role of Law and Contracts in East–West Commercial Relations', *Virginia Journal of International Law*, 41: 427, 440 (quoting in part Arthur T. von Mehre (1984) 'Some Reflections on Japanese Law', *Harvard Law Review*, 71: 1486, 1494, n. 25).

[16] ibid., 443.   [17] ibid.

[18] T. Olawale Elias (1956) *The Nature of African Customary Law*, 268–9.

[19] ibid., quoting Arthur Philip (1945) *Report on Native Tribunals*, Ch. IV, para. 188–92. Further noting that 'The native method would tend to adjust disturbances of social equilibrium to restore peace and goodwill, and to bind or rebind the two disputing groups together in a give-and-take reciprocity. The European method would tend to widen the gulf between two groups by granting all the rights to one of them to the exclusion of the other, because it would in general concern itself with acts and legal principles and take no cognizance of social implications.' ibid., quoting Arthur Philip, *Reports on Native Tribunals in Kenya*, 176.

resulted in the 'complete deformation' of customary law.[20] Although China did not have the exact same experience, as China modernized its laws, 'the confucianization of the law' remains a part of it.[21] As Professor James Nafziger writes, 'Today, the Chinese continue to be concerned about the propriety and attitudinal change just as they are intent on rapidly developing formal law.'[22]

It is within this complex historical and cultural milieu that China and Africa are now attempting to order their economic relations by formal agreements, laws, and legal institutions. The following section details the sources and contents of the available substantive norms that govern China–Africa trade, investment, and other types of commercial interactions.

11.3 China–Africa Economic Agreements and Substantive Contents and Norms

For purposes of legal analysis, China–Africa agreements could be broadly classified into trade agreements, investment agreements, commercial agreements, and other types of agreements. Since 2000, China–Africa economic relations have been coordinated under the Forum on China–Africa Cooperation (FOCAC).[23] Although it has been nearly two decades since its initiation, no effort seems to have been made to transform FOCAC into a formal economic partnership agreement of any kind. All types of agreement discussed herein are thus necessarily distinct and sectoral.

11.3.1 *Trade Agreements*

At the most general level, China and forty-seven African member states trade within the World Trade Organization's (WTO) legal regime.[24] The preponderance of the world's trade today takes place within the WTO legal framework. Although the WTO itself is a relatively recent addition to the world order (1995), 'it is not so young'[25] because the principles it is predicated on

---

[20] René David and John E. C. Brierley (1985) *Major Legal Traditions of the World Today*, 561.

[21] This notion represents the inclusion of the teachings of Confucius described in James Zimmerman (2010) *China Law Deskbook: A Legal Guide for Foreign-Invested Enterprises*, 36–8. ('To the confucianist, legal institutions were secondary to the judgment of moral men.' p. 40.)

[22] James A. R. Nafziger and Ruan Jiafang (1987) 'Chinese Methods of Resolving International Trade, Investment, and Maritime Disputes', 619, 624.

[23] Comprehensive information on China–Africa economic relations is available on FOCAC website at http://www.focac.org/eng/.

[24] See WTO, Membership list and map at https://www.wto.org/english/thewto_e/whatis_e/tif_e/org6_e.htm.

[25] K. C. Kennedy (2008) *International Trade Regulation, Readings, Cases, Notes, and Problems*, 5.

developed over a period of several decades beginning from the end of the World War II under the General Agreement on Tariffs and Trade (GATT).[26] Created by a binding multilateral treaty[27] for the purpose of providing 'common institutional framework for the conduct of trade relations'[28] in goods, services, and intellectual property,[29] the WTO enshrines some basic substantive principles, most notably: (1) the most-favoured nation (MFN) treatment; (2) national treatment; (3) tariff reduction on imports; (4) elimination of quotas; and (5) transparency of trade-related domestic laws.[30]

Technically, China and African member states of the WTO carry on their trade relations under these principles. In reality, however, many of these principles are supplanted by China's unilateral trade concessions and bilateral trade agreements with more than forty African states.[31] Presumably WTO compatible,[32] these trade concessions and bilateral agreements,[33] according to the Chinese Ministry of Foreign Commerce, offer qualifying African states preferential treatment including duty-free privileges to nearly all imports from Africa to China.[34] As yet, China has not taken a meaningful step to formalize its trade relations by free trade agreements with Africa. As of this writing, the first such effort is underway with Mauritius.[35] If it materializes, the China–Mauritius FTA could signal a significant step in formalizing China's

---

[26] General Agreement on Tariffs and Trade, 55 UNTS 194 (30 October 1947). Comprehensive information on GATT and WTO is available on the official website of the WTO at https://www.wto.org/. For scholarly commentary, see generally, J. H. Jackson (2000) *The Jurisprudence of GATT and the WTO: Insights on Treaty Law and Economic Relations*.

[27] See 'Agreement Establishing the World Trade Organization', on the WTO website at <http://ww.wto.org/. There are approximately sixty associated agreements and decisions, for a total of 550 pages. See the WTO's legal texts at www.wto.org/english/docs_e/legal_e/legal_e.htm.

[28] WTO Treaty, Article II.

[29] The texts of all these agreements are available on the official website of the WTO.

[30] See Kennedy (2008), 4.

[31] See Chinese Ministry of Foreign Commerce sources at http://english.mofcom.gov.cn/article/zt_minister/lanmua/201102/20110207420927.shtml.

[32] Although WTO compatibility of regional trade agreements is in principle not optional, a combination of expansive reading of the exceptions and lack of feasible enforcement has made the issue of compatibility a rarely raised matter. Indeed, some have suggested that the large number of preferential treatments contained in regional and bilateral trade deals have converted the WTO's MFN principle into LSN (Least Favoured Nation) principle. See Report by Consultative Board to the Director-General Supachai Panitchpaki (2004) 'The Future of the World Trade Organization: Addressing Institutional Challenges in the New Millennium' (2004), para. 60, reproduced in Kennedy (2008), 435–6.

[33] One such example is the Sino-Ethiopian Agreement for Trade, Economic and Technological Cooperation (1996). [The text of this agreement is not publicly available. Text available with the author]. References to China's other bilateral trade agreements (not including any African states) are available at http://www.china.org.cn/business/node_7233287.htm#a5 but texts are not available.

[34] See Chinese Ministry of Foreign Commerce sources at http://english.mofcom.gov.cn/article/zt_minister/lanmua/201102/20110207420927.shtml

[35] See China's free trade agreements at http://fta.mofcom.gov.cn/enarticle/chinamauritiusen/enmauritius/201712/36683_1.html (In November 2016, China and Mauritius announced the launch of the FTA Joint Feasibility Study which becomes the first joint feasibility study China has ever launched with an African country. The study showed that signing the FTA is in line with

trade relations with African states and may even offer a possible model, if done well, for future use.

11.3.2 Investment Agreements

Unlike international trade, international investment does not benefit from a multilateral treaty regime.[36] As a result, nations order their investment relations through bilateral investment treaties often called BITs. BITs are essentially reciprocal promises by and between the contracting states for the benefit of their respective nationals, natural or juridical. They set forth international rules or introduce external standards for the treatment of foreign investors in each other's territories. As of this writing, China has concluded BITs with thirty-five African countries.[37] Of the thirty-five concluded BITs, sixteen have come into force.[38]

When China began concluding BITs as it was opening up in the early 1980s, its principal focus was primarily to attract investment from the developed world of the North. As such, a great majority of the thirty BITs that it signed in the 1980s was with European nations, with only one with an African state (Ghana).[39] Unlike most, if not all, developing countries, China pursued its BIT programme using its own BIT model that changed considerably over time. The model that China concluded in the 1980s, called first-generation BIT,[40] was rudimentary but contained certain basic principles such as non-discrimination, MFN, fair and equitable treatment, some compensation for expropriation, but not the principle of national treatment.[41]

---

both the interests of China and Mauritius and will help further deepen the bilateral trade and economic relations between China and Mauritius.

As China's first free trade area with an African country, the completed China–Mauritius free trade area will not only help further expand the bilateral trade and investment exchanges between China and Mauritius, and will inject fresh momentum to the transformation and upgrade of the relationship between China and Africa and promote the Belt and Road Initiative in Africa.)

[36] The reasons for the absence of a multilateral investment treaty are complex and no attempt is made here to elaborate; however, it is useful to note that there is an element of power relations meaning that the economically powerful nations would prefer to negotiate with less developed nations individually rather than in groups, which may include developed countries. See, e.g. Jeswald W. Salacuse (2010) 'The Emerging Global Regime for Investment', 427, 464.

[37] The list and texts of almost all 145 Chinese BITs including the thirty-four African BITs are available on the official website of UNCTAD at http://investmentpolicyhub.unctad.org.

[38] ibid.   [39] See list and treaty status at http://investmentpolicyhub.unctad.org.

[40] See Norah Gallagher and Wenhua Shan (2009) *Chinese Investment Treaties*, 35 (describing the three generation of Chinese BITs with an emerging fourth one).

[41] See, e.g. China–Ghana BIT (12 October 1989); see also China–Sweden BIT (29 March 1983). It must be noted here that although China used its own model BOT text, there was notable variability within the model. At last one closer study of these BITs has concluded that the variability did not demonstrate a North–South or South–South bias. See Won Kidane (2016) 'China's Bilateral Investment Treaties with African States in Comparative Context', pp. 141, 175–6.

Chinese BITs concluded in the 1990s, called second generation, add a modified form of national treatment. A good example of what is called a modified national treatment clause is the following: 'Either Contracting Party shall, to the extent possible, accord treatment in accordance with the stipulations of its laws and regulations, to the investments of the investors of the other Contracting Party the same as that accorded to its own investor.'[42] Although this provision is contained in some of the second-generation BITs, its permissive formulation and limited use has made it an unremarkable distinguishing feature. The main difference between the two generations is on dispute settlement (see Section 11.4).

Chinese BITs concluded since 2000 are modern in the sense that they include not only the basic principles of non-discrimination, MFN, fair and equitable treatment but also national treatment.[43] They also enshrine what is called the Hull Rule[44] for expropriation.[45]

In legal terms, therefore, Chinese investors in some African nations, and investors of some African nations in China benefit not only from each other's domestic investment laws but also from external or international standards of treatment contained in these BITs.

In addition to the protection that emanates from these state-to-state investment treaties, investors or other Chinese entities doing business in Africa or African persons or entities doing business in China almost invariably order their affairs through commercial or other types of private agreements no matter who is on the other side; that is to say whether the other contracting party is a state agency or instrumentality, a state-owned enterprise or a purely private person or entity. The Section 11.3.3 takes a brief look at these commercial agreements.

---

[42] China–Iceland (31 March 1994), Article 3(3).

[43] See e.g. China–Uganda BIT (27 May 2004).

[44] The Hull Rule requires 'prompt, effective and adequate compensation'. For a discussion see Frank G. Dawson and Burns H. Weston (1962) '"Prompt, Adequate, and Effective": A Universal Standard of Compensation?', 727, 733–4.

[45] See China–Uganda BIT (27 May 2004), Article 4.

Expropriation

1. Neither Contracting Party shall take any measures of expropriation or nationalization or any other measures having the effect of dispossession, direct or indirect, of investors of the other Contracting Party of their investments in territory, except for the public interest, without discrimination and against compensation.

2. Any measures of dispossession which might be taken shall give rise to prompt compensation, the amount of which shall be equivalent to the real value of the investments immediately before the expropriation is taken or the impending expropriation becomes public knowledge, whichever is earlier.

3. The said compensation shall be set not later than the date of dispossession. The compensation shall include interest at a normal commercial rate from the date of expropriation until the date of payment. The compensation shall also be made without delay, be effectively realizable and freely transferable.

11.3.3 *Commercial Agreements (Infrastructure)*

According to data compiled by CARI, in 2016 alone, Chinese companies entered into construction contracts worth US$50 billion.[46] The Addis Ababa–Djibouti[47] and Nairobi–Mombasa rail projects are examples of mega Chinese projects.[48] Operationalizing any one of these projects requires a series of contracts and sub-contracts ranging from financing agreements to construction to management. Each contract presumably sets forth the basic terms of the agreement, choice of law, judicial forum selection, and alternative mechanisms of dispute settlement such as arbitration.

Because these contracts are not publicly available, the contents cannot be analysed here; however, a few foundational points are worth highlighting. First, although these agreements are in principle arm's length, given the element of hierarchy inherent in providing the financial resources and know-how, it is fair to expect that they manifest themselves in the contracts both in terms of the substantive contents and dispute resolution. Second, major international project contracts often use form contracts such as model contracts published by the International Federation of Consulting Engineers (Fédération Internationale des Ingénieurs-Conseils) (FIDIC). These kinds of contracts regulate the details of the relationship including the allocation of risk, claims procedures, milestones, supervision, performance bonds, dispute settlement, and so on. The Chinese international infrastructure agreements would presumably follow this or similar form contracts with the required modifications. Third, because most of the projects are financed and executed by Chinese companies, it is fair to assume that there would be some level of uniformity of terms. Finally, some anecdotal evidence suggests that in at least some of these contracts, Chinese law is selected as the applicable law and dispute settlement is referred to China International Economic and Trade Arbitration Commission (CIETAC) in Beijing or some other Chinese arbitral institution.

The terms of agreements are demonstrations of the perception and reality of the inherent balance of power between the contracting parties, and as such are excellent indicators of the sustainability of the relationship. That is because they offer clear and enforceable evidence of the exact power balance.

---

[46] See CARI data at http://www.sais-cari.org/data-chinese-contracts-in-africa.

[47] See Andrew Jacobs (2017) 'Joyous Africans Take to the Road, with China's Help' (reporting the project's cost as US$4 billion).

[48] Conor Gaffey (2017) 'Kenya Just Opened a $4 billion Chinese-Built Railway, Its Largest Infrastructure Project in Fifty Years' (reporting the project's cost as US$4 billion).

11.3.4 *Other Types of Agreements*

China also has other types of bilateral agreements with African states, including judicial assistance treaties, taxation, and currency treaties. China has entered into at least thirty-six judicial assistance treaties including with at least five African states.[49] These treaties cover such areas as court judgement enforcement (thirty-three of thirty-six), the taking of evidence (thirty-six of thirty-six), service of process (twenty-eight of thirty-six), arbitration (twenty-eight of thirty-six), information exchange (thirty-six of thirty-six), criminal (nineteen of thirty-six), and judicial record (one of thirty-six).[50] A good example of China–Africa judicial assistance treaties is the one signed between China and Ethiopia on 4 May 2018.[51] This treaty covers such areas as reciprocal enforcement of each other's courts' judgements (articles 21–27), arbitral awards (articles 28–31), service of judicial documents (article 9–12), and taking of evidence (articles 13–19). These provisions appear standard with no notable peculiarities.

China has signed at least 104 bilateral tax treaties as of 2016; fourteen of these are with African states.[52] These countries include Botswana, Egypt, Zambia, Zimbabwe,[53] and South Africa.[54] The agreements seek to harmonize the tax laws and avoid double taxation.[55]

Chinese tax treaties are reportedly based on the OECD Model Tax Convention and the UN Income and Capital Model Tax Convention.[56]

---

[49] Ratification status is available at http://www.fmprc.gov.cn/web/ziliao_674904/tytj_674911/wgdwdjdsfhzty_674917/t1215630.shtml.

[50] For a discussion of these treaties and more references see generally, King Fung Tsang (2017) 'Chinese Bilateral Judgment Enforcement Treaties', 1, 5–7.

[51] Copy on file with author.

[52] See Chinese government sources at http://www.chinatax.gov.cn/eng/n2367726/c2370422/content.html.

[53] See http://www.internationaltaxreview.com/Article/3120687/New-landscape-of-Chinese-tax-treaties.html.

[54] The text of the China–South Africa Tax Treaty is available at http://www.chinatax.gov.cn/n810341/n810770/c1153605/part/1153607.pdf. Its basic task is to eliminate the possibility of double taxation. One of the core provisions states: ARTICLE 23

METHODS FOR ELIMINATION OF DOUBLE TAXATION
Double taxation shall be eliminated as follows:

(a) in China, where a resident of China derives income from South Africa the amount of the South African tax paid on that income in accordance with the provisions of this Agreement, may be credited against the Chinese tax imposed on that resident. The amount of the credit, however, shall not exceed the amount of the Chinese tax on that income computed in accordance with the taxation laws and regulations of China;

(b) in South Africa, Chinese tax paid by residents of South Africa in respect of income taxable in China, in accordance with the provisions of the Agreement, shall be deducted from the taxes due according to South African fiscal law. Such deduction shall not, however, exceed an amount which bears to the total South African tax payable the same ratio as the income concerned bears to the total income.

[55] ibid.

[56] http://www.internationaltaxreview.com/Article/3120687/New-landscape-of-Chinese-tax-treaties.html

Although these treaties are model and principle based, great variability is to be expected. Some have caused concerns about their equitability.[57]

China's currency agreements also appear to be on the rise.[58] It is reported that Angola, Ghana, Nigeria, South, Africa, Zimbabwe, and Zambia, among others use the renminbi as their reserve and settlement currency.[59] The use of the renminbi is presumably regulated by agreements, the texts of which do not appear to be publicly available.

11.4 Dispute Settlement in China–Africa Economic Agreements

Economic agreements designed to regulate the behaviours of two or more contracting parties do not always achieve their objectives in the ways desired and anticipated by both or all parties. A certain percentage of agreements inevitably lead to disagreements, and a smaller percentage of those escalate to legal dispute requiring formal resolution. In modern times, the number of formal disputes is often one indicator of the scale and complexity of the economic relations. For example, before opening up, China did not have many, if any, trade, investment, or commercial disputes with foreign entities because the economy was at a standstill and there were limited or no foreign interests doing business in China. As its economy grew, the number of economic disputes of all types grew exponentially. A good demonstration is provided by CIETAC's caseload statistics. It shows that in 1985, it administered a total of thirty-seven cases. By 2016, that number grew to 2,183, of which 485 involve foreign-related cases.[60] Similarly, but to a less extent, the Cairo Regional Center for International Commercial Arbitration (CRCICA) has also registered a rise in the number of cases over the last decade. For example, the total number of cases filed with the CRCICA in 2008/9 was 637.[61] That number rose to 1,161 by 2016.[62] As the scale of the economic relations between China and Africa increases so will the number of disputes. With this reminder, this section focuses on formal dispute settlement

---

[57] See, e.g. 'KRA Says Kenya Risks Losing Billions in China Tax Treaty', *Daily Nation* (3 December 2017) at https://www.nation.co.ke/business/996-4212418-52miiaz/index.html (The taxman says the country risks losing billions of shillings in tax exemptions if the deal, signed in Nairobi on September 21 but yet to be enforced, is not amended.)

[58] See http://www.un.org/africarenewal/magazine/august-2014/chinese-yuan-penetrates-african-markets.

[59] ibid.

[60] See CIETAC statistics at http://www.cietac.org/index.php?m=Page&a=index&id=40&l=en.

[61] See CRCICA Annual Report for 2008/9, p. 9, available at http://crcica.org/FilesEnglish/Annual%20Report_2016-10-31_08-59-10_0.pdf.

[62] See CRCICA Annual Report 2016, p. 4, available at http://crcica.org/FilesEnglish/Annual%20Report_2017-05-31_11-51-17_0.pdf.

mechanisms in trade, investment, and commercial agreements between China and African parties.

11.4.1 *Trade*

The principal dispute settlement mechanism in world trade today is the WTO dispute settlement system. The WTO has an elaborate and perhaps relatively successful dispute settlement mechanism. This system grew out of the GATT dispute settlement mechanism.[63] The WTO has an independent treaty on dispute settlement to which every member state is required to accede as a condition of membership. It is called Dispute Settlement Understandings (DSU).[64] The DSU's twenty-seven articles set forth the details of the dispute settlement mechanism. Without getting into the details, a case is at first referred to the Dispute Settlement Body (DSB), which is the General Assembly itself. And the DSB sets up a panel for the resolution of the particular dispute. The panel's resolution would be adopted by the DSB unless all members decided to reject it unanimously. The losing party would have an opportunity to appeal to the seven-member Appellate Body.[65]

China has been an active participant since it joined the WTO.[66] As of this writing, China has had fifteen cases as complainant, thirty-nine cases as respondent and 142 cases as third party.[67] Only the United States and the European Union have been more active participants.[68] Africa's participation is limited, with South Africa having the largest number of cases—five cases as respondent and seven as third party.[69] The complainants against China were Canada, the European Union, Guatemala, Japan, Mexico, and the United States.[70]

---

[63] For a description of the evolution of the GATT dispute settlement system from its inception in 1948 to its end assimilation into the WTO system, see A. Lowenfeld (2008) *International Economic Law*, 145–60. For GATT cases and analyses, see William J. Davey and Andreas F. Lowenfeld (1991) *Handbook of WTO/GATT Dispute Settlement*.

[64] Final Act Embodying the Results of the Uruguay Round of Multilateral Trade Negotiations, opened for signature 15 April 1994, Marrakesh, Morocco, 33 I.L.M 1140–1272 (1994), 'Annex 2, Understanding on Rules and Procedures Governing the Settlement of Disputes (DSU)'.

[65] Information about the Appellate Body and its working is available at https://www.wto.org/english/tratop_e/dispu_e/ab_members_descrp_e.htm.

[66] A summary of all cases since 1995 is available at https://www.wto.org/english/res_e/publications_e/dispu_settlement_e.htm.

[67] See WTO case database at https://www.wto.org/english/tratop_e/dispu_e/dispu_by_country_e.htm.

[68] See WTO case database at https://www.wto.org/english/tratop_e/dispu_e/dispu_by_country_e.htm (United States, 115 as complainant, 135 as respondent, 142 as third party; European Union, 97 as complainant, 84 as respondent, 169 as third party).

[69] See WTO case database at https://www.wto.org/english/tratop_e/dispu_e/dispu_by_country_e.htm.

[70] ibid.

So far, no African state has filed a case against China. Similarly China has not filed a trade case within the WTO system against any African state as of this writing.[71] This is not surprising given the volume of trade and the unilateral concessions that China grants to African states. As the trade relations grow in scale and complexity, disputes are likely to arise and when they do the WTO mechanism remains available for all member states.

11.4.2 Investment

All of China's BITs with African states provide for investor–state arbitration and state-to-state arbitration. These provisions have shown significant evolution since the first China–Africa BIT in 1989, i.e. China–Ghana BIT. This BIT limited international arbitration on the quantum of compensation only.[72] As a part of China's first-generation BIT, this BIT did not permit the arbitrability of the lawfulness of expropriation or allegations of any violations of the substantive treaty protections limiting access to domestic legal processes.[73]

The second-generation Chinese BITs, including those with African states such as Egypt concluded in 1994, made minor modification to dispute settlement, limiting arbitrability to quantum but permitting the ICSID Secretary General to make the default appointment authority (i.e. when the parties disagree on the chair of the tribunal).[74]

The most contemporary Chinese BITs with African states makes no limitations on arbitrability. A good example is the BIT with Tunisia concluded in 2006.[75] It states in relevant part:

Article 9 Settlement of Disputes between investors and one Contracting Party

(1) Any dispute between a Contracting Party and an investor of the other Contracting Party, related to an investment, shall be as far as possible settled amicably through negotiations.

(2) If the dispute cannot be settled amicably through negotiations within six months from the date it has been raised by either party to the dispute, it shall be submitted: to the competent court of the Contracting Party that is party to the dispute; or to the International Center for settlement of Investment Disputes (the Center) under the Convention on the Settlement of Disputes between States and Nationals of Other States, done at Washington on

---

[71] ibid.

[72] See China–Ghana BIT (1989), art. 10. Text available at http://investmentpolicyhub.unctad.org/Download/TreatyFile/737.

[73] ibid.

[74] See China–Egypt BIT (1994), art. 9. Text available at http://investmentpolicyhub.unctad.org/Download/TreatyFile/730.

[75] China–Tunisia BIT (2006). Available at http://investmentpolicyhub.unctad.org/Download/TreatyFile/788.

March 18, 1965; Once the investor has submitted the dispute to the jurisdiction of the concerned Contracting Party or to the Center, the choice of one of the two procedures shall be final.[76]

This BIT appears to be China's most recent formulation of dispute settlement. Although China became a member of the International Center for the Settlement of Investment Disputes (ICSID) in 1991, it has not been an active player until very recently. Indeed, while about 20 per cent of all ICSID cases since ICSID's inception has involved African states,[77] China has appeared as a respondent state in only three cases, with Chinese parties initiating two ICSID cases since its inception.[78]

This shows that China has been able to avoid investment claims for more than two decades despite intense investment activity. Unlike China, many African countries have not been able to avoid investment cases against them despite lower investment volumes. Recent China–Africa investment relations have not so far led to formal investor–state disputes but some infrastructure projects have already produced disputes. Section 11.4.3 looks at these types of commercial dispute settlement.

11.4.3 Commercial (Infrastructure, Loan Agreements, etc.)

All types of transnational commercial agreements contain dispute settlement provisions. In modern times, the preferred means of dispute settlement is international arbitration. This is particularly true in contractual relationships coming from developing domestic judicial processes such as China and most, if not all, African states. International arbitration as a means of commercial dispute settlement has grown exponentially in both China and Africa, as we have seen above. This is largely because parties coming from different states could avoid jurisdictional problems and local parochialism and potentially obtain an award that they can enforce in multiple states through the New York Convention.[79] However, to be a reliable means of dispute settlement, international arbitration needs to be structured equitably.

In the past, Africa's experience with international arbitration vis-à-vis the developed world of the global North has been unequal, with the cases

---

[76] China–Tunisia BIT, art. 9. Text available at http://investmentpolicyhub.unctad.org/Download/ TreatyFile/788.

[77] See ICSID Caseload Statistics Special Focus Africa (May 2017) available at https://icsid. worldbank.org/en/Documents/resources/ICSID%20Web%20Stats%20Africa%20(English) %20June%202017.pdf.

[78] See UNCTAD Database at http://investmentpolicyhub.unctad.org/ISDS/CountryCases/42? partyRole=2.

[79] The Convention on the Recognition and Enforcement of Foreign Arbitral Awards (New York Convention) (1958) currently has 157 state parties. The text and comprehensive information is available at http://www.newyorkconvention.org/.

arbitrated outside of Africa before all non-African arbitrators[80] largely because of Africa's economically and politically subordinate position even in the post-colonial period. Because most China–Africa contracts (infrastructure, loans, etc.) are not publicly available, it is difficult to assess the fairness and equitability of the choice of the seat of the arbitration, the choice of law, and means of appointment of arbitrators. It is hoped that these choices are dictated by principles of fairness and equity including impartiality and independence of the decision makers and the institutions that administer these proceedings, and not by economic hierarchy.

11.5 Other Agreements

A notable example of what falls under other agreements is China's tax treaties with African states. An example of this is the China–South Africa tax treaty. This treaty has its own dispute settlement provision but what it envisions is exclusively domestic administrative and possibly judicial processes. The relevant provision of this treaty provides:

ARTICLE 25 MUTUAL AGREEMENT PROCEDURE

1. Where a resident of a Contracting State considers that the actions of one or both of the Contracting States result or will result for him in taxation not in accordance with the provisions of this Agreement, he may, irrespective of the remedies provided by the domestic law of those States, present his case to the competent authority of the Contracting State of which he is a resident or, if his case comes under paragraph 1 of Article 24, to that of the Contracting State of which he is a national. The case must be presented within three years from the first notification of the action resulting in taxation not in accordance with the provisions of the Agreement.

2. The competent authority shall endeavour, if the objection appears to it to be justified and if it is not itself able to arrive at a satisfactory solution, to resolve the case by mutual agreement with the competent authority of the other Contracting State, with a view to the avoidance of taxation which is not in accordance with the provisions of this Agreement.

3. The competent authorities of the Contracting States shall endeavour to resolve by mutual agreement any difficulties or doubts arising as to the interpretation or application of the Agreement. They may also consult together for the elimination of double taxation in cases not provided for in this Agreement.

4. The competent authorities of the Contracting States may communicate with each other directly for the purpose of reaching an agreement in the sense of paragraphs 2 and 3. When it seems advisable for reaching agreement,

---

[80] See generally, Won L. Kidane (2017) *The Culture of International Arbitration*.

representatives of the competent authorities of the Contracting States may meet together for an oral exchange of opinions.[81]

China seems to have used exactly the same formulation with its other economic partners outside of Africa.[82] These treaties do not offer international arbitration to individual taxpayers. Unlike BITs, they also do not anticipate state-to-state arbitration for violations of the terms of the agreement. Presumably, therefore, if a dispute arises, the aggrieved state party's choice appears to be limited to seeking judicial resolution before the World Court inasmuch as consent could be established or obtained.[83]

11.5.1 *Belt and Road Initiative Agreements*

A passage from *The Economist*'s 3 August 2017 print edition captures the economic scale and geographic reach of One Belt, One Road (OBOR) very well:

> Launched by China in 2013, the One Belt, One Road policy, known as OBOR, has two parts. There is a land-based 'belt' from China to Europe, evoking old Silk Road trade paths, then a 'road' referring to ancient maritime routes. OBOR will span 65 countries, and China has so far invested over $900bn in projects ranging from highways in Pakistan to railway lines in Thailand. Western multinationals, spotting a bonanza, are selling billions of dollars of equipment, technology and services to Chinese firms building along it.[84]

The same article, citing credible sources, suggests that about 87 per cent of the projects are executed by Chinese firms.[85] Belt and Road Initiative (BRI) directly touches and concerns several African countries, primarily Egypt, Ethiopia, Morocco, and South Africa.[86]

---

[81] Double Taxation Agreement between China and South Africa, art. 25, text available at http://www.dezshira.com/library/treaties/double-taxation-agreement-between-china-and-south-africa-3652.html.

[82] See Double Taxation Agreement between China and Malaysia. Text available at http://www.chinatax.gov.cn/n810341/n810770/c1153105/part/1153106.pdf.

[83] The International Court of Justice's (the World Court's) jurisdiction is consent based, however, there are instances where the Court may have compulsory jurisdiction based on a pre-existing consent. For basis of jurisdiction see ICJ official website at http://www.icj-cij.org/en/basis-of-jurisdiction.

[84] *The Economist* (2017) 'Western Firms Are Coining It along China's One Belt, One Road'. Digital version available at https://www.economist.com/news/business/21725810-general-electric-got-23bn-orders-infrastructure-project-last-year-western-firms.

[85] See ibid. (A database of open-source information collated by the Reconnecting Asia Project, run by the Centre for Strategic and International Studies, a think tank in Washington, DC, shows that '86% of OBOR projects have Chinese contractors, 27% have local ones and only 18% have contractors of foreign origin.')

[86] See Hong Kong Trade Development Council (HKTDC) Research at http://china-trade-research.hktdc.com/business-news/article/The-Belt-and-Road-Initiative/The-Belt-and-Road-Initiative-Country-Profiles/obor/en/1/1X000000/1X0A36I0.htm.

Chinese government sources indicate that as of the last BRI summit in May 2017, 270 BRI agreements were signed with sixty-eight countries. The details of these agreements are not public.[87] What is clear is that China has detailed implementation plans and has also begun signing cooperation agreements.[88] Because BRI is a fairly young initiative, the legal paperwork that it has generated so far is largely in the form of action plans, declarations, and similar types of what are often called 'soft law'[89] instruments.[90] An example is the Action Plan for the Harmonization of Standards along the Belt and Road (2015–17).[91] This Action Plan envisions the signing of standardization cooperation agreements.[92] For example, the China–Egypt BRI cooperation Five-Year Plan envisions a broader and lasting economic cooperation possibly governed by a complex web of cooperation agreements, treaties, contracts, etc. The following passage demonstrates the complexity of the legal relationship: 'In further moves, the two countries will seek greater co-operation in terms of production capacity, while strengthening bilateral investment ties, developing the China–Egypt Suez Economic and Trade Co-operation Zone, and nurturing financial co-operation between their respective financial institutions and enterprises.'[93]

[87] See Wu Gang (2017) 'China Touts More Than 270 Belt and Road Agreements'. This statement is attributed to Chinese president Xi Jinping. Article available at https://www.caixinglobal.com/2017-05-15/101090756.html.

[88] See HKTDC at http://china-trade-research.hktdc.com/business-news/article/The-Belt-and-Road-Initiative/The-Belt-and-Road-Initiative-Implementation-Plans-and-Cooperation-Agreements/obor/en/1/1X3CGF6L/1X0A3857.htm.

[89] *Black's Law Dictionary* defines 'soft law' as collectively, rules that are 'neither strictly binding nor completely lacking in legal significance'. *Black's Law Dictionary*, 8th ed. (2004). For a scholarly discussion of soft law v. hard law, see Gregory C. Shaffer and Mark A. Pollack (2010) 'Hard Law vs. Soft Law: Alternatives, Complements, and Antagonists in International Governance'.

[90] See HKTDC, The Belt and Road Initiative: Implementation Plans and Cooperation Agreements (10 January 2018) available at http://china-trade-research.hktdc.com/business-news/article/The-Belt-and-Road-Initiative/The-Belt-and-Road-Initiative-Implementation-Plans-and-Co-operation-Agreements/obor/en/3/1X3CGF6L/1X0A3857.htm.

[91] See http://china-trade-research.hktdc.com/business-news/article/One-Belt-One-Road/Action-Plan-for-Harmonisation-of-Standards-Along-the-Belt-and-Road-2015-2017/obor/en/1/1X3CGF6L/1X0A443L.htm.

[92] See ibid. It says in particular: 'As part of the *Action Plan*, China is looking to deepen mutually beneficial co-operation with regard to the standardisation and recognition of standards with a number of key countries along the Belt and Road routes. This will include prioritising the signing of standardisation co-operation agreements with the national standards bodies of several countries, including Mongolia, Russia, Kazakhstan, Vietnam, Cambodia, Thailand, Malaysia, Singapore, Indonesia, India, Egypt, and Sudan, as well as with members of the Gulf Co-operation Council (such as Saudi Arabia). In a number of infrastructure sectors, such as the power, railway, marine, aviation, and aerospace industries, as well as in the emerging industries of energy conservation and environmental protection, new-generation information technology, smart transportation, high-end equipment manufacturing, biotechnology, new energy sources and new materials, China will invite key countries along the Belt and Road routes to undertake studies with regard to the desired international standards. The objective will be to jointly develop international standards and improve the internationalisation level of those standards.'

[93] HKTDC, 'China and Egypt Announce Five-Year Plan for Strengthening their Comprehensive Strategic Partnership' (21 January 2016) available at http://china-trade-research.hktdc.com/business-news/article/One-Belt-One-Road/China-and-Egypt-Announce-Five-Year-Plan-for-Strengthening-their-Comprehensive-Strategic-Partnership/obor/en/1/1X3CGF6L/1X0A52O6.htmv.

As the projects take shape and mature, and the action plans move to the level of execution, it is hoped that more and more of the various agreements will become publicly available allowing scholarly scrutiny in the years to come.

11.6 Conclusion

China uses modern and formal legal agreements to order its economic relations with African states with a mix of modernity and lingering cultural hesitation. Formal and legally binding agreements appear to play a secondary role to instruments of overall understanding and exchange of tentative promises such as declarations, action plans, and memoranda of understanding. As a demonstration of this suggestion, it is enough to note that the principal platform of economic cooperation, FOCAC, remains the same kind of platform that it was eighteen years ago with no sign of being transformed into a formal economic partnership agreement. In Western-led economic initiatives, as a matter of cultural practice, formal rules and institutions precede major initiatives and projects. Although the rate of success of formal rules and informal approaches would require a deeper scientific study, the lack of formality and transparency appear to impact public perception of fairness and predictability.

In any case, this chapter has discussed China's agreements and dispute settlement in three broadly classified areas: trade, investment, and commerce. In trade relations, China and most of its African trade partners operate within the multilateral trading system of the GATT/WTO legal regime. They not only share the fundamental substantive rules and principles but also the mechanisms of dispute settlement under the DSU. More importantly, however, China has bilateral trade agreements with more than forty African states. It is fair to assume that the more than forty bilateral treaties provide more favourable trade terms and concessions than required under the WTO on reciprocal terms. It also appears that China routinely offers unilateral trade concessions to many African states outside of bilateral treaties.

The investment legal framework is a bit more systematic primarily because of BITs and domestic investment laws that give them effect or regulate investment without them. The relative permanency and the involvement of private interests enable policymakers to ensure the relative stability, durability, and transparency of the investment legal frameworks. The China–Africa investment regime, dominated by BITs as everywhere else, appears to have some of these characteristics, although many of the BITs would require significant modification to account for modern developments in the areas of both substantive rules and dispute settlement.

In the area of commerce, the legal landscape is even more sporadic. The substantive rules come from the domestic contract laws that the parties select in each individual case. In terms of dispute settlement, however, many China–Africa deals, like most other transnational deals, select international arbitration as the preferred means of resolving disputes. The availability of the New York Convention for the enforcement of awards across international borders has made international arbitration the preferred means of dispute settlement because it avoids jurisdictional obstacles and improves the potential for enforcement as there are no equivalent treaties for the enforcement of court judgements. As indicated above, however, unless equitably structured to ensure impartiality and independence of the decision makers as well as institutions selected to administer it, international arbitration could be a source of injustice and even abuse.

Finally, as they attempt to grow their trade, investment, and commercial relations, whether within the OBOR initiative or otherwise, China and Africa need to make sure that they avoid the inequities that often accompany relationships of power not only because these are morally wrong but also because that is the only way that the relations can be profitably sustained.

References

Bhala, R. (2016) *Understanding Islamic Law*. Durham, NC: Carolina Academic Press.

Black's Law Dictionary (2004) 'Soft Law'. Eagan, MN: Thomson Reuters.

Brautigam, D. (2009) *The Dragon's Gift: The Real Story of China in Africa*. New York: Oxford University Press.

Cairo Regional Centre for International Commercial Arbitration (CRCICA) (2016) 'CRCICA Annual Report 2008–2009', http://crcica.org/FilesEnglish/Annual%20Report_2016-10-31_08-59-10_0.pdf.

Cairo Regional Centre for International Commercial Arbitration (CRCICA) (2017) 'CRCICA Annual Report 2016', https://crcica.org/FilesEnglish/Annual%20Report_2017-05-31_11-51-17_0.pdf.

China–Africa Research Initiative (2017) 'China–Africa Annual Trade Data', http://www.sais-cari.org/data-china-africa-trade/.

China–Africa Research Initiative (2017) 'China–Africa FDI Data', May, http://www.sais-cari.org/chinese-investment-in-africa.

China–Africa Research Initiative (2018) 'Chinese Contracts in Africa', January, http://www.sais-cari.org/data-chinese-contracts-in-africa.

China–Africa Research Initiative (2018) 'Chinese Loans to African Governments', August, http://www.sais-cari.org/data-chinese-loans-and-aid-to-africa.

China and International Economic and Trade Arbitration Commission (CIETAC) (2015) 'CIETAC Annual Caseload', http://www.cietac.org/index.php?m=Page&a=index&id=40&l=en.

China.org (2018) 'China's Free Trade Agreements', http://www.china.org.cn/business/node_7233287.htm#a5.

Davey, W. J. and A. F. Lowenfeld (1991) *Handbook of WTO/GATT Dispute Settlement.* Ardlsey, NY: Transnational Publishers.

David, R. and J. E. C. Brierley (1985) *Major Legal Systems in the World Today.* London: Stevens and Sons.

Dawson, F. G. and B. H. Weston (1962) 'Prompt, Adequate and Effective: A Universal Standard of Compensation?' *Fordham Law Review*, 40(4), https://ir.lawnet.fordham.edu/flr/vol30/iss4/4/.

Dollar, D. (2016) *China's Engagement with Africa: From Natural Resources to Human Resources.* Washington, DC: The Brookings Institution.

Economist, The (2017) 'Western Firms Are Coining It along China's One Belt, One Road', 3 August, https://www.economist.com/business/2017/08/03/western-firms-are-coining-it-along-chinas-one-belt-one-road.

Gaffey, C. (2017) 'Kenya Just Opened a $4 Billion Chinese-Built Railway, its Largest Infrastructure Project in 50 Years' *Newsweek*, [online] 31 May, https://www.newsweek.com/kenya-railway-china-madaraka-express-618357.

Gallagher, N. and W. Shan (2009) *Chinese Investment Treaties.* Oxford International Arbitration Series. New York: Oxford University Press.

Gang, W. (2017) 'China Touts More Than 270 Belt and Road Agreements', *Caixin*, https://www.caixinglobal.com/2017-05-15/101090756.html.

Guardian, The 'Next Stop the Red Sea: Ethiopia Opens Chinese-Built Railway to Djibouti', [online] 5 October 2016, Available at: https://www.theguardian.com/world/2016/oct/06/next-stop-the-red-sea-ethiopia-opens-chinese-built-railway-to-djibouti.

Head, J. W. and Y. Wang (2005) *Law Codes in Dynastic China: A Synopsis of Chinese Legal History in the Thirty Centuries from Zhou to Qing.* Durham, NC: Carolina Academic Press.

HKTDC Research (n.d.) 'The Belt and Road Initiative: China Country Profile', http://china-trade-research.hktdc.com/business-news/article/The-Belt-and-Road-Initiative/The-Belt-and-Road-Initiative-Country-Profiles/obor/en/1/1X000000/1X0A36I0.htm.

HKDTC Research (n.d.) 'China and Egypt Announce Five-Year Plan for Strengthening their Comprehensive Strategic Partnership', http://china-trade-research.hktdc.com/business-news/article/The-Belt-and-Road-Initiative/China-and-Egypt-Announce-Five-Year-Plan-for-Strengthening-their-Comprehensive-Strategic-Partnership/obor/en/1/1X000000/1X0A52O6.htm.

HKDTC Research (2015) 'Action Plan for Harmonisation of Standards along the Belt and Road (2015–2017)', http://china-trade-research.hktdc.com/business-news/article/One-Belt-One-Road/Action-Plan-for-Harmonisation-of-Standards-Along-the-Belt-and-Road-2015-2017/obor/en/1/1X3CGF6L/1X0A443L.htm.

HKDTC Research (2018) 'The Belt and Road Initiative: Implementation Plans and Co-operation Agreements', http://china-trade-research.hktdc.com/business-news/article/The-Belt-and-Road-Initiative/The-Belt-and-Road-Initiative-Implementation-Plans-and-Cooperation-Agreements/obor/en/1/1X3CGF6L/1X0A3857.htm.

International Centre for Settlement of Investment Disputes (2017) 'The ICSID Caseload Statistics: Special Focus Africa (May 2017)', https://icsid.worldbank.org/en/Documents/resources/ICSID%20Web%20Stats%20Africa%20(English)%20June%202017.pdf.

International Court of Justice (n.d.) 'Basis of the Court's Jurisdiction', http://www.icj-cij.org/en/basis-of-jurisdiction.

Jackson, J. H. (2000) *The Jurisprudence of GATT and the WTO: Insights on Treaty Law and Economic Relations*. Cambridge: Cambridge University Press.

Jacobs, A. (2017) 'Joyous Africans Take to the Rails, with China's Help', *The New York Times*, 7 February, https://www.nytimes.com/2017/02/07/world/africa/africa-china-train.html.

Kennedy, K. C. (2008) *International Trade Regulation: Readings, Cases, Notes, and Problems*. New York: Aspen Publishers.

Kidane, W. L. (2016) 'China's Bilateral Investment Treaties with African States in Comparative Context', *Cornell International Law Journal*, 49(1), https://scholarship.law.cornell.edu/cilj/vol49/iss1/5/.

Kidane, W. L. (2017) *The Culture of International Arbitration*, New York, NY: Oxford University Press.

Legal Information Institute (n.d.) 'Parol Evidence Rule', https://www.law.cornell.edu/wex/parol_evidence_rule.

Lowenfeld, A. (2008) *International Economic Law*, 2nd edn. New York: Oxford University Press.

McConnaughay, P. J. (2001) 'Rethinking the Role of Law and Contracts in East-West Commercial Relations', *Virginia Journal of International Law*, 41(427), https://heinonline.org/HOL/LandingPage?handle=hein.journals/vajint41&div=21&id=&page=.

Mehre, A. T. von (1984) 'Some Reflections on Japanese Law', *Harvard Law Review*, 71(25): 1486–94.

Ministry of Commerce of the People's Republic of China (2011) 'China-Africa Economic and Trade Cooperation', http://english.mofcom.gov.cn/article/zt_minister/lanmua/201102/20110207420927.shtml.

Ministry of Commerce of the People's Republic of China (2017) 'China's Free Trade Agreements', http://fta.mofcom.gov.cn/enarticle/chinamauritiusen/enmauritius/201712/36683_1.html.

Ministry of Foreign Affairs of the People's Republic of China (n.d.) 'China's Foreign Judicial Assistance and Extradition Treaty', https://www.fmprc.gov.cn/web/ziliao_674904/tytj_674911/wgdwdjdsfhzty_674917/t1215630.shtml.

Modern Power Systems (2016) 'The Chinese in Africa: An Electrifying Story', http://www.modernpowersystems.com/features/featurethe-chinese-in-africa-an-electrifying-story-4991516/.

Mukeredzi, T. (2014) 'Chinese Yuan Penetrates African Markets', *Africa Renewal*, August, https://www.un.org/africarenewal/magazine/august-2014/chinese-yuan-penetrates-african-markets.

Nafziger, J. and R. Jiafang (1987) 'Chinese Methods of Resolving International Trade, Investment, and Maritime Disputes', *Willamette Law Review*, 23(69): 619–24.

Olawale Elias, T. (1956) *The Nature of African Customary Law*. Manchester: Manchester University Press.

Panitchpakdi, S. (2004) 'The Future of the WTO: Addressing Institutional Challenges in the New Millennium', World Trade Organization, Geneva.

Phillips, A. (1945) *Report on Native Tribunals*. London: Gerald Duckworth.

Pilling, D. (2017) 'Chinese Investment in Africa: Beijing's Testing Ground', *Financial Times*, 13 July, https://www.ft.com/content/0f534aa4-4549-11e7-8519-9f94ee97d996.

Salacluse, J. W. (2010) 'The Emerging Global Regime for Investment', *Harvard International Law Journal*, 51(2): 427–73.

Schaffer, G. C. and M. A. Pollack (2010) 'Hard vs. Soft Law: Alternatives, Complements and Antagonists in International Governance', *Minnesota Law Review*, 94: 706–99.

Scissors, D. (2018) 'China Global Investment Tracker', American Enterprise Institute, http://www.aei.org/china-global-investment-tracker/.

Smith, D. (2015) 'China Denies Building Empire in Africa', *The Guardian*, 12 January, https://www.theguardian.com/global-development/2015/jan/12/china-denies-building-empire-africa-colonialism.

Snow, P. (1988) *The Star Raft: China's Encounter with Africa*. New York: Grove Press.

Taylor, I. (2006) *China and Africa: Engagement and Compromise*. London: Routledge.

Tsang, K. F. (2016) 'Chinese Bilateral Judgment Enforcement Treaties', *Loyola of Los Angeles International and Comparative Law Review*, 40(1): https://digitalcommons.lmu.edu/cgi/viewcontent.cgi?referer=https://www.google.com/&httpsredir=1&article=1744&context=ilr.

United Nations Conference on Trade and Development (UNCTAD) (1989) 'China–Ghana BIT', http://investmentpolicyhub.unctad.org/IIA/country/42/treaty/906.

United Nations Conference on Trade and Development (UNCTAD) (1994) 'China–Egypt BIT', http://investmentpolicyhub.unctad.org/IIA/country/42/treaty/894.

United Nations Conference on Trade and Development (UNCTAD) (2004) 'China–Tunisia BIT', http://investmentpolicyhub.unctad.org/IIA/country/42/treaty/983.

USLegal.com (n.d.) 'Lex Mercatoria', https://definitions.uslegal.com/l/lex-mercatoria/.

Warren, H. (2015) 'Spanning Africa's Infrastructure Gap: How Development Capital Is Transforming Africa's Project Build-Out', The Economist Corporate Network Report, Baker & Mackenzie, http://ftp01.economist.com.hk/ECN_papers/Infrastructure-Africa.

World Trade Organization (n.d.) 'Members and Observers of the WTO', https://www.wto.org/english/thewto_e/whatis_e/tif_e/org6_e.htm.

World Trade Organization (n.d.) 'Appellate Body Members.' Available at: https://www.wto.org/english/tratop_e/dispu_e/ab_members_descrp_e.htm.

World Trade Organization (n.d.) 'Dispute Settlement: Disputes by Member.' Available at: https://www.wto.org/english/tratop_e/dispu_e/dispu_by_country_e.htm.

World Trade Organization (2017) 'WTO Dispute Settlement: One-Page Case Summaries (1995–2016)', https://www.wto.org/english/res_e/publications_e/dispu_settlement_e.htm.

Zimmerman, J. (2010) *China Law Deskbook: A Legal Guide for Foreign-invested Enterprises*. 3rd edn. Chicago, IL: American Bar Association.

237

Treaties

Agreement between the Government of the People's Republic of China and the Government of Malaysia for the Avoidance of Double Taxation and the Prevention of Fiscal Evasion with Respect to Taxes on Income, opened for signature 23 November 1985, entered into force 1 January 1987.

Agreement between the Government of the People's Republic of China and the Government of The Republic of South Africa for the Avoidance of Double Taxation and the Prevention of Fiscal Evasion with Respect to Taxes on Income, opened for signature 25 April 2000, entered into force 1 January 2001.

China and Zimbabwe Signed Tax Treaty, opened for signature 4 December 2015, entered into force 29 September 2016.

The Convention on the Recognition and Enforcement of Foreign Arbitral Awards (New York Convention), opened for signature 10 June 1958, entered into force 7 June 1959.

Final Act Embodying the Results of the Uruguay Round of Multilateral Trade Negotiations, opened for signature 15 April 1994, entered into force 1 January 1995.

General Agreement on Tariffs and Trade 1947, 55 UNTS 194, opened for signature 30 October 1947, entered into force 1 January 1948.

Marrakesh Agreement Establishing the World Trade Organization, opened for signature 15 April 1994, entered into force 1 January 1995.

Sino-Ethiopian Agreement for Economic and Technological Cooperation, 1996. [The text of the agreement has not been made available to the public.]

12

Labour Regimes and Workplace Encounters between China and Africa

Carlos Oya

12.1 Introduction: Workplace Encounters and Economic Transformations

A Chinese foreman wearing a large straw hat in the scorching sun gives instructions to a group of five Angolan workers giving the finishing touches to a pavement on a new road in Angola. Another group of workers surrounds a Chinese employee in blue uniform, who is handing out payslips for signature, which workers take to a tin shed at the end of the building site. Nearby an Angolan worker is operating a large motor grader sitting alongside a Chinese operator who monitors every single movement with an intense look. Further away, in Ethiopia, a Chinese factory manager walks around a couple of production lines shouting orders to an Ethiopian line supervisor while dozens of young women are busy stitching parts into a model for trousers. One of the lines is lagging behind and disrupting the workflow in other lines. Another Chinese supervisor summons a group of workers to quickly move to the refectory for the lunch break, uttering a few basic words in Amharic while using hand-to-mouth signs.

These workplace encounters are becoming increasingly common in many African countries. Images of Chinese and African workers together in construction sites and factories have become an important area of interest in much of the reporting on China–Africa encounters. What these images have in common is the emergence of new jobs in non-primary sectors at a time when debates on the imperative of structural transformation in Africa are raging. The opportunities arising from the investments and projects of Chinese and many other Asian enterprises in the manufacturing and construction sectors in many parts of Africa are highly visible even if official statistics still depict an image of agrarian-based economies.

Chinese foreign direct investment (FDI) to sub-Saharan Africa (SSA henceforth) has grown substantially since the early 2000s (see Chapter 2). A large proportion of these investments are from medium-sized enterprises in the manufacturing and services sectors, often oriented towards domestic markets (McKinsey, 2017; Shen, 2015; see also Chapter 13). Meanwhile, the presence of Chinese construction companies has boomed in Africa during the same period at an even more impressive pace. The construction boom in Africa, both for residential and infrastructure investments, has attracted a large number of Chinese contractors, mostly state-owned enterprises (SOEs). As a result, SSA is the second most important overseas market for Chinese construction firms, with US$40.6 billion (Wolf and Cheng, 2018). By 2017 Chinese contractors accounted for nearly 60 per cent of the African construction market for the top 250 international contractors. In fact, the value of Chinese construction projects and contract revenues far exceeds the flows (and even stocks) of Chinese FDI to the African continent, reaching almost US$45 billion compared with just over US$30 billion of FDI stocks by 2015 (Wolf and Cheng, 2018).

While there are different labour intensities associated with different subsectors and types of construction, there is no doubt that the expansion of industrial investments and construction projects has created a huge number of non-agricultural jobs across African economies. Thus, increasing numbers of Chinese firms, as well as companies originating elsewhere, especially the Middle East and Asia, are gradually contributing to the process of building an industrial labour force in Africa (Oya, 2019). Yet, much of the journalistic reporting focuses on the presence of Chinese workers throughout the continent. There is also much talk about sub-standard working conditions and whether China is exporting poor labour practices (Baah and Jauch, 2009; Shelton and Kabemba, 2012).

This chapter has the following objectives. First, it critically engages with popular claims about job creation, working conditions, and skill development in Chinese companies across Africa, and offers an alternative, more empirically nuanced view of these realities. Second, it proposes a labour regime analytical framework, and different research questions, to understand the interaction of global, national, and local forces in the determination of labour outcomes, to question the often-assumed Chinese 'exceptionalism' in labour relations, and to better understand workplace relations in Africa in the sectors where Chinese firms are particularly present. Third, it illustrates through emerging case-study research how different labour practices arise in different countries and sectors, underscoring the importance of sector and context specificity, management practices, and local (African) agency in determining labour outcomes.

12.2 China–Africa Labour Encounters: Dominant and Emerging Questions and Debates

There are a growing number of studies and journalistic material reporting on the employment effects of Chinese firms in Africa. While China is seen as a popular partner, primarily because of its contribution to infrastructure development,[1] Chinese employers do not enjoy the same popularity (Sun, 2017). Although the literature on labour effects of Chinese firms in Africa is still in its infancy, there are three types of common claims and perceptions that are often found in media reports, some academic publications, and indeed when interviewing different kinds of respondents in business and government settings. First is the claim that Chinese firms mostly or often employ large numbers of Chinese workers in positions that should be filled by African workers. Second, it is often reported that working conditions are sub-standard and exploitative in Chinese firms in Africa. Third, the limited localization is compounded by very limited efforts to develop the skills of local workers. We will discuss each of these claims in turn and compare with the best available evidence.

12.2.1 *Workforce Localization: Do Chinese Firms Rely on Chinese Labour?*

On the issue of job creation and localization, a common perception is the reliance on Chinese labour and the limited hiring of local labour (French, 2014). At one extreme of this widespread narrative are ludicrous stories that have survived over time about the issue of Chinese prison labour in Chinese construction sites in Africa.[2] Yet, this kind of story continues to be reproduced by journalists and even researchers (see Sautman and Yan, 2016, for some examples). This perception is now fortunately more widely questioned thanks to the growing availability of evidence to the contrary,[3] even if such claims persist among uninformed commentators, firm managers, journalists, and even some African government officials, as we encountered in our own research in Angola and Ethiopia in 2016–17.

More reliable statistics on Chinese workers in Africa, as compiled by SAIS-CARI, show a marked increase between 2001 (nearly 47,000 workers) and 2016 (227,000 workers) with a peak of over 263,000 in 2015. Of these, the proportion of Chinese workers in SSA countries has been steadily declining

---

[1] https://edition.cnn.com/2016/11/03/africa/what-africans-really-think-of-china/index.html.

[2] The origin of this bizarre claim can be traced back to a *New York Times* column in 1991 https://www.nytimes.com/1991/05/11/opinion/l-china-has-used-prison-labor-in-africa-540291.html. See also Brautigam's blog on the matter http://www.chinaafricarealstory.com/2010/08/is-china-sending-prisoners-to-work.html.

[3] https://www.reporting-focac.com/5-china-africa-myths.html.

from a peak of 78 per cent in 2011 to only 58 per cent in 2016, so that North Africa has a disproportionate share of Chinese workers and lower levels of localization. In absolute terms, after years of growth, the number of Chinese workers in SSA declined by nearly 20 per cent, a sign that workforce localization has been gaining force both in absolute and relative terms.[4]

There are already a number of large studies and plenty of specific case-study evidence suggesting that levels of workforce localization (as proportions of African workers in Chinese firms in Africa) are high and have been increasing across several countries in the past ten years. The most recent and comprehensive source of evidence on workforce localization is the survey of over a thousand Chinese firms in eight countries conducted by McKinsey (2017). This report shows how these firms largely rely on local labour, despite some significant variation by project and sector. The average rate of localization is 89 per cent. Sector matters and in manufacturing this proportion reaches 95 per cent (McKinsey, 2017: 41). This is consistent with another large-scale compilation of more than four hundred firms/projects from several hundred interviews and thousands of documents (Sautman and Yan, 2015), which concludes that the average localization rate is 85 per cent, with most firms clustered within the 80–95 per cent band largely depending on sectors. In our own project, we compiled nearly sixty studies/cases covering the wide spectrum of projects from very low to very high levels of localization and a weighted average of 85 per cent (see Appendix Table A12.1 for an illustrative selection of these sources).[5] About two-thirds of these cases/studies had localization rates exceeding 80 per cent. Moreover, comparisons between firms of different (foreign) nationality are rare but Rounds and Huang (2017) provide unusual evidence of roughly similar rates of localization between Chinese and American firms in Kenya (78 and 82 per cent respectively). More comparisons would surely show that the proportion of 'expat' labour in other foreign firms is not negligible, but such comparative evidence is generally missing.[6]

Claims of widespread use of Chinese workers contrast with significant differences in workforce localization rates, with certain countries like Angola or Equatorial Guinea receiving more Chinese labour in absolute and relative terms compared to other countries where the presence of Chinese expat labour is more limited (see Appendix Table A12.1 for examples of variation). Moreover, SAIS-CARI databases on Chinese workers in Africa show a stable pattern between 2009 and 2016, when the recorded number was just over

---

[4] All these calculations are based on analysis of data provided by SAIS-CARI at http://www.sais-cari.org/data-chinese-workers-in-africa.

[5] The simple arithmetic mean is 75 per cent.

[6] For example, according to our own interviews, three well-established Angolan road contractors employed 5, 20, and 30 per cent of expat labour in 2016 respectively, with differences being partly related to the relative scarcity of projects during that period.

200,000 workers. Given the rapid increase in Chinese FDI and construction projects (Wolf and Cheng, 2018), and assuming a similar rate of growth in job creation, most of the expansion in employment during that period must have gone to African workers. Cheru and Oqubay (see Chapter 14) show that Chinese FDI has created many more thousands of jobs (nearly forty thousand between 2000 and 2016) than other foreign companies. This dominance in absolute number of jobs created is compatible with the use of some Chinese labour for strategically critical positions. Especially in the early period of expansion of construction projects and FDI, Chinese firms saw advantages in using Chinese workers for management, engineering, and skilled positions as they were more familiar with 'companies' organization and process', quicker for the process of installing new equipment imported from China, and to make sure the first projects with some political significance were completed in very short timeframes, compared to competitors (Tang, 2016: 110).

Variation in rates of localization and job creation for African workers is linked to several factors. First, variation across countries may be due to differences in the requirements set out by host countries with regard to the type of expat labour that can be imported into the country as well as to the structural deficits in technical/skilled labour (Sautman and Yan, 2015). Countries like Angola or Equatorial Guinea are more affected by skill shortages in the labour market than other countries like South Africa, Ghana, or Kenya. Some countries (e.g. Ethiopia) have strict visa policies and only very limited categories of workers were allowed to obtain work visas, suggesting this is an important policy tool that can determine the rate of localization by imposition. Second, ownership (private or state) seems to have mixed effects. Our own analysis of several cases/studies of construction projects suggests that state-owned enterprises (SOEs) tend to have higher percentages of local workforce, partly due to more compliance with legal requirements when these are set by host countries, partly because of the costs of hiring Chinese labour in SOEs. However, the McKinsey report (2017) finds the opposite for their sample of firms across different sectors, where private firms tend to rely more on local labour (92 per cent) than SOEs (81 per cent). The main reason for this is the dominance in their sample of private firms operating in manufacturing and services, where localization rates are higher since skill demands may be lower than in many infrastructure projects that also suffer from the imperative of timely project completion. In other words, sector matters and the specific technology used by a firm also shapes the need for expat labour in foreign firms. Third, the type of project also matters: we observed in Angola that in flagship infrastructure projects with demanding technical standards firms had no option but to bring in specialized experienced workers in order to meet the tight time schedule and the quality expectations of the client (i.e. the Angolan authorities). Fourth, the longer Chinese companies operate in a country, the more settled they are, the more they rely on local workers (Corkin, 2011; Lam, 2014; Sautman and Yan, 2015; Tang, 2016). There are different forces at play in this case. On the one hand, as Chinese firms settle in new markets and gradually build a core local labour force, their recruitment processes adapt to the new context and the skills developed among local workers pay off after an initial transitional period. On the other hand, since the early 2000s, the rapid growth in labour costs in China has meant that Chinese workers have become increasingly expensive and less affordable for companies operating overseas, even for large SOEs. Economic crisis and foreign exchange shortages may also force firms to reduce their expat labour force given the difficulties of paying in foreign currency.[7] In any case, the evidence reviewed here shows that the contribution to the mass creation of unskilled and semi-skilled jobs for African workers is beyond doubt, and the implications for processes of structural transformation are significant since many of these jobs contribute to the gradual building of an industrial labour force in Africa.

12.2.2 *Working Conditions*

Evidence on working conditions is also patchy and largely anecdotal. Most available empirical studies suggest that Chinese firms comply with national minimum wage legislation but in some cases offer lower wages than their competitors in the same sector. This does not mean wages lower than national or sector averages, just that pay may be lower than other firms in the same sub-sectors. However, overall the evidence is not conclusive and lacks comparative quantitative rigour (Oya et al., 2018).

Tang (2016) provides various examples where reported wages were 'low' in relation to the 'national average' or other foreign firms.[8] Baah and Jauch (2009) also conclude that Chinese firms in Angola, Ghana, Namibia, South Africa, and Zambia tended to pay the lowest wages when compared to local and other foreign firms. A much-debated Human Rights Watch (HRW) report on Zambian mines (2011) emphasized that Chinese-owned copper mines offered the lowest salaries compared to other OECD-owned mines despite paying above the national minimum wage, but these comparisons have been criticized for lack of empirical rigour (Lee, 2017; Sautman and Yan, 2016). There are also examples where wages are not as low as expected. A very recent survey in the Eastern Industrial Zone in Ethiopia suggests that

---

[7] This evidence is based on interviews with several SOE managers in Angola and Ethiopia.

[8] An important limitation of some of these comparisons is that data on wages in most African countries are scarce and typically representative of the most advanced formal enterprises, i.e. excluding the informal activities where most jobs are found. Therefore a 'national average' may be very high compared to the average conditions of most workers in the country.

average wages among Chinese factories in the zone are considered 'low' by workers but they are well above a reported national average in the formal sector (Fei, 2018). In a 2012 World Bank survey of firms in Ethiopia, median wages in Chinese firms were 60 per cent higher than in domestic firms (Bashir, 2015: 8). At GUMCO, a Chinese ceramic manufacturer in Ghana, wages of Ghanaian workers (ranging between US$2.2 and US$10 per day) were both above the national minimum wage of US$1.9 per day (as of 2008) and also above the Indian comparator plant offering US$1.9 per day (Akorsu and Cooke, 2011).

Beyond wages, evidence is more abundant on harsh working conditions in terms of long working hours, lack of written contracts, resistance to unionization, and more frequent breaches of labour regulations compared to other foreign companies (McKinsey, 2017; Rounds and Huang, 2017). Labour conflicts seem more frequent in Chinese-owned firms, but this may reflect the greater attention that these firms have received compared to companies of other nationalities and especially domestic ones (Rounds and Huang, 2017; Sautman and Yan, 2016). More conflictual relations have also been blamed on perceived resistance by Chinese employers to the presence of unions and communication barriers (Sautman and Yan, 2016; Tang, 2016). Various studies have, however, shown that Chinese private firms may start operations with relatively unfavourable non-wage conditions but can gradually and sometimes quickly adapt and meet demands from collectively organized workers or from the host states (Lee, 2017; Tang, 2016). Our own research in Ethiopia and Angola also seems to point to wide variation in comparative wages among Chinese firms, depending on sector, firm size, market structures, and management behaviour. Where wages are lower than comparators, there are different reasons, such as low initial profitability after important capital investments (mines in Zambia), tighter profit margins for small-medium firms subject to fierce global competition, or reliance on more labour-intensive methods (Tang, 2016). In contrast, other firms opt to pay wage premia and out-compete other players in the sector to attract higher-quality workers as observed in Ethiopia's industrial zones. The relative strength of labour institutions, especially unions, also contributes to wage equalization among foreign firms in the same sectors, as in South Africa (Huang and Ren, 2013).

These findings should also be put in perspective and understood within the wider context of labour market deregulation and privatization following structural adjustment reforms. All African countries, after decades of structural adjustment and waves of liberalization and privatization, have experienced a systematic weakening of labour institutions and mass informalization and casualization of labour (Lee, 2017; Meagher, 2016). The majority of Chinese firms have entered African markets at the peak of neoliberal hegemony on the continent. Conditions found in Zambian mines, for example, are more strongly linked to the crisis and reforms in the sector in the 1990s than to the nationality of foreign firms (Lee, 2017).

12.2.3 *Skill Development*

Sometimes low wages in early processes of industrialization are compensated for by the prospect of acquiring new skills and more stable jobs (Fei, 2018). Hence skill development is seen as one of the potential contributions from new Chinese investors especially in manufacturing. While construction projects provide some form of short-term transferable capabilities, factories have the advantage of contributing with long-term capability development. However, there are some claims that Chinese firms make a very limited contribution to skill development (Baah and Jauch, 2009). More recent survey work suggests that training is provided but workers arrive with higher expectations and find that training provision is not enough, although those working for globally integrated firms certainly receive substantial and more frequent training. The literature almost unanimously confirms that, contrary to popular belief, Chinese firms do engage in labour training (e.g. Bashir, 2015; Corkin, 2011; Lam, 2014; Rounds and Huang, 2017; Shen, 2015; Tang, 2016). The McKinsey report (2017) confirms that nearly two-thirds of over a thousand surveyed Chinese firms engage in training of local employees (43 per cent in the form of apprenticeship) but in construction and manufacturing, where skills are particularly important for African workers, 73 per cent of firms offer training/apprenticeship.

Variation among Chinese firms is important and useful policy lessons can be extracted from these differences. First, some sectors/industries tend to be more skill intensive and necessarily engage in more training, whereas basic assembly jobs in light manufacturing produce a more limited range of skill transfer (Chen et al., 2016). Second, larger and more globally integrated firms have fairly sophisticated training systems, including combinations of local training centres, periods of intensive learning and skill development in China (especially for managers, skilled personnel, and semi-skilled workers), and continuous on-the-job training with career development attached (Sun, 2017; Tang, 2016).[9] Third, getting serious about building local skills and capabilities is also a way of meeting expectations from host states, which are important for the accumulation logic of many Chinese SOEs (Lee, 2017). Fourth, in some countries the state (through investment agencies and labour

---

[9] Not less important is the Chinese government contribution to education and training in Africa, through scholarships, professional courses, infrastructure investments, and various forms of partnership (Bashir, 2015). It is, however, beyond the scope of this chapter to discuss the impact of these programmes.

institutions) and lead firms in global production networks (GPNs) can put pressure on suppliers to boost skill formation in host countries and potentially contribute to the gradual development of skill development 'systems' associated with priority sectors.

One important reason why firms feel compelled to train their new workers is dissatisfaction with existing technical and vocational training systems in host countries, which makes managers prefer to 'hire someone off the street who's a blank slate' and directly invest in the most relevant skills for the company (McKinsey, 2017: 40). This is a strategy that is common to many other foreign investors, especially in export-oriented factories. Indeed job experience is the most effective form of training in the long-term process of industrial development (Amsden, 2001). Gerschenkron (1962) recognized long ago that the availability of cheap labour in latecomers was no guarantee of rapid industrialization, because in most agrarian-based economies the kind of labour force that suits the demands of industrial factory work (time management, discipline, effort, reliability, etc.) is actually very scarce (see also Oya, 2019). Thus, besides the existence or not of formal training programmes, these experiences suggest that hundreds of thousands of African workers who are often migrants finding entry-level non-agricultural jobs are learning the basic skills of the occupations that are likely to grow in the next decades, thereby making a contribution to the prospects of further structural transformation.

12.2.4 *Summary*

This section has taken stock of the published evidence on labour outcomes in Chinese enterprises in Africa. The literature on labour issues and outcomes within the broad 'China in Africa' field is still in its early days. Much more empirically grounded analysis is needed. Many of the debates and claims that have dominated the headlines in the intersection of media representation and some academic research lack analytical basis and empirical foundations. While an emerging body of ethnographic and qualitative research has helped debunk some myths, there is still a lack of rigorous quantitative evidence. Indeed, in our survey of the literature we have not found any large-scale quantitative survey of working conditions from the perspective of labour (i.e. workers' surveys rather than self-reported data from company management).[10] More alarming is the scarcity of comparative evidence, which is needed to overcome biases that reinforce ideas of Chinese 'exceptionalism'. Indeed, an important problem with the way labour issues

[10] A SOAS research project currently under way aims to fill this gap with a survey of over 1,500 workers in nearly eighty firms in Ethiopia and Angola, but statistical results are not yet available. See https://www.soas.ac.uk/idcea/.

(and many other aspects) in the 'China in Africa' field have been analysed is the 'methodological nationalism' which assumes intrinsic characteristics that apply to all sorts of Chinese actors in Africa. Thus, more quantitative and qualitative comparative evidence on different kinds of Chinese and non-Chinese firms is sorely needed.

Overcoming 'Chinese exceptionalism' requires a different set of questions. Is there one Chinese 'labour regime'? Is it different from labour regimes in developed or developing countries? If so, when firms travel overseas, do they travel with their labour practices? If not, what determines variation in labour outcomes among different firms in African countries?

Whether or not working conditions in Chinese-owned enterprises in Africa are worse than relevant comparators, or mixed according to which sector or type of firm, a more important question is *why*. There is emerging research that seeks to tackle these questions, as we shall see. Before we extract key insights from such studies, we next consider the complexity of factors shaping the labour implications of Chinese investments and projects in Africa, and contextualize the modus operandi of Chinese firms by considering the different labour regimes found in China and some of China's labour market shifts in the past three decades.

12.3 Understanding Labour Regimes in China

12.3.1 *Labour Regimes and Capitalism*

In order to understand labour outcomes (as working conditions and standards), several relevant factors must be considered. Different levels of analysis, from more abstract to more concrete, from the global to the local, are necessary to make sense of the multiple aspects that affect the conditions workers face in particular workplaces. The notion of 'labour regime' is useful as a conceptual tool to explore interconnections between multiple factors and the differences between practices in different sectors and workplaces. Bernstein (2010: 125) defines a labour regime as 'the different methods of recruiting labour and their connections with how labour is organized in production (labour process) and how it secures its subsistence'. Labour process theory is useful to understand the workplace dynamics and antagonistic interests of capital and labour, the former driven by the logic of accumulation to control and extract as much labour as possible from workers, and the latter resisting such pressures. Bernstein's definition, however, implies an extension of the analysis to understand how labour is mobilized to become available beyond the workplace, as well as how it is reproduced in a capitalist labour market. This analytical extension is exemplified by Burawoy's notion of the 'factory regime' (Burawoy, 1985), encompassing labour relations in production in conjunction with relations of production more broadly, by connecting the micro of the workplace with the macro politics of capital–labour relations in a national or global context.[11] Lerche et al. (2017) add the relation between productive and reproductive realms to the concept of labour regime.[12] As Selwyn (2016) notes, labour regime analysis is 'necessarily multiscalar', incorporating the global, national, regional, and local. The analytical extension also combines relations of production (and the capital–labour conflict) with relations to the market (i.e. commodification, especially of labour, land, and money) (Burawoy, 2013). These two relational processes in capitalism reflect both class struggle in the Marxian sense, and the movements and counter-movements in the Polanyi sense, or, as Selwyn (2014: 1020) puts it, 'Marx-type and Polanyi-type struggles (offensive and defensive struggles)'.

Drawing from this analytical framework, it is possible to operate at three different and interconnected levels of analysis to explain the multiple determinants of labour outcomes in a given context (see Figure 12.1). First, starting at the bottom, are the micro workplace dynamics and 'raw' encounters between employers and workers over wages, productivity imperatives, safety, effort, and labour time. Second are the characteristics and dynamics of a particular sector or global production network, which cuts across national boundaries and generates specific imperatives of labour control and standards,

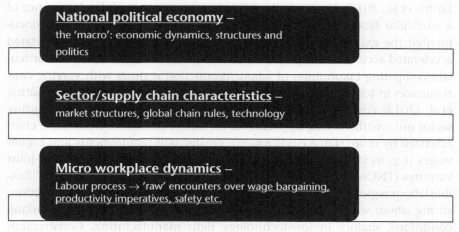

Figure 12.1. Levels of labour regime analytical framework
Source: Author's elaboration

[11] Lee (1999) uses the notion of 'factory regime' to encompass the institutional and political apparatus that regulates workplace politics (at macro level) and the labour process and social organization of production at micro-factory level.
[12] In plain language, employers operate different mechanisms of labour control that affect workers' lives beyond the factory floor.

through market structures, competition, global chain rules, and technology, and which are intimately linked with skill requirements, spatial dimensions of labour processes, and even prevailing work culture and management ethos. Third is the national political economy, and particularly the macroeconomic dynamics shaping economic transformations and structural change alongside the macro politics of production and state–society relations which shape labour supply dynamics and the arenas of different struggles, whether over the extent of commodification, the limits to labour reproduction, or claims over representation. In this case, the relations between state, capital, and labour and the institutions that underpin these relations are critical to understand labour outcomes. Through such an analytical lens, it is possible to explore the combination of a wide range of factors in determining labour standards for a particular firm and sector.

12.3.2 *Labour Regimes in China: Variation and Shifts*

This framework helps us overcome the trap of 'methodological nationalism' and 'Chinese exceptionalism' if we consider the potential variety of labour regimes in China. Empirical research on labour relations in China originates from an array of disciplines, from economics and industrial sociology to economic geography and political economy (Lee, 1999; Lerche et al., 2017; Lüthje et al., 2013). However, there is no consensus around the dominance of a particular labour regime, even though much of the literature has documented the extent to which labour control and repression have facilitated accelerated accumulation and transformations in China. Most studies articulate competing taxonomies of labour/production regimes with varying consequences in terms of labour standards and their evolution over time. Lüthje et al. (2013) consider up to five production regimes in the manufacturing sector only, with varying implications for labour standards: from those characterized by more stable employment, greater skill requirements and higher wages (e.g. in state-bureaucratic sector and transnational corporations-joint ventures (TNCs-JVs) in petrochemicals, automobile, steel) to 'low-wage' flexible labour regimes encompassing more or less globally integrated production, strong labour segmentation, reliance on migrant workers, and poor working conditions, mainly in low-technology light manufacturing. Construction labour regimes, driven by the project nature of work in this sector, share such characteristics of strong labour segmentation and flexible insecure employment. In construction, a dominant pattern is the widespread presence of footloose migrant workers employed through complex subcontracting chains that makes them prey to the discretion of labour brokers/gangmasters and widespread informalization of labour relations (Swider, 2015). A dualism between more stable secure labour relations on the one hand and flexible, insecure, and informalized relations on the other hand straddles both the state–private ownership divide and sector boundaries, even if some regimes are more dominant in some sectors (Lüthje et al., 2013). This segmentation and flexibilization has arguably contributed to the empowerment of employers vis-à-vis workers, especially in those sectors characterized by flexible employment and reliance on migrant workers. In this regard, a particularity of China's labour regimes is the role of the *hukou* (household residential) system, which maintained the umbilical cord between urban migrant workers and their rural households, thereby facilitating low-wage regimes (Lee, 1999; Lerche et al., 2017).

However, these snapshot descriptions of prevailing working conditions in China mask two additional types of variations within each sectoral labour regime. First are cross-sectional variations based on market structures (and degree of sector/internal competition), whether firms are export or domestic-market oriented, as well as on type of ownership, and especially the three leading categories in China: SOEs, JVs with TNCs, and domestic private firms. Second, longitudinal variations led by the rapid economic transformations and series of reforms that have gradually reconfigured the political economy of production and labour relations since the 1980s. It is worth noting, in particular, the role of corporatization of the SOE sector, and the concomitant growth in the private sector, which generally strengthened the authority of managers and weakened workers' bargaining power in the 1990s, leading to the emergence of a labour regime of 'disorganized despotism', different from the neo-traditional regime of 'organized dependence' attributed to the pre-reform SOEs or to SOEs with monopoly power (Lee, 1999). Particularly in the sectors pertaining to the flexible mass production and 'low-wage classic' regimes (e.g. textile and garment, toys, and other consumer goods) employer interests were well organized and coordinated, and their influence on local implementation of labour policies and exemptions has been noticeable (Lüthje et al., 2013). The fragmentation of the working class into multiple administratively and contractually defined categories reinforced the empowerment of capital, especially in the 1990s and early 2000s (Pringle, 2017). The rapid influx of FDI to China's 'sunbelt' and the incorporation into global production networks operating with a logic of flexible accumulation and subject to fierce competition between 'capitals' sourcing from different parts of the world, also generated pressures towards labour segmentation and flexible just-in-time (JIT) employment practices (Lerche et al., 2017). In the most exploitative labour regimes (garment and construction), characterized by the increasing role of labour intermediaries, there is a 'triple absence': (1) the absence of recognized labour relations and recognized employers (because of the role of intermediaries); (2) the absence of the right to organize (resistance to unionization); and (3) the absence of rights other than those directly related to labour relations (Lerche et al., 2017). In sum, during the 1980s and 1990s, both national-level political economic dynamics and the penetration of highly dynamic and flexible GPNs produced the conditions for the emergence of labour regimes with weak workers' bargaining power, leading to 'despotic' workplace relations.

At this point, two caveats are fundamental. First, as stated above, the most exploitative labour regimes coexist with other regimes where labour outcomes are different and better, reflecting legacies of the neo-traditional regime of 'organized dependence' (Lee, 1999). Second, the conditions observed in the export-oriented industrial 'sunbelt' of coastal China or in its booming construction sector are similar and not necessarily worse than what is observed in other parts of Asia (Lerche et al., 2017) and generally in the developing world, lending credence to the fallacy of Chinese exceptionalism (Chan, 2015).

Chinese exceptionalism in labour relations can also be questioned on the grounds of dynamics of change in the past three decades, and especially trends in the past fifteen years, which make us doubt that Chinese workers are powerless vis-à-vis the more exploitative labour regimes. Silver's work (2003) on historical tendencies in labour resistance and mobilization shows that capitalism's technological fixes, such as flexible sourcing, automation, and other innovations may partly weaken labour's bargaining power in some places but ultimately provoke new instances of potential resistance and enhanced bargaining power. This has happened in China in recent times. Real wages of urban workers, including migrant workers, have grown substantially between 2000 and 2016—five-fold in the case of real urban wage rates and four-fold for migrant workers, an unprecedented change in China's contemporary history (Lo, 2018).

Labour 'striking back', if this is what rapidly rising wages mean, is linked to a range of competing explanations. First, JIT systems in globally integrated production networks and industrial upgrading (as experienced in Guangdong) increase the vulnerability of capital to workplace disruption at key nodes of the chain (Pringle, 2017; Silver, 2003). These shifts may empower certain worker segments, in transport and communications sectors, while other segments remain stuck in low gear, so the outcomes are uneven (hotels, retail, restaurant and other seasonal service workers). Second, state intervention, especially through new labour legislation enacted in 2008 and 2013 and its relatively enhanced enforcement, have strengthened a set of new 'hard rules', with an important role for minimum wages and moves towards reducing segmentation and insecure employment (Chan, 2015; Lüthje et al., 2013). Third, despite a rather weak official union system, labour militancy and Marx-type 'offensive' struggles seem on the rise, often on issues of closures and compensation (Pringle, 2017). Fourth, demographic change, population ageing and the gradual exhaustion of the vast pool of rural young labour may explain emerging evidence of labour shortages and a 'Lewis turning point', which have strengthened industrial workers' bargaining power (Yao, 2014). It is difficult to establish which of these factors is more important, not least because they are all interrelated, especially the increasingly 'pro-labour' state interventions since 2008 and growing labour conflict, both feeding one another.

It is in this context that the 'flying geese' hypothesis has been revived in connection with the potential relocation of Chinese supply chains overseas, and particularly to Africa (see Chapter 13). The rise of industrial GPNs and its associated FDI dynamics since the 1980s have engendered a global pattern whereby, wherever capital (automobile, garment, electronics) moves to, new labour–capital conflict arises, and when that happens and threatens profits, capitalists resort to technological (automation) and/or spatial fixes (Silver, 2003: 81). Thus the overview of labour regime features and of their changes over time in China provides some important lessons to understand (a) the drivers of investments towards Africa—what new 'spatial fixes' GPNs and Chinese firms will generate—and (b) what kinds of labour regimes will be associated with these investments in the new host countries. Whether Chinese capital flowing to Africa produces a new wave of 'race to the bottom' is a matter of empirical investigation that is still scarce on Africa, and will not in any case manifest any kind of 'exceptionalism', given common global patterns. Some illustrations of the diversity of new Chinese labour regimes in SSA and the importance of context follow in Section 12.4.

12.4 Capital–Labour Relations from the African Ground: Illustrations from Case Studies

Understanding labour relations in Chinese firms in Africa requires an understanding of what kinds of capital move, in what sectors, and how they adapt to what political and economic contexts. This section uses evidence from selected case studies to show how variations in labour regimes in Chinese enterprises in Africa contribute to some of the outcomes discussed in the previous section.[13] Evidence on Chinese firms in Africa points to a variety of patterns depending on countries. In most countries, we find SOEs in construction, small and medium-sized firms in light industry and building materials sectors, a mix of SOEs and private firms in extractive sectors (mining and oil),

---

[13] The evidence selected for this section comes primarily from high-quality ethnographic research on Chinese firms in mining and construction in Zambia (Lee, 2017), longitudinal qualitative evidence on labour practices in Angola (Tang, 2010, 2016) and recent comparative qualitative research in construction and manufacturing in Angola and Ethiopia from a SOAS project in progress (https://www.soas.ac.uk/idcea/).

and small firms in services (McKinsey, 2017; Shen, 2015; Wolf and Cheng, 2018). Labour processes and regimes differ a lot between these sectors and across firm types, particularly between construction and mining, and between construction and manufacturing. Our own research in Angola and Ethiopia also points to important differences within same sectors and types of firms, driven by the national political economy context, particularly labour market structures, labour supply dynamics, government policy, and local labour institutions. In sum, variation in labour practices as illustrated in this section confirms the need to analyse labour outcomes in Chinese firms as the result of complex interactions between the three levels proposed under our labour regime analysis (Figure 12.1).

Lee (2017) produces unusual longitudinal comparative ethnographic research on accumulation regimes and labour outcomes in Zambia, in mining and construction, two sectors where the presence of Chinese firms is significant alongside other foreign companies. Lee grounds her theoretically informed work in the direct experiences of workers, managers, policymakers, and politicians, reflecting fluid encounters that defy generalizations, while suggesting some analytically relevant patterns. Thus a distinction is made between varieties of capital (i.e. different types of Chinese capital) to overcome the trap of 'methodological nationalism' or 'national institutionalism' inherent in a 'varieties of capitalism' approach (Lee, 2017: 9). The combination of systemic forces (inherent accumulation logic of capital, competition imperatives, etc.) and contingent events (1970s and 2008 crises, technological breakthroughs, 'Going Out' of Chinese enterprises) produces outcomes that cannot be simply deducted from some form of historical determinism. Chinese state capital (SOEs), for example, 'at home and abroad, is Janus faced, both centrally controlled and also capable of decentralized and local improvisation' (Lee, 2017: 10). Therefore, Lee shows that in order to explain labour outcomes in Chinese mines and construction sites in Zambia, it is critical to understand the dual logic of Chinese state capital (accumulation for profit, and securing resources and political/diplomatic influence) compared with the single-minded profit-driven logic of private capital, whether Chinese, other foreign, or domestic. Historical and country contextualization is also essential as all 'capitals' faced a common labour law regime that had been liberalized after decades of structural adjustment and deregulation in Zambia. Through this nuanced empirical immersion, Lee reveals contradictory labour outcomes in mining, whereby Chinese state capital workplaces are characterized by stable but low-wage employment, whereas private TNCs may display seemingly less exploitative practices in a more flexible labour regime where retrenchment is the immediate response to market volatility, as experienced in the 2008–9 crisis. This research also shows the importance of sector specificities and particularly the exploitative features of construction labour regimes, whether in

China, Zambia, or Europe, in contrast with the tradition of labour militancy and important political effects of the copper-mining sector. Lee (2017: 29) argues that 'the footloose and project-based nature of construction undermines the collective capacity of construction labour in its struggle with capital, whether state or private'. Finally, at the analytical level of the national political economy, the Zambian context suggests that 'politics—and, more precisely, a political synergy between state and society—not bureaucracy or technocracy . . . is the key to leveraging Chinese state capital for development' (Lee, 2017: 158).

Ongoing SOAS comparative research on Angola and Ethiopia also places emphasis on the politics of production at the national political economic level. In Angola the imperative of rapid post-war infrastructure reconstruction in the period 2005–15 and the political expediency of Chinese-financed and -built projects meant much less attention to job creation and local linkages, an omission partly exacerbated by a weak and resource-poor trade union system. The lack of voice from civil society and the absence of electoral contestation to the ruling party MPLA left priorities in the hands of the narrow Angolan political elite. By contrast, in Ethiopia, the imperative of structural transformation was linked to rapid job creation so workforce localization was far more important and politically important. Indeed, the promises of industrialization and rapid job creation have also generated expectations that shape the politics of production in the country, paradoxically leading to more labour militancy alongside protests around the appropriation of development outcomes. There are implications for labour outcomes, either in terms of different rates of workforce localization for SOEs, or in terms of the attraction of labour practices from globally integrated manufacturing production in Ethiopia compared to more informalized labour relations in factories oriented to the Angolan domestic market. These differences also entail different paths towards structural transformation and the building of an industrial workforce, which are more dynamic in Ethiopia than in Angola.

SOAS comparative research in these two countries also reminds us of the context specificity of sectors, which makes the 'methodological nationalism' of comparisons between firms of different nationality questionable. Lee (2017: 156) illustrates how different varieties of capital, Chinese state or global private, may in certain sectors adopt labour regimes that share international and industry-wide tendencies. While it is true that informalized and casualized labour is a central tendency in construction labour practices across countries, the preliminary findings of SOAS research suggest that the national context is crucial to understand differences in labour outcomes even for the same varieties of capital. Chinese SOEs are present in both Angola and Ethiopia but they adapt their labour practices to the labour market context they find, whether as a function of labour legislation and its enforcement (more liberal and less enforced in Angola) or in relation to the relative scarcity of skills in the two countries. In both countries, all forms of capital (state or private) in the construction sector find it hard to adopt the cascade subcontracting practices found in China and other countries with 'thick' construction business networks, and are forced to engage in direct employment and processes of recruitment and retention as in the manufacturing sector. Labour intermediaries are therefore absent, especially in Angola, so employers and employment relations are explicitly recognized, even if this does not necessarily translate into better working conditions in terms of wages, security, and benefits, given the weakness of labour legislation and labour institutions.

Various authors also pay attention to the particularities of management ethos in different varieties of Chinese capital across different sectors (Lee, 2017; Sun, 2017; Tang, 2016). Lee (2017: 13) does refer to the particular management ethos present in Chinese state capital characterized by 'eating bitterness' and a form of 'collective asceticism' that contrasts with the dynamic individual careerism of managers in global private capital. Tang (2016) also suggests that language barriers, lack of communication, and a tendency towards isolation from local host society create perceptions that affect labour encounters and fuel negative perceptions. Perhaps the main specific aspect of labour encounters between Africa and China that may result from 'Chinese characteristics' is language barriers and communication problems, which may exacerbate some of the work culture clashes and contradictory expectations common to all varieties of capital within and across sectors.[14] Chinese managers and firms do adapt though, after long periods of observation and interaction, thus gradually overcoming initial barriers. Notwithstanding these differences, there is a risk of describing differences and 'clashes' as static attributes of culture, as there are also important similarities across different national boundaries. It is possible to speak of management ethos that is specific to certain sectors or production regimes, rather than nations/cultures; for example, a disciplinary and time-efficiency oriented ethos in labour-intensive garment factories, with work culture clashes that happen between African workers newly arrived to a low-wage factory labour regime and foreign factory managers often coming from China, India, Bangladesh, and Sri Lanka (in the case of Ethiopia). Many of the negative perceptions about workers' qualities and employers' behaviour essentially reflect the fact that 'factory owners have always complained about their workers during early phases of industrialization and Chinese bosses in Africa are no exception' (Sun, 2017: 99). Many authors have given examples of negative representations of workers in the early phases of industrialization

---

[14] Tang (2016) provides ample evidence of these barriers affecting labour conflicts and the effectiveness of training and labour management more generally in several African countries.

in today's industrial giants: Germany, Japan, and China (Chang, 2008; Oya, 2019). Management ethos and associated labour practices also depend on some structural factors and strategic decisions, such as between labour-intensive and capital-intensive production, and between international customers (exporting to global markets) and domestic markets (Sun, 2017: 52–5).

12.5 Chinese Exceptionalism? African Agency and Context

This chapter explores the labour implications of the rise of Chinese FDI and building contractors in Africa, and their encounters with workers, states, and unions in African countries. A selective survey of the available literature on labour practices in Chinese firms in Africa shows the widespread negative *perceptions* of exploitative management despite very limited systematic and comparative evidence. There is plenty of anecdotal evidence on rates of localization (or the extent to which these firms rely on imported Chinese labour), poor working conditions, and limited skill development, but emerging scholarly research paints a more nuanced picture of labour outcomes, and much greater variation than usually recognized. There is an urgent need for more systematic, comparative, and larger-scale mixed-methods evidence to assess the extent to which Chinese firms adopt labour regimes that are similar to those found in China and how they adapt to new national political economy and labour market contexts as they travel. The chapter proposes different sets of questions grounded in a labour regime framework to understand the variety of labour regimes found in China and in Africa, and the shifting trends of the past two decades. This analysis suggests that labour practices and outcomes are fluid and that the 'methodological nationalism' inherent in emphasizing labour 'Chinese characteristics' is misplaced. Through illustrations from more recent case-study evidence of labour encounters in different African countries, this chapter stresses that, in order to make sense of the multiplicity of outcomes in labour relations in Chinese enterprises in Africa (and elsewhere) it is crucial to understand and document: (a) the diversity of 'Chinese capitals'; (b) the importance of African labour market contexts and their current historical conjuncture; (c) the dynamics of state–society and state–capital relations in each country; and (d) the particularities and structural features of different sectors and production regimes in which Chinese firms are investing and operating. More rigorous evidence on these dimensions is necessary to extract policy-relevant lessons, so that African countries and their governments can act to maximize the positive employment effects of the rise of Chinese actors in Africa. Indeed, the chapter has shown that the process of job creation and the quality of jobs can be substantially influenced by policy in host countries in the form of 'sticks' and 'carrots' that can enforce and induce better labour

Appendix: Table A12.1. Estimated employment localization rates in Chinese firms in Africa from most significant studies/cases

Study	Year	Country	Sector	Firm/Project	African workers	Chinese workers	African workers (% total)
Akorsu and Cooke (2011)	2009	Ghana	manufacturing	GUMCO	250	3	99%
Baah and Jauch (2009)	2008	South Africa	manufacturing	FIDA, IINCOOL, KaRITA (all clothing)	958	27	97%
CARI-SAIS (Survey by Chinese official)	2011	Rwanda	construction	China Road & Bridge Corp. (Road building)	2,000	110	95%
Lee (2017)	2007	Zambia	mining	Chambishi copper mine	2,063	189	92%
Chen et al. (2016)	2018	Nigeria	manufacturing	16 Chinese firms (cumulative number of workers)	5,656	540	91%
Warmerdam and Dijk (2013)	2012	Uganda	various	42 companies in Kampala	9,845	1,004	91%
World Bank (2012)	2011	Ethiopia	manufacturing, services, and construction	Survey of 69 Chinese firms	23,723	2,728	90%
CARI-SAIS (Reuters)	2011	Zimbabwe	mining	Anjin: Joint venture diamond mining	1,700	210	89%
McKinsey report (2017)	2016-17	8 countries	various	Survey of over 1,000 companies	300,000	37,079	89%
Brautigam and Tang (2012)	2011	4 countries	manufacturing	Firms in 4 SEZs	13,592	1,979	87%
CARI-SAIS (Hans E. Petersen and Sanne van der Lugt's report)	2011	DRC	construction	DRC Reconstruction of Lubumbashi (N1)—Kasenga (Zambian Border) Road Reconstruction	600	100	86%
Sautman and Yan (2015)	2007–13	12 countries	various	Surveys and reports for over 400 firms/projects	N/A	N/A	85%
CARI-SAIS (China Africa Business Council)	2013	Africa	various	193 Chinese companies in Africa	34,000	6,400	84%
Baah and Jauch (2009)	2008	Ghana	construction	Bui hydroelectric dam (Sino Hydro)	560	110	84%
Huang and Ren (2013)	2012	S. Africa	various	16 companies	4,160	779	84%
Baah and Jauch (2009)	2008	Angola	construction	Sinohydro	715	312	70%
CARI-SAIS (The Africa Report)	2010	Mozambique	construction	Mozambique stadium	1,000	500	67%
Tang (2010)	2007	Angola	various	55 companies	5,482	3,353	62%
CARI-SAIS (Enrique Martino reports)	2013	Equatorial Guinea	construction	China Road and Bridges	60	600	10%

Source: Author's elaboration based on sources reported in first column; CARI-SAIS sources are available from their database at http://www.sais-cari.org/data-chinese-workers-in-africa

standards. Only more rigorous comparative approaches to these questions and constructive suggestions for policy will help us overcome some of the myths that have marred our understanding of the subject until now.

Acknowledgment

'The research informing this chapter was funded by the ESRC-DFID grant ES/M004228/1. All errors and omissions are my sole responsibility'

References

Akorsu, A. D. and F. L. Cooke (2011) 'Labour Standards Application among Chinese and Indian Firms in Ghana: Typical or Atypical?' *The International Journal of Human Resource Management*, 22(13): 2730–48.

Amsden, A. H. (2001) *The Rise of 'The Rest': Challenges to the West from Late-Industrializing Economies*. Oxford: Oxford University Press.

Baah, A. Y. and H. Jauch (eds) (2009) 'Chinese Investments in Africa: A Labour Perspective', African Labour Research Network, Accra and Windhoek.

Bashir, S. (2015) 'The Imperative of Skills Development for the Structural Transformation of Sub-Saharan Africa', Investing in Africa Forum, World Bank, Washington, DC, https://openknowledge.worldbank.org/handle/10986/22380.

Bernstein, H. (2010) *Class Dynamics of Agrarian Change*. Sterling, VA: Kumarian Press.

Brautigam, Deborah, and Xiaoyang Tang (2011) 'African Shenzhen: China's Special Economic Zones in Africa', *Journal of Modern African Studies*, 49(1): 27–54.

Burawoy, M. (1985) *The Politics of Production: Factory Regimes under Capitalism and Socialism*. London: Verso Books.

Burawoy, M. (2013) 'Ethnographic Fallacies: Reflections on Labour Studies in the Era of Market Fundamentalism', *Work, Employment and Society*, 27(3): 526–36.

Chan, A. (2015) 'The Fallacy of Chinese Exceptionalism', in A. Chan (ed.), *Chinese Workers in Comparative Perspective*. Ithaca, NY: Cornell University Press, pp. 1–20.

Chang, H. J. (2008) *Bad Samaritans: The Guilty Secrets of Rich Nations and the Threat to Global Prosperity*. London: Random House.

Chen, Y. et al. (2016) 'Learning from China? Manufacturing, Investment, and Technology Transfer in Nigeria', Working Paper No. 2016/2, China Africa Research Initiative, School of Advanced International Studies, Johns Hopkins University, Washington, DC.

Corkin, L. (2011) 'Chinese Construction Companies in Angola: A Local Linkages Perspective', MMCP Discussion Paper No. 2, University of Cape Town and Open University.

Fei, D. (2018) 'Work, Employment, and Training through Africa–China Cooperation Zones: Evidence from the Eastern Industrial Zone in Ethiopia', Working Paper No. 2018/19, China Africa Research Initiative, School of Advanced International Studies, Johns Hopkins University, Washington, DC.

Gerschenkron, A. (1962) *Economic Backwardness in Historical Perspective: A Book of Essays*. Cambridge, MA: Harvard University Press.

Huang, M. and P. Q. Ren (2013) 'A Study on the Employment Effect of Chinese Investment in South Africa', Discussion Paper No. 4/2013, Centre for Chinese Studies, Stellenbosch.

Lee, C. K. (1999) 'From Organized Dependence to Disorganized Despotism: Changing Labour Regimes in Chinese Factories', *China Quarterly*, 157: 44–71.

Lee, C. K. (2017) *The Specter of Global China: Politics, Labor, and Foreign Investment in Africa*. Chicago, IL: University of Chicago Press.

Lerche, J. et al. (2017) 'The Triple Absence of Labour Rights: Triangular Labour Relations and Informalization in the Construction and Garment Sectors in Delhi and Shanghai', Working Paper 32/17, Centre for Development Policy and Research, SOAS University of London, https://eprints.soas.ac.uk/23863/1/file118684.pdf.

Lo, D. (2018) 'Perspectives on China's Systematic Impact on Late Industrialization: A Critical Appraisal'. Working Paper No. 03, Industrial Development Construction and Employment in Africa, SOAS, University of London.

Lüthje, B., S. Luo, and H. Zhang (2013) *Beyond the Iron Rice Bowl: Regimes of Production and Industrial Relations in China*. Frankfurt: Campus Verlag.

McKinsey (2017) 'Dance of the Lions and Dragons: How Are Africa and China Engaging, and How Will the Partnership Evolve?' McKinsey & Company, New York.

Meagher, K. (2016) 'The Scramble for Africans: Demography, Globalisation and Africa's Informal Labour Markets', *Journal of Development Studies*, 52(4), 483–97.

Oya, C. (2019) 'Building an Industrial Workforce in Ethiopia: Historical Lessons and Current Dynamics', in F. Cheru, C. Cramer, and A. Oqubay (eds) *The Oxford Handbook of the Ethiopian Economy*. Oxford: Oxford University Press.

Oya, C., C. Wolf, and S. K. Cheng (2018) 'Chinese Firms and Employment Dynamics in Africa: A Literature Review', Working Paper No. 04, Industrial Development Construction and Employment in Africa, SOAS, University of London.

Pringle, T. (2017) 'A Class against Capital: Class and Collective Bargaining in Guangdong', *Globalizations*, 14(2): 245–58.

Rounds, Z. and H. Huang (2017) 'We Are Not So Different: A Comparative Study of Employment Relations at Chinese and American Firms in Kenya', Working Paper No. 2017/10, China Africa Research Initiative, School of Advanced International Studies, Johns Hopkins University, Washington, DC.

Sautman, B. and H. Yan (2015) 'Localizing Chinese Enterprises in Africa: From Myths to Policies', No. 2015–05, HKUST Institute for Emerging Market Studies, Hong Kong.

Sautman, B. and H. Yan (2016) 'The Discourse of Racialization of Labour and Chinese Enterprises in Africa', *Ethnic and Racial Studies*, 39(12): 2149–68.

Selwyn, B. (2014) 'Capital–Labour and State Dynamics in Export Horticulture in North-East Brazil', *Development and Change*, 45(5): 1019–36.

Selwyn, B. (2016) 'Global Value Chains and Human Development: A Class-Relational Framework', *Third World Quarterly*, 37(10): 1768–86.

Silver, B. J. (2003) *Forces of Labor: Workers' Movements and Globalization since 1870*. Cambridge: Cambridge University Press.

Shelton, G. and C. Kabemba (2012) 'Win–Win Partnerships: China-Southern Africa and the Extractive Industries', Southern Africa Resource Watch, Johannesburg.

Shen, X. (2015) 'Private Chinese Investment in Africa: Myths and Realities', *Development Policy Review*, 33(1): 83–106.

Sun, I. Y. (2017) *The Next Factory of the World: How Chinese Investment Is Reshaping Africa*. Cambridge, MA: Harvard Business Review Press.

Swider, S. (2015) *Building China: Informal Work and the New Precariat*. Ithaca, NY: Cornell University Press.

Tang, X. (2010) 'Bulldozer or Locomotive? The Impact of Chinese Enterprises on Local Employment in Angola and DRC', *Journal of Asian and African Studies*, 45(3): 350–68.

Tang, X. (2016) 'Does Chinese Employment Benefit Africans? Investigating Chinese Enterprises and their Operations in Africa', *African Studies Quarterly*, 16(3/4): 107–28.

Warmerdam, W. and M. P. Van Dijk (2013) 'What Is your Story? Chinese Private Enterprises in Kampala, Uganda', *Journal of Asian and African Studies*, 52(6): 873–93.

Wolf, C. and S. K. Cheng (2018) 'Chinese Overseas Contracted Projects and Economic Diversification in Angola and Ethiopia 2000–2015', Working Paper No. 02, Industrial Development Construction and Employment in Africa, SOAS, University of London.

World Bank (2012) 'Chinese FDI in Ethiopia: A World Bank Survey', Addis Ababa.

Yao, Y. (2014) 'The Lewis Turning Point: Is There a Labour Shortage in China?', in S. Fan et al. (eds) *The Oxford Companion to the Economics of China*. Oxford: Oxford University Press, pp. 388–92.

Part IV
China and Africa's Economic Transformation

Part IV

13

China's Light Manufacturing and Africa's Industrialization

Justin Yifu Lin and Jiajun Xu

13.1 Introduction

Industrialization is back at the top of the development agenda. At the global level, Sustainable Development Goals (SDGs) place high priority on the objective to 'build resilient infrastructure, promote inclusive and sustainable industrialization and foster innovation'.[1] At the regional level, in its Agenda 2063 the African Union has articulated a strategic framework for economic transformation, with a special focus on manufacturing-based industrialization to escape from the commodity dependence trap.[2]

Yet Africa is experiencing premature de-industrialization. Developing countries have experienced falling manufacturing shares in both employment and real value added, especially since the 1980s. This de-industrialization trend is 'premature', because these developing countries are 'running out of industrialization opportunities sooner and at much lower levels of income compared to the experience of early industrializers' (Rodrik, 2016). Despite recent rapid growth, manufacturing is a smaller share of output and employment in Africa today than it was in the mid-1980s (Brookings, 2014). For example, in the case of Tanzania the manufacturing sector's share in GDP and growth rate has remained relatively stagnant over the past decade (Wangwe et al., 2016). In 2017 sub-Saharan Africa's average share of manufacturing value added in GDP was only 10 per cent, down from over 20 per cent in the 1980s (see Figure 13.1).[3]

[1] United Nations, Sustainable Development Goals, https://www.un.org/sustainabledevelopment/sustainable-development-goals/, accessed 15 May 2017.
[2] African Union, Agenda 2063, https://au.int/en/agenda2063, accessed 15 May 2017.
[3] World Development Indicators.

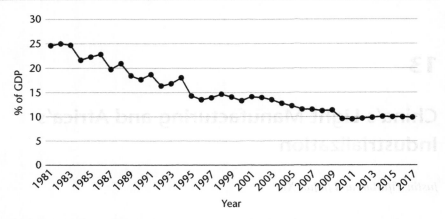

Figure 13.1. Manufacturing, value added (per cent of GDP) in sub-Saharan Africa
Source: World Development Indicators, World Bank

Most successful industrializers, including those in East Asia after World War II, captured the opportunity to transform their agrarian economies to industrialized economies presented by the global relocation of light manufacturing from higher-income countries when the latter were losing comparative advantage in light manufacturing due to rising wages (Lin, 2012b). As wages have been rising rapidly in China in recent years, labour-intensive light manufacturing firms are losing their comparative advantages. Will these light manufacturing firms, like their predecessors in the past, relocate their production capacity to low-wage developing countries, especially sub-Saharan African countries with abundant labour forces? Will such industrial transfer help to drive Africa's industrialization? This chapter aims to explore whether and how China's light manufacturing transfer can help to promote Africa's industrialization. The key argument of the chapter is that the pending relocation of Chinese light manufacturing sectors presents an unprecedented opportunity for African countries to foster industrialization in line with their latent comparative advantage but that the facilitation of key stakeholders, especially African governments, is required in order to realize this huge potential.

The chapter proceeds as follows. First, it examines the opportunities and challenges presented by the transfer of light manufacturing from contemporary China to low-wage developing countries from the historical perspective of the 'flying geese' pattern. Second, it uses first-hand survey data in China's Yangtze River and Pearl River Delta regions to explore how Chinese light manufacturing firms have coped with rising labour costs, what types of firms are more likely to relocate their manufacturing capacity to low-wage destinations, and where firms tend to relocate their production lines. Third, it examines how 'pilot' Chinese light manufacturing firms transferring their production capacity to help create jobs and promote exports in Africa have overcome first-mover challenges. Finally, using the analytical framework of New Structural Economics, it makes policy recommendations on how to mitigate binding constraints to help African countries seize the window of opportunity of industrial transfer from China to achieve economic structural transformation.

13.2 From Flying Geese to Leading Dragons

Historically, the era of economic globalization has witnessed a 'flying geese' model in which a more advanced country (the 'lead goose') opens the market space, transfers capital, technology, and management skills to a less developed country (a 'follower goose') and so facilitates their economic structural transformation (Akamatsu, 1962).[4] Since beginning to open up its economy and embark on market reform in the late 1970s, China has seized the window of opportunity by attracting light manufacturing firms from the East Asian 'tigers', especially Korea, Hong Kong, and Taiwan. Labour-intensive light manufacturing sectors were well in line with the latent comparative advantage of mainland China, which helped to tap into its abundant and cheap labour forces. China's economic miracle has defied the conventional wisdom that developing countries on the periphery of the global economy suffer from deteriorating terms of trade and are unable to converge with developed countries in the core. Yet this does not mean that latecomers will automatically benefit from industrial transfer from advanced economies, as the transformation process entails proactive efforts to seize the opportunity and realize the potential for moving up global value chains.

Real wages in Chinese manufacturing sectors are much higher than those in Africa. Moreover, real wages have been rising since the mid-2000s; the annual rise of about 10 per cent from 2003 to 2016[5] is also likely to be much greater than that in African countries.[6] This trend towards an enlarging relative wage gap has sparked heated debates on whether rising wages in China will herald a new wave of relocation of manufacturing jobs to less prosperous low-wage developing countries.

[4] Akamatsu (1962) coined the term 'flying geese' to describe the relocation of manufacturing from Japan to other lower-income countries. Lin (2012b) uses the term 'leading dragons' to reflect the much larger size of relocation from China to other countries.

[5] China Bureau of Statistics, see http://data.stats.gov.cn, accessed 1 September 2018.

[6] For example, real wages in Ethiopia grew at an annual average rate of 3 per cent from 2005 to 2013 (based on International Labour Organization statistics). Yet due to limitations in data availability, the statement here can only be interpreted as a preliminary judgement.

The need to answer this question is more urgent than ever before. The immense scale of China's manufacturing is unprecedented. With China losing its competitiveness in labour-intensive industries, it is estimated that about 85 million factory jobs fall into the category of light manufacturing industry in China (Lin, 2012b).

On the one hand, optimists maintain that the unparalleled scale of relocation of Chinese manufacturing could foster economic structural transformation on the African continent and in other parts of the developing world, as a surging youth population enters their labour market (Lin, 2012b). While data limitations make it hard to calculate the exact amount of Chinese outbound light manufacturing FDI into Africa, there is a visible sign of growing Chinese engagement with Africa as far as light manufacturing is concerned. According to the 'Statistical Bulletin of China's Outward Foreign Direct Investment', Chinese outward FDI into Africa grew from US$0.07 billion in 2003 to US$2.4 billion in 2016. A Brookings Institution study used official Chinese data—company registrations of their outward investment plans with the Ministry of Commerce (MOFCOM)—to estimate that there were about two thousand Chinese enterprises in Africa (Chen et al., 2014). Of these, the authors suggest that about 1,170 firms are in a category they label 'agricultural and manufacturing'. Of these, about 250 firms are in light manufacturing-linked sectors. Yet MOFCOM's ODI registration data underestimate Chinese overseas direct investment, as it is an administrative database rather than a representative survey of Chinese overseas investors (Rosen and Hanemann, 2009; Tan, 2013).[7] To address the limitation of this official dataset, McKinsey conducted a bottom-up survey in Africa and discovered that there were about ten thousand Chinese firms on the continent, of which about one-third are in manufacturing. It found that in the eight selected African countries, the number of Chinese-owned firms was between double and nine times the number registered by MOFCOM (Sun, Jayaram, and Kassiri, 2017). In other words, there may be many Chinese relocated firms under the radar. This comes with a caveat that despite the rapid growth in Chinese FDI into Africa, the relative share of Chinese FDI inflows in Africa remained around a modest 5 per cent in terms of stock from 2013 to 2016.[8]

---

[7] The main reason for firm compliance with time-consuming official approvals is to obtain a certificate of overseas investment that can then be used to purchase the foreign exchange required for the transaction. This is a product of controls on China's capital account. Firms may reinvest their retained earnings offshore without repatriating them to China.

[8] Ministry of Commerce of the People's Republic of China, *Statistical Bulletin of China's Outward Foreign Direct Investment*, various years.

On average, inward FDI in Africa accounts for a small part of gross fixed capital formation at an average rate of around 11 per cent from 2015 to 2017. Source: UNCTAD, Country Fact Sheet: Africa, http://unctad.org/en/Pages/DIAE/World%20Investment%20Report/Regional-Factsheets.aspx, accessed 1 September 2018.

Sceptics, on the other hand, contend that a series of secular trends have dimmed the upbeat prospects that light manufacturing jobs will be relocated from China to other low-wage developing countries on an unparalleled scale, unleashing their potential for economic transformation. First, global demand for traditional light manufacturing products, especially in Europe and North America, is declining. Second, labour absorption capacity in light manufacturing sectors is lower than before. Automation may further render more and more of the labour force redundant. This means that the potential for job creation has been undermined even if industrial transfer does occur. Last but not least, economic transformation in low-wage developing countries will not come to fruition unless the right conditions are created. Relocating manufacturing jobs from China to other developing countries will not happen unless roads, power supplies, and ports are adequate. Relocation to low-wage developing countries is unlikely to happen unless there is political stability and policy consistency. Without these soft and hard infrastructures in place, low-wage developing countries will lose the opportunity of industrial upgrading and economic transformation. Hence, realizing this great potential requires effective policy levers to put the right conditions in place.

Despite the above debates, little empirical research is available exploring the opportunities and challenges of Chinese manufacturing relocation to Africa. This is the gap that the pilot survey described below aims to fill.

13.3 A Pilot Survey of Chinese Light Manufacturing

In order to have a better understanding of the opportunities and challenges of relocating Chinese light manufacturing production capacity to low-wage developing countries in general and Africa in particular, it is important to collect first-hand firm-level empirical data. Although household surveys, such as the China Health and Retirement Longitudinal Study (CHARLS), are well developed in China, firm surveys face several challenges, especially in relation to access to the firms and to quality control.[9] To overcome these challenges, the Institute of New Structural Economics (INSE) and the Overseas Development Institute (ODI) collaborated on a pilot survey in 2017 to find out how Chinese light manufacturing firms cope with rising labour costs, what types of firms are more likely to relocate their manufacturing capacity to low-wage destinations, and where firms tend to relocate their production lines (Xu et al., 2017).

---

[9] An example of pilot firm-level efforts is the micro and small enterprises survey led by Professor Xiaobo Zhang at Peking University. But surveys on big export-oriented firms are scarce, as challenges such as access to firms are more compelling.

This pilot firm-level survey was complemented by in-depth case studies on garment firms.

To make the pilot survey feasible, we selected four labour-intensive light manufacturing sectors—home appliances, garments, footwear, and toys—collectively employing about 16 million workers in China. We focused on light manufacturing firms from the four selected sectors in the Yangtze River Delta (YRD) and Pearl River Delta (PRD) regions, where light manufacturing firms are geographically concentrated.[10]

A cluster-based sampling strategy was used, since industrial clustering is crucial in the development of Chinese manufacturing.[11] The sampling frame used in the project is the database of above-scale industrial firms with revenue from their principal business of above RMB 20 million (US$3 million) in 2013 according to the National Bureau of Statistics in China.[12] The sample also took into account realistic potential for outward investment, by restricting inclusion to 'above-scale' firms which were exporting more than half of their turnover. In the end, we surveyed 640 firms, with the response rate of over 40 per cent much higher than initially expected (see Table 13.1 for the detailed distribution of firms by sector and region).

A key finding from the survey is that rising labour costs have been the number one challenge facing firms. With annual wage growth rate of 10–20 per cent from 2014 to 2016, more than 80 per cent of firms considered rising labour costs (including wages, welfare, and social insurance) one of their three main challenges. Nearly half of these firms regarded rising labour costs as the top challenge. In addition, the rising costs of raw material inputs and shrinking demand for their products have squeezed profitability. As a result, many Chinese firms are losing competitive advantage.

---

[10] In line with the official definition of the YRD and PRD, the following cities were selected: nine in the PRD—Guangzhou, Shenzhen, Zhuhai, Foshan, Jiangmen, Dongguan, Zhongshan, Huizhou, and Zhaoqing; and twelve in the YRD—Shanghai, Nanjing, Hangzhou, Ningbo, Zhoushan, Shaoxing, Huzhou, Jiaxing, Suzhou, Wuxi, Changzhou, and Nantong.

[11] Counties/districts within the two selected provinces, Guangdong and Zhejiang, were ranked in terms of the number of firms within each selected sector. A shortlist was constructed of counties/districts that cumulatively accounted for 30 per cent of the total number of firms in each sector in each province. Accordingly, we conducted our survey in a small number of cities: three cities (Guangzhou, Zhongshan, and Dongguan) in the PRD and one, Ningbo, in the YRD.

[12] The enterprise survey has been widely used in other studies (Brandt et al., 2014; Xu and Hubbard, 2018). It provides detailed financial information from the enterprises' financial accounts, including total wages, assets, revenue, profit, and ownership, as well as data on their industrial sector and location. Data in the database come mainly from the quarterly and annual summary reports submitted by companies to their local Bureau of Statistics. The database includes basic information such as address and phone number, industry, type of ownership, affiliation, and year of starting operation. It also includes economic and financial information, such as number of employees, balance sheet, turnover, operating costs (including labour and intermediate input costs), profits earned, taxes paid, and exports. We focus on export-oriented firms whose export value accounts for over 50 per cent of total annual output.

Table 13.1. Details of enterprises by sector and region

	Surveyed firms			Sampled firms		
	YRD	PRD	Total	YRD	PRD	Total
Home appliances	146 (23)	129 (20)	275 (43)	274 (19)	247 (17)	521 (37)
Garments	75 (12)	121 (19)	196 (31)	257 (18)	324 (23)	581 (41)
Footwear	0	89 (14)	89 (14)	0	188 (13)	188 (13)
Toys	0	80 (13)	80 (13)	0	133 (9)	133 (9)
Total	221 (35)	419 (65)	640 (100)	531 (37)	892 (63)	1,423 (100)

Note: 1. Brackets are percentages of total survey (640) in 'Surveyed Firms' column, or total sample (1,423) in 'Sampled Firms' column. 2. In the end, we selected firms in the footwear and toy sectors only from Guangdong Province, as both sectors are geographically concentrated in Guangdong.

Source: Institute of New Structural Economics and the Overseas Development Institute

In response to rising labour costs, more than half of the enterprises surveyed regarded technological upgrading as their preferred strategy to reduce labour costs and increase labour productivity. While replacing labour with machines appears to be the dominant strategy adopted by firms, automation, as a principal form of technological upgrading, has its own limitations in its application to light manufacturing sectors. First, the investment required for automated equipment is so large that it goes beyond the capacity of small and medium firms. Second, many manufacturing processes in specific sectors such as garments or footwear are difficult to automate. For example, cutting, sewing, buttoning, ironing, and garment inspection cannot be entirely undertaken by machines. Third, automation also has maintenance costs and technical personnel requirements. Other strategies adopted by a number of respondents in response to rising labour costs were tightening cost control over inputs and production, and changing product lines or expanding markets.

It seems that the wave of relocations of production lines abroad is yet to occur. Only 10 per cent of the firms surveyed had invested abroad in the past or planned to do so in the next three years. Yet this may be an underestimate of the number of 'flying geese' for two reasons. First, the survey could not include firms which had already relocated in their entirety.[13] Second, investments abroad by parent companies of surveyed firms were not reported in responses.[14] Even using this conservative ratio of 10 per cent, a rough estimate

[13] Casual observations suggest that a large proportion of labour-intensive factories originally from Hong Kong, Taiwan, and Korea have left China.

[14] The survey also under-reports opportunities for low-income, labour-abundant countries. If firms in China fail to cope with the challenge of rising wages by automation or relocation and close down, the market for their exports will be freed up for firms in other countries to fill as global buyers are looking for low-cost destinations to maximize their profits.

of potentially relocated Chinese light manufacturing jobs stands at about 8.5 million.[15] While this is relatively small, as an additional 185 million of the labour force will be searching for jobs by 2030 in Africa, it is still significant in absolute terms.

But it is worth noting that relocating light manufacturing capacity abroad is gaining pace. Despite the relatively small numbers of 'flying geese' up to now, a large proportion of relocations to low-wage developing countries have occurred since 2010.

When we have a close look at the 'flying geese', it turns out that large foreign-owned footwear and garment firms engaging in original design manufacturing (ODM) are more likely to relocate their production capacity. This finding helps to shed light on the question of what kinds of firms have a greater tendency to become 'flying geese'.

First, larger firms were in general more likely to expand or transfer production abroad than smaller firms. About 12 per cent of large firms with more than 1,000 employees relocated, compared with 7 per cent of medium firms with 300–999 employees and 4 per cent of small firms with 20–299 employees. Relocating production capacity abroad entails high risks especially when the host country suffers from political instability and macroeconomic fluctuations. Big firms may have greater capacity to mitigate risks and cope with challenges.

Second, foreign-owned firms have a greater tendency to relocate abroad than domestic-owned ones. Though only 8 per cent of foreign-owned firms preferred relocation abroad as their strategy for coping with rising costs, they were four times more likely to choose this option than domestic-owned firms. One possible reason is that foreign-owned private enterprises located in the Pearl River Delta (a large group within the survey) already have experience of overseas investment. In other words, foreign-owned firms are experienced 'flying geese' which can anticipate the wave of relocation in advance instead of taking a wait-and-see attitude.

Third, firms in the footwear and garment sector are considerably more likely to relocate abroad than firms in the home appliances and toy sectors. Twenty-seven per cent of footwear firms and 5.6 per cent of garment firms either had already invested abroad or planned to do so in the next three years, compared with 1.8 per cent in the home appliances sector and 1.3 per cent in the toy sector. This intriguing pattern begs further investigation. One possible reason is that mechanization in production is difficult in the footwear and garment sectors. In other words, labour cannot be readily replaced by machine so that

---

[15] As our survey shows that there may be variation in the relocation decision across different light manufacturing sub-sectors, the estimate here should not be interpreted as prediction but rather a hint for further investigation.

firms have to relocate to low-wage regions to bring down production costs. A second possible reason is that supply chains are relatively simple in footwear and garments compared to household appliances and toys, so reducing wage costs is more likely to compensate for rising logistical costs.[16] Another possible reason is that Chinese firms in the footwear and garment sectors can enjoy substantial tariff savings if they relocate their production lines to low-income developing countries that are eligible for preferential tariff schemes. These schemes include the US African Growth and Opportunity Act (AGOA), which provides for duty-free garment imports from many sub-Saharan African countries, and the EU's Everything But Arms (EBA) for forty-nine least-developed countries (LDCs), which gives duty-free and quota-free access for all products except weapons.[17] This allows for substantial price advantages in the US or EU markets for garments and footwear imported from these countries, compared with goods imported directly from China.[18]

Last but not least, the survey found that ODM firms were much more likely to establish production abroad than original brand manufacturing (OBM) firms. Nearly 14 per cent of ODM firms had already invested abroad compared with less than 4 per cent of OBM ones. The survey found that OBM firms had larger profit margins, which enabled them to pursue a diversification strategy. One example is the FIOCCO Group in the YRD region. According to a first-hand interview, the predecessor of the FIOCCO Group was established in 1992 as Huayi Fashion, a joint venture between a rural economic cooperative and a Taiwan company. After operating as an original equipment manufacturer (OEM) for about a decade, it started to establish its high-end women's fashion brand in 2006. In response to the challenge of rising labour costs, the FIOCCO Group diversified by venturing into the international logistics business, while still maintaining its foreign trade assembly business in order to provide much-needed capital to develop its own brand.

Where, then, have the flying geese gone? A close look at the destinations of overseas direct investment by the light manufacturing firms surveyed reveals that China's neighbours in South Asia and South-east Asia with low wages are the first to benefit from this potentially accelerating trend. Vietnam and Cambodia have been the most popular destinations. But it was reported during

---

[16] For example, Huajian, the first footwear firm to relocate to Ethiopia in 2012, had its logistics costs increased from 2 per cent to 8 per cent of total costs but its labour costs reduced from about 25 per cent to 5 per cent, compared to the cost structure in China (based on an interview with the owner of Huajian Industrial Holding Company).

[17] 'GSP+' provides for zero tariffs for sixteen countries that have met certain human rights and labour rights standards.

[18] For example, non-silk knitted and crocheted headbands and ponytail holders (HTS No. 6117.80.85.00) are imported into the United States duty free if coming from AGOA countries, compared with a 14.6 per cent duty rate from China; sports footwear with leather uppers (HTS No. 6404.11.20) is duty free from AGOA countries but carries a 10.5 per cent rate if made in China; and footwear with a protective metal toe-cap (HTS No. 6401.10.00.00) avoids a 37.5 per cent tariff.

the fieldwork that due to the relatively small labour pool, wages have been rising rapidly in South Asian and South-east Asian countries. For instance, the minimum wage rose from US$24 in 2009 to US$68 in 2013 in Bangladesh.[19] A similar trend of rising minimum wages can be found in Vietnam: the minimum wage rose from US$51 in 2010 to US$174 in 2018 in Hanoi and Ho Chi Minh City.[20] The average wage of garment factory workers rose from US$56 in 2010 to US$103 in 2017.[21]

Another prospect is that companies might be moving to Africa in search of lower wages. Indeed, the first pioneer wave of relocated Chinese plants can be seen in Ethiopia, for example, the Huajian shoe factory. The current labour force in sub-Saharan African countries is about 415 million, much larger than that of Vietnam and Cambodia combined (66 million).[22] The labour force in sub-Saharan Africa is forecast to grow to over 600 million by 2030.[23] While labour productivity is relatively low in Africa compared with that in China, it can be enhanced by providing training. Hence, Africa has a huge potential for undertaking labour-intensive light manufacturing.

In summary, rising labour costs are the most compelling challenge faced by Chinese light manufacturing firms. In response to this huge challenge, the majority of firms have chosen technology upgrading as the top strategy. But firms are more likely to become 'flying geese' if they are large foreign-owned footwear and garment firms engaging in ODM. While South-east Asian and South Asian countries are currently the most popular destinations for relocating Chinese light manufacturing firms, sub-Saharan African countries may become the next frontier as they possess abundant labour forces.

13.4 Flying Geese First Movers

While rising labour costs are the most severe challenge faced by Chinese light manufacturing firms, there are other significant challenges to investing outside China. These challenges are even more compelling for first movers venturing into a new destination, especially sub-Saharan African countries.

First movers have to overcome the fear of the unknown, which is exacerbated by information asymmetry. For most owners of Chinese light manufacturing firms, Africa is a remote continent afflicted with civil wars, infectious diseases, and macroeconomic instability. Although abundant young labour forces make

[19] Current prices, from International Labour Organization (ILO) Statistics.
[20] Current prices, from the official websites of the Ministry of Commerce and the Ministry of Human Resources and Social Security of the People's Republic of China, as the ILO only provides data for 2014 and 2016.
[21] Current prices, from CEIC data.   [22] World Development Indicators.
[23] ILO statistics.

Africa a potentially attractive destination for relocation, the misperception of risks has discouraged light manufacturing firms from relocating their production capacity to Africa.

The first-mover challenge has been further aggravated by the poor soft and hard infrastructure in Africa. A salient symptom of underdevelopment is that institutions and policies are not conductive to the development of the private sector due to cumbersome red tape, poor administration capacity, and rampant corruption. For instance, many African countries rank very low in the World Bank's Doing Business Indicators due to the poor business environment nationwide. Meanwhile, many African countries also suffer from infrastructure deficits making it difficult or prohibitive to transport goods to international markets, hindering the development of export-oriented manufacturing sectors.

One way to overcome the first-mover challenge is to attract anchor firms[24] to provide a 'demonstration effect'. An illustrative case is the pilot success of the Huajian Industrial Holding Company in Ethiopia. The company, which was established in 1996 with headquarters located in the city of Dongguan in Guangdong Province, specializes in high-end women's shoes, producing over 20 million pairs of shoes a year for renowned international brands such as Guess, Marc Fisher, Coach, and Calvin Klein Nina.[25]

A key ingredient in the pilot success of the Huajian Industrial Holding Company is that the Ethiopian government has targeted light manufacturing sectors in line with its latent comparative advantages: abundant cheap labour and leather. The Ethiopian government has been actively deploying an industrial policy to support prioritized sectors through five-year development plans. It was with the launch of the Growth & Transformation Plan (GTP I) covering 2010/2011–2014/2015 that the government placed great emphasis on FDI and manufacturing exports, with a special focus on leather goods, textiles, and garments in order to build up foreign exchange and accelerate technology transfer (Federal Democratic Republic of Ethiopia, 2010).

Another key element of success is very proactive investment promotion by high-level political leaders. The World Bank's Light Manufacturing in Africa project found that Ethiopia had factor-cost advantages in the shoe industry but suffered from binding constraints including backward infrastructure, poor business environment, and a lack of international buyer confidence in Ethiopia's ability to deliver products of consistent quality in a timely fashion. To win the confidence of international buyers, it is crucial to attract FDI from

---

[24] Anchor firms are large and reputable international firms that lead their industries in terms of production processes and best practice. They can encourage other foreign investors to follow suit.
[25] 'An Introduction to the Huajian Industrial Holding Company', http://www.huajian.com/hjgk/hjjj.html, accessed 1 July 2018.

Chinese light manufacturing enterprises which already have a track record of success. The then chief economist at the World Bank, Professor Justin Lin, reported the findings to the late prime minister Meles Zenawi in March 2011 and suggested he come to China to personally invite shoe manufacturers to invest in Ethiopia's Eastern Industrial Park. Prime Minister Zenawi took swift action, visiting the city of Dongguan in Guangdong Province in August 2011, once the frontier of mainland China that had seized the window of opportunity of industrial transfer from the East Asian 'tigers'. At the invitation of Prime Minister Zenawi, Huajian visited Addis Ababa in October 2011 and decided to invest on the spot. To overcome the challenge of the lack of skilled labour, Huajian recruited eighty-six Ethiopian workers to be trained in China. Two production lines with 600 employees were set up in January 2012, and the first shipment was exported to the United States in March 2012. By May 2012 Huajian had become the largest shoe exporter in Ethiopia, and by December 2012 employment had expanded to 2,000 workers. Huajian's exports comprised 57 per cent of Ethiopia's total leather export in 2012. The number of jobs created by the Huajian shoe factory had risen to 3,500 by December 2013.

Apart from sensible sectoral targeting and proactive investment promotion, special economic zones (SEZs) act as a 'nest' for the pilot 'bird' of this leading Chinese shoe company. The first SEZ in Ethiopia, Eastern Industrial Park (EIP), was planned and constructed from 2007 and hosted its first firm, the Zhongshun Cement Company, in 2010 (Gakunu et al., 2015). Since then, the government has made substantial investments in improving both the infrastructure and institutional frameworks required to develop a national SEZ programme. The EIP is a private zone developed by Jiangsu Yongyuan Group—originally a Chinese steel pipe and aluminium producer. While the EIP suffered from some early problems which can be expected in a pilot project, it helped provide basic infrastructure to Chinese firms to make their relocation feasible.

The success of Huajian has had a snowball effect in attracting FDI to Ethiopia. The twenty-two factory units in Bole Lemi, a new industrial park, were leased out in just three months in 2013. The Ethiopian government's proactive approach to attracting foreign direct investment bore further fruit. Phillips-Van Heusen Corporation (PVH), the second-largest apparel company in the world, chose Ethiopia as the base for its new business model of a fully vertically integrated, from ground to finished product, socially responsible supply chain. PVH came to lead a group of its top suppliers to build factories and a fabric mill in Ethiopia's Hawassa Industrial Park (HIP). The construction of HIP started in July 2015 and the park was inaugurated on 13 July 2016. Within a year, on 4 March 2017, one of HIP's tenants had exported HIP's first dress shirt (Mihretu and Llobet, 2017). Ethiopia has shared its pioneer experiences with Rwanda and Senegal. Delegations from other African countries have also visited Ethiopia to learn from its experience. In light of Ethiopia's success, C&H Garments invested in the Kigali Special Economic Zone in February 2015 and production began within two months. Over five hundred jobs were created by August 2015, 300 women were trained in embroidery to enable household manufacturing, and employment reached 2,000 in 2017. In Senegal, the first SEZ was created in 2015 to attract FDI in light manufacturing and international buyers such as Carrefour. Success stories have sparked further high-level political commitment to achieve quick wins for pan-African industrialization (Hai and Xu, 2016).

13.5 Policy Recommendations

The potential for the relocation of Chinese light manufacturing capacity to Africa is huge and relocation is gaining pace, but it is not automatic.[26] Unleashing this vast potential requires key stakeholders, especially host-country governments, to play an enabling and facilitating role. From the perspective of New Structural Economics (Lin, 2012a), economic structural transformation is achieved by creating synergies between an effective market and a facilitating government. New Structural Economics (NSE) as proposed by Professor Justin Yifu Lin applies a neoclassical approach to the study of economic structures and their evolution. NSE aims to address the limitations of traditional development thinking, including old structuralism with its overemphasis on state intervention and neoliberalism with its excessive focus on the free market. NSE is 'new' at least in two ways. First, it proposes that developing countries focus on what they can do well (latent comparative advantages) based on what they have (current factor endowments). In other words, it is an industrial policy that works with latent comparative advantages. It contrasts with 'old' industrial policies that failed, often because they involved supporting industries that were not going to be viable in the setting in which they were promoted. Second, it is new in the sense that it posits that a 'facilitating state' is necessary to provide the infrastructure and services needed by export industries, and that even in the poorest developing countries this is possible through cluster-based approaches in the form of industrial parks linked to ports. The 'facilitating state' is committed to generating a

---

[26] Although Chinese labour-intensive firms may decide to close their operations instead of relocating to other low-wage countries in the face of rising wages, the market they used to serve will not disappear but is open to be filled by other suppliers. If African countries can attract the relocation of some Chinese firms, as long as they can use them as catalysts to enhance domestic labour-intensive firms' capacity, improve logistics, and gain access to foreign buyers, they may be able to capture the market left by those firms that have closed in China and start a dynamic industrialization process.

dynamic capacity-development process that leads over the course of a generation to middle-income status, as has already been witnessed in recent history. The mainstream neoliberal framework does not provide for a facilitating government, hence the failure of neoliberal economists to predict or explain the Asian growth miracles.

In the case of today's industrial transfer from China to Africa, while labour-intensive light manufacturing sectors align well with the latent comparative advantage of African countries, these sectors cannot become competitive advantages in the international market unless the government plays a crucial role in identifying and mitigating binding constraints.

The first enabling condition is that the host government can build SEZs, strategically utilizing limited resources to improve soft and hard infrastructure in a geographically demarcated area of a country beset with poor overall infrastructure and business environment. This approach can achieve quick wins by turning the country's latent comparative advantages into competitive advantages and provides a demonstration effect to win the confidence of international investors and buyers. Yet SEZs often fail to live up to their initial expectations of helping African countries to kick-start economic structural transformation. There are at least four main reasons for these failures. First, SEZs have no sectoral targets or are too ambitious in targeting sectors beyond the country's comparative advantages where factor costs are much higher than international competitors', meaning they cannot compete in international markets. Second, lack of high-level political commitment makes it difficult, if not impossible, to put special policy incentives in place due to conflicts between zone authorities and line ministries. Third, basic connective infrastructure is missing so that firms face significant challenges such as electricity shortages. Last but not least, if zones are located in remote areas such as the hometowns of political leaders, export-oriented firms encounter much higher transport costs. Hence, host governments need to undertake a proactive learning process to fulfil the full potential of SEZs.

A second enabling element is that host African governments need to undertake proactive and targeted investment promotion. As shown in Section 13.4, the Ethiopian government has successfully managed to incentivize international firms to start investing in Ethiopia. This high-level commitment to supporting private-sector investment was reported to be a major driver of investment decisions, particularly among Chinese firms that are accustomed to collaborative relationships with local and national government. It is worth noting that not all African governments are ready to undertake proactive investment promotion as the Ethiopian government has done (Calabrese, Gelb, and Hou, 2017). Only those African governments that are ready to play a facilitating role in solving binding constraints faced by investors can successfully attract Chinese light manufacturing FDI. Furthermore, to create quick wins, African governments can target investment promotion more effectively by attracting those Chinese light manufacturing firms that are most likely to make the relocation. Based on our survey findings, large foreign-owned footwear firms engaging in processing trade in the Pearl River Delta region could be the initial focus for targeted investment promotion.

A third recommendation is that development agencies can play a catalytic role in overcoming first-mover challenges. Private enterprises often tend to take a wait-and-see attitude when untested markets entail huge risks. One challenge is lack of basic infrastructure in SEZs, as host governments are often fiscally restrained and private capital suffers from short-termism. In such circumstances, development agencies can provide much-needed patient capital to build infrastructure so as to lay the foundation for the pending relocation of Chinese light manufacturing firms. Another challenge is high political risks and policy uncertainties. Development agencies such as the International Finance Corporation (IFC) can offer equity investment to help mitigate risks and build the confidence of pilot investors. A third challenge is information asymmetry exacerbating the fear of the unknown. Development agencies can act as honest brokers by providing neutral information to potential investors and disseminating the pilots' success in an effort to attract a wider wave of investors. It is worth emphasizing that these types of incentive packages provided to first movers should include an exit clause under which special support should be phased out when pilot firms become economically viable after overcoming binding constraints. Meanwhile, it is necessary to collect first-hand information on the spillovers such as additional FDI, technology transfer, and labour productivity brought about by first movers in order to ensure that special support is justified by actual performance. In short, overcoming first-mover challenges can help to create a snowball effect in the future.

Last but not least, African governments need to play a proactive role in incentivizing foreign firms to provide on-the-job training. As discussed earlier, labour productivity is relatively low in Africa compared to China. African countries may be stuck in a predicament of low wages and low productivity, as foreign investors may not voluntarily provide training and simply take advantage of cheap labour to produce low-end products or segments while keeping the high-end ones in their home countries. As on-the-job training is one key avenue for creating spillovers from FDI in the local economy, African governments should proactively incentivize foreign investors to train local workers and upgrade value chains.

In summary, key stakeholders need to play an enabling and facilitating role in helping African countries to seize the window of opportunity of the pending relocation of Chinese light manufacturing firms.

A final note of caution is that this window of opportunity may be closing if African countries do not act urgently. Two secular trends may risk the loss of such unprecedented opportunities for African countries. First, preferential trade agreements may be affected by huge political uncertainties which may discourage Chinese light manufacturers from relocating to African countries. For example, the Trump administration in the United States recently decided to suspend duty-free benefits for Rwandan textile imports.[27] AGOA was enacted by the United States in the year 2000 under President Bill Clinton, but its current preferences and privileges may expire in 2026 if no further extension is authorized.[28] Second, an overall trend towards automation in the manufacturing sector may result in fewer manual jobs for low-income countries, though there are limitations on fully applying automation in some light manufacturing sectors. In a nutshell, there is a much-needed sense of urgency for African countries to seize the window of opportunity presented by the unprecedented relocation of Chinese light manufacturing firms to promote their economic structural transformation.

References

Akamatsu K. (1962) 'A Historical Pattern of Economic Growth in Developing Countries', *Journal of Developing Economies*, 1(1): 3–25.

Brandt, L., J. Van Biesebroeck, and Y. Zhang (2014) 'Challenges of Working with the Chinese NBS Firm-Level Data', *China Economic Review*, 30: 339–52.

Brookings (2014) 'Learning to Compete: Industrialization in Africa and Emerging Asia' Learning to Compete Working Papers, Washington, DC, https://www.brookings.edu/research/learning-to-compete-industrialization-in-africa-and-emerging-asia/.

Calabrese, Linda, Stephen Gelb, and Jun Hou (2017) 'What Drives Chinese Outward Manufacturing Investment? A Review of Enabling Factors in Africa and Asia', ODI Supporting Economic Transformation Background Paper.

Chen, Wenjie, and Heiwai Tang (2014) 'The Dragon Is Flying West: Micro-Level Evidence of Chinese Outward Direct Investment', *Asian Development Review*, 31(2): 109–40.

Federal Democratic Republic of Ethiopia (2010) 'Growth and Transformation Plan (GTP I) 2010/11–2014/15', Ministry of Finance and Economic Development (MoFED), Addis Ababa.

Gakunu, Peter, et al. (2015) 'Comparative Study on Special Economic Zones in Africa and China', Working Paper No. 06/2015, United Nations Development Programme; the International Poverty Reduction Center in China, http://www.cn.undp.org/

---

[27] Sarah McGregor, 'US Suspends Duty-Free Benefits for Rwandan Textile Imports', 20 March 2018, https://agoa.info/news/article/15401-us-suspends-duty-free-benefits-for-rwandan-textile-imports.html, accessed 30 August 2018.

[28] AGOA FAQ, https://agoa.info/about-agoa/faq.html#what_is_AGOA, accessed 30 August 2018.

content/dam/china/docs/Publications/UNDP-CH-Comparative%20Study%20on%20SEZs%20in%20Africa%20and%20China%20-%20ENG.pdf.

Hai, Yu and Jiajun Xu (2016) 'Industrialization and Job Creation for Africa', in *Good Practices in South-South and Triangular Cooperation for Sustainable Development*, United Nations Office for South-South Cooperation, pp. 9–10.

Lin, Justin Yifu (2012a) *New Structural Economics: A Framework for Rethinking Development and Policy*. Washington, DC: The World Bank.

Lin, Justin Yifu (2012b) 'From Flying Geese to Leading Dragons: New Opportunities and Strategies for Structural Transformation in Developing Countries', *Global Policy* 3(4): 397–409.

Mihretu, Mamo, and Gabriela Llobet (2017) 'Looking beyond the Horizon: A Case Study of PVH's Commitment to Ethiopia's Hawassa Industrial Park', World Bank Group, Washington, DC.

Rodrik, Dani (2016) 'Premature Deindustrialization', *Journal of Economic Growth*, 21(1): 1–33.

Sun, Irene Yuan, Kartik Jayaram, and Omid Kassiri (2017) 'Dance of the Lions and Dragons: How Are Africa and China Engaging, and How Will the Partnership Evolve?' McKinsey & Company, New York.

Rosen, Daniel H., and Thilo Hanemann (2009) 'China's Changing Outbound Foreign Direct Investment Profile: Drivers and Policy Implication', Policy Brief 09–14, Peterson Institute for International Economics, Washington, DC.

Tan, Xiaomei (2013) 'China's Overseas Investment in the Energy/Resources Sector: Its Scale, Drivers, Challenges and Implications', *Energy Economics*, 36: 750–8.

Wangwe, Samuel, et al. (2016) 'The Performance of the Manufacturing Sector in Tanzania: Challenges and the Way forward', Learning to Compete Working Paper No. 22, Brookings Institute, Washington, DC.

Xu, Jiajun, et al. (2017) 'Adjusting to Rising Costs in Chinese Light Manufacturing: What Opportunities for Developing Countries?' Center for New Structural Economics and Overseas Development Institute, Peking University, Beijing.

Xu, J. and P. Hubbard (2018) 'A Flying Goose Chase: China's Overseas Direct Investment in Manufacturing (2011–2013)', *China Economic Journal*, 11(2): 91–107.

14

Catalysing China–Africa Ties for Africa's Structural Transformation

Lessons from Ethiopia

Fantu Cheru and Arkebe Oqubay

14.1 Introduction

The development landscape for Africa has changed drastically with the emergence of new development partners from the South, such as China, India, Brazil, and Turkey. While the OECD countries will remain important partners for Africa for the foreseeable future, the centre of gravity is irrevocably shifting South–South and eastwards (Alden, 2007; Cheru and Obi, 2010; Manning, 2006). The impressive growth registered over the past decade in many African countries has been underpinned by the insatiable appetite of emerging economies for African oil, gas, and mineral resources, coupled with expanded investment in Africa's infrastructure sector, which has enabled African countries such as Ethiopia to raise their productive potential, diversify their economic base, and move goods to local, regional, and global markets relatively quickly (*The Economist*, 2011; UNECA, 2013). Improved access to transport and energy has been critical in the observed productivity gain in agriculture and other sectors.

This positive portrayal of China's role in Africa does not suggest that there are no tensions between the two trading partners over economic policy. As a rising global power with a huge stake in the global economy, China behaves in the same way as the United States or any other developed country in the conduct of its economic relations with Africa. Despite the official rhetoric of mutual interest and solidarity with African nations, China's national interest is always paramount. Possible areas of tension between China and Africa could include, among others: (a) direct competition in domestic markets from cheap manufactured Chinese goods, displacing small and medium-sized African producers; (b) indirect competition in export markets of interest to Africa, namely in sectors such as textiles, footwear, and leather (Geda and Meskel, 2010); (c) limited local in-sourcing and sub-contracting opportunities for medium-sized African firms (Axelsson and Sylvanus, 2010; Wethal, 2018); and (d) poor environmental and labour practices by Chinese firms operating in Africa (Human Rights Watch, 2011). While these tensions are unavoidable, it is up to individual African countries to craft the necessary regulatory frameworks and enforcement mechanisms to resolve emerging tensions and to ensure that Chinese investment becomes a catalyst for Africa's industrialization and structural transformation (Cheru and Obi, 2011; Mohan et al., 2014).

This chapter examines the strategies adopted by the government of Ethiopia to engage China strategically in its quest for industrialization and structural transformation. The chapter aims to decipher the role of Ethiopia's developmental state in framing a long-term development vision for the country to harness the catalytic effect of economic ties with emerging powers from the East, particularly China, to achieve rapid economic growth and diversification, and develop domestic capabilities for sustained growth through a process of experimentation and learning by doing (Oqubay, 2015, 2019a). The chapter concludes by distilling the lessons learned in policymaking, negotiation strategy and capacity, knowledge acquisition, and absorption that might be relevant for other African countries seeking new pathways to structural transformation.

14.2 Beyond Theory and Ideology: the Role of History and African Agency

The literature on China–Africa relations has proliferated over the past decade. There are contending perspectives in the literature purporting to identify the real impact of China on Africa's development, and these can be classified into two broad camps: the 'alarmists' and the 'cheerleaders'. The first frames China as an 'imperialist' power intent on exploiting African resources and dominating the African market (Moyo, 2013; Sautmann and Hairong, 2008; Southall and Melber, 2009), while the second portrays China as a natural partner that will catalyse Afro-centric development in the context of South–South solidarity (Wenping, 2007: 23–40; Brautigam, 2009; Cheru and Modi, 2013; French, 2014). Bordering on xenophobia, scholars in the 'alarmist' camp characterize China's foray into Africa as being synonymous with a 'new form of imperialism' (Naim, 2007; Pillsbury, 2015; Zakaria, 2008).

By contrast, the second camp—the 'pragmatic cheerleaders'—regard the rise of China and other emerging southern actors as an opportunity rather than a threat. These scholars take the position that the rise of China and other emerging countries could open new possibilities for African countries to experiment with alternative development models without the strong-arm tactics of Western aid agencies and creditor institutions (Brautigam, 2009; Carmody, 2013; Cheru and Obi, 2010; Mohan and Power, 2008; UNCTAD, 2010). They further point to the fact that China, in a relatively short thirty years, overcame the legacies of colonialism, built one of the most powerful economies in the world, and lifted more than 700 million of its people out of poverty. Therefore, African countries can learn many lessons from the Chinese economic reform experience without having to export them to Africa in their entirety (see Chapters 3 and 14).

The relationship between China and Africa is more complex than the contending perspectives suggest. In this chapter, we try to put centre stage the issue of 'African agency' (Mohan and Lampert, 2013). We take the position that the rise of China neither necessarily produces a new 'colonial-type' relationship nor does it automatically guarantee African countries the freedom to determine their own development path without external intrusion. Transforming the new relationship with China into a 'win–win' partnership will ultimately depend on the nature of the state and political leadership in each African country; whether the government has articulated a long-term national development vision and strong institutions to drive the structural transformation agenda (Zenawi, 2012). In short, the government must set priorities, decide policy content, create necessary conditions, be responsible for implementing and monitoring projects, and be prepared to engage its external partners strategically and without surrendering its sovereignty.

Recent empirical evidence shows that, far from being powerless in the face of China's economic might, some African states have been able to turn the opportunities and resources provided by Chinese engagement to their own advantage (Mohan and Lampert, 2013: 92–3; Cheru, 2016). Ethiopia represent one such example where the EPRDF-led government has been able to strategically harness its relationship with new as well as traditional Western development partners to implement its ambitious programme of industrialization. What is even more unique in the case of Ethiopia has been the government's ability to use its strategic partnership with China as an explicit bargaining chip in its negotiations with European donors and vice versa (Cheru, 2016). This has allowed the EPRDF elites to choose from a wider range of development models that are relevant to Ethiopia than was previously the case. Indeed, Ethiopia features economic philosophy, policy capability, and growth performance that are more akin to those of East Asia's industrializing economies. The country also exhibits a high degree of political ownership and reasonably well-developed institutional capacity for implementation of policies and strategies.

It must, however, be pointed out at the outset that Ethiopia's successful development experience in the post-1991 period cannot be understood without a full grasp of the ideological underpinnings and strategic orientations of the post-liberation Ethiopian 'national project'. Since assuming power in May 1991, the EPRDF-led government has been engaged in a highly political state-building project, underpinned by a long-term political and development vision aimed at empowering the 90 per cent of Ethiopians who happen to be impoverished small-scale subsistence farmers. Central to the post-liberation national development project was the urgent need to radically transform the economy away from subsistence agriculture and towards agricultural-led industrialization to lift millions of subsistence farmers out of abject poverty, achieve full food security, and tap into the growing opportunities of the global economy. It is in this broader quest for structural transformation that China–Ethiopia relations must be examined.

14.3 Ethiopia–China Relations: Background and Context

Ethiopia is one of a few African countries that has taken a more 'strategic' approach to engaging China while maintaining strong ties with its traditional Western development partners. As it is a non-oil exporting country, Ethiopia's policymakers have enabled the country to embark on its ambitious industrialization agenda by mobilizing large amounts of investments both from China and other emerging economies, and from traditional Western development partners (e.g. WB, AfDB, OPEC Fund).

From the mid-1970s until the collapse of communism in Eastern Europe in the late 1980s, Ethiopia's foreign policy was strategically aligned with the Soviet Union. From the mid-1990s onwards, things began to change. The late prime minister Meles Zenawi visited China in 1995 and the Chinese reciprocated when Chinese president Jiang Zemin visited Ethiopia in 1997. During his first visit to China, Prime Minister Meles personally persuaded Chinese investors to come and invest in Ethiopia and assured them that his government was prepared to offer them all the necessary incentives for success. During the two exchange visits, Ethiopia and China signed several bilateral economic and educational agreements. A year later, in 1998, a Joint Ethiopia–China Commission (JECC) was established between Ethiopia's Ministry of Finance and Economic Development (MOFED) and China's Ministry of Commerce (MOFCOM).[1] The JECC serves as a platform for coordinating economic and technical cooperation agreements between the

[1] Interview with programme officers at the China Coordination Desk of MOFED, Addis Ababa, 17 August 2015.

two parties. Technical teams from both sides meet every two years and the meetings are held alternately in Beijing and Addis Ababa. Decisions on large-scale loans from China take place on a case-by-case basis, often at the highest political level.

A second channel that facilitates relations between China and Ethiopia is the respective political parties of both countries—the Ethiopian People's Revolutionary Democratic Front (EPRDF) and the Chinese Communist Party (CCP). Each year up to two hundred officials from Ethiopian regional and national administrations travel to China to attend training and experience-sharing programmes. Party-to-party meetings provide a channel to discuss development experiences, the role of the party in the state, or party succession strategies.

The decision to engage China constructively coincided with the strategic shift in economic policy that was underway in Ethiopia from the mid-1990s onwards. While the EPRDF reluctantly embraced neoliberal policies in the first decade after assuming power, its commitment to bring about structural trans-formation under the guidance of the state predates the party's accession to power in May 1991. During the transition period in the early 1990s, Western donors consistently pressed the government to open the economy to foreign investors and introduce far-reaching market-oriented reforms. Despite having serious misgivings about the relevance of a neoliberal economic policy in post-conflict Ethiopia, the EPRDF reluctantly began to implement IMF/World Bank-supported market-oriented reforms in exchange for accessing badly needed donor funding to kick-start the economy and undertake post-conflict reconstruction and rehabilitation projects. These donor-supported reform programmes had, by and large, limited impact on reversing the productivity decline in Ethiopian agriculture and on generating enough jobs for the population.

The poor state of the economy called for more radical and counter-hegemonic thinking on development policy. After a series of internal discus-sions and debates within the party in the early 2000s, a consensus was reached within the EPRDF on the need to counterbalance the excessive meddling of Western donors by diversifying Ethiopia's foreign and economic relations through closer engagement with the emerging countries of Asia, and to place centre stage the role of the state in national development. South Korea and Taiwan were Prime Minister Meles's favourite examples of developmental states that had succeeded in subverting the neoliberal dogma (De Wall, 2012; Zenawi, 2006).

Central to the East Asian economic miracle, according to Meles, was the role played by the Chinese state in guiding the market through disciplined plan-ning, and the willingness of the state to experiment with 'heterodox' policies to revive the economy, compete in global markets, and reduce poverty in the process while moving in a free-market direction. This strategy is in stark contrast to the failed policies of the Washington Consensus that Ethiopia and other African nations followed faithfully without any success.

While the ideological roots of a 'developmentalism and developmental state' approach appears to date from the period of the liberation struggle, its substantive parts were developed in successive development plans, starting with the Programme for Accelerated and Sustained Development to End Poverty (PASDEP–2005/10). PASDEP aimed at moving Ethiopia from dependence on subsistence agriculture towards industrialization and the export of value-added products under the guidance of a strong and development-oriented state (MOFED, 2005; Zenawi, 2012). Based on the lessons learned from implementing PASDEP, the government formulated the first Growth and Transformation Plan (2010–15) in 2010 (MOFED, 2010). The GTP's approach of 'state-led' systemic transformation drew its inspiration from the East Asian model of development.

The key vectors of interaction between Ethiopia and China include measures to expand trading opportunities, soft loans for infrastructure projects, direct investment, technical assistance, and training programmes.

14.3.1 *Trade Patterns*

As a non-oil exporting country, Ethiopia's trade with China has grown dramatically over the past decade. China is Ethiopia's second most important trading partner, behind the European Union, but ahead of the United States. However, it is important to note that Ethiopia's exports to China are negligible: a mere US$288 million compared to its imports from China which stood at US$4.8 billion in 2017, leaving a trade deficit of US$12.16 billion in China's favour. Imports from China grew at the rate of 37 per cent during the period 2000–10 and 17 per cent from 2011 to 2017 (ERCA, 2018; see also Appendix, Table A14.2).

14.3.1.1 EXPORT GROWTH AND COMPOSITION
While Ethiopia's export to China has grown substantially over the last decade, reaching US$288 million in 2017, the European Union remains Ethiopia's top trading partner (US$881.45 million), followed by the Middle East (US$553.82 million). China accounts for 10 per cent of Ethiopia's total exports while the United States and the European Union accounted for 29.1 per cent of total Ethiopian exports in 2017 (Figure 14.1).

Ethiopia's exports to China are dominated by unprocessed agricultural products such as sesame seeds, oil seeds, leather, and spices. Ethiopia benefits from the preferential trade arrangement that China announced in 2006. The number of products covered under the zero-tariff programme grew from 190

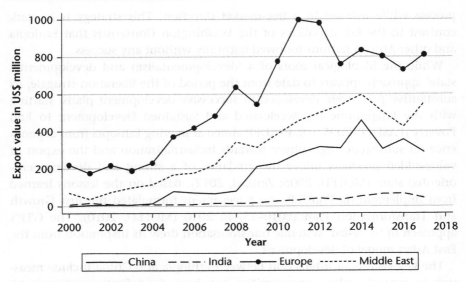

Figure 14.1. Ethiopia's export comparison, 2000–17

Source: Ethiopian Revenue and Customs Authority (2018) (based on Appendix Table A14.1 unpublished)

in 2006 to 440 in 2012 (Anshan et al., 2012). There is still considerable room for Ethiopia to take advantage of the preferential trade arrangement with China through expanded value addition to its agricultural products and by developing niche markets in highly selected agricultural products to meet the demands of a growing Chinese middle class. The rapid growth of the Ethiopian wine industry and its success in penetrating the Chinese market is a good illustration of what Ethiopia can do to expand its trade with China.

14.3.1.2 IMPORT VOLUME AND STRUCTURE

Imports from China have grown exponentially since the adoption of Growth and Transformation Plan I in 2010, reflecting the high level of investment by the government in mega infrastructure projects and the boom in private construction of housing and office buildings. Ethiopia's imports from China include finished manufactured goods, machinery, iron and steel, construction materials, power generation and transmission equipment, and industrial parts. As shown in Figure 14.2, the total value of imports in 2000–17 was US$142.39 billion, of which imports from China accounted for 26 per cent (or US$37 billion) of the total import bill. The other import destinations for the same period were: India US$11.6 billion (8 per cent), Europe US$26.93 billion (19 per cent), the Middle East US$30.96 billion (22 per cent), and other countries US$36.32 billion (25 per cent) (ERCA, 2018).

The structure of Ethiopia's import–export trade with China is heavily in favour of China and the trade deficit between the two countries has grown substantially in recent years, contributing to the balance-of-payments crisis. Ethiopia's inability to export its way out of the crisis has further deepened the debt burden with China and other trading partners. Overall Ethiopia incurred a trade deficit of US$11.8 billion in 2017, down by 14.2 per cent from the US$13.8 billion in the red for 2016 (see Table 14.1). These cashflow deficiencies clearly indicate Ethiopia's competitive disadvantages, but also present key opportunities for Ethiopia to develop country-specific strategies to strengthen its overall position in international trade.

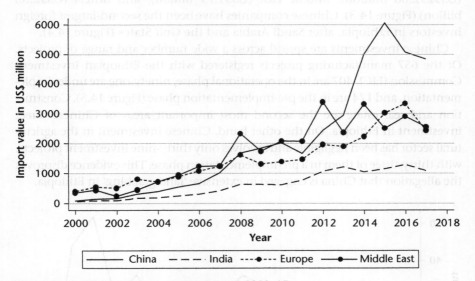

Figure 14.2. Ethiopia's import comparison, 2000–17

Source: Ethiopian Revenue and Customs Authority (2018) (based on Appendix Table A14.2, unpublished)

Table 14.1. Ethiopia's trade deficits with key trading partner countries, 2017 (in US$ millions)

China	−4,600
India	−1,000
United States	−984
Italy	−584
Japan	−579
Kuwait	−563
Turkey	−557
Malaysia	−340
Morocco	−286
Saudi Arabia	−247

Note: Rounded to single digit.

Source: UN Comtrade data and Trade Map, International Trade Centre

14.3.2 *The Productive Nature of Chinese FDI Inflow*

Although Ethiopia is not an oil-exporting country, it has been successful in attracting investment from many countries and covering a wide range of sectors. The total number of new manufacturing firms in Ethiopia from 2000 to 2017 was China (407), India (123), Europe (60), and Middle East (112). Of the 407 Chinese firms, eighty-seven were joint ventures (ERCA, 2018).

In terms of the value of FDI inflows in the manufacturing sector from 2000 to 2017, the total was close to US$5.65 billion. This is distributed as follows: China (US$851.74 million), India (US$261.95 million), Europe (US$292.08 million), Middle East (US$1.71 billion), and others (US$2.53 billion) (Figure 14.3). Chinese companies have been the second-largest foreign investors in Ethiopia, after Saudi Arabia and the Gulf States (Figure 14.4).

Chinese investments are spread across a wide number and range of projects. Of the 657 manufacturing projects registered with the Ethiopian Investment Commission (EIC), 407 are in the operational phase, ninety-one are under implementation, and 174 are in the pre-implementation phase (Figure 14.5). Construction and real estate are the second most important areas of Chinese direct investment in Ethiopia. On the other hand, Chinese investment in the agricultural sector has been negligible and involves only thirty-nine investment projects, with thirty-three of them in a pre-implementation phase. This evidence disproves the allegation that China is engaged in extensive 'land grabbing' in Ethiopia.

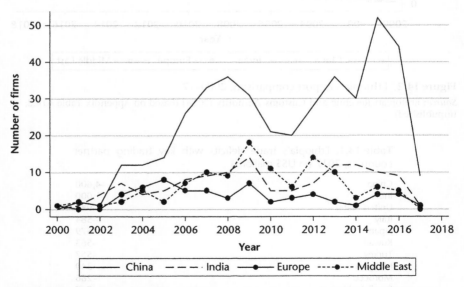

Figure 14.3. Total number of new FDI manufacturing firms in Ethiopia, 2000–17

Source: Ethiopian Investment Commission (2018) (based on Appendix Table A14.3, unpublished)

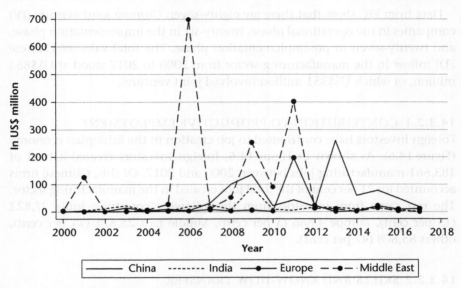

Figure 14.4. FDI inflow to Ethiopia, 2000–17
Source: Ethiopian Investment Commission (2018) (unpublished)

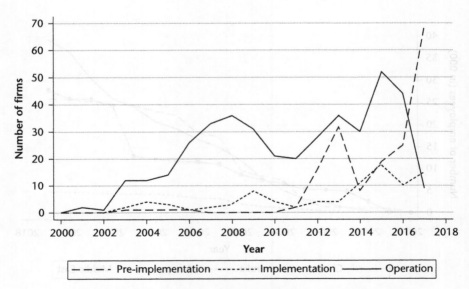

Figure 14.5. New Chinese manufacturing firms in three phases
Source: Ethiopian Investment Commission (2018) (unpublished)

Data from EIC show that there are eighty-seven Chinese joint venture (JV) companies in the operational phase, twenty-six in the implementation phase, and twenty-seven in pre-implementation phase. The total value of Chinese FDI inflow in the manufacturing sector from 2000 to 2017 stood at US$852 million, of which US$351 million involved joint ventures.

14.3.2.1 CONTRIBUTION TO PRODUCTIVE EMPLOYMENT

Foreign investors have contributed to job creation in the Ethiopian economy (Figure 14.6). As shown in Figure 14.6, foreign investors created a total of 183,661 manufacturing jobs between 2000 and 2017. Of this, Chinese firms accounted for 21 per cent of the total jobs created in the manufacturing sector. The rest came from investors from the following countries: India 27,822 (15 per cent), Europe 4,866 (3 per cent), Middle East 25,871 (14 per cent), others 85,808 (47 per cent).

14.3.2.2 SKILLS AND KNOW-HOW TRANSFER

The most visible part of the Chinese attempt to transfer knowledge and skills has been the experiment to set up special economic zones (SEZs). The first export processing zone (EPZ) was set up in Lebu, on the outskirts of Addis Ababa in 2015. The EPZ aimed to employ 30,000 workers and provide housing and schooling on site. Initial funding for Lebu came from the Huajian Group—a Chinese leather shoe manufacturer—and interested investors

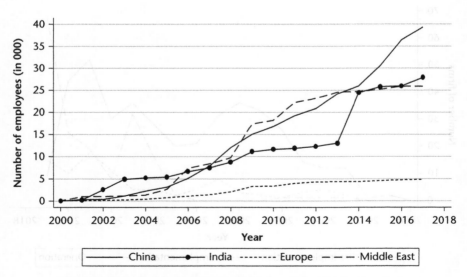

Figure 14.6. Employment generated (cumulative) by foreign firms
Source: Ethiopian Investment Commission (2018) (unpublished)

include the China–Africa Development Fund (CAD) and the International Financial Corporation (IFC). The developer claims that the zone is projected to require US$2 billion dollars of investment and yield US$4 billion dollars in return over ten years. Six private new SEZs or industrial parks were planned during the period of GTP II (2015–20).

In addition, China supported the establishment of the Ethiopia–China Polytechnic College in 2009 and continues to grant scholarships to large numbers of Ethiopian students to study in Chinese universities, including short-term training for large numbers of government officials and technocrats from line ministries.

14.3.3 *Financing and Infrastructure Development*

In addition to Chinese private investment, Chinese firms are extensively engaged in huge infrastructure projects carried out by the government of Ethiopia. These projects, which cover roads, rail, hydro-power, and telecommunications, are largely financed by multilateral institutions, such as the World Bank, the African Development Bank, the Arab Fund, the China Development Bank, and the Export-Import (Exim) Bank of China.

Accurate figures on the total amount of loans (concessional and non-concessional) that Ethiopia has been able to secure from China are difficult to come by (see Chapter 7). The best available data is provided by the China Africa Research Initiative (CARI) at Johns Hopkins University. According to a CARI briefing paper issued in August 2018, 'Chinese creditors have loaned at least US$12.1 billion to Ethiopia since 2000, yet Ethiopia has also borrowed heavily from the Middle East, the World Bank, and others, with a total debt of US$29 billion' (CARI, 2018: 2). We have attempted to provide a more comprehensive overview of the scale of Ethiopia's external borrowing, for example, but a complete breakdown of lending countries and institutions was difficult to come by due to the different reporting requirements of government institutions responsible for power, roads, and rail transport. In addition, there are sensitivities on the part of the government regarding disclosures on foreign loans. In some other cases, the reasons were more prosaic and practical. For example, Table A14.4 (in Appendix) presents a listing of Chinese loans for various infrastructure projects in 2012/13.

14.3.3.1 POWER SECTOR

Under the GTP, the Ethiopian government aims to enhance power projects from 2,178 MW to 10,000 MW. The Chinese are involved in nearly all power generation projects in the country. In addition to dam construction and transmission tower construction, Chinese engineering companies, such as Bonle International, China Wanbao Engineering Corporation, Zhejiang

Holley International, and China National Electric Equipment Corporation, have been the main suppliers of electrical accessories for several AfDB II-financed universal access projects worth millions of dollars (see Table A14.5 in Appendix).

14.3.3.2 TRANSPORT INFRASTRUCTURE

Chinese companies have dominated the transport infrastructure sector in Ethiopia. Chinese firms have been engaged in about 60 per cent of the road works being carried out in the country and have brought with them the financing for over 2,000 kilometres of the national rail network and about 30 kilometres of the Addis Ababa railway construction. The railway deal with China is estimated a total commercial loan of US$3 billion, which included US$2.5 billion for the Ethiopia–Djibouti railway and the remaining US$500 million for light city railways in Addis Ababa.

It is important to point out, however, that not all large-scale construction projects in Ethiopia are financed by official Chinese entities. As shown in Table A14.6 in the Appendix, most of the road and rail network projects are Ethiopian government investments financed either from Ethiopia's own resources or from loans secured from IDA, AfDB, and other Gulf-based Arab development finance institutions. The Chinese construction companies happen to be the ones who ended up winning.

14.3.3.3 TELECOMMUNICATIONS

The third area of Chinese engagement in Ethiopia is the telecommunications sector. The government granted exclusive rights to two Chinese telecommunication companies, ZTE and Huawei. ZTE, which is owned by the Chinese state, offered the Ethiopian Telecommunication Corporation a credit line (vendor financing) to the tune of US$1.5 billion on condition that the company secured the contract without competitive bidding. A second line of credit was granted by ZTE in 2013 to extend 4G services to Addis Ababa and 3G services to the rest of the country. In a reversal of fortunes, however, the Ethiopian government decided to award the ZTE portion of the contract to a Swedish telecoms company, Eriksson, in December 2014 when ZTE failed to fulfil its contractual obligations.

While the IMF and the World Bank have been urging the government to open the telecommunications sector for competition, the government has until recently refused, claiming that if it was left to private providers, millions of customers on low incomes would be denied access to telecoms services. Instead, the government opted for technological upgrading of the system to reduce costs for consumers and improve efficiency as a better option than wholesale privatization.[2] With the appointment of a new prime minister in March 2018, however, several state-owned companies, including Ethio Telecom, are slated for privatization. This is bound to affect the operations of Chinese telecoms companies in Ethiopia as competition between service providers will intensify.

In summary, Chinese trade with and investment in Ethiopia have been extensive over the past two decades. While Ethiopia's exports to China remain miniscule at present, Chinese loans and investment in the infrastructure sector have played an important role in unleashing Ethiopia's productive potential.[3] By improving trade logistics, Ethiopia is becoming a manufacturing hub in East Africa to which Chinese investors wishing to escape the high labour costs in China can easily relocate. This gives another boost to Ethiopia's economy. With the government's GTP II firmly focused on expanding manufacturing's share in GDP by 20 per cent in 2025, China's role as an investor and as a source of concessional loans will remain important if Ethiopia is able to service these debts by expanding its export volume.

14.4 Engaging China Strategically: Learning from Ethiopia

Ethiopia is one of a few African countries that has taken a more 'strategic' approach in its engagement of China while continuing to maintain strong ties with its traditional Western development partners. In practice, this involves the adoption of 'heterodox' policies of strategically opening the economy to world markets as opposed to 'indiscriminate opening'. Through disciplined planning, policy actions are properly evaluated, based on how they support the national interest of the country in terms of promoting economic growth and structural change, before they are adopted. This pragmatic approach has given the government enough policy space to embark on an ambitious industrialization agenda. Among the key ingredients for Ethiopia's success are the following.

[2] Personal communication with Dr Arkebe Oqubay, minister and special adviser to the prime minister, 12 May 2015.

[3] In August 2018, the Ethiopian government opened the logistics industry to international companies for 49 per cent joint ventures with local firms. In June 2018, the Ethiopian government decided to allow up to 49 per cent joint ventures in telecom and railway sectors and also to divest the sugar sector which was under the Ethiopian Sugar Development Corporation. Despite the fact that MOFEC does not make the loan figures public, estimates show that out of the total US$10 billion commercial loans, the railway projects account for 30 per cent, the telecom sector accounts for 30 per cent, and the remaining percentage is accounted for by the energy and sugar sectors (for instance, see China Africa Research Initiative (CARI) database at Johns Hopkins University).

14.4.1 *Articulation of Long-Term Development Vision*

The architects of Ethiopia's industrialization agenda point to two factors that were central to the industrialization strategy of China and the other East Asian countries: (a) the freedom of the governments to control basic economic policy; and (b) the development of the administrative, legal, and regulatory capacity of the state to guide the market in a way favourable to national development. Following this logic, the Ethiopian government developed a long-term vision for the country's industrialization and structural transformation that does not subscribe to the dominant neoliberal dogma of the Washington Consensus (Oqubay, 2019a, 2019b). The late prime minister Meles Zenawi emphasized the critical importance of securing 'policy space for countries like Ethiopia to pursue alternative development strategies' (Zenawi, 2006).

The first Growth and Transformation Plan (2010/15) was the culmination of many years of thinking within the EPRDF on the appropriate development path that Ethiopia should follow (MOFED, 2010). The GTP aimed at transforming the economy away from subsistence agriculture and towards industrialization and value addition in agriculture with the goal of becoming a middle-income country by 2025. Given the big emphasis accorded by the government to infrastructure as a foundation for growth, the decision to engage China made good political and economic sense since the Chinese, besides having the expertise, were willing to provide the necessary financing for large-scale infrastructure projects.

14.4.2 *Committed Political Leadership and Strong Political Ownership*

Ethiopian authorities made sure that they had the freedom to set priorities, decide policy contents, create necessary conditions, and be responsible for implementing and monitoring projects. The state developed the administrative, legal, and regulatory capacity of the government to guide the market in a way favourable to national development and Ethiopia's insertion into the global economy (Oqubay, 2015). A highly committed political leadership, backed by strong institutions for implementing and monitoring projects, has made it possible for Ethiopia to benefit from its strategic engagement with China.

14.4.3 *Prioritizing Investment in Infrastructure and Energy*

Investment in infrastructure has a central role in the development agenda and is critical for supporting economic growth and poverty reduction. Infrastructure affects growth through two channels: directly through physical capital accumulation and indirectly through improvement in productivity. At a micro level, investment in infrastructure enhances private-sector activities by lowering the cost of production and opening new markets, presenting new production and trade opportunities. At the same time, infrastructure investment in power generation, water, sanitation, and housing improves the social well-being of citizens. Ethiopia currently invests about 15 per cent of its GDP in infrastructure—roads, rail, dams—enabling the country to unlock its productive potential and to position itself as the manufacturing hub in East Africa.

14.4.4 *Learning by Doing and Emulation*

Latecomers such as Ethiopia cannot hope to industrialize by simply copying models that worked elsewhere. Nor can they afford to flatly reject external models as irrelevant. Smart governments are those that take a systematic and pragmatic approach to learning from international best practices (and even failures) and to designing their own policy package. In this regard, industrial policy has been at the heart of development policies and strategies in Ethiopia. Ethiopia has made efforts to learn from the Chinese experience while recognizing the local context and peculiarities which matter in learning (Oqubay, 2019a; Oqubay and Ohno, 2019; Oqubay and Tesfachew, 2019). For instance, Ethiopian policymakers critically studied (both positive and negative lessons from) the Chinese experience of hub development and industrial parks, together with those of other countries, such as Singapore, South Korea, Vietnam, and Mauritius. Lessons on building national champions, successive insertion into the global production network, the use of SEZs for the successful promotion of FDI and technological upgrading, and the shift from investment-led to innovation-led transition can be learned from the industrial policy of China (Lin, 2012; Lin, Xu, and Hager, 2019; Nolan, 2014; Oqubay, 2019c).

Policy learning in Ethiopia is an ongoing process. Training was conducted, institutions were created, funds were mobilized, and officials and experts were mobilized to execute projects stipulated in the long-term plan. The government built its own policy capability through trial and error, and hands-on struggles to attain specific nationally defined targets—not targets developed and imposed by donors (Oqubay, 2015; Oqubay and Tesfachew 2019). This pragmatic approach has several advantages: concentration of limited human and financial resources on priority projects, clear criteria by which to assess performance, flexible shifting of resources and organizations where they are needed, and the sense of pride and achievement that emerge as concrete projects are accomplished one by one.

14.4.5 *Pragmatism and Policy Flexibility*

Despite its socialist background, the post-1991 government adopted a pragmatic approach to economic reforms (as happened in China from 1976 onwards) and adapted the capacity of its economic agents to this process. This implies being open to foreign ideas but selectively picking out elements that are considered useful and adapting them to local context. While the long-term goal is to leapfrog technologically, Ethiopian policymakers take a more realistic approach to industrialization and lay emphasis on climbing the ladder in proper steps (Oqubay, 2019b). In this regard, priority has been given to ensuring road connectivity and stable power supply, including technical education programmes—things that are needed before plunging into programmes and projects aimed at achieving high industrial goals. The government has devoted a lot of energy not only to learning from best practices, but also to how to learn.

14.5 The Bigger Picture: Constraints and Pathways to Africa's Economic Transformation

The economic ties between Africa and China have expanded in recent years. China is today Africa's largest trading partner, and the leading contributor to Africa's development of infrastructure. As President Xi Jinping pointed out at the fifteenth anniversary of FOCAC, 'The past fifteen years have seen fruitful progress in China–Africa practical cooperation across the board. Two-way trade and China's total non-financial investment in Africa in 2014 were 22 times and 60 times that of 2000 respectively, which shows China's contribution to Africa's economic development has risen significantly.'[4] The contributors to this volume concur with President Xi's assessment of the state of China–Africa economic ties.

Despite these positive developments, however, the catalytic effect of Chinese economic engagement with Africa has been uneven. The authors in this volume argue that the key driver for variation of outcomes is a strategic approach and policy ownership by the host African country. Ethiopia is a typical case study of a country that has benefited from China–Africa economic cooperation, demonstrating the proactive policy of the government as well as the extensive room for improvement that is available. There is considerable room for enhanced China–Africa economic ties in the years ahead. However,

[4] President Xi Jinping's speech on 5 December 2016 at FOCAC VI, Johannesburg Summit, http://english.cri.cn/12394/2015/12/05/4083s906994.htm.

there are a number of issues that both partners must address to create conditions for 'win–win' outcomes. These include the following.

14.5.1 *Persistent Trade Imbalances*

The trading partnership is marred by major weaknesses. First, there are fundamental imbalances in terms of the volume and composition of exports/imports. African exports are dominated by primary commodities, which are characterized by declining value, while Africa is a net importer of both cheap manufactured goods (such as garments and footwear), machinery, and high-value goods from China. This will limit the growth dynamics and sustainability of trade. Promotion of Chinese FDI in manufacturing will help to improve and substitute the low-value imports to Africa, which also helps to create employment and improve purchasing power (Yueh, 2013, and Chapters 2 and 13). This will help to relax the constraints on the balance of payments, as well as helping African countries develop production capabilities. Additional instruments of duty-free access to China's market may be explored to fully support this strategy.[5]

14.5.2 *Excessive Debt Burden and Finance Sustainability*

The financing of infrastructure through concessional and commercial loans has immensely helped accelerate rapid economic growth and promote industrialization, as observed in Ethiopia. However, high dependence on commercial loans has become unsustainable as countries struggle with debt-servicing problems. The major drawbacks are that Africa's exports are too weak to cover the foreign exchange requirements, domestic savings too weak to reduce overdependence on external financing, and investment and economic activities too weak to fully utilize the infrastructure outlays. The current financing scheme, which is dominated by commercial loans, must give way to an alternative financing scheme that is not punitive to African countries. This requires a new approach to expand the concessional loans component (see Chapter 7). New modalities to widen opportunities for private–public partnerships in various infrastructure developments should also be explored to reduce the burden on African governments. However, these measures will not bear fruit unless they are linked to improving the trade imbalance, supporting the export sector, and expanding productive investment.

---

[5] The duty-free opportunities to Europe and the United States through 'Everything But Arms' and AGOA are examples that would potentially help fulfil the strategic aim. As a newcomer to production of industrial goods, a period of duty relief would help to develop the competitiveness of the African manufacturing sector.

14.5.3 *Quality FDI and Productive Capacity*

From the perspective of the economic transformation of African countries, arguably the most critical component of China–Africa cooperation is the FDI inflow in productive sectors as it helps address structural constraints. Such investments are central to developing the export sector and relaxing the balance-of-payments constraints, to generating employment and improving income levels, to developing domestic linkages and boosting productive investment, and to improving technological capability. According to the McKinsey survey (2017) and other studies, Ethiopia has succeeded in attracting massive manufacturing investment relative to the rest of Africa. But this is limited, considering the much larger investment that can be harnessed, given China's position as a leading economy and a manufacturing powerhouse.

14.5.4 *Limited Knowledge Transfer Impact*

The transfer of know-how and domestic capability has been limited and is below the desired level. Designing infrastructure projects to develop technological capability and know-how transfer as well as coming up with new models to improve post-construction operation and management is critical to gain the best value for money and to better serve the goal of economic transformation of host countries. A special fund for capacity building and know-how transfer, and incentives to encourage local products and services, is critical for sustained benefits to African countries.

14.5.5 *Transforming FOCAC as an Effective Platform*

FOCAC has emerged as the largest South–South economic partnership, and this partnership has been based on robust principles of mutual respect, non-intervention in internal affairs, and a prime focus on mutually beneficial economic development (PRC, 2006). China continues to demonstrate its commitment towards Africa by increasing its financial and economic support from year to year. As an example, at the 2015 FOCAC VI Summit in Johannesburg, China pledged a US$60 billion package to Africa, a significant proportion of which has been implemented (CARI, 2018). At the opening session of the FOCAC VII meeting held in Beijing on 3–4 September 2018, President Xi Jinping announced US$60 billion of development financing for African countries, centred around an eight-point plan.[6] The pledged resource includes:

---

[6] FOCAC Secretariat (2018), 'Full Text of Chinese President Xi Jinping's Speech at the Opening Ceremony of 2018 FOCAC Beijing Forum', ⟨https://focacsummit.mfa.gov.cn/eng⟩.

- US$15 billion in aid;
- US$20 billion credit line;
- US$10 billion for developing financing;
- US$5 billion special fund to accelerate non-resource-based imports to China; and
- US$10 billion investment from Chinese companies.

China will remain an important source of development finance and investment for African countries. Yet, many African countries have so far not taken advantage of the FOCAC platform to strategically engage China in enhanced economic relations, or to systematically use the platform to address any contentious issues that might emerge in the relationship. It is imperative that the African countries concerned develop coherent policies and take a strategic approach to economic partnerships with China. Governments that lack home-grown policies and strategies would fail not only on this front but also when it comes to broader economic transformation. This strategy must be supported by evidence-based research and analysis. It is imperative that African countries invest heavily in the development of strong national think tanks and research institutes that can provide an accurate picture of China's role in the world economy and its implications for Africa. Currently, think tanks that focus on such cooperation are few and far between, or are ideologically driven.

14.5.6 *Improving the Business Climate on Both Sides*

Chinese investors face major obstacles that could potentially be addressed by both African countries and China. African host economies should improve the business climate and provide much more effective support.[7] Industrial parks and SEZs have played an important role in this respect (Lin, Xu, and Hager, 2019). But these interventions alone will not be enough to have a strategic impact. Financing for Chinese investors cannot be addressed by host countries, considering the resource constraints they face. Incentives and additional support by host countries as well as China will be required because of the difficult conditions in which they operate and the constraints they face. As studies show, the focus on training and upgrading local skills, networking with local firms, and promoting domestic linkages is uneven and relatively weak (McKinsey, 2017; Oqubay, 2019c; World Bank, 2012). Chinese investors have perception gaps when it comes to Africa and lack an understanding of Africa's potential.

---

[7] See Kidane (2011, 2019) on bilateral investment agreements between China and African countries.

14.5.7 *Narrowing the Knowledge and Cultural Gaps*

Knowledge of Africa on the part of the Chinese and African understanding of China remain underdeveloped on both sides. As a result, Chinese investors prefer to invest in Asia, which is familiar and perceived as less risky to most investors. Chinese policymakers and think tanks have a limited understanding of Africa and the economic potential of the continent. Promotion of Africa as an investment destination for Chinese investors by the central government, provinces, and local governments has not been uniform and consistent. More proactive joint action from China, African host governments, and private-sector associations is needed to deepen economic and cultural ties between China and Africa. Similarly, there is also a lack of understanding on the part of African institutions about how economic partnership initiatives such as FOCAC and the Belt and Road Initiative are structured and how they might be of relevance to Africa. There is a clear need on both sides to communicate better to citizens and the private sectors about the nature of China–Africa economic ties and to improve cultural understanding between the peoples of Africa and China. Greater engagement by non-state actors from both sides can broaden common understanding of both societies.

Addressing the above-mentioned challenges through joint action will go a long way to improving and strengthening China–Africa relations in the coming decades.

14.6 Conclusion

Africa's relations with China and other development partners are changing fast and the future is uncertain. The word 'turbulence' best captures the state of the world today. China's ambition to reorganize the old-world order brings with it risks but also opportunities; however, Africa cannot wait for its partners to define the nature of the relationship. It must take control of its own future. The continent must move from being a passive onlooker to global debates and rulemaking to become an active participant in shaping those rules.

Second, African countries must do their homework before jumping into complicated trade and investment relationships with China in the hope of replicating the Chinese development experience. It is too naïve to assume that Africans can simply transplant institutional practices from China with little attention to their fit in the African context. The focus must be on 'learning', not on 'copying'. As Premier Deng Xiaoping, the architect of Chinese economic reform, once told a visiting young Ghanaian leader, Jerry Rawlings, in 1985: 'Please don't try to copy our model. If there is any experience on our part, it is to formulate policies in light of one's own national conditions. Seek truth from facts.' There is indeed a lot that African countries can learn from China's experience. The key, however, is to adapt that experience to African realities.

Appendix

Appendix Table A14.1. Destination of Ethiopia's exports, 2000–17

Year	Export value in US$ millions				% share (of total export)				Growth rate (%)	
	2000	2005	2010	2017	2000	2005	2010	2017	2000–8	2009–17
China	1.05	78.93	228.21	288.16	0.28	9	11	10	62	3
India	8.29	8	27.51	44.69	2	1	1	2	6	10
Europe	220.50	370.35	774.47	881.45	46	41	36	28	12	4
Middle East	72.40	168.11	386.68	553.82	15	19	18	19	19	6
Others (US$ bn)	0.18	0.27	0.73	1.09	36.72	30	34	41	1	77
Total (US$ billions)	0.48	0.90	2.15	2.86	100	100	100	100	100	100

Source: ERCA (2018) (unpublished)

Appendix Table A14.2. Ethiopia's import comparison

Year	Import value in US$ billions				% share (of total import)				Growth rate (%)	
	2000	2005	2010	2017	2000	2005	2010	2017	2000–10	2011–17
China	0.10	0.55	2.02	4.86	8	15	24	32	37	17
India	0.07	0.25	0.62	1.09	5	7	7	7	25	10
Europe	0.40	0.90	1.40	2.43	32	24	17	16	14	10
Middle East	0.36	0.95	2.08	2.55	28	25	25	17	23	7
Others	0.34	1.15	2.21	4.09	27	29	27	28	1	56
Total	1.27	3.80	8.33	15.02	100	100	100	100	100	100

Source: ERCA (2018) (unpublished)

Appendix Table A14.3. Total number of new manufacturing (foreign) firms

Year	Number of firms			Cumulative no. of firms	Cumulative no. of firms in %
	2000–5	2006–11	2012–17	2000–17	2000–17
China	41	167	199	407	32
India	21	51	51	123	10
Europe	19	25	16	60	5
Middle East	13	61	38	112	9
Others	97	263	197	557	44
Total	191	567	501	1,259	100

Source: EIC (2018) (unpublished)

Appendix Table A14.4. Chinese loan commitments to Ethiopia, 2012/2013 (by creditor and type)

	Signature date	Economic sector	Amount in US$ millions	Terms		
				Interest rate %	Grace period (years)	Maturity (years)
Central government						
Exim Bank of China	27/03/13	Electric light and power products	292,250,000.00	2	8	20
Government guaranteed						
CDB	19/12/12	Sugar manufacturing	25,000,000.00	Libor+2.6	3	10
China Elect. Power	26/04/13	Electrical distribution	1,002,970,414.05	3.08	3	15
Exim Bank of China	15/05/13	Rail transport infrastructure	220,471,000.00	Libor+3.0	6	15
Exim Bank of China	15/05/13	Rail transport infrastructure	981,260,000.00	Libor+3.0	6	15
Exim Bank of China	15/05/13	Rail transport infrastructure	1,289,029,000.00	Libor+3.0	6	15
Non-government guaranteed						
Huawei	10/01/13	Telecommunications	800,000,000.00	Libor+1.5	3	13
ZTE	10/01/13	Telecommunications	800,000,000.00	Libor+1.5	3	13

Source: MOFED (2012), 'Public Sector Debt Statistical Bulletin No. 9' (2007/8–2011/12), Debt Management Directorate, Ministry of Finance and Economic Development, Addis Ababa, October

Appendix A Table 14.5. Chinese engagement in the Ethiopian power sector

Project	Company	Type of work	In US$ millions (at 2009 rate of 12.45/$)
POWER GENERATION			
Tekeze Hydroelectric Project	CWGS JV	Construction of Arch Dam head race tunnel	220.57
Tekeze Hydro project	CWBEC	Design, supply, and electro-mechanical equipment	23.60
Tekeze Hydro	JV JPCC & CCC	Design, supply, and erection of 230Kv S/S	4.26
Tekeze Hydro	JPCC	Design, supply, and construction of transmission line	6.32
Finchaa-Amertimulti-purpose project	CGGC	Design, procurement, and construction of plant	97.92
Beles Hydroelectric	CMEC	Design, manufacture CIF supply, transport, building materials	49.26
Genale Dawa hydro project	CGGC	Design, manufacture CIF supply	463.51
Chemoga-Yeda power project	Sinohydro	Design, manufacture CIF supply	570.32

Harena Messobo & Adama Nazret wind power project	Hydro China	Design, manufacture CIF supply and transport, loading/ unloading equipment test	256.90
Power generation total			**1,692.65**
POWER TRANSMISSION PROJECTS			
Tekeze-IndaSelassie-Humera		China	12.05
Tekeze-IndaSelassie-Humera		China	16.99
Bedele-Metru power transmission		China	9.24
Bedele-Metu power transmission		China	7.60
Bahir Dar-Debre Markos-Addis Ababa power transmission project		China CAMC Engineering Ltd	32.98
Bahir Dar-Debre Markos-Addis Ababa power transmission		Shingai Electric Group Co. Ltd	31.23
Bahir Dar-Debre Markos-Addis Ababa transmission project		Shingai Electric Group Co. Ltd	48.97
Gibe III-Addis Ababa transmission line contract		TBEA (China)	75.00
Fincha-Gedho-Gefersa power transmission project		CWBEC (China)	10.84
Fincha-Gedho-Gefersa power transmission project		CGGC (China)	19.82
Koka-Dire Dawa power transmission project		CWBEC & JPPC (China)	89.28
Transmission total			**353.99**
UNIVERSAL ACCESS PROGRAMME			
Sawla Afer project	China Wanabo Engineering Co.	Supply of S/S and power transformer	4.57
ADB II-financed project	CAMCO International	Supply of OHL accessories	0.79
ADB II-financed project	China National Elec. Equip. Corp.	Supply of MV & LV insulators	2.29
ADB II-financed project	Zhejiang Hilley Int. Co.	Supply of MV & LV switch gears	2.01
ADB II project	China Wnbao Engineering Corp.	Equipment	6.51
EAREP I	Bonle, China	Supply of MV and LV insulations	2.11
EAREP I	CE Lighting Co.	Supply of energy-saving compact fluorescent bulbs	3.40
EAREP I	Bonle, China	Procurement of street lighting	0.49
Total universal access			**23.17**

Source: Ethiopian Electric Power Corporation

305

Appendix Table A14.6. Partial listing of Chinese companies engaged in Ethiopia's road sector (2009)

Name of Chinese firm	Name of project	KM road constructed	In US$ millions	Financed by
CGGC	Shire-Siraro-Humera Lugdi lot 1	156	49.51	GOE
HUNAN HUNDA	Shire-Shiraro-Humera lot 2	161	50.42	GOE
Hunan Hunda	Gonder-Humera	117	27.40	GOE
CGC Overseas	Kombolcha-Gundewoin, Contract 1	173	55.75	GOE
CGC Overseas	Kombolcha-Godewoin, Contract 2	136	72.63	GOE
Hunan Hunda	Harar-Jijiga	106	28.11	GOE
CGC	Dodola-Junction-Goba	130	29.85	IDA
CGC Overseas	Magna-Mechara	120	37.60	IDA
CGC	Dondola-Junction-Goba	130	7.60	IDA
China Railway Eng. Corp.	Adigrat-Adiabun	108	22.75	IDA
Sinohydro Corp.	Nazreth-Assela	79	14.24	IDA
Sinohydro Corp.	Nekempt-Mekenajo	127	24.15	IDA
CRBC	Butajira-Hossana	95	17.47	ADB
China Sichuan Int.	Mekenajo-Dengoro-Billa-Hena	61	11.13	OPEC
CRBC	Nejo-Mendi	74	11.87	OPEC
CRBC	Merawi-Gonder	208	31.77	IDA
CRBC	Alemgena-Butajira	120	17.96	ADB
CRBC	Awash-Hirna	140	20.61	IDA
CRBC	Kulubi-Dengego-Harar	80	13.03	IDA
China Won.	Woldiya-Alamata	78	12.07	IDA
China Won	Betemariam-Wukro	117	16.34	IDA
China Won.	Debre Markos-Merawi	220	26.27	IDA
CRBC	Gashena-Woldiya/Woreta-Woldya	108	29.78	IDA
Total			**628.34**	

Source: Based on Ethiopian Road Authority data

References

Alden, Chris (2007) *China in Africa*. London: Zed Books.

Anshan, Li, et al. (2012) 'FOCAC Twelve Years Later: Achievements, Challenges and the Way Forward', Discussion Paper No. 74, The Nordic Africa Institute and Peking University, Uppsala.

Axelsson, L. and N. Sylvanus (2010) 'Navigating Chinese Textile Networks: Women Traders in Accra and Lomé', in F. Cheru and C. Obi (eds) *The Rise of China and India in Africa*. London: Zed Books, pp. 132–44.

Brautigam, Deborah (2009) *The Dragons Gift: The Real Story of China in Africa*. Oxford: Oxford University Press.

Carmody, P. (2013) *The Rise of the BRICS in Africa: The Geopolitics of South-South Relations*. London: Zed Books.

Cheru, Fantu (2016) 'Emerging Southern Powers and New Forms of South-South Cooperation: Ethiopia's Strategic Engagement with China and India', *Third World Quarterly*, 37(4): 592–610.

Cheru, Fantu and R. Modi (eds) (2013) *Agriculture and Food Security in Africa: The Impact of Chinese, Indian and Brazilian Investments*. London: Zed Books.

Cheru, Fantu and C. Obi (2010) *The Rise of China and India in Africa: Challenges, Opportunities and Critical Interventions*. London: Zed Books.

Cheru, Fantu and C. Obi (2011) 'Decoding China–Africa Relations: Partnership for Development or Neo-Colonialism by Invitation?' *World Financial Review*, September–October: 72–7.

China-Africa Research Initiative (CARI) (2018) 'The Path Ahead: The 7th Forum on China–Africa Cooperation', Briefing Paper No 1, prepared by Janet Eom, Deborah Brautigam, and L.Benabdallah. https://static1.squarespace.com/static/5652847de4b033f56d2bdc29/t/5b84311caa4a998051e685e3/1535389980283/Briefing+Paper+1+-+August+2018+-+Final.pdf.

De Wall, Alex (2012) 'The Theory and Practice of Meles Zenawi', *African Affairs*, 112 (446): 148–55.

Economist, The (2011) 'Africa Rising', 401(8762): 3 December 2011.

ERCA (2018) Unpublished raw data collected from the agency. Ethiopian Revenue and Customs Agency, Addis Ababa. Unpublished.

French, Howard (2014) *China's Second Continent: How a Million Migrants Are Building a New Empire in Africa*. New York: Alfred A. Knopf.

Geda, Alemayehu and A. Meskel (2010) 'China and India's Growth Surge: The Implications for African Manufacturing Exports', in Fantu Cheru and C. Obi (eds) *The Rise of China and India in Africa: Challenges*. London: Zed Books, pp. 97–106.

Human Rights Watch (2011) 'You Will Be Fired If You Refuse: Labor Abuse in Zambia's Chinese State-Owned Copper Mines', Human Rights Watch, New York.

Kidane, Won L. (2011) *China–Africa Dispute Settlement: Law, Economics and Culture of Arbitration*. Alphen aan den Rijn: Walters Kluwer.

Kidane, Won L. (2019) 'The Legal Framework for the Protection of Foreign Direct Investment in Ethiopia', in Fantu Cheru, Christopher Cramer, and Arkebe Oqubay (eds) *The Oxford Handbook of the Ethiopian Economy*. Oxford: Oxford University Press.

Lin, Justin (2012) *Demystifying the Chinese Economy*. Cambridge: Cambridge University Press.

Lin, Justin, Jiajun Xu, and Sarah Hager (2019) 'A New Structural Economics Perspective on Special Economic Zones in Ethiopia', in Fantu Cheru, Christopher Cramer, and Arkebe Oqubay (eds) *The Oxford Handbook of the Ethiopian Economy*. Oxford: Oxford University Press.

Manning, R. (2006) 'Will Emerging Donors Change the Face of International Cooperation?' *Development Policy Review*, 24(4): 371–85.

McKinsey (2017) 'Dance of the Lions and Dragons: How Are Africa and China Engaging and How Will the Partnership Evolve?' McKinsey, New York.

MOFED (2005) 'A Plan for Accelerated and Sustained Development to End Poverty (PASDEP) 2005/6–2009/10', Government of Ethiopia, Addis Ababa.

MOFED (2010) 'Growth and Transformation Plan, 2010–2015', Federal Democratic Republic of Ethiopia, Addis Ababa.

Mohan, G. and B. Lampert (2013) 'Negotiating China: Reinserting African Agency into China–Africa Relations', *African Affairs*, 112(446): 92–110.

Mohan, G., et al. (2014) *Chinese Migrants and Africa's Development: New Imperialists or Agents of Change?* London: Zed Books.

Mohan, G. and M. Power (2008) 'New African Choices? The Politics of Chinese Engagement in Africa and the Changing Architecture of International Development', *Review of African Political Economy*, 35(1): 23–42.

Moyo, D. (2013) *Winner Take All: China's Race for Resources and What It Means for Us,* London: Allen Lane & Penguin Books.

Naim, M. (2007) 'Rogue Aid: What's Wrong with the Foreign Aid Programs of China, Venezuela and Saudi Arabia?' *Foreign Affairs*, 159: 96.

Nolan, Peter (2014) *Chinese Firms, Global Girms: Industrial Policy in the Era of Globalization*. New York: Routledge.

Oqubay, Arkebe (2015) *Made in Africa: Industrial Policy in Ethiopia*. Oxford: Oxford University Press.

Oqubay, Arkebe (2019a) 'Ethiopia: Lessons from an Experiment', in Justin Lin and Celestin Monga (2019) *The Oxford Handbook of Structural Transformation*. Oxford: Oxford University Press.

Oqubay, Arkebe (2019b) 'Industrial Policy and Late Industrialization in Ethiopia', in Fantu Cheru, Christopher Cramer, and Arkebe Oqubay (2019) *The Oxford Handbook of the Ethiopian Economy*. Oxford: Oxford University Press.

Oqubay, Arkebe (2019c) 'Structure and Performance of the Ethiopian Manufacturing Sector', in Fantu Cheru, Christopher Cramer, and Arkebe Oqubay (2019) *The Oxford Handbook of the Ethiopian Economy*. Oxford: Oxford University Press.

Oqubay, Arkebe and Kenichi Ohno (2019) *How Nations Learn: Technological Learning, Industrial Policy, and Catch Up*. Oxford: Oxford University Press.

Oqubay, Arkebe, and Taferre Tesfachew (2019) 'Learning and Catch Up in Africa', in Arkebe Oqubay and Kenichi Ohno (eds) *How Nations Learn: Technological Learning, Industrial Policy, and Catch Up*. Oxford: Oxford University Press.

People's Republic of China (PRC) (2006) 'Declaration of the Beijing Summit and Beijing Action Plan, 2007–2009', Forum on China–Africa Cooperation (FOCAC), Ministry of Foreign Affairs, the People's Republic of China, Beijing.

Pillsburry, M (2015) *The Hundred Year Marathon: China's Secret Strategy to Replace America as Global Superpower*. New York: Henry Holt Co.

Sautmann, B. and J. Hairong (2008) 'Fu Manchu in Africa? Distorted Portrayal of China in Africa', *South African Labor Bulletin* 31(5): 34–6.

Southall, Roger and Henning Melber (eds) (2009) *A New Scramble for Africa? Imperialism, Investment, and Development*. Scottsville: University of Kwazulu-Natal Press.

UNCTAD (2010) 'Economic Development in Africa Report 2010: South-South Cooperation: Africa and the New Forms of Development Partnership', UNCTAD, Geneva.

UNECA (2013) 'Economic Report on Africa 2013: Making the Most of African Commodities—Industrializing for Growth, Jobs and Economic Transformation', UN Economic Commission for Africa, Addis Ababa.

Wenping, He, (2007) 'China Policy Balancing', *China Security*, 1(3): 23–40.

Wethal, Ulrikke (2018) 'Beyond the China Factor: Challenges to Backward Linkages in the Mozambican Construction Sector', *Journal of Modern African Studies*, 56(2): 325–51.

World Bank (2012) 'Chinese FDI in Ethiopia: A World Bank Survey', Addis Ababa.

Xi, Jinping (2018) Speech at the opening of FOCAC VII, Beijing.

Yueh, Linda (2013) *China's Growth: The Making of an Economic Superpower*. Oxford: Oxford University Press.

Zakaria, F. (2008) *The Post-American World*. New York: W.W. Norton & Co.

Zenawi, M. (2001) 'States and Markets: Neoliberal Limitations and the Case of a Developmental State', in A. Norman et al. (eds) *Good Growth and Governance in Africa: Rethinking Development Strategies*. Oxford and New York: Oxford University Press, pp. 140–74.

Zenawi, M. (2006) 'Africa's Development: Dead End and New Beginnings', unpublished master's dissertation, Erasmus University, Rotterdam.

15

The Future of China–Africa Economic Ties

New Trajectory and Possibilities

Arkebe Oqubay and Justin Yifu Lin

The research and publication of *China–Africa and an Economic Transformation* was concluded at an important historical moment shortly after the 2018 China–Africa Summit (FOCAC VII) held in Beijing in September 2018, making the volume relevant and timely. During the Summit, the Chinese government announced new initiatives that are informed by a thorough review of FOCAC accomplishments and gaps since its inception in 2000, the lessons learned in promoting China–Africa economic ties, emerging new possibilities due to China's economic rebalancing, and Africa's own changing conditions in the global political economy (Xi, 2018). The volume editors hope to have contributed to a better understanding of the dynamically evolving economic ties between China and Africa, and the implications for African economic transformations.

The concluding chapter does not aim to summarize the various chapters in the volume. Its purpose, rather, is to highlight the common themes that cut across the volume, and to discuss the strategic implication of the FOCAC VII outcome document which outlined new directions and frameworks for strengthening China–Africa economic ties over the coming decades. The chapter concludes by highlighting key insights on how African countries can strategically engage China for greater economic benefit.[1]

[1] The authors thank Fantu Cheru, James Mittelman, Scarlett Cornelissen, Mohamed Salih, Linda Yueh, Ian Taylor, Carlos Oya, Daniel Poon, and Dirk Willem for their suggestions and inputs. Their comments as well as the discussion during the Addis Ababa workshop on 30–31 August 2018 have been valuable. We are also grateful for copyedits by Deborah Kefale and Binyam Arkebe.

15.1 Countering 'Anti-Chinese' Narratives: Let the Facts Speak

The myth that has surrounded China–Africa cooperation for almost three decades has intensified and today has reached extreme levels. 'New colonialism' has become a catchphrase used, especially by Western media, to define the nature of the relationship. For example, a recent article in the *Financial Times* headlined 'China Model Is Failing Africa' predicted that 'after more than a decade of vaulting growth in trade, finance and investment, China's weighty engagement is jeopardising future development prospects in Africa . . . The fanfare of next week's forum is likely to be short-lived—the China model is failing Africa' (*Financial Times*, 2018).[2] In a speech at the African Union on 8 March 2018, former US Secretary of State Rex Tillerson said, 'We think it's important that African countries carefully consider the terms of those investments, and we witness the model that the Chinese follow. They do not bring significant job creation locally; they don't bring significant training programs that enable African citizens to participate more fully in the future; and oftentimes, the financing models are structured in a way that the country, when it gets into trouble financially, loses control of its own infrastructure or its own resources through default' (Tillerson, 2018).

Several African leaders have rejected the charge of 'Chinese colonialism' or 'imperialism' and vehemently defended China's positive role in Africa's economic transformation.[3] Given the violent nature of 'real' colonialism, the use of this term to characterize the current dynamics is insulting. Likewise, Chinese leaders were explicit and bold in pronouncing China's 'five-no' approach, which is to be adhered to by other countries as well:

> We respect Africa, love Africa and support Africa. We follow a *'five-no' approach* in our relations with Africa: no interference in African countries' pursuit of *development paths* that fit their national conditions; no interferences in African countries' *internal affairs*; no imposition of *our will* on African countries; no attachment of *political strings* to assistance to Africa; and no seeking of *selfish political gains* in investment and financing cooperation with Africa. We hope this 'five-no' could apply to other countries as they deal with Africa . . . Ultimately, it is for the peoples of China and Africa to judge the performance of China–Africa cooperation.
>
> (Xi, 2018, authors' emphasis)

Between 2015 and 2018, the Chinese government organized numerous conferences and workshops, and deployed multiple think tanks that focused on studying the economic ties, constraints, and ways of exploring and improving

[2] https://www.ft.com/content/ca4072f6-a79f-11e8-a1b6-f368d365bf0e.
[3] For the full interview, see https://www.caixinglobal.com/2018-09-06/qa-south-africas-president-dismisses-accusations-against-beijing-of-new-colonialism-101323312.html.

the partnership. It was evident that China–Africa relations were based on well-informed, evidence-based decisions and new learning.

Contrary to polemical and sensational assertions and stories that focus on 'China in Africa' narratives, there is an increasing number of empirically grounded studies that focus on China–Africa economic ties, and on Africa's political economy and its structural transformation (for instance see, among others, Alden and Large, 2018; Brautigam, 2009, 2015; Cheru and Obi, 2010; China Africa Research Initiative, 2018; Lee, 2017).[4] Brautigam's works debunked the myth around the Chinese in Africa and in Africa's agriculture. Anchored in comparative ethnography, Lee (2017) has brought novel insights that show 'the unique nature of Chinese investment in Africa', the diverse nature of investments from China, and how Chinese state investment is distinct from global private investment.[5] Such studies, while dispelling conventional misperceptions, may open up new avenues of research and inform the policymaking of African countries and China.

15.2 Unevenness, Diversity, and Shifting Dynamics

A major theme that has emerged in this volume is that China–Africa economic ties are neither static nor uniform. The primary nature of the partnership is that it exhibits *unevenness*, *diversity*, and *dynamic shifts* over time. Understanding the nature of the multifaceted relationship requires appreciation of the current international context and evolving international order. It also requires deeper analysis of the contemporary trajectories of China and individual African countries (rather than 'Africa' as a whole) in their integration in this global order. The evolving global division of labour and power has far-reaching implications for the trajectory of African development.

At a time when global commitment to multilateralism is declining, and unilateralism and protectionism are on the rise, China has emerged as one of the leading countries advocating greater rule-based multilateralism, and

---

[4] Alden and Large refreshingly review questions of how Africa–China is being studied and on new directions for future studies (Alden and Large, 2018). They highlight that the current literature has been narrowly limited to assessing China in Africa, China–Africa, or China and Africa rather than all-encompassing (epistemology, theory, and method) in-depth research studies of 'field of power embedded in deeper, historically produced questions about African studies'.

[5] Lee (2017) highlights that Chinese state capital is characterized by its own 'logic of accumulation, regimes of labour, ethos of management', with uneven capacity and uncertain outcomes across different industrial sectors and countries or regions. According to Lee (2017) the major imbalances shaping Chinese investment are 'overcapacity, falling profit rates, underconsumption, shrinking demand from traditional export markets, and scarcity of strategic resources'.

globalization and integration. President Xi Jinping's new leadership has played a more assertive role globally and geopolitically. President Xi has also become an advocate of globalization and multilateralism (Cornelissen, Cheru, and Shaw 2015; Shambaugh, 2013).[6] China also increased its economic internationalization strategy, with 'Going Global' and the Belt and Road Initiative bringing new dynamism to its historical relationship with Africa.[7] This process embodies the unfolding global division of labour and power (GDLP), and power asymmetry (Fröbel, 2009; Mittelman, 2011). The rise of China and the expanding China–Africa economic ties cannot be comprehended out of this context.

In addition to the global power structure, it is important to understand not only the implications for Africa of China's rise as a global economic power, but also the history and the complex changes and processes in Chinese domestic politics (Yueh, 2013). As Chapters 4, 5, and 6 show, China's policies have been shifting with the changes in dynamics of domestic politics. Mao's policy towards Africa (in the 1960s and 1970s) was predominantly shaped by China's role in the non-aligned movement and support for anti-colonial liberation struggles. After the 1980s, consideration of economic complementarity and market economy reflected the transformation ushered in by the then 'opening and reform' (Lin, 2011). After the 1990s, the initial experimentation of 'Going Global' reflected new strategy and self-confidence, and a new Chinese approach to policymaking. Furthermore, Chinese policy thinking mirrors its long history, experiences, and Confucian culture, as past history and culture are a social fabric that will help to predict a more likely behaviour. Chinese nationalism has played an important role as a vehicle for the 'Chinese Dream'. The unforgettable memories of colonial domination by Western and Japanese imperialism have in particular shaped Chinese nationalism and the determination to defend Chinese sovereignty and the right to determine China's own development path autonomously (Chow, 2007; Nayyar, 2016; Nolan, 2016).[8] Considering this history, China is less likely to be associated with predatory and 'new' colonial power and more likely to associate itself with other developing countries.[9]

[6] Shambaugh (2013) highlights China's 'partial power' in view of China's expanding economic might, trading dominance, growing military power, diplomatic dominance, and increasing 'soft power' (despite the relative lag in its 'soft power' to become 'partial power').

[7] It is less clear how the Belt and Road Initiative (BRI) and FOCAC intersect.

[8] Nolan (2016: 3–4) highlights: 'For over 2,000 years from the Han Dynasty (206 BC–220 AD) through to the late eighteenth century, China was the most economically and technologically advanced part of the world . . . Many of the key technologies of the Industrial Revolution had their origin in China.'

[9] Yueh (see Chapter 2) highlights that China is the first developing country to become a global economic power.

15.3 Bringing in Africa's Economic Transformation

A central theme of this volume is the structural transformation of African economies and the perspective that China–Africa economic ties should be examined through the lens of structural transformation and their catalytic effect on Africa's economic transformation measured. The definition provided by Ocampo, Rada, and Taylor (2009: 7), conceptualizing structural transformation as central to economic development, looks a more plausible conceptual alternative within the context of this volume:

Economic development is a process of structural transformation. Structural transformation is associated with ... the composition of production activities, the associated patterns of specialization in international trade, the technological capabilities of the economy, including the educational level of the labour force, the structure of ownership of factors of production, the nature and development of basic state institutions, and the degree of development and constraints under which certain markets operate ... the reallocation of productive factors from traditional agriculture to modern agriculture, industry and services ... shifting resources from low-to-high productivity sectors ... a capacity to diversify domestic production structure: that is, to generate new activities, to strengthen economic linkages within a country and to create domestic technological capabilities.

In applying a structural transformation perspective, it is important to focus on the process of economic diversification, the development of technological capabilities, and the promotion of domestic linkages, with a policy focus that gives prominence and centrality to the development of the manufacturing sector, the vitality of exports and international learning, and the modernization of agriculture.

The overall conclusion of this volume is that, while African countries have benefited greatly from their engagement with China, they are far from achieving industrialization and structural transformation. The economic ties between China and Africa have largely been asymmetrical. This is expressed in multiple ways.

First, the catalytic effect of Chinese economic engagement with Africa, despite the positive developments, has been uneven across countries.

Second, countries that have benefited most from China–Africa economic cooperation demonstrate the proactive policy of the government as well as the extensive room for improvement that is available. The key driver for variation of outcomes is a strategic approach and policy ownership by the host African country.

Third, there is considerable room for enhanced China–Africa economic ties in the years ahead, and both partners must address some issues to create conditions conducive to 'win–win' outcomes. These include: persistent trade imbalances; excessive debt burden and finance sustainability; selective targeting on quality and appropriate FDI and productive capacity; the potential to expand knowledge transfer and local content through Chinese FDI; lagging business climate; narrowing knowledge and cultural gaps; and transforming FOCAC into a more effective platform and institution.[10]

The FOCAC VII Summit has made significant progress in addressing the constraints and weaknesses in China–Africa economic partnerships in terms of their increasing alignment towards the economic transformation of Africa. The matrix in Table 15.1 provides strategic responses that may help to improve the alignment of China's eight initiatives for Africa's economic transformation.

15.4 Strategic Approach to China–Africa Economic Ties: the Way Forward

As China undergoes major economic rebalancing to enter the fourth industrial revolution and upgrade to an innovation-driven economy, this is bound to affect China–Africa relations in multiple ways, offering both opportunities and challenges (see Chapters 2 and 3). For example, China's new internationalization strategy, the Belt and Road Initiative, is a strategic initiative that covers not only Africa, but other continents, and represents China's 'Going Global' strategy and the potential to attract FDI in light manufacturing. Reaping the opportunities offered by China's economic rebalancing and the 'Going Out' of Chinese enterprises will primarily depend on the capacity of African actors to make the most of these opportunities.[11] Considering China's global ambitions, African policymakers need to understand the contributions as well as the limitations of economic ties with China in a rapidly changing context. There are instructive lessons from China's rapid rise that are relevant for African countries.

15.4.1 *China as a Source of Learning: Writing their Own Script*

China has lifted more than 700 million people who had been living below the poverty line and has successfully climbed the ladder of industrialization, emerging as the largest exporter and the second-largest economy in the course of a generation.[12] These lessons are important not only for Africa but for other

---

[10] See Altman (2018) on imbalances of China–Africa trade. See also Taylor (2009), and Cheng and Taylor (2017) on Chinese new role in African and Chinese aid.

[11] See also Lin and Monga (2017, 2019) on Africa's structural transformation.

[12] The volume editors note the analytical danger of an over-simplistic view that looks at the Washington Consensus versus a Beijing consensus. The Washington Consensus is a term coined to

Table 15.1. Strategic approach by African countries to FOCAC VII initiatives (2018–21)

Strategic cooperation areas	Chinese 8 initiatives (2018–21)	Strategic implication for African governments
FDI and productive capacity	**Industrial promotion initiative (1):** Increase investment in Africa; upgrade economic and trade cooperation zones; support modernization of Africa's agriculture; China–Africa Development Fund; Special Loan for Development of African SMEs	• Develop development strategy with a focus on industrialization and structural transformation • Develop coherent industrial policies (with a focus on manufactured exports, in sectors with scope for learning, dynamic linkages, stimulate domestic learning) • Develop manufacturing clusters in SEZs based on productive criteria • Design targeted investment promotion package on selectivity, single window, appropriate incentive structure and performance requirements of FDI • Promote research on industrial policy and hubs development • Enhance coordination among government agencies and dialogue with investors[a]
Trade and exports	**Trade facilitation initiative (3):** Increase imports, particularly non-resource products from Africa; trade facilitation schemes; support African Continental Free Trade Area; promote e-commerce cooperation; local currency settlement; support trade expos[b]	• Modernization of transport and logistics industry, and regional connectivity • Reform banking and customs system, enhance harmonization and automation • Surveillance of products to be exported to China and focus on value addition • Ensure lead agency is strengthened and requirements are monitored • Central banks institutionalize currency settlement schemes • Critically review bilateral trade negotiations
Financing and infrastructure development	**Infrastructure connectivity initiative (2):**[c] Formulate China–Africa infrastructure development on energy, transport, ICT; support Single African Air Transport Market; expand China–Africa air connectivity; new models of infrastructure financing; promote bond issuance by African countries; access to Asian Infrastructure Investment Bank, the New Development Bank, and the Silk Road Fund;	• Develop infrastructure development strategy and master plans (>10 years) with key priority given to utilities critical for manufacturing and exports (such as energy, industrial infrastructure, and transport) • Capacity building of focal agencies and enhanced coordination • Robust procurement process, project management, and contract administration • Avoid the pitfall of neglecting the operation and management of infrastructure • Know-how transfer, skill formation, boosting local content, links with local firms • Use alternative financing schemes, and debt sustainability as critical concerns • Environmental sustainability consideration
Sustainability and environment	**Green development initiative (5):** Low-carbon, circular economy and sustainable development; fifty green projects; policy dialogue, exchanges, and research	• Develop green economy strategy (industrialization, infrastructure development, climate-resilient agriculture) and focal agencies • Develop focal agencies, introduce and enforce laws • Education and awareness campaigns

Human capital and capacity building	**Capacity-building initiative (6):** Support in development planning and experience sharing; innovation cooperation centres; 1,000 innovators exchange; 50,000 scholarships	• Develop the capacity to manage these initiatives and selection transparency • Define the required skills in view of the focused industries and knowledge • Support with research on skills formation and demand • Focus on ensuring trained experts are deployed in key priorities • Enhance twining among learning institutions and staff exchanges
Health care	**Health care initiative (6):** African Centre for Disease Control and Prevention; hospitals; campaigns on HIV-AIDS, malaria, communicable diseases	• Develop health care strategy • Focus on capacity building and healthcare systems • Develop pharmaceutical industry (where viable economically)
People-to-people	**People-to-people exchange initiative (7):** Institute of African Studies; joint research; people-to-people exchange; expand Confucius institutes; promote African tourism	• Promote new think tanks and research • Use research input in reviewing process and outcome, and setting priorities • Develop aviation hub (such as Ethiopia) to build on their competitive advantage • Develop tourism strategy with Chinese tourists in mind (requires distinct approach)
Security and stability	**Peace and security initiative (8):** Pursuing peace and development; scale up UN peace-keeping role; fight piracy and terrorism (Gulf of Aden and Guinea, Sahel); joint security forum	• Tap into training opportunities and experience sharing in peace-keeping operations • Enhance intelligence capacity and coordination for synergy • Strengthen sub-regional organizations (IGAD, SADC, etc.)
Resources	**Total of US$60 billion financial resources:** Government assistance, investment and financing by financial institutions and firms: US$15 billion grants, interest-free loans and concessional loans; US$20 billion of credit lines; US$10 billion special fund for development financing; US$5 billion special fund for financing imports from Africa; US$10 billion investment by Chinese firms; cancellation of interest-free Chinese government loans of LDCs and landlocked and small islands	• The prime focus should be developing relevant strategies and policies to ensure economic transformation, focus on capacity building and building key institutions, support with research, and enhance joint effort among African countries and through the AU. Promoting mutual learning is critical • Build capacity within ministries of finance, national planning agencies, agencies responsible for infrastructure planning, development and operation, and the development of skilled human resource. • Focus on experience and know-how transfer between China and Africa, mutual learning and experience sharing among African countries, tap into technical support from international organizations • Enhance research to study ways of improvement
International order and governance	Multi-polarity; economic globalization; participative global governance; uphold international order; boost regional and international coordination	• Enhance joint and coordinated efforts to change international governance systems • Strengthen the AU as strategic institution and regional organizations • Close coordination with UN agencies such as UNECA, UNCTAD

(continued)

Table 15.1. Continued

Strategic cooperation areas	Chinese 8 initiatives (2018–21)	Strategic implication for African governments
		• Strengthen South–South cooperation
		• Engage international organizations and economic ties with other advanced and emerging economies
Cooperation principles and new ideas	Strengthen comprehensive, strategic, cooperative partnership; mutual learning; 'five-no' approach; complementarity; people-oriented approach; improve institution building; develop new ideas; expand cooperation areas; China–Africa community; shared future; co-existence of civilizations	• Design comprehensive strategic approach to China–Africa economic ties • Maximize efforts to be a proactive and vigilant partner • Conduct relevant research • Policy learning as central in the cooperation • Deepen knowledge about China (policymaking, dynamics, etc.)

Notes: The key challenges are uneven political will, the presence of policies and strategies, and implementation capacity.
[a] See Lin and Zhang (2019) on a review and new survey on inducement of Chinese investors in light manufacturing. [b] See Reuters (2018) reaction by the US Treasury Department's response to local currency settlement. Billingslear noted that 'it is of something of great concern to us as well'. [c] See also Brautigam (2018) on a review of financial flow related to FOCAC VII.
Source: Authors' own compilation and summary (2018).

developing countries and emerging economies. China has successfully inserted itself into the international market and leveraged FDI to develop domestic firms.[13] Rodrik (2012: 153) states: 'China's ability to shield itself from the global economy proved critical...In sum, Chinese policymakers maintained their manoeuvring space and exploited it skilfully.'[14] Mittelman probes, 'how can a developing country capture the advantages of globalization?' (2006: 377). He adds:

Largely overlooked in this search for a key is the range of China's internal debates. This creative dialogue could help overcome the despair of antidevelopment, a multipronged attack on the whole developmentalist paradigm...It is a compelling case of a home-grown strategy of transformation, hope and self-confidence, and a large measure of self-determination. In other contexts, the Chinese narrative

capture neoliberal thinking and IFIs prescription, while the Beijing consensus is a loosely defined term that will not help to understand the nature of China–Africa economic ties.

[13] Akyüz (2017) highlights China as an example of managing FDI for structural transformation by increasing domestic value-added content and forcing joint ventures (in exchange for accessing China's domestic market). See Akyüz (2017) who argues that developing and emerging economies should 'identify correctly the capabilities of foreign firms, the channels through which they could stimulate growth and structural change, and the policies needed to deploy them'.
[14] Kozul-Wright (2018) highlights, 'China has drawn from the same standard playbook that developed countries used when they climbed the economic ladder.'

prompts the question of how to write a fresh script for development within the compass of neoliberal globalization. (Mittelman, 2006)

Indeed, the most important lesson has been China's homegrown strategy (not a prescription by others) of transformation, policy learning (such as 'finding truth from facts', and policy experiment or 'feeling the stones to cross the river'), self-confidence, and its choice of its own development path. Xiaoping (1994: 137) highlights that 'the special economic zones are an experiment... Our entire policy of opening to the outside is an experiment too.'[15] This continues to be the core belief in the development thinking of its present leaders: 'China's affairs must be handled in accordance with Chinese national conditions and reality. This is the only correct way to address all our problems' (Xi, 2017: 13). Opening to the outside world or building special economic zones, building national champions, and education were strategies aimed at speeding up technological transformation (Xiaoping, 1994: 43, 61; Lanqing, 2011).[16] From this perspective there is no such thing as the Chinese model to be copied by Africans. In sum, African leaders should aim to be a strategic partner and driver of the partnership.

15.4.2 *Prioritizing and Focusing on Productive Investment*

Financial resources and infrastructure development are two facets that dominate the China–Africa narrative and debate. From the perspective of structural transformation of Africa, investment in productive capacity—economic infrastructure in particular—has significant spillover effects in accelerating industrialization and modernization of agriculture, building technological capabilities and domestic linkages, boosting exports to improve the imbalances in trade terms, and debt servicing (CNN, 2018). The development of human capital and infrastructure, electricity and transport in particular, should be geared towards developing productive capacity and leveraging optimum returns. Another fundamental issue related to policy learning is that African policymakers and scholars may overlook China as a source of learning or may fail to follow a systematic learning approach (Oqubay, 2015; Oqubay and Ohno, 2019; Oqubay and Tesfachew, 2019).

---

[15] See also Langqing (2011) on Chinese characteristics of reform and opening.

[16] Xiaoping (1994: 269) who highlights, 'from a long-term point of view, we should pay attention to education and science and technology' and adds (1994: 43) 'We should open our country wider to the outside world... so as to speed up our technological transformation... It is a matter of strategic importance.' See also Nolan (2014) on China's industrial policy on building national champions and the active role of the state. See also Chu (2019) on the role of the state and industrial policies.

15.5 Policy Autonomy and Being in the Driving Seat

A strategic approach to China–Africa economic ties implies that African countries have development strategies, industrial policies, and long-term indicative plans which need to be aligned to ongoing China–Africa initiatives and long-term structural transformation frameworks (UNECA, 2016).[17] This is a dynamic process that enforces learning and continuously nurtures partnerships. In addition to this, African policymakers should understand the initiatives, and design new programmes to maximize them and to bring in new ideas to further improve the process. Learning among African countries is vital in itself and such mutual learning could reinforce the strategic nature and complementarity of China–Africa relations. This should be supported by evidence-based research to feed into policymaking.

African policymakers also need to engage other emerging and advanced economies and 'traditional' partners to accelerate structural transformation. Better coordination and synergy among partners will result in better outcomes. In this respect, the focus should not be limited to financial resources but more importantly should include promoting FDI inflow and promoting exports. Knowledge transfer and experience sharing need to be given more strategic importance. The guiding principle should therefore be to sit in the 'driving seat' and ensure policy independence. Joint efforts should be increased that seek to change global governance to ensure Africa receives better benefits and leverages.

15.5.1 *Investing in Innovation, Research, and Development*

A fad of the day among some international figures and influential scholars is that African countries should abdicate policy that focuses on manufacturing because of saturating international export markets, the competition posed by the rise of China, and rapid technological development (robotization and artificial intelligence), as manufacturing will not be a growth driver. The reality is that the special properties of manufacturing are still robust and valid for the twenty-first century, and accelerated technological advancement implies that industrial policies should focus on fostering technological learning.[18] Yülek (2018) highlights that manufacturing is 'the hotbed of technology, productivity, and innovation', which continues to be the engine of growth, and export-led growth is stellar for industrial policy in

---

[17] Although Agenda 2063 is important, what matters most is the national development strategies and industrial policies of respective countries. Action will depend on the development direction and trajectory of each country.

[18] On special properties of manufacturing and the strategic role of exports, see Kaldor (1967) and Thirlwall (2013).

the twenty-first century.[19] Much of the expansion of modern services also depends on manufacturing development. African countries should embrace industrialization and industrial policy to generate employment, promote exports, develop technological capabilities, and speed up economic transformation. This has to be supported with human capital development and infrastructure development directed at accelerating economic transformation. From this perspective, not many African countries have succeeded in leveraging China–Africa economic ties to foster industrialization and structural transformation.

15.5.2 *Mapping out a New Research Agenda*

While research on China–Africa relations has expanded over the past decade, huge gaps remain on a several critical themes. Among the gaps that merit further investigation is fostering technological learning between universities in China and Africa. While there is a robust flow of African students to China and numerous workshops for training, substantial programmes for joint basic and applied research with spillovers to industry do not exist to date. A shift in approach and urgent action is necessary to connect knowledge institutions such as universities and research entities to industries and firms in Africa, and to intensify capacity building in universities and in local firms. Second, as China prepares to enter the fourth industrial revolution and prepare the groundwork to become an innovation-driven economy, there is a need to probe the implications of digital technology, artificial intelligence, and the reach of algorithms for the future of China–Africa economic ties. Besides the economic consequences of digital technology and artificial intelligence, research is needed on modalities of governance and regulations to be adopted to pre-empt the harms and ethical abuses of technological innovation, as with robotics and automation, encountered in other parts of the world.

References

Akyüz, Yilmaz (2017) *Playing with Fire: Deepened Financial Integration and Changing Vulnerabilities of the Global South*. Oxford: Oxford University Press.

Alden, Chris and Daniel Large (eds) (2018) *New Directions in Africa–China Studies*. New York: Routledge.

Altman, Miriam (2018) 'Taking China–Africa Trade Relations to New Heights', *China Daily*, 5 September.

---

[19] See also Lee (2019) on the importance of innovation and absorptive capacity.

Brautigam, Deborah (2009) *The Dragon's Gift: The Real Story of China in Africa*. Oxford: Oxford University Press.

Brautigam, Deborah (2015) *Will Africa Feed China?* Oxford: Oxford University Press.

Brautigam, Deborah (2018) 'China's FOCAC Financial Package for Africa 2018: Four Facts.' 4 September, http://www.chinaafricarealstory.com/2018/09/chinas-focac-financial-package-for.html.

Cheng, Zhangxi and Ian Taylor (2017) *China's Aid to Africa: Does Friendship Really Matter?* New York: Routledge.

Cheru, Fantu, and Cyril Obi (eds) (2010) *The Rise of China and India in Africa*. London: Zed Books.

China Africa Research Initiative (2018) 'The Path Ahead: The 7th Forum on China–Africa Cooperation', Briefing Paper No 1, Janet Eom, Deborah Brautigam, and Lina Benabdallah, https://static1.squarespace.com/static/5652847de4b033f56d2bdc29/t/5b84311caa4a998051e685e3/1535389980283/Briefing+Paper+1+-+August+2018+-+Final.pdf.

Chow, Gregory (2007) *China's Economic Transformation*. 2nd edition. Oxford: Blackwell Publishing.

Chu, Wan-wen (2019) 'Catch-Up and Learning by Newly Industrializing Economies: The Case of Taiwan', in Arkebe Oqubay and Kenichi Ohno (eds) *How Nations Learn: Technological Learning and Catch Up*. Oxford: Oxford University Press, ch. 6.

CNN (2018) 'Skyscrapers, Trains and Roads: How Addis Ababa Came to Look Like a Chinese City', 3 September, Jenni Marsh, https://edition.cnn.com/2018/09/02/africa/addis-ababa-china-construction/index.html.

Cornelissen, Scarlett, Fantu Cheru, and Timothy Shaw (eds) (2015) *Africa and International Relations in the 21st Century*. London: Palgrave Macmillan.

Financial Times (2018) 'The Chinese Model Is Failing Africa', Luke Patey, 26 August, https://www.ft.com/content/ca4072f6-a79f-11e8-a1b6-f368d365bf0e.

Fröbel, Folker (2009) *The New International Division of Labour: Structural Unemployment in Industrial Countries and Industrialisation in Developing Countries*. Cambridge: Cambridge University Press.

Kaldor, Nicholas (1967) *Strategic Factors in Economic Development*. Ithaca, NY: New York State School of Industrial and Labour Relations, Cornell University.

Kozul-Wright, Richard (2018) 'The Global Economy's Fundamental Weakness', *Project Syndicate*, 13 September, https://www.project-syndicate.org/commentary/global-economy-fundamental-weakness-by-richard-kozul-wright-2018-09.

Lanqing, Li (2011) *Breaking Through: The Birth of China's Opening-Up Policy*. English edition. Oxford: Oxford University Press, and China: Foreign Language Teaching & Research Press.

Lee, Ching Kwan (2017) *The Spectre of Global China: Politics, Labor, and Foreign Investment in China*. Chicago, IL: University of Chicago.

Lee, Keun (2019) 'Catch-Up and Learning in South Korea: Formation and Absorptive Capacity', in Arkebe Oqubay and Kenichi Ohno (eds) *How Nations Learn: Technological Learning, Industrial Policy, and Catch Up*. Oxford: Oxford University Press, ch. 7.

Lin, Justin Y. (2011) *Demystifying the Chinese Economy*. Cambridge: Cambridge University Press.

Lin, Justin Y. and Célestin Monga (2017) *Beating the Odds: Jump-Starting Developing Countries*. Princeton, NJ: Princeton University Press.

Lin, Justin Y. and Célestin Monga (2019) *The Oxford Handbook of Structural Transformation*. Oxford: Oxford University Press.

Lin, Justin Y. and Jun Zhang (2019) 'China: Learning to Catch up in a Globalized World', in Arkebe Oqubay and Kenichi Ohno (eds) *How Nations Learn: Technological Learning, Industrial Policy, and Catch Up*. Oxford: Oxford University Press, ch. 8.

McKinsey & Company (2017) 'Dance of the Lions and Dragons: How Are Africa and China Engaging, and How Will the Partnership Evolve?' June. Irene Yuan Sun, Kartik Jayaram, and Omid Kassiri.

Mittelman, James (2006) 'Globalization and Development: Learning from Debates in China', *Globalizations*, 3(3): 377–91.

Mittelman, James (2011) *Contesting Global Order: Development, Global Governance, and Globalization*. New York: Routledge.

Nayyar, Deepak (2016) *Catch Up: Developing Countries in the World Economy*. Oxford: Oxford University Press.

Nolan, Peter (2014) *Chinese Firms, Global Firms: Industrial Policy in the Era of Globalization*. New York: Routledge.

Nolan, Peter (2016) *Understanding China: The Silk Road and the Communist Manifesto*. New York: Routledge.

Ocampo, José A., Cordina Rada, and Lance Taylor (2009) *Growth and Policy in Developing Countries: A Structuralist Approach*. New York: Columbia University Press.

Oqubay, Arkebe (2015) *Made in Africa: Industrial Policy in Ethiopia*. Oxford: Oxford University Press.

Oqubay, Arkebe (2019) 'Industrial Policy and Late Industrialization in Ethiopia', in Fantu Cheru, Christopher Cramer, and Arkebe Oqubay (eds) *The Oxford Handbook of the Ethiopian Economy*. Oxford: Oxford University Press.

Oqubay, Arkebe and Kenichi Ohno (2019) *How Nations Learn: Technological Learning, Industrial Policy, and Catch Up*. Oxford: Oxford University Press.

Oqubay, Arkebe, and Taferre Tesfachew (2019) 'Learning to Catch up in Africa: Lessons and Complexity', in Arkebe Oqubay and Kenichi Ohno (eds) *How Nations Learn: Technological Learning, Industrial Policy, and Catch Up*. Oxford: Oxford University Press, ch. 14.

Rodrik, Dani (2012) *The Globalization Paradox: Why Global Markets, States, and Democracy Can't Coexist*. Oxford: Oxford University Press.

Shambaugh, David (2013) *China Goes Global: The Partial Power*. Oxford: Oxford University Press.

Taylor, Ian (2009) *China's New Role in Africa*. Boulder, CO: Lynne Rienner.

Thirlwall, Anthony (2013) *Economic Growth in an Open Developing Economy: The Role of Structure and Demand*. Cheltenham: Edward Elgar.

Tillerson, Rex (2018) 'Africa: Press Availability with African Union Commission Chairperson Moussa Faki', 8 March, US State Department, Washington, DC.

Xi, Jinping (2017) *The Governance of China, Volume II*. Beijing: Foreign Language Press.

Xi, Jinping (2018) Speech at the Opening of FOCAC Beijing Summit (FOCAC VII), 3 September.

Xiaoping, Deng (1994) *Selected Works of Deng Xiaoping, Volume III: 1982–1992*. Beijing: Foreign Languages Press.

UNECA (2016) 'Transformative Industrial Policy for Africa', United Nations Economic Commission for Africa, Addis Ababa.

Yueh, Linda (2013) *China's Growth: The Making of an Economic Superpower*. Oxford: Oxford University Press.

Yülek, Murat A. (2018) *How Nations Succeed: Manufacturing, Trade, Industrial Policy, and Economic Development*. London: Palgrave Macmillan.

Name Index

Please note that page references to Footnotes will be followed by the letter 'n' and number of the note.

Adunbi, Omolade 10
Agubamah, E. 195
Akamatsu, K. 267n4
Akyüz, Yilmaz 318n13
Alden, Chris 5n5, 8, 312n4
Alves, A. C. 118, 184–5

Baah, A. Y. 244
Bao, Q. 22
Bernstein, H. 248
Bigsten, A. 21
Braudel, Fernand 36
Brautigam, Deborah 9, 91, 312
Brierley, John E. C. 220n20
Burawoy, M. 248–9

Carey, Richard 9–10
Chen, S. 48–9
Chen, Y. 195, 201–2
Cheru, Fantu 12, 175, 183–4, 243
Corkin, L. 110

David, René 220n20
Dees, S. 22
Deng, X. 35n1
Denghua, Zhang 116
Dobson, W. 23
Dollar, David 161, 217n6

Easterly, W. 46n8
Eisenman, J. 201
Elias, T. O. 219

Farole, T. 205
Fleisher, B. 22
Fröbel, F. 6n7

Gaffey, Conor 224n48
Gagliardone, Iginio 166
Gallagher, Norah 222n40
Gerschenkron, A. 247

Gu, Jing 9–10

Hameiri, Shahar 176
Harry, D. 205
Heinrichs, J. 6n7
Hua Guofeng 68
Huang, H. 242
Hurtley, J. 45n7

Jacobs, Andrew 224n47
Jauch, H. 244
Jiabao, Wen 74
Jianxin, Chi 109
Jones, Lee 176

Kang, J. S. 48–9
Kidane, Won 11
Kozul-Wright, Richard 318n14
Kreye, O. 6n7
Krugman, P. 163
Kuo, C. C. 22–3

Lai, M. 22
Lampert, Ben 175, 179
Large, Daniel 5n5, 312n4
Lasswell, Harold 149
Lee, Ching Kwan 249n11, 254, 255, 312
Le Pere, Garth 93–4
Lerche, J. 249
Li, Guangzhong 22
Li, H. 22
Lieberthal, Kenneth 99
Lin, Justin Yifu 12, 47, 84, 157, 276, 277
Liu, X. 21
Lowenfeld, A. 227n63
Lüthje, B. 250

McConnaughay, Dean Philip 219
Meles Zenawi 285, 286–7
Mittelman, James 2n2, 318–19
Mohan, Giles 175, 179

Name Index

Monga, Célestin 7, 36n2
Moyo, Dambisa 88

Obi, Cyril 10
Ocampo, José 314
Okonjo-Iweala, Ngozi 137–8
Olawale Elias, T. 219
O'Neill, J. 41
Oqubay, Arkebe 12, 243
Oya, Carlos 2n2, 11

Paltiel, J. 101
Panitchpaki, Supachai 221n32
Parikh, A. 21
Patey, Luke 176, 186
Peng, S. 22
Philip, Arthur 219n19
Pilling, David 216n4
Prebisch, Raul 197

Qoba, Mzukisi 93–4
Quigley, Sam 182

Rada, Cordina 314
Ran, Jimmy 22
Renne, E. 196, 201, 204
Rodrik, Dani 22, 318
Rounds, Z. 242

Sachs, Jeffrey 216n4
Safarian, A. E. 23
Salacuse, Jeswald W. 222n36
Selassie, Abebe Aemro 145
Selwyn, B. 249
Shan, Wenhua 222n40
Shinn, David 8, 201, 202
Silver, B. J. 252
Singer, Hans 197
Smith, Graeme 116
Snow, Philip 216n1

Solow, R. 46n8
Spence, M. 52
Stein, Howard 10, 205
Strange, Susan 149, 153
Sun, H. S. 21, 22
Sun Yun 101

Tang, X. 91, 244, 256n14
Taylor, Ian 9, 183–4
Taylor, Lance 314
Tillerson, Rex 311

Umejei, Emeka 182

Van Reenen, J. 23, 24
Voon, Jan P. 22

Wang, Y. 157
Warren, H. 217n8
Wei, S. J. 21
Wen, M. 22
Wenping, He 118
Whalley, J. 21
Wolf, M. 46, 55n15
Woo, W. J. 22

Xin, X. 21
Xu, Jiajun 12

Yang, C. H. 22–3
Yasheng, Huang 99
Yi, Wang 101
Yi-Chong, Xu 114
Yueh, Linda 7, 24
Yülek, Murat A. 320–1

Zhang, Xiaobo 269n9
Zhao, M. Q. 22
Zheng, J. 21
Zimmerman, James 220n21

Subject Index

Please note that page references to Footnotes are followed by the letter 'n' and number of the note, Figures and Tables are indicated by *f* and *t* after the page number.

Ababa–Djibouti construction project 224
Academy of International Business Officials, China 108
Addax (Geneva-based oil company) 182, 183
Addis Ababa Action Plan (2004–6) 118
Addis Ababa Light Rail System 90
Africa
  'China effect' on 4, 12, 25
  and China's think tanks 112–13
  Chinese firms in, conditions 11
  debt management concerns 145–6
  East Africa 28, 29, 135, 295, 297
  economic transformation 4, 6, 12, 314–17
    FOCAC initiatives, strategic approach 316–18*t*
  independence 63, 64, 66
  industrialization of 4, 5, 12–14, 30, 81, 193, 283, 321
    debates/outlooks on China–Africa economic relations 84, 90, 93, 95
    Ethiopia 5, 89, 283, 284, 285, 287, 295, 296, 299
    Kenya 28
    light manufacturing 265–81
    limitations and shortcomings 314
    Nigeria 203
  infrastructure development *see* **development finance and African infrastructure development**
  integration into global value chain 8
  liberation movements, China's support for 8, 64
  medical teams in 67–8
  neoliberal structural adjustment programmes 132
  North Africa *see* **North Africa**
  petro-states and Chinese SOCs, case studies 180–1
  relations with Mao Zedong (1949–76) 62–6
  soft power, increasing 76
  South Africa *see* **South Africa**
  struggle against colonialism and imperialism 2

sub-Saharan Africa *see* **sub-Saharan Africa (SSA)**
  West Africa 164, 207, 210
  see also *specific African countries*
Africa Research Centre 112–13
Africa Research Office 112
African Capacity-Building Foundation (ACBF), Harare 158, 168
African Development Bank 41n5, 168
African Growth and Opportunity Act (AGOA), US 272, 280
African Union (AU) 265, 311
  development finance and African infrastructure development 153, 168
  historical context of China–Africa relations 62, 74–5
  institutional framework of China–Africa relations 112, 119
Afro-Asian People's Solidarity Organization (AAPSO) 63
Agence Française de Développement (AfD) 161
Agenda 2063 320n17
agreements 216–38
  Belt and Road Initiative (BRI) 231–3
  currency 226
  dispute settlement 226–30
    commercial agreements 229–30
    investment agreements 228–9
    trade agreements 227–8
  economic
    bilateral tax treaties 225–6
    commercial 224, 229–30
    cultural factors 218–20
    currency 226
    dispute settlement 226–30
    economic and technical cooperation agreements 133
    investment 222–3, 228–9
    substantive contents and norms 220–6
    trade 220–2, 227–8
  judicial assistance treaties 225
  post-colonial modern world order 217–18, 220

Subject Index

Agricultural Development Bank 9
agricultural sector 91–2
Agricultural Technical Demonstration
   Centres (ATDCs) 91, 92–3
aid *see* foreign aid
'alarmists' 283
Algeria
   Front de Libération Nationale, Chinese
     support for 64
   medical teams sent to 67
   recognition of PRC (1958) 64
All-China Students' Federation 65
anchor firms, attracting 275
Angola
   borrowing by 141, 143
   Chinese involvement 87, 242, 255
   civil war (1975–2002) 140, 194
   Eurobond issue (2015) 137
   oil and gas engagements 184–5
   as petro-state 185
   risk of lending to 143
   skill shortages 243
Anticipated Impact Measurement and
   Monitoring (AIMM) system 158
arbitration 224, 225
   commercial agreements 229–30
   International Centre for the Settlement of
     Investment Disputes (ICSID), Chinese
     membership 229
   investor–state 228
   preferred means of dispute settlement
     229, 234
   state-to-state 228, 231
arms assistance 68, 70, 75
   small arms 72, 74
Arrangement on Guidelines for Official
   Supported Export Credits 159
Asian Infrastructure Investment Bank
   (AIIB) 94, 161
Asian-African Conference, Bandung
   (1955) 63
AU *see* African Union (AU)
AU/NEPAD Partnership for Infrastructure
   Development in Africa
   (PIDA) 156

Bandung Asian-African Conference (1955),
   Ten Principles 63
Bangladesh 25, 256
Bank of China 9, 136, 137
   see also People's Bank of China (PBOC)
Banking Regulation Commission,
   Chinese 152
banks *see* commercial banks/loans; lending
   institutions, China; policy banks,
   China; *individual banks and financial
   institutions*

Belt and Road Forum for International
   Cooperation 152
Belt and Road Initiative (BRI), China 5, 8, 19,
   101, 315
   Action Plan for the Harmonization of
     Standards along the Belt and Road
     (2015–17) 231
   agreements 231–3
   development finance and African
     infrastructure development 147, 150,
     163–4, 168
   global political economy (GPE)
     approach 152–3
   historical context 77
   and Kenya 28–30, 31
   launched by Xi Jinping (2013) 152
   summit of 2017 232
Berlin Conference (1884) 163
bilateral investment agreements 29
bilateral investment treaties (BITs) 233
   Chinese 222–3, 228
   first-generation 222
   second-generation 223, 228
bilateral tax treaties 225–6
Bole Lemi (Industrial Park), Ethiopia 276
bonds, renminbi-denominated 137, 152
branded goods 27, 275
   original brand manufacturing (OBM) 273
Bretton Woods system 38, 162
   post-Bretton Woods global economy 39
BRICS Inter-bank Co-operation
   Mechanism 154
BRICS New Development Bank (NDB) 94,
   154–5, 161
bridge construction 140
Bui Dam, construction of 143–4
Bui Hydropower 144
Busan High-Level Forum of Development
   Effectiveness (2011) 156

CAD Fund *see* China–Africa Development
   Fund (CAD Fund)
Cairo Regional Centre for International
   Commercial Arbitration
   (CRCICA) 226
Calabar Free Trade Zone 202
Cambodia 273, 274
capital
   accumulation of 24
   'Chinese capitals' 12, 256
   controls, use of 51–2
   dual logic of Chinese state capital 254
   human 24, 319
capitalism
   critiques 85
   and labour regimes 248–50
   restoration of 99, 120

'cascade' concept 158
cement 109, 141, 193
China
   admission to the UN (1971) 66
   as Africa's strongest trading partner 2, 3
   aid framework 106–9
   Belt and Road Initiative (BRI) *see* **Belt and Road Initiative (BRI), China**
   as competitive threat 25–6
   Cultural Revolution 8, 35, 62, 66, 67, 79
   economic development *see* **Chinese economic transformation**
   economic rebalancing 12
   foreign exchange reserves, holding 42
   Great Leap Forward 8, 62
   impact on global/African infrastructure investment framework 155–64
   imperialism, perceptions of 3–4, 175
   industrialization of 2, 6, 13, 25, 89, 296, 315
   labour regimes, variation and shifts 250–3
   light manufacturing firms 12
   media 76
   as middle-income economy 20, 25, 27
   Ministry of Commerce (MOFCOM) *see* **Ministry of Commerce (MOFCOM)**
   National Bureau of Statistics 267
   neo-colonialism, perceptions of 3–4, 175
   non-interference principle 167
   oil imports 173, 174*t*
   overseas investments 25
   overseas lending institutions in 132–7
   policy buffers 50
   political risks within 52
   post-crisis historical precedents inapplicable to 49–50
   provinces 116–17
   public entrepreneurship model 10, 147, 149–50, 153
   as recipient of FDI 21
   Sino-Soviet hostility 64, 67
   state–market relations 149
   Tiananmen Square crisis (1989) 53, 69, 71
   transition economy 20
   and United States 67
   see also **People's Republic of China (PRC)**
China Aerospace Science and Technology Corporation (CASC) 114
China Civil Engineering Construction Corporation (CCECC) 194n2, 207
China Construction Bank 136
China Development Bank (CDB) 110, 132, 135, 140
   development finance 147, 148, 152, 159, 161
   Institute of Development Finance 152
   International Development Finance Club member 161

Investing in Africa Forum (IAF) 162
   as policy bank 109, 150, 151–2
   Special Fund for SME loans 145
'China effect' 4, 12, 25
China Export Import Bank (Eximbank)
   development finance 147, 148, 159
   loans from 132, 134–7, 139, 143, 145
   as policy bank 109, 110, 150, 151
   World Bank–China Exim Bank Memorandum of Understanding on Cooperation (2007) 161
China Global Energy Finance database 110
China Health and Retirement Longitudinal Study (CHARLS) 269
China Institute of International Studies (CIIS)
   Blue Book of International Situation and China's Foreign Affairs 113
China International Centre for Economic and Technical Exchanges (CICETE) 106, 107
China International Economic and Trade Arbitration Commission (CIETAC) 224, 226
China International Water and Electric Corporation (CWE) 136
China Islamic Association 65
China model 311
China National Offshore Oil Corporation (CNOOC) 10, 173, 181, 182, 185
China National Petroleum Corporation (CNPC) 10, 173
   and Sudan 186, 187
'China paradox' 20
China Petroleum and Chemical Corporation (Sinopec) 10, 173, 180, 182, 184–5
China–Africa Cooperative Partnership for Peace and Security 74–5
China–Africa Development Fund (CAD Fund) 109, 206, 293
China–Africa Fund for Industrial Cooperation 94
China–Africa Infrastructure Cooperation Plan 153
China–Africa Joint Business Council 118
China–Africa labour encounters 241–8
   skill development 246–7
   workforce localization 241–4
   working conditions 244–6
China–Africa Products Exhibition Centre 118
China–Africa relations
   asymmetrical economic ties 314
   China as Africa's strongest trading partner 2, 3
   complementary economic partnership 13–14
   context 1–4

China–Africa relations (*cont.*)
coordination and friction 119–21
Ethiopia 285–95
Chinese FDI inflow, productive
nature 292–5
export growth and composition 287–8
financing and infrastructure
development 293–5
import volume and structure 288–9
power sector 293–4
productive employment 292
skills and know-how transfer 292–3
telecommunications 294–5
trade patterns 287–9
transport infrastructure 294
FOCAC as formal institutionalization of 117
future of 310–24
'anti-Chinese' narratives,
countering 311–12
China as a source of learning 315, 318–19
diversity 312
dynamic shifts 312
economic transformation of Africa,
bringing in 314–15
FOCAC initiatives, strategic
approach 316–18*t*
investment in innovation and R&D 320–1
new research agenda 321
policy autonomy 320–1
prioritizing/focusing on productive
investment 319
strategic approach 315–19
unevenness 312
history *see* **historical context of
China–Africa relations**
institutional framework 98–125
principles guiding relations with African and
Arab countries 65
strategic approach to 315–19
trade *see under* **trade**
uneven nature 4, 12
China–Africa Research Centre 113
China–Africa Research Initiative (CARI),
Johns Hopkins University's School of
Advanced International Studies 110,
129, 216n4, 217n5
China–Africa trade 2, 3
Ethiopian trade patterns 287–9
historical context 64, 68, 70, 76, 78, 79
textiles and Nigeria–Chinese trade
relations 195–9, 200*t*, 201–2
see also **China–Africa relations; trade**
China–DAC Study Group 156
China–Egypt BRI cooperation Five-Year
Plan 232
China–Egypt Suez Economic and Trade
Co-operation Zone 232

China–Ghana BIT 228
China–IMF Capacity Development
Centre 157–8
China–Mauritius FTA 221–2
China–Tunisia BIT 228
Chinese Academy of International Trade
and Economic Cooperation
(CAITEC) 107, 113
Chinese Academy of Social Sciences (CASS) 112
'Chinese capitals' 12
'Chinese dream' concept 77, 313
Chinese economic transformation 1–4,
19–21, 24, 178, 283, 313
China as large, open economy 25, 26
Chinese economy as a global public good
1, 37–42, 43*t*, 44–5, 50
directed development 2
foreign investment 22
global impact 19, 20, 25–6
intellectual property rights (IPR)
requirements 20–1
market-oriented reforms 20
meaning and global externalities 35–57
'open door' policy 21
poverty in China prior to 2, 6, 20, 36
pragmatism 2
regional growth 22, 23
size of China's economy 41
unique nature of China's economy 20
Chinese-African People's Friendship
Association 65
climate change policies 74
Cold War 62, 63, 70
colonialism 2, 177, 195, 284, 313
historical context of China–Africa
relations 63–5
'new' 311
post-colonial modern world order
217–18, 220
see also **imperialism**
commercial agreements, infrastructure 224
commercial banks/loans 136–7, 148
commercial suppliers' credits,
Chinese 135–6
Commission on the Economy and
Climate 162
commodity prices 25
Commonwealth Development Corporation
(CDC), UK 135
Communist Party of China (CPC) 53, 54n13,
63, 64, 65, 77, 286
Central Committee
Foreign Affairs Office (FAO) 100, 117
general secretaries of 69, 73, 76
Dialogue with World Political Parties
High-level Meeting 111
International Department (ID) 111–12

International Liaison Department 111
Twelfth National Congress (1982) 69
comparative advantage 26, 39, 50
concession foreign aid loans 104, 110, 134
Congo, Republic of
hydropower plant funding (1980) 139
National Road No. 2. 140
oil production 184
contracting and procurement 157–8
cost-cutting 29
CPC *see* **Communist Party of China (CPC)**
credit
commercial suppliers' credits 135–6
cycles, impact 48–9
excessive growth 48
export credits and tied aid 159
lines of 129, 130
oil-backed 184
Cultural Revolution 8, 35, 62, 79
impact on Africa 66, 67
currency agreements 226
currency controls 50

Dakar–Bamako railway 138
debt 47–50
African debt management capacity,
concerns 145–6
African lending, risk reduction 143–4
cancelling by China 143
debt finance for African infrastructure
development *see* **infrastructure
development in Africa, Chinese aid**
Debt Sustainability Framework 165
excessive burden of, and finance
sustainability 299
global total debt 47
international debt finance system, new
activism 161–4
official debt problem cases, managing 159
relief 142–3
de-industrialization 199, 201, 265
demography 164–5
Deng Xiaoping *see* **Xiaoping, Deng**
Department of Aid to Foreign Countries 107
depreciation, of renminbi 51–2
Development Assistance Committee (DAC),
OECD 104, 159
OECD/DAC Blended Finance project 158
**development finance and African
infrastructure development**
entrepreneurialism, Chinese 147
global political economy (GPE)
approach 149–55
history 147–8
impact of China on global/African
infrastructure investment
framework 155–64

infrastructure as a development
priority 155–6
international development finance system,
China's new activism on 161–4
see also **infrastructure development
in Africa**
development finance institution (DFI) 152
developmentalism 287
digital economy 165–6
Dispute Settlement Body (DSB) 227
dispute settlement, economic
agreements 226–30
commercial 229–30
investment 228–9
trade 227–8
**Dispute Settlement Understandings
(DSU)** 11, 227

East Africa 28, 29, 135, 295, 297
Eastern Industrial Park (EIP), Ethiopia 276
ECC *see* **Economic and Commercial
Counsellor (ECC)**
econometric methods 22
**Economic and Commercial Counsellor
(ECC)** 103, 104, 106, 108–9
**economic and technical cooperation
agreements** 133
**Economic Community of West African States
(ECOWAS)** 210
**Economic Cooperation and Trade Zones
(ECTZs)** 91, 92
economic geography 163
economic growth/transformation
in Africa 4, 6, 12, 314–17, 318t
Belt and Road Initiative (BRI) 166
causes 165
of China *see* **Chinese economic
transformation**
'China effect' on African economic
growth 4, 12
cycles 145
endogenous 23, 47
evolutionary approach to 23
export-led 39, 40
FDI and trade 21, 22
'heterodox' policies to accelerate 3,
286, 295
infrastructure development 296, 299
and Ministry of Foreign Affairs (MFA) 103
open economy 25, 26
regional, in China 22, 23
research and development (R&D) 22
in Sub-Saharan Africa 30–1
and TFP 24
and workplace encounters 239–40
economic miracle, East Asia 286–7
efficiency spillovers 22

Egypt
  Fourth Ministerial Conference (2009) 74
  recognition of PRC (1956) 64
  trade with 63
electric power/electrification 136, 140,
  164–5
employment
  Ethiopia 292
  labour regimes *see* **labour regimes**
  management ethos and associated labour
    practices 257
  real wages, in manufacturing sector 267
  skill development 246–7
  variation among Chinese firms 246–7
  wage gap 267
  workforce localization 241–4
  working conditions 244–6
  workplace encounters 239–40
    China–Africa 241–8
energy sector
  oil industry *see* **oil and gas engagements**
  prioritizing investment in 296–7
**engineering, procurement and construction
  (EPC) projects** 137, 157
Enlai, Zhou *see* **Zhou Enlai (Chinese Premier
  1949–76)**
**environmental, social and governance (ESG)
  standards** 160
Equatorial Guinea *see* **Guinea**
Ethiopia 2, 12, 28
  Chinese SOEs 255
  Eastern Industrial Park (EIP) 276
  Eastern Industrial Zone 244–5
  elites 284
  foreign policy 285
  Hawassa Industrial Park (HIP) 276
  imports from China, volume and
    structure 288–9
  industrial park, financing for 142
  and industrialization of Africa 5, 89, 283,
    284, 285, 287, 295, 296, 299
  murders of Chinese workers in 120
  New York contrasted 46
  policy learning 297
  relations with China
    background and context 285–95
    Chinese FDI inflow, productive
      nature 292–5
    committed political leadership and strong
      political ownership 296
    export growth and composition 287–8
    financing and infrastructure
      development 293–5
    import volume and structure 288–9
    long-term development vision 296
    political parties 286
    power sector 293–4

  prioritizing investment in infrastructure
    and energy 296–7
  productive employment 292
  skills and know-how transfer 292–3
  telecommunications 294–5
  trade deficit 289
  trade patterns 287–9
  transport infrastructure 294
  road construction/repair 46n8, 140
  special economic zones (SEZs) 292, 301
  structural transformation 255, 283, 284,
    286, 296
  successful development in post-1991
    period 285, 295–8
Ethiopia–Djibouti railway 294
**Ethiopian People's Revolutionary
  Democratic Front (EPRDF)** 284–6, 296
**Ethiopian Telecommunication
  Corporation** 294
ethnographic research 254, 312
European Union (EU) 25, 50, 156, 164
  Everything But Arms (EBA) 272
  trade 227, 287
exceptionalism, Chinese 9, 11
  African agency and context 257–8
  fallacy of 240, 250, 252, 253
exchange rate stability 50–2
**Executive Bureau of International Economic
  Cooperation, China** 106, 107
Eximbank *see* **China Export Import Bank
  (Eximbank)**
export credits, and tied aid 159
export processing zones (EPZs)
  Ethiopia 292
  Nigeria 204–5
Export-Import Bank of China 9
externalities
  credit growth, excessive 48
  economic threats 46
  financial stability concerns 48
  global financial crisis 26, 28, 46
  Great Recession 26, 46
  infrastructure and structural
    transformation 157
  investment quality 46–7
  investment slowdown 45–7
  leverage 48–9
  potential negative externalities, mitigating
    factors 45–54
  risk-taking, excessive 48–9
  scenarios 45–6

factors of production 46
factory regime 248–9
fair and equitable treatment 223
FDI *see* **foreign direct investment (FDI)**
financial stability concerns 48

FIOCCO Group 273
first-mover challenge 267, 274–7
Five Principles of Peaceful Coexistence
(PRC) 63, 74
fixed-proportions production function 46
'flexigemony,' defining 178
'flying geese' model 12, 253
first-mover challenge 267, 274–7
light manufacturing 266, 267–9, 272
origins of term 267n4
underestimation of 'flying geese' 271
see also light manufacturing
FOCAC see Forum on China–Africa
Cooperation (FOCAC)
Foreign Affairs Leading Small Group
(FALSG) 101
Foreign Affairs Office (FAO), CPC 100, 117
foreign aid, Chinese
aid framework 106–9
Academy for International Business
Officials (AIBO) 106, 108
Chinese Academy of International Trade
and Economic Cooperation
(CAITEC) 107, 113
Department of Aid to Foreign
Countries 107
Department of West Asian and African
Affairs 103, 106–7
Economic and Commercial Counsellor
(ECC) 103, 104, 106, 108–9
Executive Bureau of International
Economic Cooperation 106, 107
budget 134–5
concession foreign aid loans 134
debt finance, for African infrastructure
development 147–72
Department of Aid to Foreign Countries 107
development finance for infrastructure see
development finance and African
infrastructure development
historical context 65, 67, 69, 72, 74, 75, 77
lending institutions see lending
institutions, China
loans see loans, Chinese
policy banks see policy banks, China
tied aid and export credits 159
zero-tariffs 74, 287–8
foreign direct investment (FDI) 11
China as recipient of 21
and economic growth 21, 22
growth of during Hu Jintao period 75
impact on growth 21, 22
inflow, productive nature 290–5, 291t
inward 28
labour regimes 251
light manufacturing 268, 275–6
outward 2–3, 4, 19, 27–8, 78, 132, 267

quality FDI and productive capacity 300
sub-Saharan Africa (SSA) 240
and total factor productivity 22
foreign exchange reserves 42, 131
foreign exchange shortages, Africa 131
foreign policy, China 2, 62, 63, 100
Foreign Trade and Economic Cooperation
Commission (FTEC) 117
foreign-invested enterprises (FIEs) 21
Forum on China–Africa Cooperation
(FOCAC) 9, 10, 71, 117–19, 143, 192
First Ministerial Conference, Beijing
(2000) 118, 193
Second Ministerial Conference, Addis Ababa
(2003) 73, 118
Third Ministerial Conference, Beijing
(2006) 73–4, 109, 118
Fourth Ministerial Conference, Egypt
(2009) 74, 118
Fifth Ministerial Conference, Beijing
(2012) 118
Sixth Ministerial Conference, South Africa
(2015) 76–7, 109, 118, 300
Eighth Ministerial Conference, Beijing
(2018) 90, 118
Action Plan 149, 161
development finance and African
infrastructure development 147–9,
153, 158
and future of China–Africa ties 310, 315
strategic approach 316–18t
establishment (2000) 117, 133, 153
financial pledges 145
Follow-up Committee 118, 119
as formal institutionalization of Sino-African
relations 117
Infrastructure Connectivity initiative 153
results, emphasis on 118–19
trade and commerce, emphasis on 118–19
transforming as an effective platform 300–1
triennial action plans 163
Four Modernizations 68, 69
Four Principles for Sino-African Economic
and Technical Cooperation 87
461 China–African Cooperation
Framework 89
fragmented authoritarianism 99
free trade agreements (FTAs) 221–2
free trade zones (FTZs)
Calabar Free Trade Zone 202
evaluation of the operation of Chinese
companies in 211–12
Lekki Free Zone (LFZ) 10, 193, 201, 206–9
Ogun–Guangdong Zone, Igbesa 10, 209–10
Onne Oil and Gas Free Trade Zone 205
see also special economic zones (SEZs)
funding gap, global financial crisis 28

Gang of Four, purge of 66
General Agreement on Tariffs and
    Trade (GATT) 221
GATT/WTO legal regime 11, 233
Ghana
    independence (1957) 63
    repayment terms, Chinese finance 143–4
    risk of lending to 143
Gleneagles Summit (2005) 155
global division of labour and power
    (GDLP) 313
global financial crisis 1, 26, 28, 48
    economic rebalancing following 12, 46, 47
    post-crisis historical precedents inapplicable
        to China 49–50
Global Infrastructure Connectivity Alliance
    (GICA) 162, 163
global integration 2, 25, 26
global political economy (GPE)
    approach 149–55
    Belt and Road Initiative (BRI) 152–3
    BRICS New Development Bank (NDB) 154–5
    Forum on China–Africa Cooperation
        (FOCAC) 153
    policy banks, China 150–2
global production networks (GPNs) 247
global public goods see public goods, global
global total debt 47
Global Witness 160
globalization 1, 2, 6–8, 30
    Chinese economy as a global public
        good 37–42, 43t, 44–5
    'global business revolution' 6
    'Going Global' strategy 3, 12–13, 24,
        26–8
    new global economy 6
globalness 37
Going beyond Aid (Lin and Wang) 157
'Going Global/'Going Out' strategy 3, 12–13,
    139, 192
    and China's economic transformation 24,
        26–8
    development finance and African
        infrastructure development 147, 151–2
    and future of China–Africa ties 313, 315
Great Leap Forward 8, 62
Great Recession 26, 46, 48
Greater Nile Petroleum Corporation
    (GNPC) 186
Group of Eight (G8) 155
Group of Twenty (G20) 155
    Hangzhou Summit (2016) 162
    policy guidelines 158
    Seoul Development Agenda 156
    Task Force on Long-term Investment 158
Growing Together Fund, African
    Development Bank 153

growth, economic see economic growth/
    transformation
Growth & Transformation Plan (GTP I)
    275, 287
Guinea
    Chinese labour 242
    independence (1958) 63
    line of credit offered to (1960) 129, 130
    Ministry of Finance 130
    skill shortages 243

Handbook of Country Risk (Sinosure) 137
'harmonious society/harmonious
    world' 73
Hawassa Industrial Park (HIP),
    Ethiopia 276
High-Level Panel on Infrastructure 156
Highly Indebted Poor Countries (HIPC)
    Initiative 142, 159
historical context of China–Africa
    relations 7–8, 61–83
    development finance 147–8
    evolution of relations 7–8
    loans 130–2
    Ming Dynasty 61
    Second Sino-Japanese War (1937–45) 61
Hu Jintao period (2002 to 2012) 8, 62,
    73–6, 193
Huajian Industrial Holding
    Company 273n16, 275
Huawei brand 27
Hubei Province, medical teams from 67
Hull Rule for expropriation 223
human capital 24, 319
Human Rights Watch (HRW) 244
hydropower plant funding 139

IBM 27
ICOR see incremental capital-output
    rates (ICOR)
imperialism 2, 196
    future of China–Africa relations
        311, 313
    historical context of China–Africa
        relations 63–5, 67
    Japanese 313
    neo-imperialism 177, 181
    'new' 175, 283
    see also colonialism
Income and Capital Model Tax Convention,
    UN 225
incremental capital-output rates (ICOR)
    46, 47
independence, Africa 63, 64, 66
Industrial and Commercial Bank of China
    (ICBC) 136
industrial zones 142

industrialization
of Africa 4, 5, 12–14, 30, 81, 193, 321
debates/outlooks on China–Africa
economic relations 84, 90, 93, 95
Ethiopia 5, 89, 283, 284, 285, 287, 295,
296, 299
Kenya 28
light manufacturing 265–81
limitations and shortcomings 314
Nigeria 203
of China 2, 6, 13, 25, 89, 296, 315
and de-industrialization 199, 201, 265
early phases 246, 256
fostering by China 85, 89–91
and investment 319
latecomers 44, 247
and low wages/cheap labour 246, 247
marketing-based 265
pan-African 277
'pathways' 6–7
pragmatic 298
promises of 255
sustainable 265
transport infrastructure 31
zone strategy 10–11, 213
inequality 52
**Infrastructure Consortium for Africa
(ICA)** 154, 155, 156
infrastructure development in Africa 319
bridges 140
cement factories 141
Chinese aid
commercial agreements 224
debt finance 147–72
debt management concerns 145–6
export credits and tied aid 159
and international debt finance
system 161–4
loans 9, 138–42
official debt problem cases, managing 159
'off-take' arrangements 144
public vs private investment 158
zero-interest loans 130–3, 141, 143
Chinese approach 156–61
cocoa security 144
connectivity infrastructure, shared platforms
for 167–8
connectivity/geospatial dimension
omitted 163
contracting and procurement 157–8
as a development priority 155–6
electric power 140, 164–5
global political economy (GPE)
approach 149–55
Belt and Road Initiative (BRI) 152–3
BRICS New Development Bank
(NDB) 154–5

Forum on China–Africa Cooperation
(FOCAC) 153
policy banks, China 136, 150–2
and growth 137–8
human and corporate capacities and
competitiveness 159–60
hydropower plant funding 139
impact of China on global/African
infrastructure investment
framework 138, 155–64
Infrastructure Connectivity initiative 153
innovation and technology, proposition
regarding 162–3
prioritizing investment in 296–7
railway construction 8, 67, 69, 138–9, 140
road construction/repair 140
shared platforms for connectivity
infrastructure 167–8
shocks 162–3
standards 160–1
and structural transformation 157
sugar refineries 141
telecommunications 140–1
transformation
digital economy and leapfrogging
165–6
electrification and demography 164–5
transport 31, 294
water supply projects 139, 140–1
see also **development finance and African
infrastructure development; foreign
aid, Chinese; loans, Chinese; railway
construction**
Institute for Capacity Development 158, 168
**Institute of New Structural Economics
(INSE)** 267, 269
**Institute of West Asian and African
Studies** 112
**institutional framework of China–Africa
relations** 98–125
China's aid framework 106–9
Academy for International Business
Officials (AIBO) 106, 108
Chinese Academy of International Trade
and Economic Cooperation
(CAITEC) 107, 113
Department of Aid to Foreign
Countries 107
Department of West Asian and African
Affairs 103, 106–7
Economic and Commercial Counsellor
(ECC) 103, 104, 106, 108–9
Executive Bureau of International
Economic Cooperation 106, 107
China's provinces 116–17
Communist Party of China (CPC),
International Department 111–12

institutional framework of China–Africa
relations (*cont.*)
Forum on China–Africa Cooperation
(FOCAC) *see* Forum on China–Africa
Cooperation (FOCAC)
institutional rivalry between MFA and
MOFCOM 105–6
liberalization, effects of 98–100
Ministry of Commerce (MOFCOM) 103–5
Ministry of Foreign Affairs (MFA) 101–3
policy banks, China 109–10, 136, 150–2
policy drivers 100–6
state-owned enterprises (SOEs) 114–16
think tanks and Africa 112–13
intellectual property rights (IPR)
requirements 20–1
interest rates 131
International Centre for the Settlement of
Investment Disputes (ICSID), Chinese
membership 229
international development finance 148
and Chinese activism 161–4
International Development Finance Club 161
International Federation of Consulting
Engineers (FIDIC) 224
International Finance Corporation
(IFC) 279, 293
international financial institutions
(IFIs) 131, 142
international knowledge spillovers 23
International Task Force on Global Public
Goods 37, 38n3
international trade agreements 11
International Working Group (IWG) on
Export Credits 159
'intra-industry' trade 26
Investing in Africa Forum (IAF) 162
investment
'cascade' concept 158
Chinese state vs global private 312
impact of China on global/African
infrastructure investment
framework 138, 155–64
and industrialization 319
in infrastructure and energy,
prioritizing 296–7
in innovation and R&D 320–1
productive, prioritizing/focusing on 319
public vs private 158
quality 46–7
slowdown 45–7
see also bilateral investment agreements;
foreign direct investment (FDI)
investment agreements 222–3

Japan 6, 313
Second Sino-Japanese War (1937–45) 61

Jiabao, Wen 55n15
Jiang Zemin period (1989 to 2002) 8, 54n13,
71–3, 118, 285
Jinping, Xi *see* Xi Jinping (Chinese leader
from 2012)
'Joint Communiqué of the Leaders
Roundtable of the Belt and Road
Forum for International Cooperation'
(2016) 166
Joint Ethiopia–China Commission
(JECC) 285–6
joint ventures (JVs) 23–4, 292
judicial assistance treaties 225

Kenya
Belt and Road Initiative (BRI) 28–30
Chinese investment in 28
Chinese management and training in 29–30
infrastructure development 19, 29
non-hiring of local managers 29–30
Keqiang, Li 89, 101, 153
know-how, positive spillover of 21
knowledge
international, spillovers of 23
light manufacturing 300, 302
limited knowledge transfer impact 300
narrowing of gaps 302

labour process theory 248
labour regimes 11, 248–53
and capitalism 248–50
case studies 253–7
concept 248
disorganized despotism 251
factory regime 248–9
hukou (household residential) system 251
JIT systems 252
state intervention 252
variation and shifts, in China 250–3
see also employment
Lagos
diplomatic relations with 193
Lagos–Kano railway 140
Lekki Free Zone (LFZ) 10, 193, 201, 206–9
Social Economic Rights Action Centre
(SERAC) 206
Latin America 25
'Leapfrogging as the Key to Africa's
Development' report (CDB/WB) 162
least-developed countries (LDCs) 273
Lekki Free Zone (LFZ) 10, 193, 201, 206–9
China–Africa Lekki Investment
Company 206
Lekki Free Zone Development Company 206
Master Land Use Plan 206
lending institutions, China 132–7
commercial banks/loans 136–7, 148

commercial suppliers' credits 135–6
Sinosure 137
see also **foreign aid, Chinese; loans,**
  Chinese; *individual banks and financial*
  institutions
Leontief production function 46
Lesotho, medical teams sent to 67
leverage 48–9
  ratios, of policy banks 152
Li Peng 69, 71
liberal capitalism 99
liberalization, effects of 98–100
Libyan crisis (2011) 137
light manufacturing 12
  anchor firms, attracting 275
  constraints 298–300
    excessive debt burden and finance
      sustainability 299
    limited knowledge transfer impact 300
    persistent trade imbalances 299
    quality FDI and productive capacity 300
  demand factors 267
  development agencies 279
  first-mover challenge 267, 274–7
  'flying geese' model 12, 266, 267–9, 272
  and industrialization of Africa 265–81
  information asymmetry 274
  pathways
    business climate, improving 301
    narrowing knowledge and cultural
      gaps 302
    transforming FOCAC as an effective
      platform 300–1
  pilot survey (2017) 269–74
  policy recommendations 277–80
  real wages 267
  relocation of Chinese manufacturing, scale
    of 268, 272
  special economic zones (SEZs) 276, 278, 279
  under development in Africa 275
  see also **manufacturing**
loans, Chinese 129–46
  accounts 130–1
  and African infrastructure 9, 138–41
  concession foreign aid 104, 110, 134
  economic and technical cooperation
    agreements 133
  to Egypt 63
  historical context 130–2
  industrial zones 142
  lines of credit 130
  loan books 148
  manufacturing, agro-industry and value-
    added production 141–2
  official development assistance (ODA) 134
  oil-backed 184
  overseas lending institutions in China 132–7

preferential 134
risky business
  African debt management capacity,
    concerns 145–6
  debt relief 142–3
  risk reduction in African lending
    143–4
  special economic zones (SEZs) 142
  and structural transformation 137–46
  three- and five-term syndicated 136
  zero-interest 130–3, 141, 143
local government financing vehicles
  (LGFVs) 151
localization, workforce 241–4, 255
  foreign direct investment (FDI) 243
  variation in rates of 243–4
longue durée 36
low-wage economies 39

McKinsey surveys/reports 4n4, 242, 243,
  267, 300
macroeconomic policies 47
macroliberalization 99
Mali, sugar project 141
manufacturing
  and Chinese loans 141–2
  light *see* **light manufacturing**
  manufactured goods, Nigeria 197
  new Chinese manufacturing firms 291*f*
  original design manufacturing (ODM) 272
  relocation of Chinese manufacturing, scale
    of 268, 272
Mao Zedong 8, 61–2, 79, 86, 131, 313
  relations with Africa (1949–76) 62–6
  Three Worlds Theory 67
Maoism 66
market-oriented reforms 20
Marxism 35
Masai tribe 29
McKinsey Global Institute analysis 166
medical teams 67–8
methodological nationalism 250, 254, 257
MFA *see* **Ministry of Foreign Affairs (MFA)**
Ming Dynasty 61
Ministerial Conferences *see* **Forum on**
  China–Africa Cooperation (FOCAC)
Ministry of Commerce (MOFCOM) 100, 113,
  195, 267, 285
  Department of West Asian and African
    Affairs 103, 106–7
  institutional framework of China–Africa
    relations 103–5
  institutional rivalry between MFA and
    MOFCOM 105–6
  loans, Chinese 132, 133–4
Ministry of Finance and Economic
  Development (MOFED) 285

Ministry of Foreign Affairs (MFA) 100–3
  Africa Desk 101
  institutional rivalry between MFA and
    MOFCOM 105–6
  as 'Ministry of Protests' 101
mixed-methods research 257
modernization, economic 69, 70
  see also Four Modernizations
MOFCOM *see* Ministry of Commerce
    (MOFCOM)
Morocco
  independence (1956) 63
  recognition of PRC (1958) 64
most-favoured nation (MFN) treatment 221,
    221n32, 223
Mozambique, Agricultural Technical
    Demonstration Centre 93
multilateral development banks
    (MDBs) 152, 155, 161
multilateralism 312, 313
multinational corporations (MNCs) 26, 28
  Western oil MNCs 177–8, 180–1, 182, 184
mutual benefit principle (South–South) 156

Nairobi–Mombasa rail project 224
National Bureau of Statistics, China 267
National Development and Reform
    Commission (NDRC) 108
national institutionalism 254
National People's Congress (NPC) 101, 108
National Petroleum Company (CNPC),
    China 87
national public goods 38n3
National Road No. 2, Congo 140
national treatment (NT) 221
  modified form 223
nationalism 313
  see also methodological nationalism
neoclassical model, Solow-type 46
neoliberalism 99, 131, 132
new economic geography 163
New Structural Economics (NSE) 267, 277
New York Convention (1958) 229
Nigeria
  Abacha dictatorship (1993–8) 194
  Chinese companies locating to 194–5
  Chinese investment in 192–215
  'Chinese textile imperialism' 196
  Commercial Agriculture Credit Scheme 203
  cooperation 194
  dependence upon oil 10
  export processing zones (EPZs) 204–5
  free trade zones 10–11
  kidnappings in 120
  Lagos–Kano railway 140
  'Look East' policy 194
  manufactured goods 197

  memorandum of understanding (MOU) with
    China (2006) 194
  National Cotton, Textile and Garment
    Policy 203
  National Industrial Revolution Plan
    (NIRP) 203
  new government measures 202–4
  Nigeria Export Processing Zone Authority
    (NEPZA) 204
  Nigeria Investment Promotion Commission
    (NIPC) 203
  oil and gas engagements 181–4
    oil exports, dependence on 197
  overview of Nigerian and Chinese
    linkages 193–5
  petro-politics 184
  Power and Aviation Intervention Fund 203
  presidential visits to China 194
  Real Sector Support Facility (RSSF) 203
  ruling elite 183
  Small and Medium-Scale Enterprises Credit
    Guarantee Scheme 203
  special economic zones (SEZs) in 192–3,
    206–10, 212
  strategic partnership with China 194
  textiles and Nigeria–Chinese trade
    relations 195–9, 201–2
    de-industrialization 201
    exports 197–9
    imports 199, 200t, 201
    modern history of textiles 196
    Textile Intervention Fund 203
  Vision 20:2020 202
Nigerian Investment Promotion Council
    (NIPC) 195
Nigerian National Petroleum Corporation
    (NNPC) 181
Niger/Niger Delta
  Addax's UDELE 3 oil well in 182
  counter-insurgency efforts 194
  repayment terms, Chinese finance 143–4
Nkrumah, Kwame (President) 66
Non-Aligned Movement (NAM) 85, 313
non-discrimination principle 223
North Africa 68, 71, 135, 242
  arms aid 72, 75, 78
Nyerere, Julius 88

Obama, Barack 159
  visit to China (2009) 36
OECD *see* Organisation of Economic
    Cooperation and Development
    (OECD)
official development assistance (ODA) 134
official policy frameworks 98
Ogun–Guangdong Zone, Igbesa 10, 206–10
oil and gas engagements 106, 173–91

agency of state and non-state actors 178
Angola 184–5
China's expanding relations with African
  petro-states 175, 176
China's oil imports 173, 174t, 175
concept approach to China–Africa oil
  relations 177–9
interplay between state and elite
  agency 178–9
Nigeria 181–4
oil-for-infrastructure deals 181, 182,
  184, 188
Shell–ONGC Videsh deal 184
state oil corporations (SOCs), Chinese 173,
  176–9, 183, 184
  and African petro-states, case
    studies 180–1
Sudan 186–7
Western MNCs 177–8, 180–1, 182, 184
Oil and Natural Gas Corporation Videsh
  (OVL), India 184, 186
oil corporations, Chinese 10
oil multinational corporations
  (OMNCs) 173
oil price shocks (1973 and 1979) 38–9, 131
One Belt, One Road (OBOR) initiative
  231, 234
'One China' policy 8, 73, 111, 132
Onne Oil and Gas Free Trade Zone 205
'open door' policy 21
open economy 25, 26
Organisation of African Unity (OAU) 85
Organisation of Economic Cooperation and
  Development (OECD)
  Development Assistance Committee
    (DAC) 104, 159
  OECD/DAC Blended Finance project 158
  Model Tax Convention 225
original brand manufacturing (OBM) 273
original design manufacturing (ODM) 272,
  273, 274
Overseas Development Institute (ODI)
  267, 269
Overseas Private Investment Corporation
  (OPIC), US 135
ozone layer 37

Paris Club of creditor countries 159
parks, industrial 142, 276, 301
parole evidence rule 218
patent applications 20–1
peacekeeping operations, UN 72, 73, 75, 187
Pearl River Delta (PRD) 267, 272
People's Bank of China (PBOC) 130, 131, 152
  see also Bank of China
People's Liberation Army Navy (PLAN) 75
People's Liberation Army (PLA) 104

People's Republic of China (PRC)
  Five Principles of Peaceful Coexistence
    63, 74
  historical relations with Africa 61–2, 63
  recognition 64, 70
  UN Security Council bid 64
  see also China
PetroChina 180, 181
Petrodar Operating Oil Company (PDOC) 186
petroleum imports 72–3
Petroleum Industry Bill (PIB) 182
Petroleum Industry Governance Bill
  (PIGB) 182
Phillips-Van Heusen Corporation (PVH) 276
policy banks, China
  development finance and African
    infrastructure development 150–2, 159
  institutional framework of China–Africa
    relations 109–10
  loans and African structural
    transformation 136
policy drivers 100–6
Politburo Standing Committee (PBSC) 100
poverty in China, prior to economic
  transformation 2, 6, 20, 36
pragmatism 2, 12
  and policy flexibility 298
  'pragmatic cheerleaders' 175, 283–4
PRC see People's Republic of China (PRC)
preferential loans 134
preferential trade 9
privatization 245, 295
procurement and contracting 157–8
profitability principles 91
Programme for Accelerated and Sustained
    Development to End Poverty
    (PASDEP) 287
provinces, China 116–17
public entrepreneurship model, China 10,
  147, 149–50, 153
public goods, global
  Chinese economy as 1, 37–42, 43t, 44–5, 50
  collective defence as 38
  defining 37–8
  imports 43t
  International Task Force on Global Public
    Goods 37, 38
  national public goods 38n3
  'pure' 38
  structural transformation 39
  technology 39
public–private sector partnerships (PPPs)
  91, 158

Qian Qichen 71
Qing Dynasty 195
Quotations of Chairman Mao 66

railway construction 29
  Ababa–Djibouti rail project 224
  Addis Ababa Light Rail System 90
  Dakar–Bamako line 138
  Ethiopia–Djibouti railway 294
  Nairobi–Mombasa rail project 224
  standard-gauge railway (SGR) 140
  Tazara Railway (Tanzania–Zambia) 8, 67, 69,
    86, 138–9, 140, 207
Reagan, Ronald 131
rebalancing, economic 12, 46, 47
'red cap' enterprises 22
regional trade agreements (RTAs) 221n32
regression analysis 49
Regulations on Outbound Investment and
    Business Activities (2017) 160
renminbi (RMB, official Chinese currency)
  bonds 137, 152
  exchange rate strategy 50–2
  internationalization 24
Republic of China (ROC) 61, 132
  replacement by PRC on the Security
    Council 64, 66
  see also Taiwan
research and development (R&D) 22–3
  investment in 320–1
Reserve Bank, South Africa 136
risk-taking, excessive 48–9
RMB see renminbi (RMB, official Chinese
    currency)
road construction/repair 140

scholarships 76, 78
Second Sino-Japanese War (1937–45) 61
SEZs see special economic zones (SEZs)
Shangkun, Yang 71
Sierra Leone, hydropower plant funding
    (1986) 139
Sino-African relations see China–Africa
    relations
Sino-Ethiopian Agreement for Trade,
    Economic and Technological
    Cooperation (1996) 221n33
Sinopec see China Petroleum and Chemical
    Corporation (Sinopec)
Sinosure 136, 137
skill development 246–7
small- and medium-sized enterprises
    (SMEs) 23
  Special Loan Facility for African SMEs 94
SOAS University of London,
    research 247n10, 255–6
Social Economic Rights Action Centre
    (SERAC), Lagos 206
SOCs see state oil corporations (SOCs),
    Chinese
SOEs see state-owned enterprises (SOEs)

Solow-type neoclassical model 46
Sonangol (Angolan SOC) 184–5
South Africa 41, 92, 195, 227, 245
  banks 136
  Chinese loans and African structural
    transformation 135, 138
  Chinese taxation 225n54
  historical official relations with China 61, 62
  Sixth Ministerial Conference (2015) 76–7,
    109, 118, 300
  tax treaty with China 230, 231
South Korea 6, 286
Soviet Union, Chinese hostility to 64, 67
special economic zones (SEZs) 9, 10, 142, 151
  in Ethiopia 292, 301
  light manufacturing 276, 278, 279
  in Nigeria 192–3, 196, 206–10, 212
  see also free trade zones (FTZs)
Special Loan Facility for African SMEs 94
spillovers
  efficiency 22
  international knowledge 23
  positive, of technology and know-how 21,
    29, 30
  research and development (R&D) 23
  technology 21, 22
Sri Lanka 25, 256
SSA see sub-Saharan Africa (SSA)
Standard Bank, South Africa 136
standards 160–1
State Council, China 101, 105, 106, 110, 115
  Foreign Aid Training Centres approved
    by 108
  'Visions and Actions' statement of principles
    and cooperation (2015) 152
State International Development
    Cooperation Agency (SIDCA) 94, 108
state oil corporations (SOCs), Chinese 173,
    176–8, 183, 184
  and African petro-states, case studies 180–1
  'latecomers' 181
  in Sudan 186
State-owned Assets Supervision and
    Administration Commission of the
    State Council (SASAC) 115
state-owned enterprises (SOEs) 10, 26,
    110, 150
  borrowing from Chinese lenders 139–40, 155
  Chinese labour 240, 243
  farms and factories 141
  institutional framework of China–Africa
    relations 114–16, 120
  labour regimes 251, 255
States and Markets (Strange) 149
structural adjustment programmes 132, 210
  labour market deregulation and privatization
    following 245

structural transformation 285, 320
in Africa 4, 6–7, 9, 12, 14, 239, 267
and Chinese finance 129, 130, 157
Ethiopia 255, 283, 284, 286, 296
and future of China–Africa ties 312,
319, 321
in China 1, 6, 89, 157, 211
economic 12, 267, 268, 277, 278, 280, 314
and infrastructure 157
see also loans, Chinese
sub-Saharan Africa (SSA) 2, 19, 28, 165,
186, 212
foreign direct investment (FDI) 240
historical context of China–Africa
relations 75, 78
light manufacturing and African
industrialization 265, 266, 273, 274
special economic zones (SEZs) 192–3
Sudan
Chinese involvement 87
independence (1956) 63
oil and gas engagements 186–7
railway construction 140
Suez crisis (1956) 63
sugar refineries 141
Sun Yat Sen 61
Sustainable Development Goals (SDGs) 28, 265

Taiwan 6, 8, 67, 194, 286
see also Republic of China (ROC)
Tanzania
Friendship Textile Factor 141
Tazara Railway (Tanzania–Zambia) 8, 67, 69,
138–9, 140
funding 142–3
taxation
bilateral tax treaties 225–6
treaties with African states 220–1
China–South Africa tax treaty 230, 231
Tazara Railway (Tanzania–Zambia) 8, 67, 69,
86, 207
funding 138–9, 140, 142–3
technology
global public goods 39
spillovers 21, 22
technology transfers 21
telecommunications
Ethiopia, Chinese relations with 294–5
funding for 140–1
Ten Principles, Bandung Asian-African
Conference 63
terms-of-trade shock 25
textiles and Nigeria–Chinese trade
relations 195–9, 200t, 201–2
cotton textiles 195–6
de-industrialization 201
exports 197–9

imports 199, 200t, 201
modern history of textiles 196
Textile Intervention Fund 203
TFP *see* total factor productivity (TFP)
Thatcher, Margaret 131
think tanks, China 112–13
'Three Networks and Industrialization
Projects' 89–90
Tiananmen Square crisis (1989) 53, 69, 71
Tillerson, Rex 311
time-series models 49
total factor productivity (TFP) 20–2
and economic growth 24
township and village enterprises
(TVEs) 22
trade
agreements 220–2
and economic growth 21
with Egypt 63
international trade agreements 11
'intra-industry' 26
persistent imbalances 299
preferential 9
see also China–Africa trade
training courses 76
Transition Assistance Group, UN 72
transnational corporations (TCs) 254
transnational corporations-joint ventures
(TNCs-JVs) 250
transport infrastructure 31, 294
trilateral cooperation platform 153
Tunisia, independence (1956) 63
twinning assistance 116n1
Two Whatevers policy 68

United Nations
admission of China to (1971) 66
Economic Commission for Africa 168
Income and Capital Model Tax
Convention 225
peacekeeping operations 72, 73, 75, 187
Transition Assistance Group 72
United Nations Development Programme
(UNDP) 107
United Nations Industrial Development
Organization (UNIDO) 107
United Nigeria Textiles Ltd (UNT) 196
United States
African Growth and Opportunity Act
(AGOA) 272, 280
and China 67
Federal Reserve 49–50
government debt, Chinese holding of 42, 44
International Development Finance
Corporation 168
Overseas Private Investment Corporation
(OPIC) 135

Vietnam 273, 274

Washington Consensus 99
water supply projects 139, 140–1
West Africa 164, 207
  Economic Community of West African States
    (ECOWAS) 210
'win-win' principle 156, 166, 314
  oil and gas engagements 177–8, 183
workers, reallocation of 24
workforce localization *see* localization,
    workforce
working conditions 244–6
workplace encounters
  China–Africa labour encounters 241–8
  and economic transformation 239–40
World Bank 41, 245
  biannual Economic Pulse reports 155
  and development finance 158, 159, 162
  Light Manufacturing in Africa project 275
  World Bank–China Exim Bank
    Memorandum of Understanding on
      Cooperation (2007) 161
World Bank Group (WBG) 158
World Economic Forum, Davos (2017) 50n12
World Trade Organization (WTO)
  Appellate Body 227
  Chinese accession (2001) 20–1, 87, 139, 227
  Chinese and African member states 221
  dispute settlement system 226–30
    commercial agreements 229–30
    Dispute Settlement Body (DSB) 227
    Dispute Settlement Understandings
      (DSU) 11, 227
    investment agreements 228–9
    trade agreements 227–8
  GATT/WTO legal regime 11, 233
  and loans 132
  most-favoured nation (MFN) treatment 221,
    221n32, 223
  national treatment (NT) 221, 223
  quotas, elimination of 221
  tariff reduction on imports 221
  trade agreements 220
  transparency of trade-related domestic laws 221

world-economies 36
WTO *see* World Trade Organization (WTO)

Xi Jinping (Chinese leader from 2012) 8,
    76–9, 93, 101, 159, 298, 313
  BRI launched by (2013) 152
  general secretary of the CPC Central
    Committee 76
  Governance of China 7n8
  as President 109
  'Xi Jinping Thought' 77
Xiaoping, Deng 35–6, 62, 99, 319
  domestic reform era (1978–92) 2,
    68–70, 86
  general secretary of the CPC Central
    Committee 69
Xiaotao, Wang 108
Xinguang International Group
    consortium 210

Yangtze River Delta (YRD) 267
Yi, Wang 44n6, 102

Zambia
  anti-Chinese riots in 120
  copper belt 86
  labour regimes 254
  mines 244, 245–6
Zemin, Jiang *see* Jiang Zemin period
    (1989 to 2002)
zero-interest loans 130–3, 141, 143
zero-tariffs 74, 287–8
Zhao Ziyang (1980–87) 69
Zhejiang province, high-tech industries
    in 23
Zheng He naval fleet 61
Zhou Enlai (Chinese Premier 1949–76) 63,
    64–5, 69, 101
  visit to Africa (1963–4) 85–6
Zimbabwe
  infrastructure development, Chinese
    finance 137, 141, 142, 145
  Iron and Steel Corporation 137, 141
  presidential visits 71, 76
  risk of lending to 143